Toronto Studies in Religion

Vol. 2

Published in association with
the Centre of Religious Studies
at the University of Toronto

PETER LANG
New York · Berne · Frankfurt am Main · Paris

Rodney Stark
William Sims Bainbridge

A Theory of Religion

PETER LANG
New York · Berne · Frankfurt am Main · Paris

Library of Congress Cataloging in Publication Data

Stark, Rodney.
A Theory of Religion.
(Toronto studies in religion; vol. 2)
Bibliography: p.
Includes index.
1. Religion. I. Bainbridge, William Sims. II. Title.
III. Series.
BL48.B33 1987 200'.1 87-4222
ISBN 0-8204-0356-3
ISSN 8756-7385

CIP-Kurztitelaufnahme der Deutschen Bibliothek

Stark, Rodney:
A theory of religion / Rodney Stark; William Sims Bainbridge.-
New York; Berne; Frankfurt am Main; Paris: Lang, 1987.
(Toronto studies in religion; Vol. 2)
ISBN 0-8204-0356-3
NE: Bainbridge, William Sims; GT

Printed by Weihert-Druck GmbH, Darmstadt (West Germany)

Dedicated to

Charles Y. Glock and George C. Homans

Note: All material in this book is new, except for Chapter 2 which appeared in a preliminary form as:

Rodney Stark and William Sims Bainbridge: "Towards a Theory of Religion: Religious Commitment," Journal for the Scientific Study of Religion 18 (1980):114–128.

EDITOR'S PREFACE

Toronto Studies in Religion is a new book series published in association with the Centre for Religious Studies at the University of Toronto. It focuses attention on empirical, analytical and theoretical studies of religion within a broad naturalistic framework. It aims to publish original research in the historical, phenomenological and social scientific study of the world's religious traditions as well as new structural and theoretical interpretations of religion in general. Philosophical and even speculative approaches to understanding religous phenomena, carried within a generally naturalistic framework, are also welcome. The series will undertake translations of works that deserve a wider readership and that will encourage international scholarly debate. Comprehensive bibliographical studies, original dissertations, symposia of special merit and other appropriate projects will be given consideration.

A Theory of Religion is a book much overdue. Students of religion are, in general, theory-shy and prefer to deal with particular historical religious traditions at the descriptive and phenomenological levels. Such a 'nomothetic anxiety', as it has been called by some, does not characterize the work of R. Stark and W.S. Bainbridge. This book is not a polemic against those who disagree with theoretical/reductionist analyses of religion but is rather an example of what such an approach to religion can do, namely, *explain* rather than merely describe religion – show how and why the phenomena of religion occur. Their theory is not, however, the mere articulation of one or two overarching generalizations about religion so characteristic of earlier periods of theorizing about religious phenomena. Rather, they formulate a sociological theory that shares the logical form and scope of theories in the natural sciences. They attempt here to construct a deductive form of theory that rests on a small set of basic principles – axioms – that are not statements about religion but from which descriptive statements about religious phenomena can be deduced. The axioms correctly describe human nature and the conditions of human existence and from them they derive the emergence of religion. Moreover, they show that they can in this fashion 'tie together' the vast wealth of insights and carefully collected and tested facts that have accumulated over the last several decades in this field of scholarly research. As they put it in the conclusion: "The purpose of this book has been to outline a theory that models the real world experienced by humans and that derives the main facts of religion from that model."

Although Stark and Bainbridge see the deductive approach as providing a maximum conceptual coherence in the understanding of religion they are well aware that their theory has not been fully formalized and that, therefore, shortcommings are likely to remain. They are aware, moreover, that the theory will need many revisions before it is even ready for such formalization. But it has the merit of testability and they see their work in its construction as an invitation to their colleagues in the field to put it to the test. Whether their work provides the template or merely the inspiration for the development of such a formalized theory matters less to them than that it should be attempted. Their work, I believe, is a most important pioneering effort in this respect and a much needed counterbalance to the overwhelmingly descriptivist character of the work in 'Religious Studies'.

Don Wiebe
Centre for Religious Studies
University of Toronto

TABLE OF CONTENTS

CHAPTER 1:
Towards a General Theory of Religion

In this book we present a general theory of religion. The theory's claim to generally rests on the large number of central questions about religious phenomena it attempts to answer. In seeking these answers, however, we have not settled for an immense generalization or two about what religion is and does. Instead, we try to specify in a relatively complete way why and how various aspects of religion occur and to do so through a structure of formal explanation.

Whatever the merits of our theoretical achievement, it will be clear that we have broken with a long tradition of "one factor" explanations of religion. We do not seek generality by reducing all of religion to a neurotic "illusion" as Freud did, or to an "opium of the people," as Marx did, or, indeed, to "society" worshipping itself as Durkheim did. Reductions such as these have great scope, but no depth. Indeed, each is a metaphor, not a theory. We seek to be general through an integrated set of formal statements meant to answer many classic questions about religion. We shall derive these statements from a handful of very general axioms. And, scores of empirical implications can be drawn from this theoretical system, thus making it falsifiable.

We think the time is ripe for a major theoretical undertaking in the social scientific study of religion. For the past several decades the field has enjoyed a major rebirth. As a result, an amazing variety of new and well-tested facts have come to light. But no sustained effort has gone into creating theories to give order and relevance to these facts. Indeed, there has been little theorizing about religion since the turn of the century. Therefore, available "theories" of religion remain largely the product of 19th century social thought and the tradition of "grand theory" associated with the founding fathers of social science. But, as already suggested, close scrutiny reveals that these theories are not so grand. For example, the actual theorizing contained in such hallowed classics as Emile Durkheim's *The Elementary Forms of the Religious Life* or William James' *Varieties of Religious Experience*, could be excerpted on a few printed pages. The rest is illustration or digression.

Thus, we set out upon our theoretical task without a masterwork either to extend or to refute. Nothing like Adam Smith's economic theory or Karl Marx's theory of revolution exists in the area of religion. One reason for this is the widespread conviction among social scientists that religion is rapidly headed for oblivion. Why give serious attention to a social phenomenon with no future?

Consider this paragraph under the heading "The Future of Religion" published in 1966 by Anthony F.C. Wallace, one of the most distinguished modern anthropologists working in the area of religion:

> . . . the evolutionary future of religion is extinction. Belief in supernatural beings and in supernatural forces that affect nature without obeying nature's laws will erode and become only an interesting historical memory. To be sure, this event is not likely to occur in the next hundred years, and there will probably always remain individuals, or even occasional small cult groups, who respond to hallucination, trance, and obsession with a supernatural interpretation. But as a cultural trait, belief in supernatural powers is doomed to die out, all over the world, as a result of the increasing adequacy and diffusion of scientific knowledge and the realization by secular faiths that supernatural belief is not necessary to the effective use of ritual. The question of whether such a denouement will be good or bad for humanity is irrelevant to the prediction; the process is inevitable. (Wallace, 1966:265)

Of course, religion has not become extinct, nor has it even begun to wither away. Shortly after Wallace wrote these lines, a great upsurge in mysticism and religious enthusiasm occured once more. And it was the religious revival of the period immediately after World War II and the continuing encounter with stubborn religious effects on such diverse matters as voting and fertility that led to the resurrection of active research on religion.

Religion is a major factor in human life and can be expected to remain so for the forseeable future. It is time, therefore, that we begin to gain a theoretical understanding of religion.

The absence of major theoretical efforts in this area provides us with an unusual opportunity. Before us lies a literature rich in profound insights and immense with carefully collected and tested facts: a wealth of resources beyond the imaginings of those 19th century scholars who gave attention to religious questions. Moreover, through the decades when no one has theorized about religion, major theoretical developments occured in many other areas of social science. These pose the opportunity to borrow some extremely powerful tools, and we have responded by ransacking the treasuries of economics, learning theory and cultural anthropology.

Our purposes in this book are theoretical. However, it is fatuous to theorize without keeping a close eye on the available data relevant to one's theoretical results. There is no virtue in putting a theory into print that already is falsified by established facts. Therefore, we have combed the empirical literature to show that various portions of our theory are congruent with what is known. Moreover, we have published a number of studies in the past several years that test important predictions from the theory, and many of them can be found in our previous book, *The Future of Religion*. However, we regard all of these tests of the theory as quite preliminary. Extensive testing can occur only after the theory is available to others. Therefore, our references to empirical results in this book are not meant to imply that the theory already is well tested.

Deductive Theories

The form of our theory is deductive. Such theories are not new to the social sciences. As long ago as 1776, Adam Smith published a deductive theory to which all present-day versions of exchange theories in sociology, psychology, and economics trace their paternity. Nevertheless, many social scientists do not understand correctly, or fully appreciate, the utility and logical structure of deductive theories. It seems prudent to touch briefly on these matters here before turning to the theoretical task itself.

A theory is a set of statements about relationships among a set of abstract concepts. These statements say how and why the concepts are interrelated. Furthermore, these statements must give rise to implications that potentially are falsifiable empirically. That is, it must be possible to deduce from a theory some statements about empirical events that could, in principle, turn out to be incorrect (Popper, 1959; 1962).

Deductive theories meet these criteria in a particularly powerful and elegant way (Braithwaite, 1953; Nagel, 1961). They consist of a small set of basic principles to which, it is thought, some group of complex phenomena can be reduced. That is, the theorists attempt to locate a relatively small set of rules about how some relevant portion of reality operates. Logical permutations of these rules (or *axioms*) give rise to a number of derivations (or *propositions*). At least some of these propositions will have empirical implications. They will predict or prohibit certain relationships among empirical indicators of the concepts contained in the theory.

In a limited sense, deductive theories are tautological, and a misunderstanding of the way in which they are has led some writers wrongly to reject the deductive approach (Abrahamson, 1970). Once a set of axioms has been stated (and their terms defined), all of the propositions are implied. The propositions are "forced" by the axioms in accord with the rules of logic. Indeed, that is the precise meaning of the verb "to deduce." Propositions are deduced by demonstrating that each is implied logically by (and therefore already present in) the axioms.

However, simply because the propositions follow tautologically from the axioms does not mean that deductive theories are not falsifiable and are therefore tautologies at the empirical level. Indeed, unless the axioms are true, some propositions derived from them will be falsified, for not all empirical outcomes can be congruent with the propositions. Thus all deductive theories (and all real theories) are gambles. The more they attempt to explain, the riskier the gamble. The more that is predicted and prohibited, the greater the opportunity for falsification.

The tautological character of deductive theories at the abstract level is their chief virtue. In this manner very general and abstract statements become subject to empirical test. Since they require that certain propositions be true, when a proposition is falsified this result is conducted back up the logical chain, casting the entire system into doubt. Alternatively one could argue that the deductive theory was not falsified, but instead it has been established that it is not applicable to the particular reality or universe in question. That is to say, in a reality in which the axioms do hold, the theory will always be congruent with empirical outcomes (barring measurement error). But since we have no interest in those hypothetical realities, when we find a deductive theory fails to hold in this reality we search for the faulty axiom or axioms, for the vital omission, or for some other correctable flaw. That is, we try to shift the theory into our reality.

Deductive theories are much more than just intellectual games (although one must play by the rules); much more than sterile cross-reference systems for organizing our data. Because deductive theories can be permutated according to logical rules, they may give rise to propositions that are wholly novel. Predictions or prohibitions frequently are generated by deductive theories about relationships never previously suspected or examined. Thus deductive theories can force intellectual innovation.

Finally, the logical structure of deductive theories offers not merely prediction, but *explanation* (Homans, 1967). For example, a number of well-known "middle-range" generalizations or assertions about religious phenomena are found to derive from our modest set of axioms. Unless or until they are so derived, they are theoretical orphans. While they stand alone without intellectual parentage, we are unable to explain why they ought to be true or how such generalizations relate to one another. But when it can be shown that such statements derive from a simple set of axioms about human beings and how they interact, then these middle-range generalizations are not simply asserted, but explained. In Chapter 2, for example, we not only deduce that religion appeals to the dispossessed (a familiar middle-range proposition), but we also deduce why, how, and under what circumstances.

To sum up: a deductive theory is an attempt to state the elementary principles that account for some phenomenon. If these are the correct principles, then we can deduce what can and cannot happen, and see why.

When a deductive theory can be formalized (represented mathematically), its logical virtues can be realized fully (Nagasawa and von Bretzel, 1977). Then, formal manipulations will reveal redundancies, ambiguities, missing assumptions, and extract the full set of propositions implied by the axioms. The theory we present here has not yet been formalized. Therefore, many shortcomings are likely to remain. Nevertheless, even in wholly verbal form the theory is sufficiently rigorous so that it runs grave risks of falsification, as any good theory must. Indeed, the theory yields some novel and possibly counter-intuitive propositions which are testable.

We also must point out that the axioms of the theory are not statements about religion. Instead they are rather noncontroversial (and often well-known) statements about the world and about how people behave or interact. Therefore, the theory is very general in that it leads easily to propositions far afield from religious behavior. This holds out the promise of synthesis between social science understanding of religion and of other spheres of social life.

On Concepts

The building blocks of theories are concepts. Concepts isolate and identify phenomena. But there are no true or false concepts. Concepts are *definitions* that identify abstract categories intended to delimit a class of "like" phenomena. Suppose one invented the concept of satyr to identify all creatures who are half man, half goat. That concept is as "true" as any other, as true, for example, as the concept of female. But, we note that no instances of satyrs are known to exist. This does not make the concept false, it merely makes it useless. The concept retains its ability to classifiy, and thus if we ever find any creature who is half man, half goat, we shall known what to call it. We ignore the concept, only because it lacks application.

Scientific concepts can be judged only on the basis of their usefulness. The utility of concepts can be judged by two criteria. First, they must be adequate for *classification*. The definition must make it possible unambiguously to identify specific phenomena as belonging or not belonging to the class of things identified by the concept. A useful concept of religion, for example, must make it clear which phenomena are religions and which are not.

Elsewhere we have been very critical of typologies as they are used in social science, because they obscure rather than clarify the classification of phenomena (Stark and Bainbridge, 1979). This occurs when correlates of a phenomenon rather than its attributes are included in the definition of a concept. Attributes are features present in all instances of a phenomenon. Correlates occur in only some instances. When we define a sect as a religious movement that occurs within a conventional religious tradition and that is in a high state of tension with its sociocultural environment, we include only those features found in *all* sects, and which together exclude from the category all phenomena we wish to exclude. Political "sects" are excluded for lack of being religious movements (which, in turn, follows from our definition of religion). Cults are excluded because they represent an unconventional religious tradition. Churches are excluded because they are in a low state of tension with their surroundings.

In contrast, the many and competing church-sect typologies in the literature are built of correlates. For example, a sect is said to be small, to have primarily a converted rather than a socialized membership, to emphasize emotionalism, and to deemphasize ritual and ceremony – to list only a few of the characteristics assigned to sects in the literature (cf. O'Dea, 1966). None of these features is to be found in all sects – indeed many sects lack each of these features. Thus when these variables are cross-classified, empirical examples can be found fitting most or even all of the possible combinations. Some sects are large. Some have virtually no converted members. Some have staid services. Some emphasize ritual and ceremony. The result is a jumble of mixed types which cannot be ordered. Which is more sectlike, an emotionalistic group with a socialized membership, or a very restrained group with a converted membership? No answer is possible.

Lacking a clear axis of variation, typologies defy theorizing. Indeed, they often lock into the definition independent factors of potentially great theoretical interest. It is impossible to ask about the impact of the arrival of a generation of socialized members on a sect, if that has already entered into the classification of groups as sects. Moreover, typologies built of correlates are not effective for classification because subtypes proliferate. Typologizing has encouraged researchers to discover how the group they are studying is different from all others, and to the extent they succeed nothing gets classified. Science requires that like things be grouped, not that we strive to show that no two things are alike.

In this book we have torn apart previous typologies to create unambiguous classification and to replace sterile definitional schemes with fruitful theories.

We are not as concerned to name small religious groups, for example, as we are to explain how they occur and why they do or do not remain small. Contemplation of the variable of *size* immediately suggests to us that contemporary sociology often deals with variables which are continuous. There are many advantages, both technical and conceptual, to a definition which identifies an axis of variation rather than merely distinguishing two or more categories. Not only may one measure differences more finely, and employ a wider range of statistical tools, but one is in a vastly better position to understand the processes of change, if one has been liberated from the restrictive mind-set of typologies and instead defined many concepts in terms of continuous variables.

Note that this does not undermine the concepts' ability to serve as adequate tools of classification. One still makes a sharp distinction between this continuous variable and that continuous variable – between utterly different concepts. The size of a religious group is quite a different thing from the age of that group. Also, the possibility of marking off intermediate points along a continuous axis of variation realistically expresses the fact that many (perhaps most) characteristics of individuals and groups can exist in varying strengths and degrees. To recognize that size, for example, is a matter of degree in no way reduces the utility of size as a concept. One can easily make a sharp distinction between the concept of size, perhaps defined as the number of members a group possesses, and other concepts like age or "sectness." And relative concepts like big and small can be measured along the axis of variation of the master concept, size.

Often we find that a traditional idea like *sect* is best understood as the conjunction of two basic concepts from our theory – "conventional religious tradition" and "tension with the sociocultural environment." But each of these basic concepts can be defined and measured unambiguously. For example, an important concept for our theory is the degree of tension with the sociocultural environment, a clearly delineated continuous variable. A theory which begins with clear, simple, unambiguous concepts is free to examine the interaction of any two or more of them. And our theory successfully builds propositions and explanations out of basic concepts, rather than being trapped in the proliferating categorical boxes of the typologizers.

This brings us to the second criterion for judging concepts, their fruitfulness. Concepts are to be preferred to the extent that they facilitate theorizing – increase the scope, precision, accuracy, or simplicity of a theory. Suppose we defined religion as all systems of doctrine that acknowledge Jesus Christ as the Son of God. This is not a false definition, for all definitions are "true." Nor is this definition too vague to permit clear classification. We would have little trouble applying it to empirical phenomena. The inadequacy of this definition is that it forces construction of very inferior theories. For example, we would be forced to conclude that religion is a relatively rare and relatively recent phenomenon. We reject this definition only because other formulations of the concept of religion are more fruitful for theorizing. Conversely, we should try to formulate concepts purely on the basis of the needs of our theories. If changing the definitions of concepts results in more powerful theories, then those definitions ought to be changed.

These remarks are intended to clarify the merit of the many concepts used in this volume. Often we have defined a well-known word in a way somewhat different from previous useage. We have not done this out of capriciousness. Our aim is not to invent a new field, but to improve this one. We have based our definitions on what makes possible more powerful theoretical results. Indeed, these are the only grounds on which it is possible to say which of several alternative definitions is the best.

We must ask readers to note carefully our precise definitions and to abide by them while following our deductive chains. The theory works only with these definitions. If you forget how we use a term, you may check it in the appendix. If you impose a definition you prefer, the result will be nonsense. We may well have written nonsense. But that can be discovered only by reference to our logical operations, and we refuse to take responsibility for formulations we did not present and deductions that do not follow from our system. We emphasize this point because some readers of preliminary drafts of this work engaged us in debates based wholly on their substitutions of key definitions and the obvious silliness that produced.

An example may underscore the problem. In this book we restrict the term *culture* to that which humans learn from each other (cf. Tylor, 1871). A colleague thought this an inferior definition to his in which culture is defined as the "way of life" of any human group. Having made this "correction" he then went on to damn many of our propositions because they did not take account of biology. In his judgment a considerable part of the human way of life is instinctual, having genetic origins. He than argued that we could not have a good theory of religion unless we included a good theory of biological evolution and a good theory of behavior genetics. That we are not so sure he is right about instincts, is beside the point in this argument. The propositions we use to explain cultural evolution do not refer to everything humans do, but only to that which they learn to do. If some patterns of behavior are not learned, we would not expect our propositions to apply to them – we would not expect them to "evolve" as culture evolves. We shall be short-tempered with those who belabor us for strange deductions we have not made. Readers are free to make up their own theories. But do not blame us for whatever flaws they have. We are certain that our theory needs no gratuitous flaws. It is bound to have enough of its own. And we shall not be short-tempered as these are discovered and pointed out. Indeed, we propose this theory only as a systematic basis to begin, and we plan to keep tinkering with this system for years to come.

An important way in which the flaws in theories are discovered is through empirical testing. Throughout the book we report on data pertinent to particular predictions and prohibitions deduced from this theory. In most cases, the need to get on with the job of theory-construction prevents us from extended comments about particuliar studies, and to avoid distraction from our line of arguments we often restrict ourselves to mere citation of empirical studies which the reader may wish to consult. Over the past several years we ourselves have published many studies devoted to some portion of the theory. In future we expect many additional empirical tests to be made – some by us, but most, hopefully, by others. For this reason it is appropriate here to examine some common misunderstandings about the nature of theories and the quality of evidence that may call them into question.

On Testing Theories

To be a theory, it is necessary that a set of axioms and definitions give rise to statements that in principle are empirically falsifiable. The theory must predict or prohibit certain empirical states of affairs. When such are found to be in contradiction to the theory, then the adequacy of the theory is called into question.

It is important to understand limits on the empirical culpability of theories. Theories always try to isolate basic processes and properties, to separate these from the disorder of particular empirical circumstances. No theory ever offers a full account of particular empirical arrays. Put another way, no theory ever offers a full account of every aspect of any concrete event. To better grasp this point, let us consider one of the most theoretically powerful fields, physics. The laws (or theories) of physics are clear, quite simple, of immense scope, and they have survived extraordinary efforts of falsification. Yet the laws of physics will not provide full and accurate portrayals of most particular empirical situations to which they apply (Toulmin, 1960)

For example, laws of classical physics tell us that two bodies of different weight will fall to earth at exactly the same acceleration – if other things are equal. The qualifying phrase is vital. For the fact is that only in the most artificial experimental conditions is the law an accurate description of what happens, for only then are the other things equal. In fact, if we took two cannon balls of differing size and dropped them simultaneously from a tower they would seldom if ever land at the same instant. This is because they will differ in their wind resistance – something else is not equal. When we want to know the rate at which a particular body will fall to earth, we start with the laws of physics, but then we must engage in considerable empirical induction in order to get the right answer. This is why engineers must use wind tunnels, not just the laws of physics.

The fact that even the laws of physics omit so much about particular empirical applications means that there is a great deal of work for engineers. But this does not falsify the laws of physics. These theories tell us what factors will be important and what the fundamental processes are, but they do not note the fall of every sparrow. By the same token, a sociological theory of revolutions cannot be required to name the date on which each new revolution will occur or even to predict which revolutions will succeed. That is asking science to do engineering.

These limits in all good theories must be kept in mind whenever one seeks to test any theory. When our theory gives rise to propositions such as "regardless of their power, humans will tend to accept religious compensators for rewards which seem not to exist," we are not asserting that all human beings will believe in life after death, for example. The phrase "other things being equal" applies to all such propositions. And it will be obvious that other things usually are not exactly equal. In this example we may note that socialization will differ from human to human and thus make some people more likely than others to believe in life after death. Similarly, one can identify groups within which individuals are rewarded highly for disbelief in life after death – scientific and intellectual circles in Western nations and Communist Party circles in the East, for example. The list of "other things" could be extended to fill many pages without exhausting the possibilities.

What this means is that tests of a theory can occur only to the extent that the research is designed to make all other things equal. It is this that makes the experimental method ideal. But for a theory of religion, often experiments will be impossible. Hence, empirical tests of our theory usually will require multi-variate analyses which try to hold certain extraneous variables constant. Such analyses are common in contemporary social science. But there is a tendency to think of them wholly in terms of spuriousness. The researcher starts with a significant zero-order correlation of interest and then attempts to wipe out this correlation by controlling for other potential "causes." But it is equally important that when one is testing a theory and a predicted zero-order correlation fails to appear, one attempts to hold constant other things that might be suppressing the relationship. Thus had Galileo actually dropped two balls off the

Tower of Pisa, and had he possessed sufficiently accurate measuring equipment, he would have discovered that they did not strike the ground at the same speed. But, before rejecting a fundamental law of physics he ought to have tried to eliminate (hold constant) variations in wind resistance. By the same token, when we looked to see if converted members of contemporary American sects were of lower social class than were members born into the group (a result predicted by our theory), we had to remove the large number of persons brought into the sects by marriage who were swamping the results (Stark and Bainbridge, 1985).

The point of this discussion is to suggest that researchers ought not to rush into print with the first zero-order correlation that they discover to be contrary to some aspect of a theory. Theory-testing is more complicated than that, and "other things being equal" means all other things that possibly could matter. Since ours is a complex theory with over three hundred already-derived propositions, the theory itself often suggests important variables which might suppress the correlation between two variables of interest.

Plan of the Book

To build our theory we start small. We identify seven very simple axioms about humans and how they behave. We then pursue these to explain how religion serves individuals and especially how religion serves people differentially depending on their power. These efforts constitute Chapter 2 which comprises the core theory on which the rest of the book is based. In subsequent chapters only new definitions are introduced, not axioms, and the book is unified by the deductive chain begun in Chapter 2.

In Chapter 3 we begin to surround the religious individual with appropriate social and cultural structures and to explain how these structures arise and change. This requires us to turn away from purely religious matters to develop first an adequate understanding of basic social and cultural processes. In the latter half of Chapter 3 we use these propositions about society and culture to explain the evolution of the gods. Chapter 4 explains how religious institutions form and develop and the emergence of religious specialists.

Against this theoretical backdrop we then turn our attention to religious movements. Chapter 5 is devoted to sect formation. Chapter 6 explains cult formation. Chapter 7 serves as a detailed analysis of how people become affiliated with sects and cults. Chapter 8 explores the contingencies that determine the fate of cults and sects, whether they grow or stagnate, become more conventional or remain deviant. In Chapter 9 we examine societies as whole systems and the conditions under which religions lose former power, when many sects can be expected to form, and when new religions are likely to develop and succeed. Finally, in Chapter 10, we review the paths of theory we have travelled together, remark on the vast number of facts about religion thus explained, consider the best future course for work in this area, and venture prophecy about the future of religion.

These are but crude hints about the contents of the rest of the book. But, they serve to indicate that our strategy is to build upon a micro theory until large macro workings of societies can be explained.

On Faith

At the start of this chapter we mentioned that social scientists have tended to ignore religion because they were hostile toward it and wished it to disappear. If Marx called religion an "opium," Freud (1927:88) called it an "intoxicant," a "poison" and "childishness to be overcome" – all on one page. An enormous list of similar examples could be placed in evidence.

Recently, however, things have changed. Many scholars with official religious connections have entered the field. Of those who published four or more social science articles on religion during the decade 1960–1970, 52 percent could be clearly identified as religionists – that is, as scholars whose employment was as minster, priest, nun, monk, seminary professor, or who were prominent lay leaders in a religious denomination. Many of the others undoubtedly hold personal religious convictions (Reed, 1974).

Partly because of this new constituency of believers, it has become conventional in social science writing on religion to lodge the disclaimer that scientific study of religion implies nothing about the truth of religion. Strictly speaking, this denial is accurate. Science has nothing to say on way or the other about assertions that are beyond empirical contradiction. Science is helpless to assess the existence of a Heaven that is a wholly immaterial realm beyond the senses. That being so, we have taken great care in this book not to write as if we knew there is no God, no Heaven, or no soul. Such cannot be known.

On the other hand, it is hypocritical to imply that work such as we present is without implications for religious faith. While at no point do we find reason to suggest that the supernatural does not exist, neither do we find any need in our theory to postulate the existence of the supernatural. This makes it clear that, by attempting to explain religious phenomena without reference to actions taken by the supernatural, we assume that religion is a purely human phenomenon, the causes of which are to be found entirely in the natural world. Such an approach is obviously incompatible with faith in revelations and miracles (Moberg, 1967; Johnson, 1977). Furthermore, when we contrast many faiths and seek human causes for variations among them, we at least imply that none possesses the revealed truth. Orthodox clergy have no difficulty seeing at a glance that work such as ours is potentially inimical to faith. On this question we believe the orthodox clergy show better judgment than do the many liberal clergy who seem so eager to embrace social science. These are, of course, very serious matters. We do not raise them lightly.

We raise them only to preface our decision to make clear at the start of this work the personal biases and commitments we bring to it. We believe such candor ought to be the rule in all social science inquiry. But certainly it must not be evaded when the topic in question engages the deepest human emotions.

Neither of us is religious as that term is conventionally understood and as we use it in this book. Neither of us belongs to a religious organization, and neither of us believes in the supernatural. On the other hand, neither of us feels antagonism toward religion. Each of us has devoted much of his career to an examination of religion because in it human beings use all their individual and social resources to confront the greatest challenges faced by our species – a fact more likely to elicit empathy in us than scorn. Our theory suggests that there is much in religion that is admirable. Moreover, we did not write this book to "enlighten" those who accept religion or to strike a blow for rationalism. While we remain personally incapable of religious faith, our theory tells us to prefer to live in a society where most people do believe. Indeed, our theory leads us to conclude that religion will endure no matter what social scientists write about it. It was Voltaire who said, "If God did not exist, it would be necessary to invent him." Our theory agrees. If the gods do not exist as facts, they will exist as hopes in the human consciousness so long as humans remain mere mortals. Humans have a persistent desire for rewards only the gods can grant, unless humans become gods.

While personal religious faith has not prompted us to write this book, our motives are based on a commitment, the truth of which cannot be demonstrated: that human behavior ought to be explained. That we have focused on religious aspects of human behavior is in great measure the result of our idiosyncratic professional biographies – an interplay of our origins and our opportunities.

Having said all this, we must qualify the importance of bias in social theory. Although the biases of theorists can play a major role in determining what they choose to theorize about, and the way they fashion their theories, in the final analysis bias ceases to be of interest. Once a theory has been developed and published, it must stand or fall on its own merits – its clarity, its parsimony, its scope, and its ability to continue to survive collisions with appropriate facts. Nowhere in the canons of science is there justification for accepting theories because their authors were "good" or rejecting them because their authors were "bad." If it were to be discovered tomorrow that Copernicus engaged in ritual cannibalism, while Ptolemy died trying to end slavery in Egypt, it would not cause the slightest re-evaluation of astronomical theory.

We are neither astronomers nor anthropophagi. But even if we were, our theory now faces the world on its own merits.

Chapter 2:
The Core Theory: Religious Commitment

About seventy years ago, Emile Durkheim searched for the "elementary forms" – or most basic features – of religion in ethnographic accounts of the primitive tribes of Australia. Today we recognize that many of Durkheim's conclusions were unsatisfactory (Pickering, 1984), but it still seems likely that he had the right idea about where to look. Religion did not first appear in a cathedral or in culturally-advanced societies. The evidence is clear that humans possessed religion far back in prehistory, that religion first developed when humans roamed in tiny bands foraging for subsistence much like other wild animals. If religion existed when human societies constituted bands of from twenty to fifty members, and when their technology consisted of little more than sticks and sharpened stones, then the fundamental aspects of religion must be very basic human needs and activities.

For this reason we begin our search for the fundamental features of religion by examining elementary principles about what humans are like and how they interact. To learn what human religion is and does we must consider what humans are and do. Unlike Durkheim, we have not focused on primitives in order to avoid the elaborate cultural and social embellishments that overlie the fundamental features of religion. Instead, we have attempted to reach bedrock by selecting axioms stripped of all such embellishments. However, once we have isolated what seem to be the most elementary forms of religion, we give primary attention to explaining how religion comes to develop along certain cultural lines and to give rise to particular social structures. That is, the social and cultural overlays of religion are embellishments only while one seeks the elementary. Subsequently, they are not embellishments but are the primary objects of interest.

In this chapter we present our model of the elementary properties of religion. In it we address such questions as: Why do humans develop religion? What do they get from religion? Why are particular kinds of people religious in different ways?

These questions pertain to religious commitment in any human group, from the smallest and most primitive, to the largest and most sophisticated. Therefore, the human actors and actions we examine are sufficiently abstract so that they escape the protective shadows of civilization. It will be time enough to discuss cathedrals and large-scale societies when we have grasped the fundamentals of human religious expression.

We begin our quest for a theory of religion, therefore, not with axioms about the macro-workings of societies, but with some simple statements about how individuals and small groups operate. In so doing we draw upon principles common to exchange theory. Some readers will find this reductionistic. To them we counsel patience. See how far we can get with this simple model, what complex macro-structures arise as our deductive chain lengthens. Furthermore, we quickly agree that our theory is reductionistic. A theorist should always be as reductionistic as possible – or, to paraphrase Occam, a theorist should try to get the most out of the least. A theory is too reductionistic only when it cannot do what it must, without more than it has. We believe it is a great merit of our theory that it derives religious phenomena from nonreligious phenomena, that it reduces a theory of religion to a general theory of human action.

In structure, our theory consists of an ordered set of connected statements, many of which can be derived from others. The most general statements are called *axioms*. Like the axioms of Euclid, they are inspired by our observation of the world and compel our belief. They might be susceptible to demonstration within some logical system of great scope, but for our present purposes they are taken as givens, and only are illustrated in our discussion, not proven. There are seven axioms.

The statements that are derived from these axioms are called *propositions*. Some are the theoretical statements about religion that it is our desire to discover. Others are intermediate steps that permit us to derive the statements in which we are most interested.

Propositions bring us close to the real world, but they cannot be tested without a further step, provided by *definitions*. Definitions are statements that link the axioms and propositions to the empirical world. They express certain observable characteristics of the *elements* of other statements, elements which might be described as variables, concepts, or simply things. Through definitions we can operationalize the statements that have been deduced, and thence test the theory or its parts.

To facilitate understanding and use of the theory, we have given numbers to the axioms, propositions and definitions. Axioms are identified by the code letter *A*, propositions by *P*, and definitions by the abbreviation *Def*. The statements are arranged and numbered in the order which permits us to derive propositions most efficiently.

A Theory of Human Action

We begin with an axiom that is so basic that standard social scientific theories seldom mention it. Yet it is essential before we can understand anything else. The first axiom places human existence in *time*.

A1 Human perception and action take place through time, from the past into the future.

Def.1 The *past* consists of the universe of conditions which can be known but not influenced.

Def.2 The *future* consists of the universe of conditions which can be influenced but not known.

The second axiom is a restatement of the first proposition in exchange theory, operant learning theory, and micro-economics (Skinner, 1938; Miller and Dollard, 1941; Homans, 1974).

A2 Humans seek what they perceive to be rewards and avoid what they perceive to be costs.

Def.3 *Rewards* are anything humans will incur costs to obtain.

Def.4 *Costs* are whatever humans attempt to avoid.

We find it facilitates comprehension and discussion to use the most familiar and widely used words in our statements. Therefore we speak of rewards and costs rather than of positive and negative reinforcers. Our definitions might be phrased in numerous ways. For example, we might say that subjectively rewards give pleasure while costs give pain. But our purpose is to explain human behavior in general, not merely to express our feelings about our own personal behavior. Therefore we are best advised to define our concepts in terms that can be operationalized through observation of other persons. We do not deny the importance of subjective states. We merely believe it is most fruitful for science to deal whenever possible with external phenomena that can be observed and measured. Our first proposition derives directly from A2, Def.3 and Def.4.

P1 Rewards and costs are complementary: a lost or forgone reward equals a cost, and an avoided cost equals a reward.

Proposition 1 extends A2 by expressing in another way the relationship between its terms. Seeking and avoiding are opposites. To obtain a reward, a person accepts costs. When a person attempts to avoid a cost, he seeks the avoidance of that cost, and this avoidance is by Def.3 a reward. If rewards and costs were not complementary, there could be no human action, but human action is still not possible without a further principle:

A3 Rewards vary in kind, value, and generality.

> Def.5 Reward A is more *valuable* than reward B if a person will usually exchange B for A.
>
> Def.6 Rewards are *general* to the extent that they include other (less general) rewards.

All our experience supports the truth of this axiom. We know we desire some things more than others. Some desires are biologically conditioned, some are conditioned by environment, others by culture, and some even depend upon an individual's unique history. Here this variation is not germane. All that is asserted is that for every individual there are things he wants more or less of. This also implies that for each individual there are rewards which the person does not possess at any given moment, while other rewards may already be in the person's possession.

The second proposition is derived from all the previous statements, and gives the condition under which human action is possible:

P2 Sometimes rewards can be obtained at costs less than the cost equivalent to forgoing the reward.

Stated another way, P2 says that sometimes human action can be profitable. This means that over time an individual may gain some desired rewards through the expenditure (as costs) of less desired rewards. If rewards did not differ in kind, then there would only be one reward, and it is difficult to see how one could make a profit through trading in it. If rewards did not differ in value, there would be no sense in giving up one to acquire another. The fact that rewards differ in generality is implied by the mathematical possibility of addition. When a person seeks a collection of rewards, by Def.3 this collection constitutes a reward in itself, and yet it includes other lesser rewards. Thus, any collection of rewards is more general than any single reward in the collection.

If reward A is more valuable than reward B, then they must differ in kind, generality, or both.

These axioms and propositions give us the context in which human action is possible, but they do not sufficiently specify the necessary characteristics of the human actor. Axiom 4 expresses the human capacity to perceive and act effectively in a complex environment:

A4 Human action is directed by a complex but finite information-processing system that functions to identify problems and attempt solutions to them.

Def.7 The *mind* is the set of human functions that directs the action of a person.

Def.8 Human *problems* are recurrent situations that require investments (costs) of particular kinds to obtain rewards.

Def.9 To *solve* a problem means to imagine possible means of achieving the desired reward, to select the one with the greatest likelihood of success in the light of available information, and to direct action along the chosen line until the reward has been achieved.

Our definition of the *mind* is extremely non-specific. We note that the mind performs certain functions, but we do not say very much about how it accomplishes this. The mind is often conceptualized by social scientists as the nervous system as modified by learning. It is more than just the brain. In cybernetic terms, the brain is hardware, while learning is software. The mind is the total combination of hardware plus software required to direct individual action. To say that the mind is finite means that it is limited in the amount of information it can store and process. We make no assumptions concerning the existence of the soul; our theory neither denies its existence nor requires it. Definition 9 is a rather long statement of how the human mind must operate if it is to achieve its task in complex circumstances. This definition reminds us of what our minds actually do, but it is also implied by the preceeding arguments.

Because rewards differ in many ways, problems also differ, and solutions must also differ if complex human action is to be possible. Solutions must often be somewhat novel, since humans constantly encounter circumstances they have not previously experienced. Yet solutions are not the result of random experimentation. Not even Skinner's stupid pigeons thrash aimlessly about, flapping their wings and pecking and clawing in all directions, whenever they encounter a slight change in the experimental contingencies. Instead, organisms attempt to deal with novel circumstances as variations on circumstances with which they are already familiar. Thus, we attack new situations as mixtures of the familiar and the unfamiliar, and attempt to break novelty down conceptually into combinations of familiar elements. Conceptual simplifications of reality, models of reality designed to guide action, may be called *explanations*.

P3 In solving problems, the human mind must seek explanations.

Def.10 *Explanations* are statements about how and why rewards may be obtained and costs are incurred.

Because humans seek explanations, and by Def.3 whatever humans seek is a reward, it follows that:

P4 Explanations are rewards of some level of generality.

Explanations differ along all the dimensions that other rewards do; for example they differ in generality. An explanation can guide action on more than one occasion, and therefore potentially can provide several lesser rewards. Thus, any explanation is relatively general. Explanations tell us what costs to expend under what circumstances and in what time sequence in order to obtain the desired reward. Given an effective explanation X_1, we can imagine another explanation X_2 identical to X_1 but with the addition of some costly action C which does not alter the value of the reward obtained. Thus we can deduce that:

P5 Explanations vary in the costs and time they require for the desired reward to be obtained.

Explanations should also vary according to the kind, value, and generality of the rewards to be obtained through them, but here we note that they vary even when the reward achieved is held constant. It is said that there are three ways of doing everything: the right way, the wrong way, and the Army way. In fact, of course, there is an infinite number of ways of attempting to accomplish anything, thus an unlimited number of competing explanations, and usually there are many routes to success, each of a distinctive length. Often, it is fairly easy to find a successful explanation and solve the problem of obtaining a desired reward. But sometimes this is not the case. Axiom 5 introduces this tragic fact and is the turning point on which the crucial parts of our argument hinge:

A5 Some desired rewards are limited in supply, including some that simply do not exist.

Def.11 A *limited* supply means that not everyone can have as much of a reward as they desire.

Def.12 Rewards that *do not exist* cannot be obtained by any person or group.

People always tend to want more rewards than they can have. Put another way, aggregate demand tends always to exceed supply. While this may not be true of a given reward at a given time, it is true of the sum of rewards. Natural resources and human productive capacities tend to limit the supply of many rewards. For example, most societies have never possessed more food than their populations would have consumed. Obviously, the extent to which any given reward is in short supply varies from society to society and from time to time. But unsated appetites always remain. And some, like the desire for honor, tend to be insatiable (Lenski, 1966).

As if the human predicament were not bad enough, many rewards are very temporary. The achievement of gratification uses up the reward. Thus, not only are many rewards scarce, but they must be acquired again and again. This is a principle of great importance for later parts of our theory, although here it may seem just an amplification of A5, and so we shall state it as an axiom.

A6 Most rewards sought by humans are destroyed when they are used.

Def.13 *Consumables* are rewards which are destroyed when they are used.

Food is the obvious example. It achieves its human purpose when it is eaten and nourishes our bodies. One way of conceiving of consumables is as means to desired ends. Some consumables are spent in exchanges with other humans. Others are resources that are depleted in the achievement of desirable states of being. Again, food gives us bodily satisfaction, a very direct kind of reward. Many consumables satisfy rather specific (rather than general) desires. Food satisfies hunger; water satisfies thirst; air satisfies the desire to breathe and our need for oxygen; heat in the furnace satisfies the desire for warmth, and so on.

More complex desires are also satisfied by consumables. A good mystery novel may temporarily satisfy the desire for entertainment, but it is an odd person who can be happy reading the same mystery novel over and over again. The rush of sexual satisfaction passes quickly, rather than being a permanent state that need only be achieved once. Repeated experiences of erotic pleasure must be achieved separately through the kind of work known appropriately as "love-making," an activity that entails new costs every time it is attempted.

How do humans get those rewards that do exist? Much of what we desire can only come from someone else, whether the reward be affection or apples. When we seek a reward from someone else, that person usually must pay a cost for providing us with the reward. Thus, in order to induce another to supply us a reward, we must offer an inducement – some other reward – in return. Proposition 2 tells us that a deal is possible. Sometimes we can offer the other person a reward that he evaluates more highly than what he gives us, while we likewise value what we get over what we give. Thus, through seeking rewards people are forced into exchange relationships (Homans, 1950, 1974; Axelrod, 1984).

P6 In pursuit of desired rewards, humans will exchange rewards with other humans.

People will not engage in these exchanges in an aimless way. All our discussion explains that they will tend to act rationally to maximize rewards and minimize costs. Thus, it follows that:

P7 Humans seek high exchange ratios.

Def. 14 *Exchange ratio* is a person's net rewards over costs in an exchange.

So far in this discussion we have been dealing with abstract "persons" who are equally constrained by our propositions. But we know that real people do not possess equal rewards, nor are they treated equally by each other. There might be many ways of expressing the fact that some individuals have greater resources than others, but the way we find most convenient for our deductions is stated in our final axiom.

A7 Individual and social attributes which determine power are unequally distributed among persons and groups in any society.

Def.15 *Power* is the degree of control over one's exchange ratio.

Power has proved elusive of definition in sociology. Usually it is defined as the capacity to get one's way even against the opposition of others. Such a definition fails to say what it means to get one's way. Obviously, getting one's way has to do with gaining rewards or avoiding costs and is lodged in exchange relationships. It proves fruitful to define power as controlling the exchange ratio with the consequence that the more powerful, the more favorable the exchange ratio.

With power defined thus, attention must turn to capacities or attributes that enable persons or groups to be powerful, to control exchange ratios with others. Some of these capacities are biological features of human organisms – height, weight, eyesight, reflexes, endurance, strength, beauty, health, agility, and intelligence, for example. But it will also be obvious that many achieved and ascribed characteristics serve as power-giving capacities. Achieved skills, training, knowledge, and experience tend to give power. Ascribed statuses such as sex, race, family background, and the like also often serve to give power. These too vary (Davis and Moore, 1945; Lenski, 1966).

Among the important determinants of power are the outcomes of previous exchanges. That is, power may be used to accumulate resources that confer still more power. This tendency may have limits. For example, some rewards may be difficult to concentrate in great quantitites, while any that are unlimited in supply cannot be concentrated at all. But rewards that exist only in limited supply are particularly susceptible to the exercise of power. Scarce rewards will tend to flow through exchanges into the hands of the powerful and away from the weak. In other words:

P8 Exchange ratios vary among persons and groups in any society.

P9 Rewards that exist in limited supply will tend to be monopolized by powerful persons and groups, thereby becoming relatively unavailable to others.

When persons seek scarce but valuable rewards, they usually do not give up at the first sign of difficulty. Humans are persistent in pursuit of strongly desired rewards. This is another way of stating that they are willing to pay great costs for great rewards, a fact that follows from P1 and from the definition of "valuable." Some problems can be solved only through extended and costly effort, and among them are the satisfactions of several strong desires. Difficulty in obtaining strongly desired rewards not only produces the emotion we call *frustration*, but also leads to a knotty intellectual and logical quandry. How do people decide if they are on the right track? How do people evaluate the explanations on which they base their action?

P10 Explanations can be evaluated correctly only by reference to their known ability to facilitate the attainment of the desired reward.

Def.16 *Evaluation* is the determination of the value of any reward, including explanations.

Def.17 The *value* of a reward is equivalent to the maximum cost a person would pay to obtain the reward.

As noted in P5, explanations do vary in the costs and time required before they can give us the desired reward. As A4 pointed out, the human mind has to compare explanations to decide which is the cheapest way of getting what is wanted. If our current situation is very similar to past situations, we can simply repeat what worked for us before. Suppose this is the third time we wanted a person to share their food with us. The first time we insulted them, and they gave us nothing. The second time we complimented them, and they gave us a bit to eat. This time we should compliment them, because that solution to the problem worked before. In thinking things over, we can evaluate the two courses of action because one worked in the past while the other did not. That means that evaluations, in the terms of Axiom 1, are used to influence the future but must be based on knowledge of the past.

In A5 we noted that some desired rewards are scarce, and others do not even exist. In saying that some rewards do not exist, we are postulating a fact which we cannot prove. Certainly, human observation demonstrates that some rewards are very scarce. No one is reliably known to have survived death. Although some religions report evidence on outstanding cases, the other religions do not accept their claims. Logically, some rewards cannot exist because their terms are contradictory. As we usually interpret the words, we cannot have our cake and eat it too. It is a fact of life that some of the most desired, most general rewards have not been shown to exist, and we suspect that they do not in fact exist. If A5 is a little unsettling as it is stated, we could interpret it to say that some desired rewards are so scarce that they do not seem to exist in this world.

However, unless the definition of a particular desired reward contains a logical contradiction, we cannot be absolutely sure that there is no solution to the problem of obtaining it. This follows from Axiom 1, because until the end of time – until we run out of future – we will not have complete information about all possible explanations, that is, we cannot evaluate the success of all possible courses of action. This is true in lesser degree for scarce rewards that can be obtained only through relatively costly action, including rewards that require lengthy sequences of exchange. Suppose we want to compare the values of two competing explanations for obtaining a scarce reward. We cannot honestly end the test until we have expended at least twice the cost required by the explanation that is in fact the cheaper of the two. We must have succeeded with one and have invested slightly more than an equal amount in the other before it is ideally justifiable to abandon the one that has not yet led to success. Until some course of action succeeds for us, we cannot completely reject any others that are possible to follow under the given circumstances. It is not surprising that people often stick with explanations that seem to work, without ever testing others that may exist. Because explanations can only be evaluated through a process that actually invests the minimum cost required to obtain the desired reward, the following propositions hold:

P11 It is impossible to know for certain that a given reward does not exist.

P12 When a desired reward is relatively unavailable, explanations that promise to provide it are costly and difficult to evaluate correctly.

P13 The more valued or general a reward, the more difficult will be evaluation of explanations about how to obtain it.

Taken together, these three propositions explain why people will often persist in following an incorrect explanation or one that has at least not proven fruitful, especially when strong desires are concerned. Some explanations will be invalidated because they set specific terms for themselves. If they state the exact interval of time required for the reward to appear, then they will be discredited if the time passes and nothing happens. If people are determined to invest in seeking a reward, false explanations that can be discredited easily will drop by the wayside, leaving explanations (whether correct or not) which are not as vulnerable. Therefore:

P14 In the absence of a desired reward, explanations often will be accepted which posit attainment of the reward in the distant future or in some other non-verifiable context.

Def.18 *Compensators* are postulations of reward according to explanations that are not readily susceptible to unambiguous evaluation.

The Compensators of Magic and Religion

The concept of *compensators* is the key to the theory of religion which follows. When humans cannot quickly and easily obtain strongly desired rewards they persist in their efforts and may often accept explanations that provide only compensators. These are intangible substitutes for the desired reward, having the character of I.O.U.s, the value of which must be taken on faith.

P15 Compensators are treated by humans as if they were rewards.

P16 For any reward or cluster of rewards, one or more compensators may be invented.

P17 Compensators vary according to the generality, value, and kind of the rewards for which they substitute.

Def.19 Compensators which substitute for single, specific rewards are called *specific compensators*.

Def.20 Compensators which substitute for a cluster of many rewards and for rewards of great scope and value are called *general compensators*.

These propositions outline a major orphan generalization in social science analysis of the functions of religion. Malinowski's (1948) celebrated theory of magic – as an attempt to provide people with a compensatory sense of control over dangerous or vital events they cannot control – is pertinent here. So are Marx's ruminations about false consciousness and opium of the people, Durkheim's analysis of primitive religions, Freud's conjectures about religion as illusion, and much of church-sect theory. As they stand, however, our propositions do not equate compensators with religion. Many compensators have no connection with religion. Consider the faithful servant of the millionaire who accepts years of poverty and self-effacement on the strength of promise to a major part of the millionaire's estate. Each day, rewards are foregone and an unfavorable exchange ratio is accepted on faith that all will be made-up in the end. If the millionaire finally dies and does leave the servant a fortune, then all comes out right in the end, and the I.O.U.s are converted into rewards. But if they are never converted, or until they are converted, they are compensators.

All societies utilize compensators. Perhaps the most universal is some promise of a triumph over death (Cook and Wimberley, 1983). If means were provided to evade death here and now, that would be a reward. But at present immortality is to be achieved somewhere (somewhen?) else, and the validity of the promise cannot be determined. Thus the desire for immortality is not satisfied with a reward but with an intangible promise, a compensator. The validity of this promise cannot be determined empirically, but must be accepted or rejected on faith alone. If the promise turns out true, then at that point compensators are redeemed as rewards. If not, not.

Some desired rewards are so general as to require explanations that also are very general – explanations which can best be described as philosophies of life, theologies, or solutions to questions of ultimate meaning (Tillich, 1948; Parsons, 1957; Kluckhohn, 1962; Glock and Stark, 1965; Wuthnow, 1976). As discussed more fully later in this chapter, humans have an irrepressible habit of asking *why*, a habit captured in our axioms. When human "whys" are repeated along certain logical chains they lead eventually to questions about the fundamental meaning and purpose of human existence and of the natural world. Some of these desired explanations are not susceptible to unambiguous evaluation. That is, we cannot establish beyond doubt whether these explanations are correct. According to our definition, such untestable and extremely general explanations are compensators. This is not to say that they are untrue. The opening line of *Genesis* states, "In the beginning God created the heaven and the earth." This may be absolutely true. But we cannot find out anytime soon. It is this, and only this, aspect of such explanations that leads us to identify them as compensators. Surely there is nothing controversial about distinguishing between statements that can be tested and those that must be taken on faith.

Insofar as the empirical world is concerned, at any given moment a more favorable exchange ratio is possible if one can obtain a reward in trade for a compensator. Unlike bonds and other financial I.O.U.s, compensators do not pay interest to the holder. On the contrary, they are often costly to keep and maintain. Any compensator entails the risk that it cannot be redeemed for the promised reward, and therefore must be judged less valuable than that reward.

> P18 Humans prefer rewards to compensators and attempt to exchange compensators for rewards.

This is merely to recognize that intangible I.O.U.s may represent a low cost to the giver. If you demand a better deal, and I can keep things as they are by issuing promises. I can continue to enjoy a more favorable exchange ratio. Drawing together many pieces of the argument to this point, we can specify when people will succeed in obtaining rewards, and when they will be forced to accept compensators instead:

P19 It is impossible to obtain a reward rather than a compensator when the reward does not exist.

P20 It is impossible to obtain a reward rather than a compensator when the compensator is mistaken for the reward.

P21 It is impossible to obtain a reward rather than a compensator when one lacks the power to obtain the reward.

Obviously, one can at best accept a compensator if the desired reward does not exist. Malinowski's Trobriand Islanders undoubtedly would have preferred ocean liners to outrigger canoes. But in their world liners did not exist. The best they could do was use magical compensators for the risk of sailing on the open sea. By the same token, humans would prefer not to die. Lacking scientific means to achieve immortality, they can at best settle for compensators in the form of hopes for the life to come.

It is equally obvious that people will often fail to obtain a reward and will accept a compensator instead if they cannot distinguish the one from the other. An important capacity influencing power is the ability or knowledge to make such discriminations. Ignorance of the contingencies of reward implies little control over one's exchange ratio. Indeed, this line of analysis reminds us how often means come to be mistaken for ends.

Finally, awareness is not enough if we are unable to control our exchange ratios. As Proposition 9 states, scarce rewards will tend to be monopolized by powerful persons and groups, leaving the powerless to content themselves with compensators. Here one thinks of the transvaluational character of religions of the poor and dispossessed. For example, folks who belonged to fundamentalist sects in Apalachia in the 1930s knew perfectly well that jewels, fancy clothes, and other material luxuries existed. They also knew perfectly well they had little chance to get any. So they defined these things as sinful and accepted the compensatory belief that by doing without on Earth, they would triumph in Heaven, where the first shall be last, and the last, first. However, in keeping with Proposition 18, when the economic circumstances of such groups changed, they tended quite rapidly to become more worldly and materialistic, an observation of some interest in church-sect theory.

We have now reached the point at which we can introduce the concept of *religion* itself. We do so in a definition appended to a proposition about compensators. Thus we show that religion must emerge in human society, and we derive its existence entirely from axioms and propositions in which religion is not an original term. At various points in this book, as in the first article introducing our theory, we show that the term *religion* is best reserved for systems of the most general compensators, while less general compensators may be found in many contexts (Stark and Bainbridge, 1979). But the proposition itself is about the sources of faith in general compensators. It follows most immediately from Proposition 13, Proposition 14, Proposition 17, and Definition 20.

> P22 The most general compensators can be supported only by supernatural explanations.
>
> > Def.21 *Supernatural* refers to forces beyond or outside nature which can suspend, alter, or ignore physical forces.
> >
> > Def.22 *Religion* refers to systems of general compensators based on supernatural assumptions.

Earlier we mentioned very general compensators that offer explanations for questions of ultimate meaning. It is evident that many humans often desire answers to such questions: "Does life have purpose? Why are we here? What can we hope? Is death the end? Why do we suffer? Does justice exist? Why did my child die? Why am I a slave?" Humans are bound to raise questions about how great rewards can be obtained and why great costs are sometimes incurred. Evidence that our rude Neanderthal ancestors performed burial rites indicates that the tendency to ask such questions and to fashion answers to them reaches far back into pre-history.

When we consider such questions it is self-evident that some of them require a supernatural answer. To seek the purpose of life is to demand that it have one. The word *purpose* is not compatible with blind chance, but assumes the existence of intentions or motives. These assume a consciousness. For the universe to have a purpose, it must be directed by a conscious agent or agents, for the capacity to form plans or have intentions is to be conscious (cf. Gorsuch and Smith, 1983).

Conscious agents on this scale are beyond the natural world. Their existence is not subject to empirical inspection. Thus, to answer certain common questions about ultimate meaning it is necessary to assume the existence of the supernatural.

Our decision to restrict the definition of religion to very general compensator systems that rest on supernatural assumptions is in keeping with a very long and fruitful tradition in social science (Tylor, 1871; Parsons, 1957; Swanson, 1960; Goody, 1961; Spiro, 1966; Wallace, 1966; Garrett, 1974). A few scholars have dissented in order to apply the definition of religion to systems of thought that inspire devotion even when these are explicitly opposed to supernatural assumptions (Luckmann, 1967; Bellah, 1970; Yinger, 1970). This minority tradition follows in the path of Durkheim (1915) and is based on giving total priority to the need to "find" religion present in all societies. While this book owes a great debt to Durkheim, we do not feel the need to follow him in this respect. Durkheim rejected the supernatural criterion because he thought Buddhism was atheistic and hence that to define religion as having a supernatural component was to fail to encompass all cases. Unfortunately Durkheim was incorrect in his conclusions about Buddhism. And he was misguided in his concerns for universality. Suppose an irreligious society did exist? Ought we hush this up with definitional changes, or ought we examine how this occurs and with what consequences? Spiro (1966) has provided a definitive treatment of this matter.

As Swanson (1960) pointed out, the members of this minority tradition blur a vital theoretical question with their all-inclusive definition of religion. For example, if scientific rationalism, Roman Catholicism and Russian Communism are all declared to be religions, we lose the conceptual tools to explore the constant and profound conflicts among them. Berger (1967:177) has demonstrated the futility of this too-inclusive definition of religion. If we define as religion all systems of very general compensators, "self-transcendent symbolic universes" as Berger calls them, then one immediately is forced to define in what way science, for example, is "*different* from what has been called religion by everyone else . . . which poses the definitinal problem all over again." For if we then adopt new terms to identify these differences we merely make superfluous the original definition of religion which classified all of them as the same. We prefer to honor the commonly understood meaning of the term *religion*, especially because we can anticipate increased theoretical utility from so doing (cf. Stark, 1981).

The insistence on limiting the definition of religion to systems of very general compensators also permits us to distinguish between religion and magic, and in turn between magic and science. *Magic* is a set of compensators of less generality than those identified as religion. That is, magic does not concern itself with the meaning of the universe, but with the manipulation of the universe for quite specific ends. Here we follow Durkheim (1915:42), who argued that since magic is directed toward "technical and utilitarian ends, it does not waste its time in speculation" as is the case with religion. Being directed towards quite specific and immediate rewards, magic becomes subject to empirical evaluation. Claims that a particular spell will cure warts or repell bullets are empirically testable (Dodd, 1961). Weber (1963:2) invoked the criterion of empirical verification to distinguish between magic and science. He wrote:

> Only we, judging from the standpoint of our modern views of nature, can distinguish objectively in such behavior those attributes of causality which are "correct" from those which are "fallacious," and then designate the fallacious attributions of causation as irrational, and the corresponding acts as "magic."

Magic flourishes when humans lack effective and economical means for such testing. Indeed, it was by learning how to evaluate specific explanations offered by magic that humans can be said to have developed science. That is, science is an efficient procedure for evaluating explanations.

Note that we have not identified magic with supernaturally-based compensators. Often magic is based on supernatural assumptions. But at the level of small, specific assumptions, concepts of the supernatural blend into ordinary views of the natural world. In particular, modern forms of magic often postulate the existence of forces and entities ("animal magnetism," "orgone," the "id," "aura") which serve the same functions as the concepts of primitive magic but which sound scientific rather than supernatural. We wish our definitions to include the present-day magical pseudosciences, unquestionably current examples of magic, even though many of them avoid supernatural explanations. Many of these are putative psychotherapies (Dianetics and est are examples) which supply compensators for relatively limited goals such as peace of mind or increased personal influence. They can be identified as compensators rather than as rewards in the manner suggested by Weber, that is, by empirical falsification of their claims. They constitute magic rather than incorrect efforts at science because they are offered without regard to their demonstrable falsity. Thus we reserve the term *magic* for compensators which are offered as correct explanations without regard for empirical evaluations and which are found wanting if they are properly evaluated.

An important reason for defining magic this broadly is because we have observed a number of cases wherein what began as magical pseudoscience evolved into a religion. In these cases, groups that began by dealing in magic, such as crank therapies, and who had no supernatural elements in their original system, began to pursue explanations of greater and greater generality until they invented a fully religious system (Bainbridge, 1978). In Chapter 6 we show how these increasingly numerous cases can be understood in terms of our theory.

Throughout this book we will examine the nature and sources of different forms of religion. One concept that brings focus to many of our discussions is that of the *religious organization*. In the modern world, when one thinks of religion one first thinks of churches. Two later chapters examine how new religious organizations come into being. Chapter 3 lays a solid basis for such analysis by demonstrating that religious organizations in fact are bound to emerge in societies that have evolved beyond the lowest levels of population and complexity.

Here we want to show the reader the utility of our theoretical approach, and do not wish to present extremely long chains of deduction merely to arrive at a few examples of the power of our propositions. The reader deserves to see some Sociology of Religion before we journey for a chapter or two in the realms of ancient history. We could assume that religious organizations exist by stating the fact in an axiom, but since we shall be able to derive the existence of religious organizations we should avoid an unnecessary postulate. Therefore, let us consider each of the following propositions to be in the form of a conditional: "if religious organizations exist, then X is true." Later, when the existence of such groups has been derived, these propostions can take on their full scientific weight. We introduce the concept of religious organizations in a definition.

Def.23 *Religious organizations* are social enterprises whose primary purpose is to create, maintain, and exchange supernaturally-based general compensators.

Commitment to Religious Organizations

As in the case for all other social groups and formal organizations, commitment to religious organizations depends on the net balance of rewards and costs humans perceive they will experience from participation (Schoenherr and Greeley, 1974). While humans will often accept compensators as if they were actual rewards, our theory has emphasized the conceptual and empirical differences between rewards and compensators. Surely the role of religious organizations in producing and promulgating compensators will be obvious. A major emphasis in religious proselytization is that religion will provide a cure for pain and trouble. Indeed, because religions have recourse to a supernatural realm they have an unmatched capacity to create and sponsor compensators. But it also should be emphasized that religious organizations, like other organizations, have the capacity to provide rewards.

Because compensators function as if they were rewards, humans are prepared to expend costs to obtain them. Religious organizations provide compensators through exchanges in which at least some measure of real rewards is collected. Proposition 18 should not be misinterpreted to mean that persons will never give up a reward to obtain a compensator. Just as they will exchange a lesser reward for a more valuable one, they will readily exchange a reward of low value for a compensator that promises to provide a reward of great value. Upon reflection it is obvious that, although religions usually cannot match the reward-generating capacity of some other societal institutions, they do in fact provide rewards. For example, through religious organizations one can gain leadership positions (with attendant status and power), human companionship, leisure and recreational activity, and the like. Any organization that provides a stage for human action and interaction will produce scenes in which all manner of rewards are created and exchanged.

P23 As social enterprises, religious organizations tend to provide some rewards as well as compensators.

This proposition permits us to introduce our derivations concerning power into the religious realm, in the three propositions that follow.

P24 The power of an individual or group is positively associated with control of religious organizations and with gaining the rewards available from religious organizations.

P25 The power of an individual or group is negatively associated with accepting religious compensators, when the desired reward exists.

Power means control of one's exchange ratio. Control of religious organizations facilitates control of one's exchange ratio by increasing one's ability to exchange compensators for rewards. Furthermore, those most able to gain rewards will tend to gain a bigger share of religious rewards too. Because the powerful are more able to gain rewards, they will find less need for compensators. But this does not mean that powerful persons and groups will have absolutely no use for compensators. Some rewards are so scarce – even nonexistent – that even the powerful will not be able to obtain them. Therefore,

> P26 Regardless of power, persons and groups tend to accept religious compensators, when desired rewards do not exist.

Some will interpret Propositions 24 and 25 in Marxist fashion – that the powerful will profit while the poor pray. If so, then by the same token the twenty-sixth proposition is unMarxist, and reflects basic functionalist assumptions: that all members of a society can have significant common interests, that they will tend to pursue these interests in a cooperative fashion, and that there will be considerable consensus on such matters (to say nothing of the integrative functions of such common interests). Of course, in a pluralist society compenting religious organizations may exist, and there is always the competition offered by secular organizations in those areas where less general compensators or demonstrable rewards are offered.

> P27 If multiple suppliers of general compensators exist, then the ability to exchange general compensators will depend upon their relative availability and perceived exchange ratios.

Religious organizations vary in terms of how well-developed and credible a set of compensators they offer. Furthermore, they vary in terms of their degree of formal organization, and the extent to which they are differentiated from other social institutions. Such variations are likely to matter.

Furthermore, in some societies other institutions and organizations offer serious competition to religion in offering both rewards and compensators. The quasi-religious character of some political movements has long been recognized. While there are substantial differences between, for example, the location and character of socialist and Christian utopias, the two nevertheless compete. By the same token, a scientific perspective may compete with religion in offering very general explanations concerning the most important human rewards and costs. Proposition 27 is crucial for understanding the great compexity found in the real world, but in present form it is so general as to be a truism. Later chapters will add specificity and explore socialization to these perspectives in detail.

> P28 All patterns of human perception and action are conditioned by socialization.

Def. 24 *Socialization* is the accumulation of explanations over time through exchanges with other persons.

Clearly it matters, for example, whether an American is raised by Baptists or Unitarians. Furthermore, regardless of the content of socialization, the effectiveness of socialization varies. Variations in socialization probably will account for much variation in religious behavior across individuals – and probably across groups as well. This is an area that deserves extensive exploration. But for present purposes it is best to pause in our exposition of the theory and conclude this chapter by showing that our key concepts can be operationalized and that once this is done we will find that much evidence supports our propositions. Other chapters present evidence as individual propositions are derived. We think the following sections will help the reader see the scientific utility of our theory, but they are also intended to let us pause and take stock of key concepts.

Operationalizing Religious Rewards and Compensators

In order to test the theory it is necessary to determine more specifically what is meant by religious rewards and compensators and select means by which they can be measured. This is not a difficult matter because in fact these are nothing but new labels for an old distinction. The distinction between churches and sects parallels the notion of rewards and compensators. Churches are characterized in terms of low key social participation and little tension with the surrounding social and cultural environment. Sects are characterized in terms of fervent commitment and rejection of the surrounding social and cultural environment (Johnson, 1963, cf. 1957, 1971). Churches, then, can be seen as placing more emphasis on direct rewards, sects on compensators.

In 1965, Demerath made an important extension of church/sect theories. He pointed out that the church/sect distinction makes as much sense within as across churches. He demonstrated that within several mainline Protestant churches, a minority of members tended to constitute a sect. Put another way, he found one group of church members who were inclined to "do" their religion, to attend services, participate in church organizations and activities, whereas a second group of members tended to "believe" and "feel" their religion, to be very concerned with religious doctrines and to express their religiousness in emotional ways. He referred to the "doers" as having a church-like religious orientation, and the "believers" and "feelers" as having a sect-like religious orientation.

Over the next several years the first major body of data on American religious belief and behavior strongly confirmed Demerath's findings (Glock and Stark, 1965; Stark and Glock, 1968). A host of findings showed that within even the most liberal Protestant denominations a subset of members could be found who constituted, in effect, a highly integrated, fundamentalistic, emotionalistic sect. In 1972, Stark classified a series of indexes of religious commitment as church-like or sect-like. He could as well have referred to them as rewards, on the one hand, and compensators, on the other.

Rewards available from American religious institutions include at least the following:

1. *Church membership*: which confers status and legitimate standing in the community, and which makes it possible to secure other religious rewards.
2. *Attendance at worship services*: which in addition to any specific religious meanings are also social occasions, and provide whatever rewards obtain from such.
3. *Participation*: in religious organizations and activities, including such disparate things as the choir, the square dancing club, or the singles club.
4. *Child socialization*: conveying a cultural and moral heritage to children as well as supplying rewards such as membership in scouting and sports groups.

Compensators available from American religious institutions include at least the following:

1. *Religious doctrines*: which promise to make the burdens of this life bearable, to make guidance and help available, and to offer reparations for earthly suffering in the life after death.
2. *Religious experiences*: a release for pent-up emotions and a source of confidence in the authenticity of compensators, such as when a person has a vision or speaks in unknown tongues.
3. *Prayer and private devotionalism*: mechanisms for seeking devine aid and guidance, for confessing guilt, for gaining comfort.
4. *Particularism or moral superiority*: reassurance that no matter how little one seems to matter in the world of affairs, one is among those chosen by God and possesses an elite religious identity. Elsewhere this concept has been developed at length (Glock and Stark, 1966).

j This listing is hardly exhaustive. Previous work has developed and examined empirical measures of each (especially in Stark and Glock, 1968). Indeed, it is particularly in connection with these measures and ones closely akin to them that many of our new facts have been piled up over the past 20 years. That means, of course, that the theory must be reconciled with a considerable number of tests of its most obvious hypotheses. We now demonstrate that the theory can survive an initial confrontation.

Socio-Economic Status and Religious Commitment

From Propositions 24, 25 and 26 a number of complex and nonobvious hypotheses can be deduced about the relationship between power-giving attributes of people and groups and religious rewards and compensators.

The most obvious and direct of these hypotheses predicts the relationship between socio-economic status (SES) and religious behavior. SES should be positively associated with religious rewards and negatively associated with religious compensators – with the exception that SES should be unrelated to belief in life after death.

Since the beginning of public opinion polls it has been known that in fact SES is positively associated with church attendance. For a long time this was a very bothersome finding because the founding fathers had been nearly unanimous in believing that the primary social function of religion was to comfort the poor. It was not until the 1960s that it was recognized that church attendance was not the way in which the lower classes tended to manifest their religiousness (Demerath, 1965; Stark, 1964; 1972). Also during the sixties it became apparent that church membership was predominately a middle and upper class affair. Even in the small sects, membership tends to be middle-class. Put another way, the half of Americans who are not members of a parish or congregation (as distinct from claiming nominal affiliation with a denomination), are very disproportionately lower SES (Stark and Glock, 1968).

SES also is positively associated with taking part in church-related organizations and activities. It is even positively associated with saying prayers before eating. Nor should it be any surprise that among church members it is disproportionately those with higher SES who hold the offices and lead activities. By the same token parents' SES is positively associated with their children's Sunday school enrollment and with the attendance of those who are enrolled. In short, everything that involves public participation, and which can be seen as constituting rewards, per se, is positively associated with SES as predicted by the theory (Stark, 1972).

So far so good. But is it possible that the sign of the relationship can turn negative, as predicted, when compensatory aspects of religiousness are examined despite robust correlations among these religious measures? Yes. Consistently negative associations are found between SES and a well-validated measure of religious orthodoxy. The same occurs when a measure of religious particularism – belief that only true Christians can be saved – is examined. Similarly, while SES is positively associated with saying grace before meals, other kinds of praying are negatively associated with SES. SES is also negatively associated with an index of religious experiences – having felt in the presence of God, having had a salvational experience, having felt punished by God (Stark, 1972).

Finally, SES is much less related to belief in life after death than to other central Christian doctrines (with the exception of belief in the existence of God, where the level of belief is so high that little variation by SES is possible statistically). That is, as the theory predicts, power is little related to compensators when no direct reward exists.

However, all of the findings reported above are subject to several important qualifications. These bear on Propositions 26 and 27 of the theory.

Proposition 28 introduces *socialization* as qualifying other aspects of the theory. The importance of this is easily demonstrated by further examination of the connection between SES and religiousness. Most of the data reported above are based on samples of church members. However, when data based on the total adult population of the United States are examined, the results differ in one important fashion. The sign of the relationship between SES and religiousness does not become negative on measures of religious orthodoxy. Thus among the general public there is a weak positive relationship between SES and accepting the compensations of religious doctrines. The reason is that so many lower SES persons in the United States are unchurched.

For religious compensators to be available, some minimal connection with religious institutions is required. Put another way, those who grow up within religious institutions, who regularly attend Sunday School and church, are more fully socialized into the whole system of religious doctrines and practices. Religion of any kind is a more hit-or-miss affair among those raised outside such institutions. Hence we find that among those who are church members, SES is negatively related to orthodoxy, as predicted. But when the unchurched are included in the data, because they are disproportionately lower SES, the relationship is weakly positive (Stark, 1972). How it is that large numbers of people in a society can be left out of religious organizations is taken up in later chapters.

Further support for the importance of socialization can be seen in comparisons across denominations. The SES-religion associations reported above were all computed within four main denominational clusters – Roman Catholics, and Liberal, Moderate, and Conservative Protestant denominations. Regardless of class, denominational group had a major impact on levels of religious belief and practice. To the extent that denomination is a proxy variable for differences in religious socialization, then socialization plays an important independent role.

Of course, traditions to which people become socialized (from which they receive their explanations) are themselves the residue of past exchanges between persons in accordance with the principles of our theory. However, for purposes of testing major propositions of our theory the central fact is that the effects of SES on religious commitment were independent of denominational group. That is, although the relative proportions of those whose religiousness was manifested primarily through rewards or through compensators differ from one denominational cluster to another, in all clusters the patterns between SES and religiousness were as predicted (Stark, 1972). Another way of viewing this matter is to suggest that the content of socialization varies across American religious subcultures, but that the SES-religion relations hold in all of them.

In Proposition 27 we have deduced competition between religious and other institutions to provide rewards and compensators. Studies show considerable incompatibility between religious commitment and support for leftist politics. Some of the tendency of lower SES groups to be unchurched, especially in Europe, is accounted for by the tendency of these groups to be involved in left politics. Furthermore, the advent of vigorous leftist movements in Europe coincided with a decline in new sect formation. Conversely, new sects continue to form in the United States, while left politics remains weak (Lipset, 1960; Stark, 1964; Glock and Stark, 1965; Martin, 1978).

Similar competition can be found between religious and scientific perspectives. In Chapter 1 we cited data by Leuba which showed that natural and social scientists in the United States at the turn of the century, and again in the 1930s, showed only a small proportion believed in God or in life after death. It is also the case that American graduate students in the arts and sciences show a much higher proportion who deny all religious affiliation than is found in the public at large. Furthermore, those enrolled in the highest quality graduate schools, and who are most committed to a scholarly self-image, are very unlikely to claim religious affiliation (Stark, 1963). Finally, in the general American public the graduate-educated differ remarkably from all others in their levels of religious belief. For example, while 80 percent of college graduates expressed belief in life after death, only 21 percent of those with post-graduate training did so

(Stark, 1972; cf. Albrecht and Heaton, 1984). In contemporary society, then, those to whom a scientific perspective is most available, or who are most likely to be rewarded for holding scientific views, are a relatively irreligious group.

The conclusion is that religion is not the only institution capable of offering compensations for the rewards one cannot gain, or which do not exist. Indeed, in the case of radical politics, the claim is made that rewards can be obtained directly thus making the comforts of faith unnecessary.

Age and Religious Commitment

Age permits examination of the somewhat subtle 26th proposition of the theory. It predicts that when there is a desire that cannot be satisfied with a direct reward, none being available, people will tend to accept a compensator regardless of their power. Data indicating that the relationship between SES and belief in life after death was very weak gave support to hypotheses operationalizing this derivation.

It is a truism that as people age they become more concerned about death. It should follow, then, that as people age they will be more likely to accept a compensator for death – faith in a life beyond death. But there is no reason to suppose that this tendency will affect religious commitment not directly linked to the fear of death, for age has but weak and fleeting connections to power. That is, age is a series of statuses through which all automatically pass merely by surviving.

The most satisfactory data available show that there is a continuous, positive relationship between age and belief in life after death. When other religious beliefs are examined, the relationship is not continuous. Cohorts who grew up before World War II show similar, and higher levels of religious belief. Those who grew up in the postwar period show similar, lower levels of religious belief. This suggests that age differences in religious belief in general reflect social changes – cohort effects – not effects produced by aging (cf. Johnson, *et al.*, 1974). Conversely, belief in life after death rises from cohort to cohort in a way most compatible with an aging interpretation (Stark, 1968).

Age has no appreciable influence on religious rewards or on other religious compensators, with one exception. The data suggest an aging effect on private prayer (Stark, 1968). Surely it is not special pleading to suggest that older people explicitly link prayer with belief in life after death – as the primary way to manifest the devotion that Christian doctrine prescribes as necessary to ensure salvation. Furthermore, to the extent that aging results in physical pain and discomfort and in emotional trauma from the death of friends and loved ones, prayer serves as a means for relieving desires for which rewards do not exist.

Obviously this brief tour of empirical findings serves as no more than a very preliminary testing of hypotheses derivable from our propositions about the relationship between power and religious commitment. Much remains to be done. Yet, at this point we feel encouraged that in being congruent with many pertinent facts, our theory may offer a parsimonious explanation of them.

Conclusion

Any effort to replace a huge, rich, and unsystematic literature with a relatively small set of quite formal statement easily can appear too simplistic. Perhaps our theory is simplistic. We must rely on our colleagues to render a judgment. Nevertheless, we find great complexity both contained in and clarified by the theory. To conclude this chapter we should like to point to some of the virtues we perceive and suggest several opportunities for extending this core theory to other questions, a task we shall undertake more systematically in later chapters.

The dominant line of thought on religious commitment is a very simple deprivation theory. The Apostle Paul believed that religion most appeals to "the weak things of the world," and from the founding fathers on down social scientists have agreed (cf. Glock and Stark, 1965). Already we have demonstrated that this deprivation thesis (Proposition 25) can be derived from our axioms and definitions. However, our theory does not merely echo the deprivation thesis. Instead, we arrive at a considerably more complex picture of religious commitment. As did Weber, we too have paid attention to the fact that religious organizations do more then comfort people for missing out on scarce rewards. Proposition 24 permits us to see that religious organizations also serve as sources of rewards. This permits us to explain religious commitment that is not prompted by deprivation, but instead is a religious expression of privilege.

We have long known that the empirical world was much too complex for religion to be encompassed by a deprivation thesis alone. Indeed, a crucial element of church-sect theory always has been incompatible with the deprivation thesis. Deprivation may be the mainspring of sect formation, but it cannot serve to explain why sects are captured and transformed into churches by the privileged. Thus Proposition 24 fills a critical void.

Finally, the theory permits us to, in effect, greatly expand the sphere of deprivation and thus to recognize that, vis-a-vis certain kinds of desired rewards, everyone is potentially deprived (Proposition 26). While relative deprivation separates the poor from the privileged, objective deprivations such as those entailed by human mortality are shared equally by all. This observation permits us to examine the profound common interests that can unite powerful and powerless alike in creating and maintaining religious organizations. In our judgment, these three propositions deal with religious commitment in a way that is neither more reductionistic nor less comprehensive than previous treatments.

For those whose interest is in the consequences rather than the sources of religious commitment, we also think our three propositions point in a fruitful direction. They specify three basic dimensions of religious commitment. The first of these (Proposition 24) could be identified as the *churchlike* dimension. Here we find all those aspects of religious commitment that can be regarded as directly rewarding to the individual. The second (Proposition 25) could be regarded as the *sectlike* dimension. This includes all those aspects of religious commitment that serve as comforts for failure to gain scarce rewards. Finally, the third (Proposition 26) could be called the *universal* dimension – those aspects of religious commitment that are rooted in the existential condition of humankind.

These three dimensions seem very compatible with the variety of schemes in the literature for conceptualizing varieties of commitment (cf. Glock, 1962; Stark and Glock, 1968). Note in particular the affinity of these dimensions for those proposed by Gordon W. Allport (1960). Allport's *extrinsic* type is weighted heavily on the sectlike dimension. Extrinsic believers seek "comfort" and "safety" and "make use of God." The *intrinsic* type is weighted heavily on the universal dimension (cf. Hood and Morris, 1983) and to a lesser extent on the churchlike dimension. Such believers do not rest their faith on "ego-centric needs."

The importance of the dimensions that derive from our theory is that they are not *ad hoc*. Both Glock's and Allport's dimensions of religious commitment were inductive products, empirically created as summaries of data. Indeed, most other dimensional schemes in the literature are based on nothing more theoretical than the results of factor analysis (cf. King, 1967; Hilty, *et al.*, 1984; Hilty and Morgan, 1985). And of course, factor analysis and similar techniques can at best uncover the pattern in a particular set of data coming from a particular historical situation and expressed through measures selected by the researcher. The trouble with inductive conceptualizations is that an infinite number of alternatives exists, and there is no way to choose among them. Since concepts are definitions, all concepts are "true." As we have said, the real test of concepts is their fruitfulness for theorizing. That is, concepts are useful only to the extent that they play an effective role in theories which have the power to explain significant, interesting sectors of reality. Social science achieves little when it merely names twists and turns in the pattern of some data. Far more of an accomplishment is successful explanation in terms of a general theory. Therefore, concepts that are not incorporated in theories may or may not be fruitful. There is no way to tell. Since our conceptualization of commitment derives from an explanatory theory, it is at least provisionally fruitful.

Finally, it will be clear to many readers that our three propositions about the relationships between power and different modes of religious commitment provide the essential starting point for a theory of church and sect movements. That is, we have deduced the existence within religious bodies of an "internal contradiction" – the presence of groups with a conflict of interests over whom the religious organization is to serve, and how. Thus the seeds of schism and of the transformation of religious organizations are inherent in the social composition of religious organizations. A host of complex predictions about the formation and transformation of sect and church movements can be deduced from our core theory.

The following chapters extend our theory to a wide range of traditional social-scientific questions. Numerous empirical journal articles published by us in recent years, many of them incorporated in *The Future of Religion*, provide strong support to major portions of our theoretical system. If our attempt to construct a general theory of religion proves successful, the gain in scope and parsimony in explaining important religious phenomena will be great. We invite the reader to participate in this difficult project, by mentally improving our insights and derivations while reading, adding the reader's own knowledge and intelligence to the mental resources that were available to us. Where we stumble, the reader can find the straight path. Our failures of imagination or unclear logic should encourage the reader to publish improvements and friendly amendments, to join us in the quest for clear and rigorous theories of religion. For if we all theorize in explicit and systematic ways, then our activities can be coordinated and cumulative. Only through these means can we achieve a systematic understanding of our subject matter. And, in our view, systematic understanding is the reward, for which proliferating facts, orphan propositions, and idiosyncratic hypotheses are merely compensators.

CHAPTER 3:
Evolution of the Gods

Since the nineteenth century, when the founding fathers of sociology and anthropology wrote, it has been believed widely that there is an intimate relationship between the nature of societies and the nature of the gods they worship.

Durkheim (1915), of course, carried this view to its logical extreme when he identified the object of religious worship as society itself. Durkheim's argument is easily shown to be deficient logically, but the general point retains its force. Variations on the theme that the religious culture reflects the overall culture of a society are prominent in the writing of Marx and Engels and in the work of a host of other social scientists beginning with Comte, Tylor and Spencer (cf. Durkheim and Mauss, 1963). More recently the theme has been sustained by Evans-Pritchard (1965), Swanson (1960; 1975), Underhill (1975), and Simpson (1984). Yet, in none of this work is a sustained effort at theorizing to be found.

One thing is certain: Any adequate theory of the relationship between the nature of societies and the nature of their gods must place major emphasis on change. Neither societies nor gods simply pop into existence. When we examine societies and their gods, we must ask how both developed, rather than treating them as static entitites.

The previous chapter gave primary attention to the ways in which religion serves the individual. In this chapter, we begin to surround the individual with a more clearly delineated social and cultural setting, giving special emphasis to the process of social and cultural change. This is a big job. At several points we only sketch the outlines of deductive arguments, so we can progress at a reasonable rate to the deductions of greatest interest in this chapter. Later chapters, especially 4 and 6, return in part to complete the outlines, providing alternative and fruitful derivations.

Despite our desire to get to the business at hand, the first half of this chapter has little to do with religion per se. In it we introduce fundamental social and cultural structures, and we deduce from our core theory some general principles of social and cultural development – of evolution. We then apply this model to discover the origins and evolution of the gods. We explain why people will think it possible to engage in exchange relations with the gods, and when they will or will nor seek such exchanges. Then we examine why gods tend to grow in scope and decrease in number. Finally, we explain why the gods fall into a dichotomy of good and evil.

In pursuit of these goals we found it unnecessary to add to our original set of seven axioms introduced in the previous chapter. We suggest this demonstrates that the core theory is not nearly so simple or excessively reductionist as it might first appear.

Social Structure

Society is not a disconnected mass of social atoms interacting unpredictably at random. Religions and societies are not exactly solid, frozen into unchanging crystals, but they are not gaseous either. Relatively stable structures exist, and the history of humanity is in great measure a process of increasing size and complexity of social organization. Structures sometimes collapse (Gibbon, 1782). But there has been more growth than decay, and the modern world is marked by institutions and markets far more vast and complicated than those known in earlier centuries (White, 1959; Lenski, 1976).

Before we can understand such structural processes as the growth of churches and the schism of sects, we must examine the nature of groups and of social relationships. We conceive of *social structure* as the network of relationships linking individuals together through regularized exchanges. In the previous chapter, we deduced propositions explaining that humans will seek exchanges with others, and that these exchanges may often be profitable:

P6 In pursuit of desired rewards, humans will exchange rewards with other humans.

P2 Sometimes rewards can be obtained at costs less than the cost equivalent to forgoing the reward.

Both parties to an exchange may profit, if both give something they value less than what they get. But of course this is not always the case. Some exchanges lead to loss rather than to profit. Human action is guided not only by our desires but also by our intellects. In our minds we compare the probable costs and rewards associated with different lines of action, with competing choices. Our basic theory contains several statements about human cognition and judgment, including the following.

P3 In solving problems, the human mind must seek explanations.

Def.8 Human *problems* are recurrent situations that require investments (costs) of particular kinds to obtain rewards.

Def.10 *Explanations* are statements about how and why rewards may be obtained and costs are incurred.

P5 Explanations vary in the costs and time they require for the desired reward to be obtained.

Propositions 6 and 3 show that the human mind must often seek explanations about which exchanges with other persons will lead to the desired reward. Some people can give you what you desire, while others cannot. And among those who can do it, only some are willing to exchange with you at the price you are able to pay. Furthermore, propositions derived from Axiom 7 demonstrate that individuals differ in the kind and quantity of rewards they control, and thus both in what they desire and what they offer to others in exchanges. Thus follows our first new derivation:

P29 Individuals will favor exchanges with certain exchange partners rather than with others, depending upon the particular rewards desired and upon the perceived exchange ratio that is experienced with different partners.

This proposition appears to introduce continuing social relationships into our deductive system, but in fact it is not quite able to achieve this. We need further specification of the nature of rewards. In our theory we avoid stating every fact about the nature of the world humans inhabit, and only state in axioms and definitions those very general observations that are absolutely necessary for our derivations. Therefore, it was for an important purpose that we said in Axiom 6 that most rewards sought by humans are consumables.

We doubt that any humanly desired rewards are permanent. So long as life is finite, all rewards will ultimately be lost. But most rewards are lost long before life ends. Many are consumed in the very act of using them. Food is the obvious example, but all material things wear out. Houses may last many generations, but they must be maintained. Those consumer items called "durable goods" generally include appliances that seldom last a decade. Many intangibles also vanish, including the good will of friends soon after we quit rewarding them.

We must give in order to get, and what we get usually is lost before long. Living is work, the constant exertion of individual action against the environment, including repeated exchanges with other humans. This line of reasoning brings us to our second new derivation.

P30 To satisfy desires for consumable rewards, humans will engage repeatedly in exchanges in which they seek the same reward.

Over such a series of exchanges, individuals will of course be concerned about the costs they expend each time. Typically, different exchange partners will provide the reward at different costs. This follows from an axiom and a proposition:

A7 Individual and social attributes which determine power are unequally distributed among persons and groups in any society.

Def.13 *Exchange ratio* is a person's net rewards over costs in an exchange.

Def.14 *Power* is the degree of control over one's exchange ratio.

P8 Exchange ratios vary among persons and groups in any society.

Individuals will not pursue consumable rewards in a series of randomly selected exchanges. Instead, they will prefer those exchange partners who give them the best deal – the most favorable exchange ratio. This follows from another earlier proposition:

P7 Humans seek high exchange ratios.

Because exchanges can be profitable for both partners, and because experimentation with new exchange partners will be somewhat expensive, individuals will tend to develop persistent patterns of exchange with the same partners. Another way of looking at these partners is in terms of explanations, as suggested above. In Chapter 2 we showed that humans will tend to cling to explanations that have worked reasonably well in the past, because of the high cost of testing alternative new explanations. Since good explanations often specify types of exchange to achieve certain rewards, the best explanations will often go so far as to name the ideal exchange partner. Except for those pathetic individuals who had utterly unsuccessful experiences with other persons, humans will settle on particular exchange partners for the achievement of particular rewards.

P31 Humans tend to develop persistent exchange relationships with particular other individuals and groups.

Def.25 A *relationship* exists between two persons if, after a series of exchanges, they have come to value each other as exchange partners and will seek more interaction in the future.

Individuals will turn to their habitual exchange partners when they desire the relevant rewards, and on a more general level will seek such a partner when one is not currently available. Because of the number and value of rewards that humans receive through exchanges, the urge to do this will be very strong. By Def.3, rewards are whatever humans seek, so:

P32 Relationships with some other human beings are rewards of high value.

There are at least two reasons why individuals are likely to develop exchange relationships with several other individuals, rather than seeking all rewards from a single source. For one thing, rewards are distributed in a very complex and uneven way throughout the human population. Perhaps the tiny baby can receive everything it desires from its mother, but more fully developed humans desire rewards that must come from a variety of sources. A second reason for multiple relationships is that a single supplier would be in a very powerful position, able to set a very high price for the rewards, and thus achieve a highly favorable exchange ratio at our expense. In pursuit of relatively low cost, humans are best advised to develop relationships with multiple suppliers, even if the number must be limited by the cost of experimenting with many exchange partners. Thus, it follows that:

P33 Humans tend to develop several relationships with other human beings, differing in value and in the particular rewards exchanged.

There is nothing novel in this line of reasoning (Meeker, 1971). Peter M. Blau has framed the argument in terms of *social attraction* which we might see as a synonym for the value persons place on other persons:

> Social attraction is the force that induces human beings to establish social associations on their own initiative and to expand the scope of their associations once they have been formed. . . . An individual is attracted to another if he expects associating with him to be in some way rewarding for himself, and his interest in the expected social rewards draw him to the other. . . .
>
> A person who is attracted to others is interested in proving himself attractive to them, for his ability to associate with them and reap the benefits expected from the association is contingent on their finding him an attractive associate and thus wanting to interact with him. Their attraction to him, just as his to them, depends on the anticipation that the association will be rewarding. (Blau, 1964:20–21)

Some might argue that an instinct of sociability urges people to interact and develop bonds, quite apart from any rewards that might come to each as a result of the relationship. Usually this hypothesis is stated only in the vaguest terms, and evidence to test it is hard to find (cf. Phillips, 1967). But there is not necessarily any incompatibility between it and our theory. We prefer not to make a formal, deductive connection between a sociability instinct and our propositions about social bonds not only because the facts are hazy at present, but because an extra axiom might be required, and we seem able to derive everything we need without it.

The fact that humans, for whatever mix of causes, do tend to develop several distinctive relationships with other human beings permits us to go beyond consideration of the individual and those few others with whom he interacts, to understand the nature of *society* and how it differs from *culture*.

Culture and Society

We must clarify that old but confusing distinction between *culture* and *society*. These words are practically mass nouns like "sand" and "wind" that seem to describe single entities but in fact refer to almost infinitely divisible aggregates composed of myriad parts. We suggest that culture is composed of explanations while society is composed of exchanges. Over time, some of these exchanges become regularized and produce social relationships. It is the relationship that provide a measure of stability to society, just as general explanations may give structure .to culture. Stable relationships form the strong skeleton of society, while the flesh is composed of more ephemeral exchanges. Thus we can define *society*:

Def.26 *Society* is the structure of social exchanges.

In Chapter 5 we discuss cleavages in social networks, breaks in the structure of society. A cleavage is a natural split in a network of exchanges, a division of the network across which there are relatively few strong relationships. Those matters get extensive coverage in Chapter 5 because our task there is to explain religious schism. Here, we introduce another concept familiar in network analysis, the degree of *closure* of a network.

Def.27 A portion of a network is *closed* to the extent that a high proportion of members' relationships are with other members.

Def.28 A portion of a network is *open* to the extent that a high proportion of members' relationships are with persons who are not members.

One could also say that a portion of a network is closed to the extent that it is surrounded by a cleavage. We can now focus the abstract concept *society* by placing the article *a* in front of it:

Def.29 A *society* is a closed structure of social relations.

The reader may object that we have really defined *a group* rather than *a society*. Not so. In sociology, the word *group* carries several connotations, including the idea that members of a group are conscious of their membership and conceive of their group as a real entity. But we might want to use the term to describe a relatively closed portion of a network. The extreme case, the structure of social relations that is extremely or thoroughly closed, is more than just a group. For it to be very closed, it must provide members with much if not all of what they seek through exchanges. Thus is must be an economic unit. There can be some trade with non-members, but if there is too much, then the cleavage vanishes and we must speak of the larger social structure as a society. Of course, closure is a relative concept, and we have considerable leeway in deciding where to draw the line (cf. Granovetter, 1973). In accordance with traditional usage, we apply the term *a society* to social structures that are significantly but not necessarily absolutely closed. The concept has theoretical utility because it describes a unit that can be understood fairly well without reference to conditions outside it. If much that goes on inside a set of social relationships cannot be explained without reference to other social groups outside it, then the set cannot properly be considered as a society.

One notable characteristic of societies is a strong tendency to "own" territory. There is much that could be said about this point, but we must be brief. We resist the bad habit of referring to societies as if they were persons, although the members of any society are apt to do this. But societies tend to act as units with respect to other societies, even though the actions are entirely those of individuals. Much has been made of the fact that even elementary societies gain much of their apparent cohesion from the need to defend the possessions of members, including territory, against alien invaders (Thrasher, 1927). There are two sides to this defensive cooperation. First, members may induce others to come to their rescue through offering rewards that range from immediate payment to the promise of reciprocal aid when it is needed. Second, it is in the direct selfish interests of any person to protect his exchange partners. If all of an exchange partner's resources are plundered by an outsider, then the series of exchanges is brought to an end. Persons value their exchange partners as future sources of rewards. Therefore they will expend costs to protect them. This adds up to the fact that the sum of resources possessed by the members of a society are treated as if they were possessed, albeit in a weaker sense, by the society as a unit. This is true even before the society has evolved a true state that is able to formalize this feeling of collective ownership.

Most traditional human resources, including essentially all natural resources and much of the wealth produced by human work, are tied to the land. From this comes the fact that societies tend to be territorial. Or, put more precisely:

> P34 To the extent that a social network is closed, its members will tend to occupy and hold a particular, bounded area of land.

Territoriality can be derived in other ways. For example, we could first note that transportation entails a cost in exchanges. The further you have to ship something to your exchange partner, the more the transaction costs you, and the more you will want the partner to pay in return. From this it follows that exchanges with nearby partners will be favored over exchanges with distant partners (cf. Homans, 1974:144). In the absence of complicating factors, such as very high population density, it will be possible, therefore, to map social networks directly on the surface of the earth (Haggett and Chorley, 1969). People will tend to have relationships with their neighbors, and gross cleavages are likely to be lines on the map which separate geographically integral closed networks. Thus, a society will cover a territory.

It is often appropriate to describe a nation as a society, although in this interdependent world it may be more appropriate to describe a bloc of nations as a society (Chirot, 1977). In nations, this territoriality is well developed, with formal ownership of land defined and sustained by complex institutions. The reader might object that many societies have been nomadic, and therefore did not exhibit territoriality. But at any given moment even nomads are someplace, and they claim certain rights concerning that place. Furthermore, nomads do not wander aimlessly, but have a territory in the sense of an established migratory trail or area.

The objection is also defeated by a close consideration of our two derivations of territoriality. In the first one, we introduced lands as an extremely important source of valuable resources. It is a practical fact, not a refutation of our logic, that under certain circumstances some other source may replace land in people's lives. The herds of animals owned by nomadic pastoralists are the functional equivalent of agricultural land, and may be regarded as "fields on the hoof" (Ekvall, 1968). Our second derivation showed that a society tends to be localized in space, and so far in human history, space has meant land. Looking at the question the other way around, it is obvious that one of the most effective conditions that keeps two societies from merging into one has always been geographical distance or barriers between them.

Societies vary along several dimensions. Some have few members, while others have many. Some have many resources, while others are destitute. Some are relatively homogeneous, while others are conglomerate. Within a large, closed social network there may be significant cleavages leading to relative closure of portions of the network. That is, within a society there may be sub-societies. When we speak of the whole as *a society*, we imply that no groups within it are completely cut off from social relations with the others. But closure, we must recall, is a relative concept that can be measured along a continuum. Unfortunately for clarity of thought, traditional social science has used the word *subculture* rather than the better *subsociety*. The two terms ought to be used for quite different concepts, because culture is not the same thing as society. While necessary for the survival of society and arising through the exchanges that make up society, culture is composed of a different element:

> P35 Human culture occurs through the accumulation and transmission of explanations over time.
>
> Def.30 *Culture* is the total complex of explanations exchanged by humans.

This proposition merely makes P28 concerning socialization collective, and is entirely in line with classical statements of cultural evolution (Ogburn, 1922). Humans seek explanations about how rewards are to be gained and costs avoided.

They do so through experimentation with the environment and through exchanges with other persons. This is called learning. As humans exchange explanations with one another, the experience of many becomes social, that is to say, shared. Because it is learned, culture is non-genetic, although of course all human action has a biological base. Culture comprises the "software" of the mind and the "hardware" of technology.

Although the term *culture* has been defined in any number of ways, there is general agreement that it is that which is learned and hence is something to be found within the human mind. But what of technology – those material artifacts and processes which enable humans to gain (or to think they gain) rewards and avoid costs? Technology, too, has its ultimate existence within the mind. It is the "software" of meanings and understandings that makes a stick into "hardware" such as a lever or club. Culture, then, is not "out there," and can be separated from the humans who create it and sustain it, in the analytical sense only.

Society is held together by social relationships, but what can unify culture? Shortly, we will explain that society can do this job, but cohesion also results from the fact that when two rewards are added the result is also a reward. Explanations are a class of reward. Therefore, two explanations can be added together to produce another, greater explanation that is their sum. Indeed, as suggested earlier, explanations tend to be composed of parts, like steps in the directions for assembling a model kit or in the recipe for baking a cake. Related explanations are connected to form a *cultural system*. For example, religions are cultural systems. In its entirety, the culture of a religion is a single vast explanation. Put most succinctly, each religion asserts that it is *the way*. Follow it, and all will be well; every religion offers a complex system of explanations that are believed to fit together and that support each other. To put it formally:

P36 The explanations of a religion are a cultural system.

Def.31 Explanations form a *cultural system* if they are parts of a greater explanation that includes them.

Purely as a matter of convenience and habit, we use the term *cultural system* primarily for explanations that include many costly sub-explanations. The word *system* inplies that there are real functional relationships that tie the parts together. The separate explanations are not complete without each other. But there is also another manner in which explanations may be aggregated. Some collections of explanations may have no logical integrity and be nothing but accidental hodgepodges of ideas. This is true of what are commonly called *cultures*, so we can refer to such an aggregate of explanations as *a culture*. If these are not systems, what can unify them and give them boundaries? The answer is, societies:

> P37 A culture is created by a society and consists of whatever explanations are accepted by the members of the society.

> P38 Social cleavages tend to produce cultural cleavages.

The latter derivation has several justifications, but for sake of conciseness we will only point out that the existence of a social cleavage retards the exchange of explanations across the line. New explanations generated on either side will be inhibited from spreading and will contribute to a growing cultural divergence. From this it follows that subsocieties tend to produce subcultures. But subcultures (without subsocieties) may also represent relatively autonomous *cultural systems*. If it is true that human societies tend to accept a wide variety of unrelated explanations, including many that are contradictory, then it follows that:

> P39 Any culture contains a number of cultural systems.

Some nations, such as Nazi Germany and Soviet Russia, have consciously attempted to enforce single cultural systems on their citizens, without complete success even though they are able to dominate the political apparatus (Milosz, 1953; Committee on the Judiciary, 1964; Viereck, 1965; Medvedev, 1971; Medvedev and Medvedev, 1971; Allen, 1984).

There is a proof that every human society must have merely a culture and cannot be organized according to a single cultural system. If there were a cultural system capable of serving the complete cultural needs of human beings, it would have to possess at its center a prime explanation that ultimately explained how all rewards can be obtained. Of course we have shown that some rewards cannot be obtained and therefore are replaced by compensators. The explanations that successfully give us rewards can be evaluated empirically. The explanations (compensators) in which people can have faith and yet promise rewards that are not obtainable must be explanations that cannot be tested empirically. Thus, the prime explanation that unites the cultural system must be verifiable and non-verifiable at the same time. This is a contradiction. Therefore there is no cultural system that can serve all human needs. This is not a proof that cultural systems cannot provide both rewards and compensators, because limited cultural systems can leave many questions open, and avoid such a contradiction.

These propositions demonstrate that it would be a mistake to equate *subculture* with *subsociety*, just as it is wrong to equate culture with society. The two will often go hand in hand, but not always, and if we wish to understand how they come into being and influence each other, we must be prepared to distinguish them. Indeed, it is quite possible for a cultural system or even a culture to be possessed, at some moment, by two different societies. This fact does not contradict P37 and P38. Sometimes a society is sundered, for example by war or migration, in such a way that separated parts initially have identical cultures. Although they will drift apart culturally, this process will take time as each adopts new explanations and discards old ones. Cultural systems, especially simpler ones composed of only a few constituent explanations, can be invented independently, without any communication between the people who create them. In fact, this is quite common in science and technology (Merton, 1973; Hagstrom, 1974; Cf. Schmookler, 1966:191; Gilfillan, 1970).

The argument above, for all its length, is only a part of the discussion that could be written about these matters. Our chief need here is merely to separate certain clusters of people from the products of their experience and creativity, in order to examine the interplay between the two. To do so has proved fruitful in past social theories and promises to be fruitful here as well. However, in drawing the distinction between culture and society we wish to make as few assumption as possible about the components and processes present in either. Therefore, we have omitted certain features commonly found in definition of culture and society, while attempting to retain the critical aspects of these concepts.

First of all, we have defined *a society* in terms of relative (but great) closure of social relations. Thus we can validly speak of "American society" without denying the fact that citizens of the U.S. may have Canadian friends or get their oil from the Mideast. Furthermore, we do not assume that every culture is a cultural system. On the contrary, our theory states that human societies will not possess logically intergrated, unambiguous, successful explanations that solve the major problems of life. We include no statement that societies have cultures because that already is established, since humans have culture. We are especially careful not to define societies as clusters of people having distinctive cultures, because we can observe cases of societies whose cultures are not very distinct. P38 does not say that social cleavages produce completely alien cultures with totally incongruent explanations. At the very least, successful human explanations will tend to have something in common because all people live in the same natural world. We especially want definitions that are at ease with the observation that quite different cultures (or subcultures) can exist within a single society.

P40 Humans retain that culture which appears more rewarding.

This is a simple extension of A2 as elaborated by other axioms. The principle of evaluation (Def.16) plays a critical role in this process through which humans accumulate culture: that which works, or appears to work, will be repeated; that which appears not to work, or to work less well than a known alternative, will be discarded. It will be evident that this proposition derives an evolutionary principle. That is, P40 introduces a vital selective process, indicating that culture will be screened on the basis of its perceived efficacy in producing desired rewards. This tells us that only certain kinds of cultural patterns are likely to be retained.

However, we have avoided all mention of "natural selection," "survival of the fittest," or "adaptation," because these terms tend to lead to circularity unless treated with great precision, and because they seem to imply that culture which is retained will be objectively more potent than that which is discarded. We suspect this is the trend (cf. Lumsden and Wilson, 1981; Cavalli-Sforza and Feldman, 1981). But we desire a selection principle that will permit humans to be in error, at least for long periods of time, and a principle that will operate despite an absence of significant external pressures on societies. A military technology that is associated with the triumph of one society over others will appear more rewarding and be retained. This will occur even if the technology was not in fact responsible for victory. For example, there are grounds to argue that the development of armored heavy cavalry in medieval Europe was based on false assumptions about its superiority to infantry. But so long as the faulty assumption appeared productive, it guided action. We grant that when societies contest for survival, their cultures encounter a very unforgiving evaluation. But we must note that cultures change even in strict isolation. As it is stated, P40 will deal with this range of changes.

P41 The greater the number and the diversity of exchanges that have occured over time, the more complex and apparently rewarding the culture will become.

Def.32 *Complexity* of culture refers to the number, scope, and detail of explanations, and the amount of technology.

Here we confront evolution even more fully. If culture is the product of exchanges, then the more exchanges that have occurred, the more explanations that will have been evaluated favorably and retained. In addition to number, the more diverse these exchanges (the greater the range of rewards that have been pursued, and the greater the variety of circumstances in which they have been pursued), the greater the scope and detail of the culture thus accumulated. For example, a society with only one enemy will have encountered less variety of military threat and will have acquired a less complex repertoire of military culture than a society that has confronted many enemies (all else being equal). Or, within a society, the greater the number of rewards that have been sought (and the greater the number of times a reward has been sought), the more explanations that will exist and the more times each will have been evaluated.

> P42 As a society grows and endures, it will come to have a progressively more complex culture.

For this to be true, there must be adequate means for accumulating culture. Accumulating is possible if explanations are invented faster than they are forgotten. Good inventions increase the wealth and number of human beings, thus contributing to increased creation of culture. Some inventions, most notably writing, have made it possible to preserve culture without the necessity of it all being carried in human memories (Childe, 1951). But population growth itself permits accumulation of culture, because the greater the number of human minds, the greater the number of ideas that may be remembered by someone, and on occasion shared with the group through exchanges.

Growth of population means a greater number of exchanges will occur within a society. Passage of time has the same consequence. Thus we derive from our seven simple axioms a fundamental principle of both classical and modern versions of social evolutionary theories. There is no reason to dispute the simple observation that a great deal of time has passed from the earliest known human societies until the present, and that over time there have been two master trends: Human societies have increased in population size, and they have acquired more complex cultures (Lenski, 1976). Proposition 42 links these three elements in explanatory fashion: As time passes and societies grow, their cultures become more complex.

It is extremely important to recognize that this proposition states a general principle and does not necessarily apply to every single society under all conditions. For the principle to be verified, most societies must display increasingly complex cultures, if they grow and persist.

Deviant cases of technically static societies may result from a set of unfavorable accidents – such as the small size and geographic isolation of Easter Island culture. Or, more interestingly, it may result from social factors which our theory predicts might retard progress. Consider tyranny and slavery, for example. When the slaves do the work, and the tyrants merely give orders, there may be no one in a position to consider new technical procedures (explanations), to evaluate them, or to be rewarded by implementation of procedures which are more effective than existing ones. What is good for the slaves may not be good for the master, and vice versa. And if communication between slave and master is poor, or communication between the workplace in Spain and the decision place in Rome is poor, the social exchanges required to implement new explanations become impossible. Thus, agricultural technology may have progressed more slowly in the years from Hesiod to the fall of Rome than in the allegedly dark but freer centuries that followed (White, 1962). Our theory explains that societies as well as individuals will achieve progressively greater rewards including more effective explanations when the marketplace of interaction is free to work its will.

But the overall trend is toward greater size and complexity, occasional deviant cases being swamped by the general development. Furthermore, growth and persistence of societies are contingencies, not assumptions in our theory of *religion*. We explain the cultural implications that ensue if societies grow, and if time passes. If they remain tiny, and little time passes before they cease to exist, little or nothing will occur culturally within them.

So let us assume societies in which culture is becoming ever more complex. Axiom 4 reminds us that the powers of the human mind are finite – there are limits on the amount of information the human mind can store and process. This permits us to deduce a vital implication:

> P43 The more complex the culture, the less of it that can be mastered by any given individual.

There comes a point in the development of culture when it constitutes too much to be fully known and understood by any one person. One easily thinks of the demise of the "Renaissance Man" as Western culture developed more fully. But the fact is that no man or woman during the Renaissance could master more than fragments of the total culture. The last true "Renaissance Man" probably died in the earliest days of the Lower Paleolithic era. Indeed he probably was not even yet a "man" in the true sense.

If no member of a society can master all of the relevant culture, it must follow that:

> P44 To the extent that its culture is complex, adult members of a society must exchange culture.

We know that children must rely on the cultural knowledge of adults, but here we see that all persons share this dependency. If individuals cannot know everything, they must rely on others to inform them when they need to know that which they do not. Put another way:

P45 The more complex the culture, the greater the degree of cultural specialization.

Def.33 *Cultural specialization* refers to the tendency of individuals to master parts of their culture and to engage in exchanges with others who have mastered different parts.

Here we have deduced the division of labor in a more general form. The core of cultural specialization undoubtedly is the tendency of people to earn their living by specializing in certain tasks of great importance for the survival of the group. These major economic specialties are referred to as the division of labor and can, to some extent, be found in all human societies about which the facts are sufficiently known. Thus, even in the simplest hunting and gathering bands essential tasks tend to be divided along sex and age distinctions (Murdock, 1949; van den Berghe, 1973). But if the division of labor is the most visible manifestation of cultural specialization, it is not the whole of it. People exchange culture all the time in ways that elude the notion of division of labor. If A tells B a story that B has never heard, and B responds with a story unknown to A, a cultural exchange has occurred even though neither A nor B makes his living as a story-teller.

We do not claim that the only source of the division of labor is increasing cultural complexity. But the other sources will themselves produce cultural specialization, and therefore contribute to social evolution in the same direction. It is often suggested that the division of labor flows from differences in native talent among people. But talents must be cultivated and combined with skill, thus producing a difference in knowledge between people who originally differed only in aptitude. The spear-thrower must know how to throw, as well as have the strength, and will therefore become more knowledgeable than other people about throwing-sticks, flint points, balance, and follow-through. The flute-player knows his instrument as well as having a good ear.

The division of labor and cultural specialization flow, in part, from the complexity and dispersion of natural resources on the earth. Miners will specialize in digging into the hillside, not because others cannot dig holes, but because the holes must be dug in certain places remote from most people's homes. Similarly, only people who live near the sea are likely to become sailors. Miners in the hills and sailors on the shore will learn different things in the practice of their separate trades. Most humans will not have the opportunity to learn either cultural system. Uneven distribution of any significant resource, including power, will stimulate culture differentiation.

It will be seen that on the basis of P42, as societies get larger and older they will exhibit more cultural specialization.

P46 Given some degree of cultural specialization, the larger societies become, the greater their degree of differentiation.

Def.34 *Differentiation* refers to cultural specialization at the level of groups rather than at the level of individuals.

This is simply to recognize that as societies with somewhat complex cultures become larger, numbers of individuals will share a given *cultural specialty*. They may compete with one another individually or in coalitions, or they may form monopolies, but in any event there will be a degree of coordination among them. That is, as groups of people develop who specialize in providing some important cultural specialty – leaders, warriors, metal-smiths, etc. – they form distinctive clusters within societies that can be distinguished easily from one another according to their specialized activities. Sociologists have long identified this tendency towards group specialization as *differentiation*. Thus, when the roles of leaders and priests, for example, are no longer performed by the same individuals, that society is said to be more differentiated than before. And, for an equally long time, it has been understood that an increase in the size of a society – in its population size or territorial expanse – is the engine pushing differentiation (Spencer, 1893).

Social scientists have long speculated that, over time, differentiation is coupled with increasing social and cultural integration within each specialization. Sometimes words like "rationalization," "formalization," "institutionalization," and "bureaucratization" are used. We wish to avoid the connotations conveyed by any one of these, and focus on the common principle they share. Certainly the outcome of greater cultural integration is suggested by the above argument, including P38 and P39. But we have not yet demonstrated that the subcultures produced by differentiation are in fact well-integrated cultural systems. The truth is that not all specializations have evolved conceptually coherent systems of explanations, but there is a strong tendency in that direction. Thus, we must derive the tendency of cultural specialties to evolve into cultural systems, while also showing what factor might inhibit this development.

It might seem that P39, by asserting that any culture contains a number of cultural systems, has already accomplished the desired derivation. But it has two defects. First, it says nothing about evolution, and instead makes a static observation about any given moment in a society's history. Second, it leaves open the possibility that many specialties that could evolve into cultural systems fail to do so, lacking any force driving them toward cultural integrity.

The motive force for this evolution is found in P3, P4, P5, and P40. In solving problems, the human mind must seek explanations. Explanations are rewards of some level of generality. Explanations vary in the costs and time they require for the desired reward to be obtained. Humans will retain that culture which appears more rewarding.

Thus, human culture evolves in the direction of finding explanations that accomplish more and cost less. Suppose that an incoherent set of explanations has accumulated for providing a number of rewards. Let us call them E_1, E_2, E_3, E_4, etc. Now suppose a new explanation, E_x, is invented which brings together the other explanations, thereby achieving some efficiency in the costs required to obtain the full set of desired rewards. This new explanation, E_x, will be retained, and by Def.31 brings the lesser explanations into a cultural system, X. Another general explanation, E_y, may accomplish the same thing for another set of specific explanations, E_a, E_b, E_c, E_d, etc. At some future time, an even more general explanation, E_z, may bring E_x and E_y together, uniting cultural systems X and Y into a single, grander system, Z.

Many examples could be provided. For thousands of years, humans accumulated myriads of facts and specific explanations about chemical processes. The invention of the periodic table of elements brought many of these subexplanations together into a cultural system, and further scientific development has attached more and more of the facts of chemistry to the central explanation.

Such a consolidation of many explanations into a cultural system is likely to render some of the explanations superfluous, thus reducing the intellectual and material cost of obtaining the desired rewards. But the facts must be willing to cooperate! The process of intellectual consolidation will be blocked if no general explanation can be found that is successful in bringing the others together. The facts of the natural world may resist. Some of them may happily combine in support of various different explanations, yet resist the merger of all cultural systems into one. Thus, P39 states that there is a limit to this evolution, and the limit is the supply of general explanations that achieve positive evaluation (Def.16). Therefore, we can state the general principle:

P47 Cultural specialties evolve into cultural systems, dependent upon the discovery of explanations that prove valuable in uniting the relevant subexplanations.

This line of thought suggests yet another source of cultural differentiation. Suppose a specialty follows this evolutionary track and reaches a point where all its culture is assembled into two cultural systems, each of great value. Further suppose that no explanation is found that can unite them. It will be efficient to follow either, but there will be inefficiencies in trying to follow both simultaneously. Depending on the details of the cultural systems and on the socioeconomic conditions in the surrounding environment, it may be an advantage for the specialty to split into two specialties, each with its own cultural system. These two can cooperate and exchange with each other to achieve the rewards sought by the original, single specialty. This leads to the following proposition:

P48 Cultural specialties tend to be divided along lines which divide cultural systems.

In P36 we asserted that the explanations of a religion are a cultural system. In using the term *religion*, we meant to refer to the well-developed manifestations of the religious phenomenon – to what are commonly called religions in large and socially advanced societies. Just as one can have social relations without having a society, one can have religious phenomena without their cohering into a system. We need to understand the emergence of a religion as a relatively integrated unit. Our original definition tells us we must explain the evolution of a system.

Def.22 *Religion* refers to systems of general compensators based on supernatural assumptions.

How does P47 apply to the cultural specialty of providing general compensators based on supernatural assumptions? It says that the specialty will indeed tend to evolve into a cultural system. This will take time, as new explanations are generated and old ones are discarded. We can think of numerous contingencies that might retard this process. But, unlike many other specialties, explanations to achieve the unification of a religious cultural system are bound to be possible. This is true because the facts of the natural world cannot disqualify many religious statements by proving them valueless. An explanation that would transform a collection of religious explanations into a cultural system must be a very general compensator based on supernatural assumptions. It cannot be evaluated through any empirical test. Later we will see that the need to provide specific compensators prevents religious culture from becoming entirely integrated and simple. But, still, we can state:

P49 A cultural specialty dedicated to providing general compensators based on supernatural assumptions tends to evolve into a cultural system, thus becoming a religion.

Perhaps the reader would prefer a definition of *religion* rather different from Def.22, a definition that stresses that religions are social organizations. Certainly, one may conceive of a religion either as a faith or a church, either as a cultural system or a social system. We have no quarrel with either approach, because in fact they ultimately converge with each other. The main disadvantage of emphasizing the extent to which a religion is a formal social organization is that this perspective might lead us to ignore loosely affiliated lay believers and to concentrate too much on the formal leadership structure of the clergy. That is, we might emphasize the business while losing sight of the customers. But at this point in our deductions we do want to stress the religion-building that goes on at the social heart of a religion. As P38 suggests, the emergence of formal religious organization will speed the differentiation of a religious cultural system.

We have now examined propositions explaining the emergence of cultural specialties within increasingly complex and larger societies, thereby producing cultural division of labor. There is another good line of derivation for the division of labor, however. It rests on earlier propositions about social relationships. Recall:

P9 Rewards that exist in limited supply will tend to be monopolized by powerful persons and groups, thereby becoming relatively unavailable to others.

P29 Individuals will favor exchanges with certain exchange partners rather than with others, depending upon the particular rewards desired and upon the perceived exchange ratio that is experienced with different partners.

Powerful persons may often seek to corner the market on a reward, not only so they will have it for themselves, but also so that they may sell it to others at a high price. Because the power of any individual is limited, it will be impossible for anyone (even the Emperor) to monopolize all rewards. Rather, individuals will specialize in providing particular rewards at prices not so high that no one will trade for them but high enough to provide a good profit. The existence of competing sources of a scarce reward will alter this only to the extent of keeping the price somewhat lower and encouraging suppliers to increase the efficiency of their operations. Coupled with propositions on cultural specialization, P9 and P27 explain the origins of the division of labor.

Once a society has progressed at all far on the road to great size and complexity, the division of labor will apply not only to individuals and categories of individuals, but also to *networks* and *groups*. No single individual will understand or be able to carry out all the actions required to provide a particular valued reward to other persons. The man who runs the grocery store does not also plant the corn and herd the beef. Really complex structures emerge when individual suppliers develop exchange relationships in order to get the components of rewards for sale to their customers. Each component is a specific reward, while the end result is a product that constitutes a more general reward. For example, the wheel of a chariot is lesser than the entire vehicle.

Examples include not only manufacture and trade, but also the military and communications (in advanced societies). The general reward sought in a military operation may be to protect the homeland and secure loot from the defeated enemy. To achieve this general reward, one must spear this individual enemy, and this one, and this one – a series of actions beyond the strength and skill of Achilles himself. But if one can organize a large army of fellow soldiers, then the general reward of victory can be secured. This example reminds us that one source of social organization is the desire to assemble the social power to accomplish monopoly which is a very general reward.

One could derive the existence of organizations directly from P29, given complexity in the nature of some rewards. Let us say person X wishes to provide customers Y_1, Y_2 and Y_3 with a complex reward R. This reward is sufficiently complex that no single individual can be master of all the means to produce it. Therefore, X will engage in subsidiary exchanges with suppliers A, B and C to obtain the components of R. A may provide the raw materials, B the tools, and C the design for R. X then takes these purchased sub-rewards, adds value through his own efforts, and offers the finished reward to Y_1, Y_2 and Y_3. If a large number of customers (or repeat customers) keeps X in the business of providing R, then he will develop lasting exchange relationships with A, B and C. This results in a network of producers and providers. To the extent that a guiding cultural specialty, the necessity of combining against competitors, or other factors make it efficient for X, A, B and C to continue exchanging as a relatively closed part of the social network, they will constitute a *group* with somewhat distinctive culture. Since they value each other as long-term exchange partners, members will expend costs on behalf of each other. The slightest consciousness of their own social relations is enough to give them the sense of being an organization.

P50 Social organizations emerge in human society.

Def.35 *Social organizations* are collective enterprises that specialize in providing some particular kinds of rewards.

P51 Religious organizations emerge in human society.

There may be some question in the reader's mind whether P51 in fact derives the existence of *churches*, large formal religious organizations of great stability and complex internal structure. P51 does not really say much about the nature of religious organizations. Chapter 4 is devoted to the evolution of the church and the development of ever larger and more monolithic religious organizations. One may also wonder why religion requires a division of labor among suppliers. We will see in Chapter 6 that production of general compensators is a difficult business. Religions generate and distribute compensators, and once society has evolved through the stages described here and in Chapter 4, most religious specialists are engaged only in distribution, not production. To have any good compensators to sell, they must link together in a system of distributors sustaining a religious tradition that affords the compensators to be distributed.

Individuals may form exchange relationships with organizations as well as with other individuals, although the actual exchanges are carried out with individuals who represent these organizations. Thus the individual may receive rewards and religious compensators from a particular priest operating from a particular local church organization within the over-all context of a particular religious denomination within a particular religious tradition. The individual has a relationship with each of these, although the relationships differ in quality.

Suppose Father Sullivan, a priest at St. Anne's Roman Catholic Church has given us comfort a number of times in the past. Suppose we again need comfort. Our best explanation tells us to seek Father Sullivan again. If he is out of town, the same explanation may tell us to seek another priest at St. Anne's. If we are a great distance from the church ourselves, the same explanation will tell us to go to another Catholic church. And if there are no Catholic churches within reach, it may even suggest we try a minister from another Christian denomination. Thus our relationship to a formal organization may be conceptualized as a hierarchical structure of related explanations and evaluations that go somewhat beyond the particular exchanges we have engaged in and that is equivalent to a complex set of relationships of varying kind and value.

Before we leave the topic of cultural differentiation, we must make one more observation about the macrostructure of societies:

P52 The more cosmopolitan societies become, the more complex their cultures.

Def.36 *Cosmopolitan* refers to the existence of plural cultures within a society.

When several distinctive cultures (or subcultures) exist within a society, the diversity of cultural exchanges is thereby increased with the result of making each distinctive culture more complex. This is simply to recognize that the principle of cultural diffusion applies within as well as across societies. Indeed, because of the greater frequency of exchanges, diffusion is more rapid across cultures contained within the same society. Cosmopolitanism occurs in a number of ways. Most typically it occurs when societies expand and thus annex other societies and their distinctive cultures. Cosmopolitanism also occurs by immigration. But it also can occur simply through the growth of societies and the subsequent formation of subcultures based on regional, class, occupational, or other grounds which promote interaction and conflict. Weber's conception of status groups is pertinent here, as is Hechter's theory of a cultural division of labor (1978), and Fischer's work on the formation of subcultures in response to urbanization (1975).

Stratification and the State

Thus far we have paid relatively little attention to power differentials associated with cultural specialization and differentiation. Axiom 7 posits the existence of inequalities of power – or stratification – among persons and groups in any society. Recall that we define *power* as the degree of control over one's exchange ratio. Now we examine more fully how this elementary aspect of individual differences becomes elaborated as societies develop.

P53 Some cultural specialties will produce greater power than will others.

This easily follows from the axiom that some rewards are of greater value than others (A3). As people and groups begin to specialize in providing particular rewards, this will give some of them advantages in exchanges with others. The rewards supplied by some will be more valuable than the rewards supplied by others.

P54 Cultural specialization and differentiation will increase stratification in societies to the degree that classes will emerge.

Def.37 A *class* is a set of persons, of all ages and both sexes, with a relatively similar degree of control over their exchange ratio with other sets.

Here we follow Weber, not Marx. We leave open the question of whether class position is obtained through ascription or achievement, whether classes are "conscious," and we do not base classes wholly on economic criteria. Control over one's exchange ratio can derive from a variety of sources and can involve the exchange of many non-economic rewards. Money is a source of power, but so is membership in a strong family, many relationships with powerful individuals, or high caste status. Castes may be defined as classes that are highly endogamous and ascriptive. The possession of religious compensators and membership in a cultural specialty that facilitates distributing them, are also valuable resources. The promise of life after death is not an economic factor, but we plan to show that it can be exchanged for wealth and that it can serve as the source of great control over exchange ratios (or power). But our immediate task is to derive the existence of the state, so we can understand the social context in which religions exist, and to do that we must turn from the more spiritual sources of power to the brute force of coercion.

Def.38 *Coercion* is the interaction strategy of threatening to inflict great costs on others, thereby imposing on them exchange ratios which are below market value.

It is assumed that everyone will seek to get the most for the least. However, coercion is only indirectly connected with exchange ratios as such. High exchange ratios may prevail without any hint of coercion. There will always exist a level of value at which people will choose to exchange a certain amount of any ordinary reward for a certain amount of another. At this point, people will voluntarily initiate exchanges. This level is the *market value*. The element of choice is crucial. No matter how much of reward X one partner in an exchange must give in order to induce another to yield however little of reward Y, this exchange represents the market value so long as nothing besides the desires (and/or needs) of each trader for the reward of the other (and the availability of alternative suppliers) enters into the exchange.

Coercion occurs when one trader is not free to refuse the deal. That is, coercion occurs when one trader would not have chosen to exchange and does so only to avoid costs in excess of the value given up – not to gain a desired reward. In the old paradigm – "your money or your life" – person A gives up his money to B, but is not rewarded in return. B does not give a reward which A would have sought voluntarily, simply by leaving A alive. A had not planned on expiring in the first place. Rather, a cost (death) greater than the reward demanded (money) is averted. If free to choose, A would not have given B anything – as the unexpected appearance of the police would always demonstrate. The threat to inflict costs out of proportion to most available rewards is therefore coercion.

It might be objected that P1 defeats this analysis. It says: "Rewards and costs are complementary: a lost or forgone reward equals a cost, and an avoided cost equals a reward." This may seem to imply that no exchange can be distinguished from another in terms of coercion, because a reward is given the coerced person. P1 seems to define the lifting of a dire threat as a very valuable reward indeed. But this objection is not well-founded.

It is worth distinguishing two different kinds of exchanges a person can accept to defend against a threat. When threatened with death by B, A can simply accept an exchange with B, perhaps surrendering the money. Or, A could call on help from some other person C. An exchange with C is not coerced, because it was B, not C, who presented the threat and initiated the series of exchanges. In principle, A has the option of dickering with C, D, E, and others over the price he must pay to get help against B. When A is not able to exercise any of these options, he is coerced by B. Thus, an exchange is coerced, when it is initiated by a threat from the party with whom one must exchange.

The main flaw in the objection based on P1 is that it makes the mistake of beginning its analysis in the midst of a series of exchanges unilaterally initiated by B, and therefore misses the overall quality of this transaction. Coercive exchanges are not initiated by their victims, but by those who have the will and the resources to use this exploitative strategy with some less powerful exchange partners. A non-coercive exchange, in which both parties benefit, logically could be initiated by either party, even if there is a great difference in their power.

Coercion could also be defined by its consequences, using a conception identical to that of Def.38, but phrased with different emphasis:

Def.39 A *coercive exchange* is one in which one party, with full knowledge, has a lower net supply of rewards after the exchange begins than before.

Put more simply, this is one kind of exchange in which one party does not make a profit, while the other may. There are, of course, other exchanges which do not fulfill P2, which says: "Sometimes rewards can be obtained at costs less than the cost equivalent to forgoing the reward." Accidents or other external factors may ruin an exchange for one party, but in coercion the high cost to the victim is intended by his exchange partner. Often, humans make mistakes, or are confused, and therefore lose in an exchange. In these cases, there is no coercion. Def.39 says we have coercion only when the party has essentially full knowledge of the relevant contingencies. Only coercion can force a person to expend costs without hope of recompense and drop to a lower net level of reward. Coercion should not be confused with "altruism." If a person wants to reward someone else without immediate repayment, then the exchange provides intangible gains to the giver.

Now that we understand what coercion is, we can define other concepts necessary to describe the sociocultural environment in which religions develop.

Def.40 *Cultural means of coercion* refers to knowledge, capacities, and technologies that can inflict unbearable costs on the human organism.

Def.41 The *state* is the monopoly of the cultural means of coercion by a clearly differentiated group of specialists.

Def.42 Those who monopolize the use of coercion are the *political elite*.

Def.43 A *repressive state* exists when the political elite use their monopoly on the cultural means of coercion to impose below market exchange ratios on non-elite members of the society.

Not all culture is potentially deadly to human organisms. In the final analysis, however, coercion rests on those parts of culture that are deadly. It is the capacity to impose physical suffering and death on one another that makes it possible for humans to coerce one another. In the simplest case, these means might be a weapon itself (club, knife, gun, etc.). In more complex cases, it might be the social resources to send a troop of soldiers to apply force indirectly.

In defining the state in this fashion, we are aware that (in a manner of speaking) the state exists in all human societies, in that the use of coercion within the group is always somewhat monopolized and subject to control. But it has become conventional to regard societies as stateless until the process of differentiation has resulted in the emergence of clearly defined specialists in monopolizing coercion. This, of course, supplements our definition of *a society*. For the organized use of coercion provides a very effective social cleavage – between those controlled by one state and those controlled by another. The state amplifies the tendencies toward territoriality in human societies, and indeed the state is highly adaptive for societies, all else being equal (cf. Weber, 1946; Nozick, 1974).

Those who run the state, those who monopolistically decide when and against whom coercion will be used, are the political elite. The number of elites involved in the state has much to do with how coercion will be utilized (see Chapter 9). But our concern here is not with an extended theory of the state, and therefore not with such matters as pluralism. It is sufficient for now to designate the repressive state. These definitions permit us to conclude this section with a proposition of great significance:

> P55 The growth, duration, and differentiation of societies leads to the emergence of the state.

We have deduced fundamental features of human societies and their development from our core theory. Thus we have provided a context in which to understand the evolution of religion. Now we will explain that gods evolve as well.

The Gods

We define religion as systems of general compensators based on supernatural assumptions. *Supernatural* refers to forces beyond or outside nature which can suspend, alter, or ignore physical forces. We have further specified that only supernatural agents can justify the most general explanations or compensators – those which give meaning and purpose to the existence of the world. We now examine more closely human conceptions of the supernatural.

P56 Humans will tend to conceptualize supernatural sources of rewards and costs as gods.

Def.44 *Gods* are supernatural beings having the attributes of consciousness and desire.

In the following chapter we will more fully derive human conceptions of the gods in a detailed examination of relationships with exchange partners who provide compensators. Here we will concentrate on the main issues. Seeking great and difficult rewards, humans imagine supernatural exchange partners who have the resources to satisfy human desires. As exchange partners, these gods are conceived of as super-humans with desires of their own. For an exchange to be possible, some of the gods' desires must concern humans, and it must be possible for humans to reward the gods. Such rewards can take material, psychic, and behavioral forms.

Humans have no experience of conscious beings without desires. In the gods, humans seek exchange partners capable of providing the greatest rewards, and exchange partners always expect something in return for what they give. Indeed, it seems unreasonable to posit the existence of supernatural beings who act upon the world yet to suppose that such beings are without intentions. As Freud (1927:25) put it:

> Nothing can be made of impersonal forces and fates: they remain eternally remote. But if these elements have passions that rage like those in our own souls . . . if everywhere in nature we have about us beings who resemble those of our own environment, then indeed we can breathe freely, we can feel at home in the face of the supernatural . . . we can have recourse to the same methods against these violent supermen of the beyond that we make use of in our own community; we can try to exorcise them, to appease them, to bribe them, and so rob them of part of their power by thus influencing them.

Freud's views are echoed by the dominant view among anthropologists, who define religion in terms of patterns of interaction (or exchange) between humans and the gods. For example, Spiro (1966:96) defines religion as "an institution consisting of culturally patterned interaction with culturally postulated superhuman beings." He then characterizes superhuman beings as

> any beings believed to posses power greater than man, who can work good and/or evil on man, and whose relationships with man can, to some degree, be influenced by . . . activities which are believed to carry out, embody,

or to be consistent with the will or desire of superhuman beings. (Spiro, 1966:97–98)

What can the gods desire? This may be answered both on logical and sociological grounds. Logically, the gods can desire whatever humans have to give. These can be material rewards such as livestock, gold, food, or even human life itself. The gods can also desire psychic rewards such as adoration, submission, and other forms of affect. Finally, the gods can demand that humans behave or not behave in various ways. That is, the gods may use humans as resources to accomplish divine purposes. Sociologically, we shall see in the next chapter that inevitably certain humans assume the role of intermediary for the gods and thus can benefit directly from the rewards others offer to the gods. It is, therefore, no surprise to find that the desires of the gods closely resemble the desires of humans.

Humans will think it possible and desireable to exchange with the gods. Indeed, the gods are the only source of some desired rewards of great value. As a result:

P57 The gods tend to enjoy high exchange ratios.

The admission fee to Heaven may be abject submission to the will of God and a considerable measure of self-denial. At least humans will expect to pay a high price. Below and elsewhere we qualify this deduction by introducing elements of a market – that is, alternative suppliers limit the costs of dealing with the gods. Nonetheless, it will always be somewhat expensive to deal with the gods. It may also be slow to do so. Explanations based on supernatural assumptions tend to offer compensators that are redeemable as rewards only in the distant future or in some other unverifiable context. It therefore follows that:

P58 People will not exchange with the gods when a cheaper or more efficient alternative is known and available.

Here we deduce one of Malinowski's (1948) most profound insights which exposed as spurious the notion that the "primitive mind" is fundamentally irrational. Malinowski argued that magic consisted of recourse to nonempirical or superempirical explanations in order to obtain rewards that are unavailable through natural empirical means. He argued that primitives always use natural or empirical-verifiable procedures to gain desired rewards, when such procedures were known and available. Thus, for example, a primitive does not try to substitute magic for work when it comes to gardening:

> He knows as well as you do that there are natural conditions and causes, and by his observations he knows also that he is able to control these natural forces by mental and physical effort. His knowledge is limited, no doubt, but as far as it goes it is sound and proof against mysticism. If the fences are broken down, if the seed is destroyed or has been dried or washed away, he will have recourse not to magic, but to work guided by knowledge and reason. (Malinowski, 1948:28)

But, Malinowski argued, many factors are beyond the control of the primitive agriculturalist. He cannot control the weather or prevent swarms of insects from eating his crops. These thwart his efforts and exceed his knowledge. "To control these influences and these only he employs magic" (Malinowski, 1948:29).

It is more efficient to pull weeds than to pray for food. It is not more efficient to spit on fields than to pray for rain. We stress this point because we wish to make clear that our theory conceives of religion as a rational human activity, not as the bursting-forth of deep, irrational impulses. That is, religious compensator systems arise out of the same processes of reasoning and of trial and error, as do other aspects of human culture. Even a primitive people's religious rites have been subjected to as much thought and creative effort as have their gardening techniques. That we may be in a position to demonstrate that rituals to ensure good crops do not work, in no way suggests that primitive farmers ought to recognize this fact or that such beliefs about the effect of rituals are irrational. No one has made this point more clearly than has Melford Spiro:

> A religious system, then, is first of all a cognitive system, *i.e.*, it consists of a set of propositions, explicit or implicit, about selected aspects of the world which are asserted to be true. Undeniably, many of these propositions, when transmitted to actors, evoke their assent because, among other reasons, they would like them to be true. . . . Others, however, evoke the assent of actors despite the fact that they would prefer that they not be true. Nevertheless, the pleasant and the unpleasant beliefs alike continue to be held because, in the absence of other explanations, they serve to explain, *i.e.*, to account for, give meaning to, and structure, otherwise inexplicable, meaningless, and unstructured phenomena. They are assumed to be true because in the absence of competing beliefs, or disconfirming evidence, there is no reason to assume that they are false. (Spiro, 1964: 105).

Elsewhere, Spiro (1966:113) pointed out that merely because the "premises" on which a religion might be based "are false does not render them irrational – until or unless they are disconfirmed by evidence." Religion arises from the human reaction against irrationality. Religious beliefs make rational a variety of things that otherwise would be irrational. It therefore is no surprise that people engage in rational behavior when they deal with the gods. When they know a cheaper or better way to gain rewards, people tend not to seek them from the gods.

Scope of the Gods

We already have seen that the more complex the culture the greater the scope of the explanations it provides. Some of these explanations serve as religious compensators, that is, they are predicated on the existence of the gods. It follows, therefore, that

> P59 The more complex the culture, the greater the scope of the gods.

> Def.45 The *scope of the gods* refers to the diversity of their powers and interests and to the range of their influence.

The greater the scope of religious explanations, the greater the scope of the gods who undergird these explanations. Gods are of greater scope when they perform a wider range of activities, offer a greater variety of rewards, impose a greater variety of costs, and when the sphere of their influence is more universal and less local. Thus a god of weather is of greater scope than a god of wind, or a god of rain. A god that controls the weather everywhere on earth is of greater scope than a god whose control of weather is restricted to a small tribal territory.

If there is any doubt that the general trend of societies toward explanations of greater scope will also apply specifically to religious culture, we can derive P59 more directly from P49 which states that religious culture will tend to evolve into a cultural system. As this happen, lesser explanations are grouped together by explanations of greater generality. New explanations of great scope replace more limited older explanations. The most distinctive religious explanations, of course, are supernatural beings. Therefore, the evolution of a religious cultural system is apt to entail the invention (or elevation by redefinition) of gods of ever greater scope to act as the unifying explanations that cap the system. From the above arguments, it also follows that:

P60 The older, larger, and more cosmopolitan societies become, the greater the scope of their gods.

We thus deduce an evolutionary tendency towards gods of greater scope. This seems consistent with the historical record (Bellah, 1964). When societies were new, small, and culturally homogeneous, the gods were coterminous with societies. Their powers were local, and their concerns were parochial. Tribe A did not suppose its gods concerned themselves with tribe B. As societies grew, the spheres of influence of their gods also grew. As societies became more cosmopolitan, the gods tended to be merged – often with the assumption drawn that the gods of two cultures were the same gods with different names.

It also follows that as gods attain greater scope there will be a reduction in their number, as many gods with limited concerns are merged into fewer gods with more general concerns. We may state this:

P61 As societies become older, larger, and more cosmopolitan they will worship fewer gods of greater scope.

Conclusion

In this chapter we have traced the emergence of religion, and the birth of the gods, from the interchange between individuals seeking valuable rewards. The evolution of society, and of systems of general compensators, entails the invention of gods of ever greater scope. But it is important to recognize that we intentionally have not pushed our deductions to the conclusion that social and cultural evolution lead towards monotheism. We have not done so because we know of no cases of large religious groups that are truly monotheistic, if by that term is meant the existence of only one supernatural being. Later, we will show that such apparent exceptions as modern Unitarianism approach very close to the brink of secularism, and in elevating God the last step, strip away the supernatural characteristics that define the religious (cf. Miller, 1976).

Extant religions that claim to be monotheistic, while they posit a superior god of great scope, identify many other supernatural beings. In Judaism, in addition to Jehovah, there exist various angels, a subordinate, but extremely powerful evil being (Satan), and a host of demons and spirits. Indeed, the Old Testament acknowledges the existence of many gods, although these are deemed inferior to Jehovah. The same multiplicity of supernatural beings is found in Christian "monotheism." In addition to the God of Judaism, Christianity adds

Christ and the Holy Spirit to form the Holy Trinity. And some Christian denominations also give significant supernatural status to Mary and the saints. Islam, too, admits to a host of lesser spirits, both benign and evil, in addition to Allah.

These similarities stem in part from the fact that diffusion played so vital a role in the development of these major faiths. Both Christianity and Islam grew out of Judaism, and there has been long and acrimonious debate over the possible origins of Judaism in the monotheism of the Egyptians (Freud, 1939; Rosmarin, 1939), or perhaps that of the Indo-Europeans (Stone, 1976). But the important point is that these cases are best described as a reduction in the number of gods, and an expansion in their scope, not as the rise of pure monotheism. That is why P61 is stated as it is. Furthermore, we attempt below to deduce that religions will not reduce the supernatural to a single entity, but will in fact dichotomize the supernatural into good and evil and thus limit the maximum potential reduction of the gods to no fewer than two.

CHAPTER 4:
Priests and Magicians

It is time to place religion inside cathedrals. In this chapter we pursue the evolutionary processes introduced in the last chapter in order to explain the development of specialists in religious culture and the sources of power that elevate such specialists into a social elite. Next, we examine the emergence of stable organizations devoted primarily to religious activities – organizations containing both an elite and an active laity. We see why magic tends to become differentiated from religion, and why magic, unlike religion, does not provide sufficient basis for sustaining stable organizations. Finally, we inspect the ways these factors influence the evolution of the gods. Once again we do not find it necessary to introduce any new axioms, but merely build on the original seven and the propositions already derived from them.

Religious Specialists

In the previous chapter, we provided the context of socio-cultural evolution in which religious organizations arose and developed. We gave propositions that began to describe characteristics of these organizations, if such existed, but we did not in fact complete the proof that they would come into being. When we stated that religious organizations will tend to emerge in society, we did not specify the steps of our argument, and we did not delineate anything about the form of these organizations. At that time, we could not yet prove that religion would be a cultural specialty, nor could we say how that specialty might be manifested in societies of different kinds. These steps can be taken now, but we must begin at the starting point of our deliberations – the individual with his desires, searching for explanations to help fulfill them.

A most intriguing psychological question is how compensators come into being and how they come to be believed. Especially in the chapter on cult innovation we will amplify on our understanding of this matter. But here we must discuss at moderate length the ways social exchange can support belief in a compensator. Recall P13:

> P13 The more valued or general a reward, the more difficult will be evaluation of explanations about how to obtain it.

Propositions 5, 11, and 12 had already shown that many explanations are costly and difficult to evaluate correctly. Proposition 13 pointed out which explanations would present persons with the greatest difficulty. From these considerations, and from the fact that the mind is limited (A4) while culture is vast (P43, P44), it follows that:

> P62 No human being can personally evaluate all the explanations he uses, including verifiable ones.

Certainly, if no human being can know all the explanations of his culture, it follows he cannot come anywhere near evaluating them all, but the fact that he must rely upon others for many explanations (P44) means that this inability to evaluate personally extends to a significant portion of the explanations the person actually uses. Many of these explanations are potentially testable, but the individual does not have the time or wealth to check them out for himself. This means that any individual must rely upon evaluations of explanations, which are reported to him by other persons. Or, more formally:

> P63 The value an individual places on an explanation is often set by the values placed on it by others and communicated to him through exchanges.

People may communicate through words, by stating or implying the value of an explanation. Or, they may communicate unintentionally through their actions, as they are seen to follow an explanation in pursuit of a reward they desire. Another way of looking at this is through the concept of a market:

> P64 In the absence of a more compelling standard, the value an individual places on a reward is set by the market value of that reward established through exchanges by other persons.

General compensators, the merchandise of religion, are not possible for an individual to test, so:

> P65 The value an individual places on a general compensator is set through exchanges with other persons.

It is not news that humans learn much about the world from each other, rather than from their own private experiences. And over forty years ago social scientists demonstrated that individuals will learn explanations from persons who previously have led them to rewards (Miller and Dollard, 1941). Here we have shown that faith derives from other persons, as do the religious beliefs that it values (cf. Gaede, 1976; Becker, 1977; Welch, 1981; Roberts and Davidson, 1984). In very simple societies, the younger generation may receive its faith entirely from the parents, and the older generation will receive no spiritual guidance form any authority other than its own memory of childhood. To a great extent, transmission of religious culture is performed by the parents in advanced societies as well, but they are backed up by formal religious organizations that act to stabilize the sacred culture (Hunsberger, 1983).

Let us consider a simple society that grows beyond a small band, but does not yet have religious organizations. The social structure becomes complex, including subgroups set off by social cleavages of greater or lesser depth, as the previous chapter explained. In the absence of an external standard, this would lead to the multiplication of different religious explanations. There would be a constant cultural drift, in which families and other groups would continually disagree about which explanations were correct. This produces a crisis of belief.

What happens when a person receives quite divergent evaluations of the same explanation, in exchanges with different partners? He might be influenced by the majority, or by those from whom he had received the best explanations in the past (cf. Miller and Dollard, 1941; Katz and Lazarsfeld, 1955; Katz, 1960; Rogers, 1960; Burgess and Akers, 1966; Sutherland and Cressey, 1974; Akers, 1977; Akers, *et al.*, 1979). But, if the individual is involved in a number of exchange relationships and there is some complexity to the religious culture, he must somehow take into account the competing evaluations. At this point we must emphasize that the ordinary person is in a very different situation from that of the religious specialist.

Consider the specialist, first. An important standard of value for him is the cost others are willing to pay in exchange for the religious compensators he offers. Crudely: how much money will they pay for the funeral ritual that he claims will smooth the departed relative's way into heaven? More subtly: how much affection will they give the specialist in return for the prayers he says on their behalf? For the specialist, the value of an explanation may be set by the maximum value it is accorded by some significant class of exchange partners. This is so, because he can then use the explanation as a compensator to exchange with them for great rewards. This observation partly explains why religious specialists often can maintain great faith even when they carry on several close relationships with nonbelievers. For them, the value of a compensator is greatly set by its exchange value with a set of customers.

The ordinary person lacks this standard, and is more affected by disagreement. To examine just how this happens, we must understand more about evaluation. For someone who wants to use an explanation to obtain a desired reward for himself, the value of the explanation is not identical to the value of the reward less the costs demanded by the explanation. To the extent that the explanation is thought to have a chance of failing, its value is further reduced. A plan that will net a hundred dollars if it succeeds, is worth no more than fifty (and perhaps much less if the investment could be lost) if it has one chance in two of succeeding.

Consider now the person who asks several friends who have already tried this plan, for their evaluations. Some will say it is good, while others will say it is bad, depending on how it worked out for each of them. At this point the person realizes that there is some question whether the plan will work for him. He seldom has the opportunity to perform valid statistical studies of his chances of success, but he will know they are somewhere between certainty and impossibility. If he has received many evaluations from others, he will be able to make a more precise estimate.

Let us take the argument one step further. People realize there is a good deal of uncertainty in human affairs. So, not only will they discount explanations according to the apparent chance they will fail, but they also will discount evaluations according to the same principle. Indeed, evaluations of explanations must be carried out according to yet other explanations which in turn will sometimes fail. Because of these uncertainties, a person will combine the evaluations of other people to arrive at a net evaluation for himself, something like an average chance the explanation will work for him.

We would like to specify the exact way this "average" will be calculated, but are not prepared to examine this difficult side issue in depth. Certainly there is no reason to believe that it will always be the arithmetic mean. The vast tradition of research on the psychology of human perception reports that our senses do not respond according to a simple linear function. Economics reports the same finding: one ton of steak is not necessarily a thousand times as valuable to a person as two pounds, if he intends to consume it himself. It is certain that this "average" will fall between the extreme values.

Furthermore, a person does not value the beliefs of his exchange partners equally. If he has received great rewards (perhaps including explanations and evaluations) from A, and relatively bad ones from B, he will tend to value what A offers in future over what B offers. If A now presents him with a general compensator, which B says is no good, A's evaluation will be given the greater weight. These considerations will take on great significance in our chapter on recruitment to religious groups, but for the moment they permit the following necessarily wordy derivation:

P66 When there is disagreement over the value of an explanation, the individual will tend to set a value that is a direct averaging function of the values set by others and communicated to him through exchanges, weighted by the value placed on such exchanges with each partner.

This proposition does not apply, of course, when the individual has successfully carried out his own evaluation. But here we are concerned with explanations he cannot test. A second point is that the proposition may not apply when the situation is extremely chaotic and the exchange partners present the individual with many logically contradictory explanations. When this is the case, the individual may disqualify all his partners as authorities, and may give each of the explanations a far lower evaluation than P66 would imply. This does not disprove the proposition, however, but refers to a situation in which the individual decides that the current exchanges are not of the same kinds he previously enjoyed with these partners, that he has had no "such exchanges" with the partners and need not believe that the proffered explanations have any value.

Even in such extreme cases, the important result is the same. When there are competing general compensators, the value of each will be driven down by the competing claims of the others (cf. Mannheim, 1936). Or:

P67 The more cosmopolitan a society with respect to religious culture, the lower the market value of any given general compensator.

This proposition has magestic implications for later parts of our theory and goes a long way toward explaining secularism in the modern world. But it also has profound implications for the birth of religious organizations in far less advanced societies. It provides us with the last insight required to understand why individuals cannot be content with their own personal religions, but must receive religion from religious specialists, in all but the simplest societies.

P65 explains that persons will, by and large, receive their general compensators from other individuals. P66 and P67 explain why an organized specialty occupation, possessing relatively stable and uniform culture, has an advantage over disorganized single providers of general compensators. The larger the proportion of providers who offer the same explanations, by P66 the greater the value of the explanations. In a society of some degree of complexity, such providers cannot rely upon popular culture to establish such uniformity. Rather, they must organize into a cultural specialty. Naturally, the construction of strong social organization defining and sustaining such a specialty takes time and some resources. It will not happen overnight. Thus, the following can be stated:

P68 The more complex the culture, the more likely that persons will specialize in producing and exchanging compensators of great generality based on supernatural assumptions.

Def.46 Persons who specialize in producing and exchanging compensators of great generality based on supernatural assumptions are *religious specialists*.

P69 The older, larger, and more cosmopolitan societies become, the more likely they will be to contain religious specialists.

Many other cultural specialties will be slow to emerge because they cannot flourish until a sufficient number of good explanations have been empirically proven to permit them to do the required practical job. For example, mining as a specialty makes no sense at all until metal working and chemistry have advanced to the point where the material dug out of the ground has some value. Nor will mining progress very far until there are ways to bring light, air, and a modicum of security to the ends of deep tunnels. But because the explanations of religion do not require (and cannot receive) empirical test, nothing inhibits the rapid emergence of the religious specialty:

P70 Religion will be among the very first cultural specialties to emerge in the development of societies.

Indeed, the ethnographic literature does report that religious specialists are among the earliest fulltime specialists to appear in human societies. With specialization, of course, comes differentiation. Therefore, propositions 68 and 69 can be restated to predict differentiation of religious specialists – the appearance of coordinated groups of persons all engaged in producing and exchanging compensators of great generality based on supernatural assumptions. In fact, P67 combines with P68 and P69 to predict that:

P71 Once religious specialists have emerged in a society, they will tend to combine in organizations seeking a religious monopoly.

A tendency toward monopoly may be opposed by other groups, but will be supported by many ordinary members of society. By P67, general compensators have the greatest value when they have no competition. There will be most faith in a set of religious beliefs, and the greatest comfort received from them, when there is a strict religious monopoly, and all providers agree.

Look at it from the perspective of practitioners of religion A in a society that also includes religion B. It will be to their advantage to drive out the priests of B. Not only would they be able to appropriate B's clients, but also the value of A's own compensators would rise, even among people already affiliated with A. In relatively small and homogeneous societies, a religious consensus can be achieved peacefully, as religious beliefs coalesce in accordance with such propositions as P49 and P61. But in large and complex societies, containing many subgroups with their own religious organizations, these principles will apply within each religion, but may not be sufficient to meld them all together. Under such conditions, there are many hurdles in the way of monopoly. Some are described in the middle chapters of this book. How, then, can one organization achieve dominance over others and approach monopoly? Only through coercion.

Where can a religious organization get the power to coerce? We could list several very special circumstances and strategies. For example, in some societies religions can be assisted by secret societies (Assassins, Thugs, Leopard Men) able to exert force outside the normal social structure. Or, if a religious group is already wealthy, it can buy the social means of coercion. But both of these possibilities point to the key to the puzzle: *the state* (cf. Frankfort, 1948).

If a well-organized state has not yet emerged in society (or has recently decayed), then there is no monopoly of the cultural means of coercion, and many specialized organizations, including religious secret societies, may possess some of these means themselves. But this will not lead to a true religious monopoly, because competing religious organizations will be able to ally themselves with other sources of coercion.

Sufficient cultural means of coercion to achieve effective religious monopoly can only come from the state itself. History shows that relationships between the state and the dominant religion in a society can be of several kinds. But no religion can achieve dominance over any but the smallest societies, unless it has established a cooperative and mutually valuable exchange relationship with the state. Later, especially in Chapter 9, we will examine this more closely. But at this point we can deduce:

P72 In socially complex and cosmopolitan societies, a religious organization can achieve an effective monopoly only through an alliance with the state.

Def.47 An *alliance* is a continuing relationship between persons or groups, in which each contributes to the power the other enjoys in exchanges with third parties.

P73 The emergence of the state in a society will tend to be followed by the emergence of a single dominant religious organization, to the extent that the state is repressive.

There may be mitigating circumstances that prevent dominance by any one organization, but we feel they probably can be reduced to the common factor of incomplete development of a centralized state. It does not undercut P73 to note that different ancient Egyptian monarchs and dynasties supported different cults, nor to note that it was in the interests of the pharaonic state to permit local cults associated with subordinate power centers which could not be suppressed easily. On the contrary, such observations support the proposition, because they point to religious pluralism associated with diffusion and fragmentation in the coercive power of the state. The extreme example is our own society, in which power flows in complex and shifting channels. There is no dominant religious organization, and myriads of new and schismatic organizations proliferate.

Historical evidence suggests that P73 applies without qualification to traditional monarchical societies in which the state first emerged. Of course these states seldom had the power to eradicate secondary religions altogether, but they could place one in dominance over its competition. It is no accident that Christianity became dominant after the last vestiges of political pluralism vanished from the Roman Empire. Many religions tumbled over each other in the highly fragmented political environments of late Republican Rome, Classical Greece, or indeed the entire Mediterranean before the coming of the Caesars. The change was not instantaneous, both because considerable political pluralism existed long after Augustus, and because generations may be required for a religion to edge out its rivals. Several religions, such as the bizarre sun cult of Elagabalus or the more popular Mithraism, nearly established alliances with the imperial state, and it is immaterial to this part of our theory that Christianity, specifically, was the winner in the contest for monopoly.

We now explore the potential for great power inherent in the role of religious specialist and how this creates elites and influential organizations. The social source of this power is the status as *intermediary* which religious specialists perform, acting not only as the middlemen between ordinary persons and the gods, but often also as double-agents mediating between citizens and the state. Our core theory derived a simple but crucial proposition on which a theory of social relations is based:

> P6 In pursuit of desired rewards, humans will exchange rewards with other humans.

At the time we did not discuss every detail of the derivation (more is given in Chapter 6), nor all of its implications. This proposition is derived, in part, from the observation stated in Axiom 5 that some desired rewards are limited in supply. Earlier we noted that "much of what we desire can come only from someone else, whether the reward be affection or apples." These two examples are more than a capriciously chosen alliteration. They represent two crudely distinguishable kinds of reward. Affection can come only from other persons, while apples sometimes may be picked right off the tree, without any exchange with another person. Suppose we want apples. At first, we may look for an apple tree, one that is not the property of anyone and is open to harvesting. Failing in this, we will consider finding a human being who has such a tree, or a cellar of apples picked earlier, and try to initiate an exchange. Thus, a corollary of P6 is:

> P74 When an individual finds he cannot obtain a desired reward by himself, he will tend to seek an exchange partner who can provide it to him.

> Def.48 An *exchange partner* is someone who participates in exchanges vis-a-vis a given other person.

Note that P74 does not say that the exchange partner must own an apple tree. He may get his apples through exchanges with some third party. There may be a lengthy chain of exchanges reaching from this person through many others to a distant orchard owner. The people between the consumer and the one responsible for the tree are all intermediaries.

Let us pass from apples to eternal life. We would like to live forever, but cannot provide such a great reward for ourselves; the fountain of youth eludes our discovery. So we might try to initiate direct exchanges with someone who has the power to grant immortality. Such an exchange partner must be a god. But, as the argument of the previous section explained, ordinary people are not very successful in contacting the gods. Therefore, we must turn to intermediaries who either talk to gods themselves, or are in touch with other persons who do. These intermediaries are religious specialists.

P75 Religious specialists act as intermediaries between their clients and the alleged sources of the desired general rewards – the gods.

Def.49 An *intermediary* is a person who receives rewards in exchanges with one party in order to provide them to another party through other exchanges.

The intermediary acts in accordance with A2 and P6. He engages in all the exchanges in order to get rewards for himself. So, too, his supplier. The intermediary must give rewards to the supplier in order to get the merchandise to exchange with us. The rewards for the supplier must, ultimately, come from us. We must give the intermediary some rewards for himself, but we must also give – through him or at least according to this instructions – rewards desired by the gods.

In P56 we explained that humans will tend to conceptualize supernatural sources of rewards and costs as gods. Definition 44 further stated that gods are supernatural beings having the attributes of consciousness and desire. Our discussion of these statements noted that the rewards desired from humans by gods can take material, psychic, and behavioral forms. The last of these is especially interesting. As we said, the gods may use humans as resources to accomplish divine purposes. But, what purposes? How can we learn what the gods demand of us? Since it has proven impossible to verify what the gods promise and desire, the terms of exchanges with the gods are freely defined by religious specialists.

P76 Religious specialists direct others to offer material, psychic, and behavioral rewards to the gods.

P77 By defining behavioral rewards desired by the gods, religious specialists can influence norms.

Def.50 *Norms* are the rules governing what behavior is expected or prohibited in various circumstances. Thus, they are equivalent to culturally shared explanations that govern the terms of exchanges.

The norms promulgated by religious specialists are supposed to serve the interests of the gods, but they may be designed to serve the interests of the specialists, instead. We will shortly see that this may be in the interests of the specialists' clients, as well, instead of being to their disadvantage. To elucidate, we can use the familiar metaphor of the shepherd and his flock, but with a non-traditional emphasis. It is to the advantage of the shepherd to promulgate the following norm among his sheep: "Go thou whither I direct thee." He does this not only by prodding but also by leading them to rewarding fresh pastures. Thus he leads them to sheepish prosperity on the way to the slaughter. If the sheep were intelligent, he might promulgate more complex norms that are unrestrictedly good for the sheep, such as: "Thou shalt not cavort with wolves." Up to a certain point, the sheep's benefit is his benefit, and to that point his norms serve both their interests.

In our original discussion of territoriality, we noted that it is in the interests of persons to protect their exchange partners, if this can be accomplished at moderate cost. We now see that many kinds of nurturance – *cultivation* we might call it – can be to the advantage of both partners, yet superficially appear like altruism entirely for the benefit of the recipient. This follows directly from a full consideration of the net economics of sequences of exchange. Of course, as sociobiologists surmise, there might be something like an "instinct" of altruism in humans; without great care given to children, the species would have died out long ago. But our theory does not need to postulate such an instinct. Apparent altruism often makes perfectly good economic sense for the giving individual. Often the gift will enable the recipient to reward us highly in future exchanges. Food given to a starving man may or may not be repaid in gratitude. But if the man survives and becomes prosperous, then there is one more possible source of rewards through exchange with whom we might profitably trade in the future. Thus, we can deduce from P77 that:

P78 Religious specialists promulgate norms, said to come from the gods, that increase the rewards flowing to the religious specialists.

P79 Religious specialists promulgate norms, said to come from the gods, that increase the ability of their clients to reward the religious specialists.

P80 Religious specialists promulgate norms, said to come from the gods, that increase the total rewards possessed by the clients as a group.

Religious specialists may make mistakes. There may be great limitations on their ability to get people to follow certain norms. Thus, their ability to increase the well-being of their clients (in order to garner more for themselves) may be severely limited. Furthermore, other organizations in society, such as the state, may follow similar principles, sometimes reinforcing the norms promulgated by religion, and sometimes conflicting. We certainly do not wish to perpetuate the extreme functionalist myth that religion inevitably serves to achieve maximum benefits for society as a whole, nor that it has an unsullied tendency to increase human happiness. But, as Parsons (1964) noted, religion may indeed be highly adaptive for human societies.

One principle operating is purely mathematical. Once a religious organization has grown to a reasonable size, or even has become dominant in a society, it receives rewards from numerous clients over long periods of time. Two habits immediately derive from this fact: 1) some concern for the greatest good for the greatest number, and 2) an emphasis on behavior that produces long-term, consistent profits instead of immediate consumption. An individual might gain by cutthroat exchanges that wipe out many of his exchange partners, partly because many other persons would remain for later looting. But an established organization, like a religion, subsists on regular exchanges with large numbers of persons. The religion will benefit if it can promulgate norms against cutthroat behavior. Similarly, other individual impulses are not in the interests of religion, nor of a society, but may be rewarding for the individual. Sexual promiscuity may be fun, but it does not build a stable congregation for a church. Therefore, established religions are likely to say the gods forbid promiscuity.

Social theorists and ordinary people have long believed that religion was good for people, even though it sometimes opposes certain natural impulses. Proposition 80 explains that this often is true, but its truth ultimately rests on the religious specialists' own quests for rewards through regular exchanges with numerous clients.

Behavioral rewards often may be translated into material rewards. God says we must carry out good works; therefore, the congregation should give money to the priests for use in missionary projects. Often it happens that the gods demand material rewards themselves. Again, the supernatural consumers remain beyond our inspection and cannot be observed receiving these rewards.

P81 It is in the nature of the supernatural that the gods are not observed to take physical possession of material rewards exchanged with them.

P82 Religious specialists act as receivers for the gods and partly define what material rewards they receive.

P83 Religious specialists share in the psychic rewards offered to the gods, for example: deference, honor, and adoration.

We can return for a moment to proposition P72, which said that, in socially complex and cosmopolitan societies, a religious organization can achieve an effective monopoly only through an alliance with the state. It was obvious what the religion wanted from the state: the cultural means of coercion to suppress competing religions. What did the state want from religion? First of all, P80 is (by and large) in the interests of the state, because a prosperous citizenry gives the state (and its elites) the possibility of extracting greater rewards for itself through exchanges with the citizens. Beyond that, the ability of religion to promulgate norms, said to come from the gods, can be turned directly to the state's purposes. The most obvious case is the doctrine of the divine right of kings (cf. Frankfort, 1948). Here, religion supports the state by encouraging citizens to accept its dominance. The doctrine of an afterlife, which primarily serves as a very general compensator appealing to every kind of person, may be adapted to encourage acceptance of even quite harsh state repression. Thus, from P72 and P78 we can deduce:

P84 In socially complex and cosmopolitan societies, a dominant religious organization will promulgate norms, said to come from the gods, that increase rewards flowing to the state.

We must not picture religion as purely the tool of the state. Religion often mediates both ways between the state and the citizenry, acting as an agent of each with respect to the other. P80 says that the aggregate well-being of the citizenry is of value to religious specialists. Further, if the state drains away all surplus rewards, then there will be none left for the churches. Therefore, they will not want to see the people squeezed dry by the state.

P85 Religious specialists promulgate norms, said to come from the gods, that limit the repressiveness of the state.

Propositions 84 and 85 appear contradictory, but they are not. They represent opposing but logically linked loops in a feedback system. In any given society, a dominant religion will seek the balance of P84 and P85 that gives the greatest net reward for the religious specialists. This gives religion a very central role in the interplay of forces that determine the course of a civilization. Also we should recall what P57 says: "The gods tend to enjoy high exchange ratios." As agents for the gods, religious specialists enjoy great power.

P86 Religious specialists can exert great influence over their exchange ratios with others, and thus over the exchange ratios experienced by others.

Remember that exchange ratio is the net of rewards over costs in an exchange. Chapter 2 showed that one's exchange ratio can be increased by exchanging compensators for rewards. This is precisely the advantage enjoyed by religious specialists. The rewards to be gained from the gods tend to take the form of compensators – I.O.U.s to be redeemed in the distant future or in some other unverifiable context, and the value of which must be accepted on faith. By utilizing compensators in exchange for rewards, religious specialists have great control over their exchange ratios. Thus:

P87 Religious specialists constitute an elite.

Def. 51 An *elite* is a group with great control over its exchange ratio.

Earlier (Def. 42) we defined a *political elite* as those who monopolize the cultural means of coercion concentrated in the state. Obviously, such a monopoly gives them great control over their exchange ratios. The more general definition here merely says that an elite is powerful, since we have defined power as the degree of control over one's exchange ratio. As forshadowed by P24:

P88 Religious organizations and positions are controlled by the powerful.

This is true both because such control constitutes power and because the powerful will seek this additional source of power. Priests are powerful because they are priests. Powerful people will seek to be (or to control) priests in order to add to their power. This conclusion loops back to Chapter 2 where we also deduced that the power of an individual or group would be positively associated with control of religious organizations and with gaining the rewards available from religious organizations. We now see additional grounds for this deduction by more fully specifying the contingencies involved in exchanges between humans and intangible trading partners. The inherent ambiguity of such exchanges, in combination with the development of religious specialists, creates an opportunity for amassing considerable power. Predictably, such opportunities are utilized.

Also in Chapter 2 we said that religious organizations will tend to emerge in societies – social enterprises whose primary purpose is to create, maintain, and exchange supernaturally-based general compensators. Basing its logic on Axiom 6, Chapter 3 gave a much fuller derivation of the emergence of religious organizations. We must now complete this task.

The most general compensators available from religion can only be realized (if at all) in the very long run. For example, rewards that can be realized only after death outdistance the life-span. Pursuit of such long-term benefits therefore can be life-long. That is:

> P89 Explanations in pursuit of very general religious compensators require individuals to exchange with the gods on a continuing basis.

It is therefore inherent in the nature of religious compensators that:

> P90 Religious elites can implicate others in long-term, stable patterns of exchange.

These long-term, stable patterns of exchange with the gods constitute *religious commitment*: patterns of belief, feelings, and activities offered in exchange for religious compensators and rewards. Religions combine a religious elite and a committed laity. Here we see that religion is not an episodic, purely individualistic phenomenon. People do not visit a priest merely when a specific need arises. Instead, religions flourish as stable organizations. As Durkheim (1915: 47) put it:

> A religion is a unified system of beliefs and practices. . . which unite into a single moral community called a Church, all those who adhere to them.

It is being embodied in stable, organized "moral communities" that religions have such impact on societies. That is, religions constitute social structures – stable social relationships among a number of persons in a society. Recently, we have published numerous empirical studies supporting this observation, including research on the classic question of suicide (Durkheim, 1897). While Durkheim may have been wrong to say that Catholic communities are more cohesive than Protestant communities, and thus have lower suicide rates (Pope, 1976; Pope and Danigelis, 1981), a strong community expressed through high rates of church membership does inhibit self-murder (Stark, Doyle and Rushing, 1983; Bainbridge and Stark, 1981c). Similar findings about the impact of religious social structures on many other kinds of behavior have accumulated rapidly (Stark, Doyle and Kent, 1980; Bainbridge and Stark, 1971a; 1981b; Bainbridge and Hatch, 1982; Stark, Kent, and Doyle, 1982). Religious socialization received early in life may have some permanent power to shape behavior in modest ways, even without the continuing support of social bonds. But such socialization represents the influence of a past moral community, not the power of a purely individualistic faith, and these studies indicate that the power of religion is greatest if supported by current moral communities. And as they express the hope and will of the community, religions are both powerful and persistent social organizations able to exert their influence on a continual and long-term basis.

Later in this book, we shall further explore relations between religious organizations and other powerful and persistent social organizations, notably the state. Here we provide theoretical balance by contrasting the organizational character of religion with the lack of organizational potential in magic.

Magic and Magicians

In Chapter 2 we distinguished between religion and magic, and we distinguished between magic and science. Religion includes very general compensators – those which promise rewards of great scope based on the existence of the supernatural. Magic, in contrast, is limited to less general compensators for fairly specific rewards, Religion may promise triumph over death; magic will be limited to recovery from a particular illness or a charm against contracting the illness. Furthermore, magic may or may not be based on supernatural assumptions. Usually it is. Religion must be based on supernatural assumptions, but not magic. The fundamental feature of magic is that it is a pseudoscience. Magic deals in such specific and immediate rewards that often it is subject to empirical verification. Indeed, it is only on the basis of such verification, as Weber (1963: 2) pointed out, that the claims of magic may be distinguished from the findings of science.

In the modern world there are many magics that are sustained as pseudosciences although devoid of explicit supernatural assumptions (Gardner, 1957; Frazier, 1981). Some forms of astrology have this non-supernatural but pseudoscientific character, as do many forms of putative psychotherapy (est and Dianetics, for example). These are magical in our cultural context, despite the fact that they do not invoke the supernatural, because they make empirically verifiable claims concerning rewards without regard for verification, often even when their claims have been falsified empirically. To return to the criteria of rationality employed by Spiro (1966:113): unlike religion, magic can consist of beliefs that are assumed true in the presence of disconfirming evidence and thus when there is reason to assume they are false.

One important feature of magic is that it deals in relatively specific compensators for relatively specific rewards. We now show that this has two significant implications: 1) it leads to the differentiation of magic and religion and to the existence of specialists in each; 2) it prevents magicians from building organizations based on long-term exchange relations with others. Because magic offers specific results:

P91 Magic is more vulnerable than religion to disconfirmation.

> Def.52 *Magic* refers to specific compensators that promise to provide desired rewards without regard for evidence concerning the designated means.

P92 It is not in the interest of religious specialists to risk disconfirmation of the compensators they supply.

Religious specialists have a wealth of compensators which involve no risk of disconfirmation. Not all the powers of modern science can raise the slightest question about the claims of even a primitive priest that the gods can grant immortality. Indeed, we have just seen that it is through possession of compensators of such immense value, and which can be achieved only in the distant furture or in another reality, that religious elites are able to create powerful and stable organizations. Clearly, it is not in the interest of persons possesssing such advantages to risk them through continually dealing in very specific, short-term, and potentially falsifiable compensators. To do so would be to risk raising doubts about the unverifiable compensators, too, as P66 suggests. In consequence, as religious elites develop and assume places of great power and privilege in societies, they can be expected to pursue their own best interests by dropping this risky line of merchandise. It will be in their interest to do so even though a substantial demand for such compensators persists. Let others with less to lose run the risks of failure.

P93 Religious specialists will, over time, tend to reduce the amount of magic they supply.

P94 To the extent that a demand for magic continues after religious specialists have ceased providing it, others will specialize in providing it.

Def.53 Cultural specialists whose main activity is providing specific compensators are *magicians*.

P95 The roles of religious specialist and magician will tend to be differentiated, as will religious and magical culture generally.

When we look around the world, we do find that magicians are differentiated from religious specialists among the more complex societies. Leach (1962) suggests that a dichotomy between religion and magic – between a priesthood that deals with the transcendental and shamans who deal with specific, pragmatic needs – is universal wherever religious specialists have appeared on a fulltime basis. In his view, religion deals with humans reaching "up to heaven," while magic deals with the gods coming "down to earth." This is another way of describing unverifiable compensators on the one hand, and compensators that might be verifiable on the other. In a major paper on this matter, Mandelbaum (1966) found this dichotomy throughout the great Eastern religions. Each religion lives in acknowledged symbiosis with a host of local magicians. People seek to ensure their general welfare and their future life through religion, but consult magicians for specific and immediate needs. Thus, Mandelbaum reported, a Brahmin priest will not (or very rarely) attempt "to cure an immediate and specific ailment." For this, people must consult a magician.

The risks of the magic business are shown by the rapid shifts in the reputations of magicians. Sometimes, even, a magician is killed by a dissatisfied client. In complex societies, magicians can cope with this difficulty by accepting a high turn-over of short-term clients, many of whom leave in anger. The precariousness of magic in the face of potential disconfirmation has been documented for preindustrial as well as for modern societies (Evans-Pritchard, 1937; Bainbridge and Stark, 1980c; Bainbridge and Jackson, 1981). Religious organizations that have delegated magic to the magicians can enjoy secure high status.

In Western societies, this same dichotomy is found, but is not so obvious. For one thing, science does tend to drive out magic. For another, the West is somewhat unique in the hostility of the major faiths to magicians and a corresponding tendency to retain magical elements within religious organizations, especially the sects. Elsewhere we will analyze these tendencies. But perhaps the main problem is that magic is much more visible in other cultures than in one's own. Thus, it may not strike Americans how much magic exists in this society. Yet, close inspection reveals that many therapists in the human potential movement are magicians, as are the many faith healers, food faddists, and other pseudo-scientists (cf. Lederer, 1959; Frank, 1961). In our judgement, Vitamin B-17, unknown to science but sold to countless Americans, is the precise counterpart of "eye of newt" or a fertility charm. Numerous apparently practical political programs, economic schemes, and even government responses to social problems are promoted with such disdain for scientific evidence about their worth, that we are safe in calling them magical, too. The important point is that while there is an abundance of magic in modern societies, it tends to be clearly differentiated from religion.

Unlike the providers of general compensators, magicians cannot substantially increase the faith of their clients by combining to form visible and well-known organizations. This is true because another standard than consensus – empiricism – operates here. Indeed, by combining they would only concentrate information about the valuelessness of their services and become contaminated by each other's failures. Because magic offers specific results over a short time-span:

P96 Magicians cannot require others to engage in long-term, stable patterns of exchange.

P97 In the absence of long-term, stable patterns of exchange, an organization composed of magicians and a committed laity cannot be sustained.

P98 Magicians will serve individual clients, not lead an organization.

P99 Magicians are much less powerful than religious specialists.

We are pleased with these propositions because they are so familiar. While it is often very fruitful when a novel proposition "falls out" of a deductive system, it greatly increases the credibility of the theoretical enterprise when a familiar finding does so. In this case we have deduced Durkheim's classic statement on the contrast between religion and magic. It may lend further credibility to our theory if we admit (with appropriate blushes) that we had long forgotten this aspect of Durkheim's work when we first developed our theory. Thus it was with profound delight and a sense of confirmation that we encountered the following passage in *The Elementary Forms of the Religious Life*:

> . . . whenever we observe the religious life, we find it has a definite group as its foundation . . . It is quite another matter with magic. To be sure, the belief in magic is always more or less general; it is frequently diffused in large masses of the population, and there are even peoples where it has as many adherents as the real religion. But it does not result in binding together those who adhere to it, nor uniting them into a group leading a common life. *There is no Church of magic*. Between the magician and the individuals who consult him, as between these individuals themselves, there are no lasting bonds which make them members of the same moral community, comparable to that formed by believers in the same god. . . . The magician has a clientele and not a Church, and it is very possible that his clients have no other relations between each other, or even do not know each other; even the relations they have with him are generally accidental and transient; they are just like those of a sick man with his physician. It is true that in certain cases, magicians form societies among themselves. . . . But what is especially important is that when these societies of magic are formed, they do not include all the adherents to magic, but only the magicians; the laymen . . . are excluded. . . . A Church is not a fraternity of priests; it is a moral community formed by all the believers in a single faith, laymen as well as priests. But magic lacks any such community. (Durkheim, 1915:44–45)

While Durkheim often got his ethnography wrong, modern anthropology supports his conclusion (and ours) that there is no church of magic. Thus, for example, Mandelbaum (1966) reported that in both the Buddhist and the Hindu cultures he examined, religion and magic enjoy a symbiotic relationship. Whereas religion is embodied in stable and powerful organizations, magic is sustained by only fleeting and instrumental exchanges between magician and client. The role of priest if based on ascription and is filled by persons of high social origins. Priests are "accorded prestige and high social rank. . . . Their clients are traditionally in a stable, bound relationship to them" (Mandelbaum, 1966:1175). Magicians, on the other hand,

> achieve the role. . . . Whatever prestige a shaman gains by the exercise of his powers accrues to himself alone and is not shared by his kin and caste fellows. His clients are not bound to him in any regular relationship, but

> patronize him as their need arises and as his reputation attracts them. . . . The shaman is usually from the lower ranks of the caste order. . . . (Mandelbaum, 1966:1176)

That magic will not sustain stable organizations, or moral communities, is an important insight for analysis of much that occurs in the contemporary occult scene. In Chapter 6 we note the tendency for some modern magical groups to evolve into religions. That is, so long as they are merely magical, occult groups cannot form into fully-fledged social movements, but are locked into a limited form of relationship that we describe as *client cults*. In order to become something more, such groups must become religions, for only when they can offer compensators of great magnitude can they gain the organizational potential present in religions. So long as magic is what is being exchanged, ralations are limited to the client cult type described by Durkheim and Mandelbaum, and which can be deduced from and explained by our theory.

Good Gods, Evil Gods, and Demigods

The preceeding discussion of magic gives a new perspective on some of our earlier derivations about religion. Several propositions deduced characteristics of religious evolution that do not apply to magic, because an essential ingredient in the proofs was the nature of general compensators. A review of their proofs will show that the following do not apply to magic:

P36 The explanations of a religion are a cultural system.

P49 A cultural specialty dedicated to providing general compensators based on supernatural assumptions tends to evolve into a cultural system, thus becoming a religion.

P59 The more complex the culture, the greater the scope of the gods.

P60 The older, larger, and more cosmopolitan societies become, the greater the scope of their gods.

P61 As societies become older, larger, and more cosmopolitan they will worship fewer gods of greater scope.

Propositions 36 and 49 are prevented from applying to magic by the observation, stated in P47, that evolution into a cultural system is dependent upon the discovery of explanations that prove valuable in uniting the relevant subexplanations. The specific explanations of magic are continually being disconfirmed. Suppose we were able to link two magical explanations, E_1 and E_2, through a larger explanation, E_x. The disconfirmation of E_1 would undercut E_x, and therefore would tend to reduce the value of E_2, as well. Certainly, some magical subexplanations can be linked through more general explanations, and it may be profitable for magicians to develop some very restricted cultural systems, within a practice that is not unified on the whole. But, because of their vulnerability to disconfirmation, magical explanations tend to proliferate. The disconfirmation of E_1 might tend to disconfirm the magician's value altogether, and magicians can protect themselves (to some extent) with a tangle of many contradictory explanations that can act as specific excuses to cover unwanted facts. The refusal to admit that the many explanations of magic constitute a logically interdependent system can indeed reduce the harm that any one disconfirmation might do to the magician's practice (Evans-Pritchard, 1937). If a magician throws caution to the winds and creates a system despite the risks, the first few disconfirmations will wreck it. Thus, instead of P36 and P49, we have:

P100 The explanations of magic are not a cultural system.

P101 In dealing with the disconfirmation of their explanations, magicians tend to generate large numbers of new and unconnected explanations.

Propositions 59, 60 and 61 about the scope of the gods, are not disproved by our discussion of magic. Of course, it might have been useful to stress in each of these propositions that we were talking about the gods of religion, not the various supernatural beings that frequently appear in magic. But there is a more fruitful way of cleaning up our nomenclature. As the scopes of certain gods increase, these deities approach closer and closer to what people today ordinarily mean by *god*. In ordinary language, we tend to use the word *god* for supernatural beings of great scope, and to use a variety of other words for supernatural beings of lesser scope: demon, spirit, angel, saint, and so forth. We like the word *demigod*, because it clearly points to a supernatural being of limited power and scope. Magic can get along without demigods, as we have said. But for now, we will skirt the issue of magic that does not use explicitly supernatural explanations, to avoid having to derive elements of secularization at this premature stage in our deductions. We can express as propositions some obvious points that derive immediately from the logic of Chapters 2 and 3:

P102 A society in which religious organizations with gods of great scope have differentiated, yet which possesses magic based on supernatural assumptions, will continue to postulate numerous demigods.

P103 To the extent that a religion provides relatively specific compensators as well as general compensators, it will tend to have a complex culture including demigods.

Proposition 103 describes the Catholic pattern. In Protestantism, a variety of needs are met by competing churches with different styles. As we explain in Chapter 5, religious schism may produce sects which dispense relatively specific compensators, though not usually as specific overall as the compensators magicians deal in. But when there is a strong central religious organization, as in Catholic countries, it will have to provide some moderately specific compensators, if it wants to prevent schism. In so doing, it must maintain a more complex set of explanations, and the supernatural agency of these compensators will be demigods like the saints and the Virgin within the Catholic tradition.

We must stress that this line of thinking does not invalidate P59, P60 and P61. In later chapters we will say more about the distinction between specific and general compensators. Two points about our earlier discussion of these propositions may help clarify this issue. First, the propositions are about evolution, so they do not assert that religions will give up all specific compensators the moment they become organizations; P93 says this tends to happen "over time." Second, the risk in providing a specific compensator depends on how easily it can be disconfirmed, and this is proportional to the degree of specificity. The more general a compensator is, the less risk in providing it. Therefore, the movement of a religion away from specific compensators will have less force the further it has gone in the direction of generality, and may decellerate markedly – and even stop – before it has jettisoned them all. Thus, P59, P60 and P61 describe a powerful tendency in one direction – they do not describe a disjunctive leap from one extreme to another.

Now consider what happens when both P94 and P95 apply, the situation when both religion and magic attempt to satisfy terrestrial desires with moderately specific compensators. Religion, of course, will be more concerned with general compensators, while magic will be active at the very specific end, but there is an overlap in many societies, when the territory of moderately specific compensators is contested. This means direct competition, and by P71, the religion will try to drive out the magicians, or, failing in this, force them to specialize in only the most specific compensators.

P104 To the extent that a religion provides specific compensators as well as general compensators, it will tend to oppose supernaturally-based magic and demigods outside its own system.

P105 To the extent that a religion does not provide specific compensators, it will tolerate supernaturally-based magic and demigods outside its own system.

Notice that P104 describes the reality within Catholicism, while P105 describes the Buddhist pattern. Consider the Buddhist tradition for a moment. There has been an open question (and ultimately an irresolvable one) whether Buddhism has a god or not. One complication – the facts of which give strong support to our theory – is that folk versions of Buddhism tend to treat the Buddha as a god, while more philosophical versions focus on cosmic principles that seem devoid of personality and desire. Philosophical Taoism postulates a cosmic principle, the Tao, which does not reach into human life like a living god, but merely expresses a sense of unity and rightness about the way the universe is arranged. That is, ethical aspects aside, philosophical Buddhism and Taoism assert the great general compensator that existence is meaningful. These systems, in their pure forms, promise no terrestrial benefits at all from a supernatural source. Therefore, by P105 these religions tolerate supernaturally-based magic and demigods outside their own organizations.

Looked at as cultural systems, these Eastern religions represent the extreme in development – God has evolved to infinite scope and become one in number, therefore he has abandoned any interest in the world. A being (call it the Tao), which is the unity or unifying principle of all things, can have no desires because there is nothing outside itself which it can act upon or seek rewards from. Therefore, humans cannot obtain rewards they desire by exchanging with an impersonal Tao. To the extent that a religion abandons specific compensators altogether, a process analyzed in Chapter 9, then P59, P60 and P61 may run their course until God vanishes completely.

Earlier, we commented that these propositions did not necessarily lead to true monotheism. Indeed, we said that we did not know of any vigorous popular religion that was monotheistic. For example, Christianity follows P103, and contains a number of supernatural entities. So long as God is conceived of as anything less than the totality of existence, then logically the residue must have some form, and that portion of the supernatural not included within God must be manifested through one or more other beings. Jehovah of the Old Testament confronts other supernatural beings, and reaches with his own hand into the world to act upon it. The God of the New Testament stands a bit further away from humans, but sends his agent, Christ, into the world to do his work. The protracted debates over the nature of Christ (the same substance as God, or only similar?), that were acted out in bloody war, were not airy philosophical speculations. Different conceptions powerfully reflected the competing desires and interest groups in human society. Philosophers and theologians, a small educated elite whose power (such as it is) comes from elegance of thought, want to achieve beautifully coherent cultural systems without flaws, thereby raising God out of terrestrial affairs. Ordinary people have many conflicting and intense desires that demand specific compensators and thus imply an active god who is not alone in the supernatural realm.

P106 If a religion evolves until it has but one god of infinite scope, it can no longer provide supernatural specific compensators as part of its cultural system, and it will have little to offer most people.

The minimum number of gods that can be the basis of a popular religion is two, one good and the other evil. To understand the nature of this duality, we must return briefly to the first principles of our theory of religion. We have already established that many explanations are very costly and even impossible to evaluate. That is, often it will be futile to attempt to choose among competing explanations on the basis of their results in providing desired rewards if such rewards are believed to be forthcoming only in the far distant future or in an inherently univerfiable context. For example, we cannot evaluate the relative efficacy of Catholicism and Lutheranism on the basis of the proportions of adherents who enter heaven. However, explanations of this kind often can be evaluated comparatively on the basis of their logical properties. Thus, an explanation with logical properties that make it appear more certain to provide the desired reward will be preferred to an explanation that logically appears less certain to provide the reward. It follows that:

P107 Explanations that assume the gods are rational offer greater certainty of reward than explanations that assume the gods are irrational.

Def.54 *Rationality* is marked by consistent goal-oriented activity.

The irrational is inexplicable and unpredictable. One cannot count on any particular outcome when the phenomenon in question in irrational. However, consistent goal-oriented behavior is predictable and understandable, given that the goals which orient that behavior are identified correctly. It will appear possible to exchange with rational gods. It will not appear possible to exchange with irrational gods. Therefore, humans will tend to choose explanations of the gods that posit rationality.

P108 Distinguishing the supernatural into two classes – good and evil – offers a rational portrait of the gods.

Def.55 *Good* and *evil* refer to the intentions of the gods in their exchanges with humans. *Good* consists of the intention to allow humans to profit from exchanges. *Evil* consists of the intention to inflict coersive exchanges or deceptions upon humans, leading to losses for the humans.

Remember that the gods are postulated by humans as explanations to serve human needs. One could invent gods with very complex plans that only incidentally intersect with human lives. Such beings certainly could appear to be mixtures of good and evil. But humans are not going to postulate irrelevant gods; instead they will postulate gods whose defining characteristics are their orientations toward humans. Of course, in societies that still imagine numerous small gods, each will have his own special personality and unique social relations with the other gods. When the scope of the gods becomes very great, their number will be reduced until it reaches two, one good and one evil.

We believe close analysis of useage of the terms good and evil reveals that humans employ these terms as synonyms for rewards and costs. Good is beneficial. Good people reward us. Evil is costly. Evil people do "bad" things to us – that is, they extract costs out of proportion to any reward we get from them. Good gods offer us the opportunity to profit in exchanges: if we love and serve Christ we are promised everlasting life, a reward immensely more valuable than the costs entailed in gaining it. The paradigm of the exchange with evil gods is the legend of Dr. Faustus. In exchange for immediate gratifications, the Devil claimed Faust's immortality – a cost immensely greater than the rewards obtained.

Good and evil, then, reflect the possible logical goal-orientations of gods – to give more than they take, or to take more than they give. A god holding either of these intentions is more rational than is a god who holds both intentions. The behavior of the latter must be judged as inherently inconsistent and hence inexplicable. A Tao beyond good and evil, we have already explained, does not make a fit exchange partner. We propose that:

P109 The more complex the culture, the clearer the distinction drawn between good and evil gods.

P110 The older, larger, and more cosmopolitan societies become, the clearer the distinction drawn between good and evil gods.

P111 Humans seek to exchange with good gods, and to avoid exchanging with evil gods.

P112 Good gods will be preferred who are thought to protect humans from exchanges with evil gods.

P113 The more complex the culture, the more likely is belief in good gods that are more powerful than evil gods.

P114 The older, larger, and more cosmopolitan societies become, the more likely they are to believe in good gods that are more powerful than evil gods.

P115 To the extent that good gods are thought to be more powerful than evil gods, the less likely it is that persons will exchange with evil gods.

This last proposition points toward one of the main features of contemporary liberal theology, the tendency to orient toward a single distant good god and to depersonalize or desacralize evil. Earlier we said that the minimum number of gods that can be the basis of a popular religion is two. We do not think contemporary liberal Protestantism is a counter-example, but rather it is a supportive example, for it is losing its popularity at a ferocious rate. The depersonalization or desacralization of evil leads quickly to the situation described by P106. When the evolution of a particular religion results in a single good god of infinite scope, the religion can no longer plausibly offer supernatural specific compensators. It can no longer render evil meaningful within a sacred context, and followers no longer have the opportunity of entering into an exchange relationship with God to gain rewards. A collapse of popularity follows. Furthermore, if evil becomes a feature of the natural world, then humans are given the impossible burden of actually vanquishing evil. And a distant, impersonal God offers little help. The conquest of evil, that is, the achievement of all desired rewards and avoidance of all feared costs, cannot be done, according to our axioms and early propositions. Thus the result of this evolution, for the given religious organization and its members, is frustrating and painful.

One senses, for example, that some Puritans conceive of God as a good spirit at war with an evil physical world of inert matter. Here the logical good/evil duality may be linked to others like cosmos/chaos, spirit/matter and life/death in a way in which the positive alternative retains a divine personality while the negative side is sketched in impersonal terms. But this occasional theological position is unstable, if only because it is highly uncomfortable, and rarely held seriously for long by a particular religious organization. It implies a dislike of Nature incongruent with the plenitude of rewards which flow from the physical world. Further, it implies a considerable self-hatred on the part of the believer who must recognize he is imprisoned in a body which is part of Nature. At best, we suspect that Puritanism which has lost Satan as a supernatural enemy is a rare minority stance at an advanced stage on the road to collapse of a religious organization or tradition.

More common but ultimately no more stable is the view that evil flows from human ignorance and improper social arrangements. If evil has a supernatural character, then we cannot hope to vanquish it entirely through our own efforts. But for decades, in several parallel sub-traditions, liberal Protestantism has been dedicated to the eradication of social ills. And what warrant have the liberal clergy possessed for leading this crusade? Their God has grown ever more distant and even in neo-orthodoxy provided little guidance. Surely, the secular social theories from which they drew some guidance failed to explain why distinctively religious leaders should be more effective than secular political leaders in achieving good results. And for many clergy, who had lost the sense of contact with a personal God, the rush into social activism therefore meant an uninhibited and dangerous return to the realm of magic. Social problems were supposed to be conquered by the application of means which, at best, had only an attenuated supernatural validation. The result has been a double failure. Evil remains strong. The liberal churches are weaker than ever (Johnson, 1982).

Conclusion

This chapter has focused on the historical emergence of religous organizations and the tendencies that shape the development of their structure and doctrines. Full consideration of the modern situation cannot be completed until Chapter 9, and it would be unbearably awkward to pepper these pages with too many hints of what is to come much later in this book. However, we should point out that our propositions about the evolution of the gods do not say religion achieves a permanent stable state if the pantheon is reduced to two gods of great scope, one good and one evil. Such a pantheon can sustain a very successful religion, that meets the need of clergy and laity alike, and thus may enjoy great stability. But two factors add complexity.

First, the character of religion is powerfully affected by the character of other institutions of society. A major collapse of the state and the economy may destroy the coherence of religious orthodoxy, thus reversing religious evolution for a time as the society in general regresses. At the other extreme, an expanding traditional society that incorporates new ethnic groups may find it politic to add their deities and rituals to its central religion, producing a Baroque complexity, like popular Hinduism or Classical Paganism. The peregrinations of fate that complicate analysis of the real world in terms of any of the sciences are really invitations to develop subsidiary theories, not refutations of basic principles.

Second, as we hinted at the end of the preceding section, the process of *secularization* can transform a particular religion beyond the dualism that otherwise is maximally stable. But this weakens the religion and leaves a sacred vacuum into which another religion can grow. The question of secularization is the main theme of our companion volume, *The Future of Religion*. There, we consider much empirical evidence on these points, as well as offering a considerable amount of less-formalized theory. Religions that abandon powerful, specific supernatural claims thereby lose their ability to serve many people's religious needs. More youthful and vigorous religions, that promise rewards and confidently explain the costs humans endure, will win converts at the expense of the more fully evolved religious organizations.

Secularization is not merely a feature of the contemporary cultural scene, but a permanent process in every religious tradition. The result, however, is not the extinction of religion, but the weakening of some particular religious organizations. The counterbalancing processes of revival and innovation keep religion, in general, alive. These processes of rebirth are the topics of the following chapters. But in the two chapters since we presented our core theory, we have already achieved much.

Perhaps the most significant feature of the propositions about religious phenomena we derived in Chapters 3 and 4 is that so many of them are familiar. We find this encouraging because our purpose is not to seek eccentric explanations of the world. Instead, we work on the assumption that we have been preceded by observant and sophisticated scholars who gained considerable insight into these matters. Our aim has been to bring order and integration to our knowledge about religion, not to invent a new field.

In consequence, we are especially pleased when we are able to deduce from our theory very familiar ideas such as Malinowski's recognition that people will not exchange with the gods when a cheaper or more efficient alternative is known and available (P58). Granted, Malinowski didn't state it quite that way. But we think our phrasing captures the essence of his point. If so, then a deductive result such as this serves to illuminate the merit of deductive theories. When Malinowski's insight about the rationality of primitives stands alone as a "middle range" generalization, we remain uncertain about why it ought to be so, and we cannot be sure what other statements about human behavior are assumed by his statement or what other statements stand in intimate relationship to it. However, when it proves possible to derive Malinowski's generalization from a unified theory, then his proposition is *explained*. We know why it ought to be true. And we know what else it is related to – that it belongs to a kinship structure made up of all of the statements that derive from this single set of axioms and definitions.

The same points apply to the fact that Durkheim's generalization about magic derived from our theory. Novel propositions can be very valuable theoretical results; they may direct our attention to important and previously unnoticed matters. But in the early stages of an effort to organize a rich, but disparate, area by means of formal theorizing, it is the discovery of many tried (and potentially true) "friends" that lends plausibility to the enterprise and encouragement to the theorists.

Thus we were especially gratified to discover how easily propositions concerning religious evolution derived from our theory and how familiar many of these propositions were. That we were able to arrive at these propositions without additional axioms suggests the power of the seven simple axioms from which we began. But more important, these propositions are not eccentric, but are accepted by virtually everyone who has examined the long history of culture. Hence, no one seriously questions that in the most simple cultures the gods are minute and numerous; nearly every rock, tree, stream, or plant is thought to be inhabited by a supernatural being of limited and local power (Stanner, 1956). Nor does anyone deny that in such societies cultural specialization has not reached the point where full-time religious specialists have appeared, nor is magic clearly differentiated from religion. By the same token, everyone recognizes that these aspects of religion changed over time. The gods grew in scope and declined in number. Religious specialists and religious organizations appeared. Religion and magic became separated. Indeed, in 1964 Robert Bellah published a paper on "religious evolution" that outlined these same trends and the wealth of evidence for their occurrence.

What is new about our work is that it is truly theoretical. Where Bellah comingled these many trends to discribe five ideal types representing stages in evolution, we have tried to explain these trends and to capture their complexity by deriving many related propositions about them. Elsewhere we have explained why ideal types, as they usually are constructed in sociology, tend to prevent theory-construction and in effect substitute premature descriptive complexity for complexity of theoretical accomplishment (Stark and Bainbridge, 1979).

Here, however, instead of preaching about what ought to be done, we have chosen to let our procedures demonstrate their own utility. Whether this demonstration is successful is for others to decide. But at least there can be little doubt about what it is we are claiming will or will not happen in the world. Therefore, it will be easy enough to discover if we are wrong. And that is a further reason why we are so fond of deriving well-known, middle-range generalizations. If our theories ultimately go down to defeat, they will take much of the sociology of religion down with them, and we shall at least have the comfort of some distinguished company.

CHAPTER 5:
Sects: Emergence of Schismatic Religious Movements

Fifty years ago Richard Niebuhr (1929) gave us the first sketch of a church-sect theory. Doubting that theological disputes were the real reasons behind the schisms in Christianity, he suggested that denominationalism was the product of class conflicts. He argued that the masses, having less stake in the world, were less worldly than the middle classes and thus were the generators of religious movements. But, he concluded, the successful religious creations of the masses soon were captured by the middle classes and accommodated to the world. This deprived the masses of a satisfactory faith, and therefore they soon launched a new one.

Niebuhr's classic book is many things: a sharp theological critique of sinful, worldly, self-satisfaction on the part of established churches; an historical investigation of the class interests that lie behind various theological doctrines; and a historical overview of Christian denominationalism. The least of the tasks Niebuhr seems to have set himself was to construct a social theory. That his theoretical insights and asides struck so responsive a chord in social science is a credit to his intellectual gifts. That for fifty years sociologists have done little to sharpen the theory beyond the form in which Niebuhr left it, adds no luster to our calling.

Indeed, sociological efforts in the church-sect area subsequent to Niebuhr have been, for the most part, retrograde. Niebuhr, the theologian and historian, realized the need for a general explanation. But most sociological contributions since have been wholly descriptive. Description had been but one of the aims of Max Weber and his student Ernst Troeltsch when they developed the concepts of church and sect. Niebuhr incorporated the terms in a truly scientific theory, but then sociologists who should have been committed to science backtracked and gave primary attention to the concepts themselves. Through the years a multitude of different church-sect typologies were added to the literature, but no significant efforts were made to advance the theory (Goode, 1967; Gustafson, 1967; Dittes, 1971; Welch, 1977). In consequence, although church-sect theory has long been a prominent topic in introductury textbooks, the theory presented today is Niebuhr's, almost without modification.

In our 1979 paper, "Of Churches, Sects and Cults," we pointed out in detail that much of the difficulty lay in typologies as such. Each new scheme repeated the failures of those that came before – no typology could order the cases, and therefore it virtually was impossible to construct theories with such recalcitrant concepts. Since 1963, however, this reason should no longer have stifled efforts to theorize about church and sect movements. For that year Benton Johnson cleared away the conceptual tangle and produced the simple tension axis along which to order religious bodies as more sectlike or churchlike. Since then it has been clear how to go about building more efficient, precise, and comprehensive theories.

Johnson postulated an underlying dimension of the *degree of tension* between a religious organization and its surrounding socio-cultural environment. The higher the tension, the more sectlike the religious organization. The lower the tension, the more churchlike the religious body. Tension is equivalent to broad subcultural deviance. The high tension group is *different* from the socio-cultural standard, mutually *antagonistic* toward the dominant groups that set that standard, and socially *separate* from them. In a second paper we have explored this concept more deeply and shown that the degree of tension experienced by a religious group can be measured easily and unambiguously (Bainbridge and Stark, 1980c).

Unfortunately, Johnson's paper appeared at what may have been the nadir of interest in sect formation. The "religious revival" of the early post World War II era was waning, its causes revealed to be little more than the baby boom and the tendency of people to be more active in church while their children are growing up. Meanwhile, the period from the 1940s until well into the 1960s seems to have been one of unusually little sect and cult formation. Or, at least, cults and sects received little media attention. Unfortunately, sociologists are subject to fads and fashions of the moment. Sect formation seemed a dying phenomenon, not the sort of thing on which to build an up-and-coming career. And so the study of religious movements languished.

As so often happens, however, trying to keep abreast of current events proved a poor guide to sociological enterprise. For, just as the subject had been laid to rest, the counter-culture turned mystical (Wuthnow, 1976, 1978). Moreover, the mysticism was not limited to new, strange or non-Western faiths (Glock and Bellah, 1976). The "Jesus freaks" were involved in traditional "Old Time" Christianity. Meanwhile, new and vigorous sectarian impulses errupted in the established churches. Over the past few years the news media have focused not on the "New Breed" of clergy (who placed so much faith in social activism, and so little in theology), but upon the massive new strength of conservative, evangelical Christianity. Even the Roman Catholic Church has been caught up in the new fervor. The Catholic Charismatic Movement – old-fashioned pentacostalism, complete with speaking in unknown tongues – has swept through the church at the parish level, threatening to produce new Catholic sects. And for sociologists, religious movements have once again become a hot topic (Flowers, 1984).

In this chapter we begin development of a church-sect theory intended to stand the test of time, not merely to satisfy the temporary perplexities of our decade. We seek to explain why sects are born at different rates under different social conditions yet are always potential outcomes of the search for religious compensators. Our theory is more comprehensive than Niebuhr's in a number of ways. First, by being based on the principles developed in earlier chapters it will be able to explain church movements as well as sect movements and to recognize that sects often break away from other sects. We seek to understand something very basic: religious schism. We want a theory explaining the forces that cause religious bodies of whatever type to develop internal conflicts that result in fission.

Secondly, we avoid Niebuhr's reliance on social class as the primary cause of schism and instead base our theory on the more general concept of power – the degree of control over one's exchange ratio. This makes it possible to examine a much broader range of deprivations and sources of conflict than the economic alone. Indeed, as we shall see, while the absolute economic status of a person is invariant at any given moment, a person simultaneously may have considerable power within a religious group and little in the surrounding society, or vice versa. This variation proves very important in our theory. Furthermore, high economic position is neither a necessary nor a sufficient condition for power. We shall see that church movements occur in part because those with the highest economic rank in a sect may have little power within the sect itself.

Finally, we attempt to isolate the specific mechanisms through which schism occurs. We shall not rest with the deduction that the powerless will tend to be discontented within a low tension religious body. It is essential to go beyond this to say why they are discontented, how they are mobilized, and from whence comes the leadership necessary for the formation of a sect or church movement.

The theory presented in this chapter deals with only one part of the dialectical process sketched by Niebuhr: Why and how schismatic religious movements occur. It does not deal with questions concerning the fate of such movements once they have formed, and therefore ignores the process by which sects sometimes are transformed into churches. These matters are the subject of Chapter 8.

Because we propose to base our theory of religious schisms on the most fundamental mechanisms, we cannot immediately restrict our focus to religious groups and organizations. First we must understand the essentials of all human groups. Specifically, if we are to explain the forces that cause religious groups to split into two or more pieces, we must understand the structures of social relations that constitute groups – forces that bind groups together or rend them apart. We must discover the dynamics of social structure. Part of this background was given in our discussion of exchanges and relationships in Chapter 2 and Chapter 3. More will come soon. First, we must take up again the question of definitions.

Basic Concepts

This chapter and the next derive the basic mechanisms that produce and shape new religious movements. Here we will discuss religious schisms and the emergence of sects; there we will discuss religious innovation and the formation of cults. Sects and cults share the quality of deviance. They depart from the standards of belief and practice (or from the organizational forms) established by the majority of members of the society or by the dominant elite. Seen the other way around, sects and cults are social movements that seek to transform the larger culture.

The terms *church, sect* and *cult* need to be defined afresh, to become unambiguous concepts identifying clear phenomena of great sociological interest. Guided by Benton Johnson and by our earlier essay, "Of Churches, Sects and Cults," we have chosen the following definitions designed for the most fruitful use in theoretical deductions:

Def.56 A *church* is a conventional religious organization.

Def.57 A *sect movement* is a deviant religious organization with traditional beliefs and practices.

Def.58 A *cult movement* is a deviant religious organization with novel beliefs and practices.

Def.59 *Deviance* is departure from the norms of a culture in such a way as to incur the imposition of extraordinary costs from those who maintain the culture.

Costs may be imposed on the deviant in either of two ways. First, exchanges with other parties may become more costly – within the immediate context of the exchanges themselves. If this were a deductive theory of deviance in general, rather than of religious deviance specifically, we would spend much time on the reasons why voluntary, mutual exchanges involving deviant individuals tend to demand exceptional costs. Recall our definition of norms:

> Def.50 *Norms* are the rules governing what behavior is expected or prohibited in various circumstances. Thus, they are equivalent to culturally shared explanations that govern the terms of exchanges.

Often, the disagreement about norms between a deviant and a non-deviant is directly relevant to the particular exchange they want to conduct. In general, when people exchange across cultural lines (or from a culture to an individual who recognizes no fixed standards of exchange) the mutual cost is high. Unless the particular exchange is instantaneous, open, and well-guarded, the cost of uncertainty is added. People are well advised to mistrust others who reject their accustomed terms of exchange. Furthermore (as we shall explain with respect to religion in this chapter) the presence of an individual or group following deviant explanations undercuts the value of conventional explanations. This raises the net cost of exchanges with these persons by non-deviants, and therefore the cost for the deviants as well. This increment in cost within exchanges may not be perceived clearly by parties, and need not represent a conscious policy.

The second way deviance incurs cost is through punishment, the conscious policy of imposing special costs on deviants outside and above ordinary exchanges with them. Sometimes, punishment may seek to change the behavior of the deviants by rendering their current patterns of behavior more costly than conformity would be. At other times, the hope may be to drive the deviants away and avoid further costly exchanges with them – at the extreme leading to the destruction of the deviants. Whether or not there is a separate category of vengeance, the infliction of costs to redress a previous exchange in which one's exchange ratio was unsatisfyingly low, we cannot say at this point in our derivations. Punishment of religious deviants may be carried out informally by small groups or individuals, or it may be practiced by the state through its organized powers of coercion. These considerations and a variety of exchange processes involving religious deviance will become clearer in the following pages.

Another way to describe religious deviance is to say that both sects and cults are in *tension* with the surrounding sociocultural environment. When Benton Johnson suggested this conceptualization in 1963 he said, "A church is a religious group that accepts the social environment in which it exists. A sect is a religious group that rejects the social environment in which it exists" (Johnson, 1963:542). As we have shown in our paper developing Johnson's ideas

(Stark and Bainbridge, 1979), what Johnson did was to propose a continuum, running from high to low tension. The ideal sect falls at one pole where the surrounding tension is so great that sect members are hunted fugitives. The ideal church anchors the other end of the continuum and virtually is the sociocultural environment, and the two are so merged it is impossible to postulate a basis for tension.

Johnson's conceptualization permits clear definition of two other important concepts: religious *movement* and religious *institution*. When we look at the low tension end of his axis we find not only churches but religious institutions. That is, we find a stable sector of the social structure, a cluster of roles, norms, values, and activities associated with the performance of a key social function or functions.

Social institutions are not social movements, if we define social movements as relatively organized groups or networks seeking to cause or prevent social change. Institutions adapt to change. Social movements seek to alter or become institutions. Thus we can see that if religious institutions are one pole of the tension axis, as we move along the axis in the direction of greater tension we discover religious movements. That is, religious movements are social movements that wish to cause or prevent change in a system of supernaturally-based general compensators. Such groups would like to become the dominant faith in their society, although they may make little effort to achieve this end if they are convinced their chances are too remote.

Johnson's axis of variation also permits us to characterize the direction taken by religious movements. When they move toward less tension with their sociocultural environment they are *church movements*, so called because they move in the churchward direction. Of course, a group may remain a sect during a long period of tension reduction if the initial level of tension was very high. When groups move toward the high tension pole they are *sect movements*. Instead of two mutually exclusive categories, *church* and *sect*, this conceptualization sees a continuous spectrum of degrees of tension, a dimension we have elsewhere shown can be measured with some precision (Bainbridge and Stark, 1980c). Degree of tension is equivalent to degree of deviance.

The sect, of course, is not the only common kind of religious movement that is in a high state of tension with the surrounding sociocultural environment. Many deviant religions have no history of prior organizational attachment to a "parent" church or to the dominant religious tradition. They are neither schismatic nor doctrinally traditional. Indeed they lack a close cultural continuity with (or similiarity to) other religious groups in the society. These non-schismatic, deviant religious groups are of two types. One type represents cultural *innovation*. Although many familiar components of religious culture may appear in the beliefs, values, symbols, and practices of the group, there is something distinctive about them. In common parlance, these innovative, deviant but non-schismatic bodies which make a distinct break with the religious tradition of the culture are called *cults* (Glock and Stark, 1965; Lewis, 1966; Nelson, 1969; Eister, 1972). They will be treated in the following chapter.

The second type represents cultural *importation*. Such groups represent a religious body well-established in another society. While our theory can easily be extended to cover the many social and cultural processes that may take place when culture is transplanted from one society to another, the complexity of the many situations that would have to be analyzed would render a discussion of religious importation excessively long for inclusion in this book.

In discussing sects and cults, we will use "tension" and "deviance" almost interchangeably, as alternate terms for the same concept. But there is a special advantage to the term "tension." It conveys the special character of religious deviance and has just the right connotation to express in a word this segment of our theory. The more general term "deviance" conjures up images of criminals, madmen and perverts, specters that have little to do with religious schism. Before we can proceed with our explanatory theory of sects, we should say how a sect can be deviant yet possess traditional beliefs and practices and why sects form through schism rather than in some other way.

Proposition 73 says, "The emergence of the state in a society will tend to be followed by the emergence of a single dominant religious organization." Thus, we have already derived the emergence of the *church*. Other religious organizations may exist, but will be relegated to the category of deviance, all the more sharply as the one church gains dominance with the help of the state. If a new organization, identical in belief and practice to the dominant church, were to appear, it also would be attacked by the state church. Not belief and ritual alone, but political and social ties to the elite mark a religious organization as the dominant church. An alternate source of compensators represents competition for the church. Given the opportunity, the church will use the coercive power of the state to suppress its rival, inflicting punishment upon those who traffic with it, identifying them as deviants.

Of course, sects commonly give a different emphasis to parts of the religious tradition they share with churches. In the following pages we will explain why this is. But despite the differences in style and leadership, the groups that concern us here do share much culture. They share most of the same supernatural explanations. Therefore, the deviant groups must be schismatic in origin. It is not beyond the powers of imagination to conceive that the same set of explanations might be invented independently by two different groups. But religions are cultural systems. Therefore, even a small number of general compensators found in one group and not the other would mark them as quite different religions. Often, a single general compensator means the difference between one major tradition and another, as *Jesus* separates Christians from Jews, (cf. Bainbridge, 1985). Therefore, the likelihood of two essentially identical religions emerging from separate origins is remote. Except for this improbable possibility, if two religious groups share the same culture, they must be offshoots of the same organizational tradition.

As Proposition 65 states, "The value an individual places on a general compensator is set through exchanges with other persons." Therefore, religious compensators are sustained and transmitted by organizations of religious specialists. People will not accept a religion unless they are in contact with the organization on which it rests. The existence of two or more groups with the same beliefs and practices implies that an earlier organization split into two or more parts at some time in history.

P116 Sects come into being through schisms from existing organizations in their religious tradition.

Def.60 A *schism* is the division of the social structure of an organization into two or more independent parts.

The simplest image of a schism is that of a congregation that fell to fighting in church one day, until one side walked out to found a new sect. But sometimes even very large denominations divide, for example along geographic lines. On other occasions, a small counter-organization develops slowly around a few individual church members, perhaps first appearing as an acceptable prayer or meditation group, then grows in size and independence until it challenges the parent church. Whatever the speed, magnitude and clarity of the split, all these are schisms.

A new religious body that is born socially detached from the other religious bodies in the society is highly unlikely to duplicate existing religious traditions, but instead will innovate as described in the following chapter, and will be a cult, not a sect. Having shown that sects emerge through schisms, we can begin to explain how group fission can occur in the rupture of social relationships.

To understand differences between relationships it will be useful to examine different aspects of the social bond. A good starting point is a list of four concepts suggested by Travis Hirschi (1969): attachment, commitment, involvement, and belief. Because we use the word *commitment* in a very general sense, we prefer to employ *investment* to name this aspect of the social bond. All four of these can be stated in the terms of our deductive theory, so it is the following definitions of four aspects of the social bond that we will follow:

Def.61 *Attachment* is positive evaluation of an exchange partner.

Def.62 *Investments* are costs expended in an exchange which have not yet yielded their full potential of desired rewards.

Def.63 *Involvement* is that proportion of one's total resources that one invests in an exchange.

Def.64 *Belief* is positive evaluation of an explanation.

In real life it may often be difficult to separate these four empirically, although each can in principle be measured separately from the others. We have already seen that relationships with exchange partners can be conceptualized in terms of explanations. Consequently, belief is implicated in each of the other three. Belief and attachment bring one to make investments in lengthy exchanges with selected partners, thus leading to the involvement of a large proportion of one's resources. But as Hirschi showed, there are a number of ways that the effects of each can be distinguished from the others. For example, one can have belief in the efficacy of explanations offered by one's religious denomination, but attachment to one's local priest. One can have made a great investment toward achieving salvation by living a righteous life, quite apart from any consideration of the particular religious denomination that encouraged one to do this. Or, one can spend much of one's time in a particular religious group, and thus have a great involvement in that group.

What relevance do these four connected concepts have for the development of religious schism? As Hirschi explains, they are the means through which social control takes place. Each points to one aspect of what Toby (1957) calls *stakes in conformity*, the controlling force of social bonds. To the extent that each binds a person to a group, that person will accept the dominance of the group and will follow its norms. To the extent that persons are bound to a religious group, they will not be free to participate in a schism. We can state this argument more fully in terms of four propositions that flow immediately from our original commitment theory:

P117 When a person is attached to an exchange partner, the person is willing to expend some costs to maintain the relationship with the partner.

P118 When a person has invested in an exchange, the person will tend to maintain the exchange relationship until the potential reward is achieved, or until the continuing cost of the relationship markedly exceeds the cost the person is willing to pay for the reward.

P119 When a person is involved in a set of exchanges, the person will have fewer resources to invest in alternative exchanges.

P120 When a person believes in a particular explanation, the person is unlikely to invest in competing explanations in which the person does not believe.

Each of these four propositions explains commitment to a person or to an organization. But relationships with a group differ in complexity from those with a single individual. *Organizations* can be conceived of as networks of persistent exchange relationships linking individuals. The concept of *network* has received renewed attention among sociologists in recent years (White, Boorman, and Breiger, 1976; Laumann, *et al*., 1977). Networks play an important role in later parts of our general theory of religion, especially in the theory of recruitment, as well as being essential to the theory of schism. Up to this point, our theory has focused on a single hypothetical individual and one or more exchange partners. But now we have the basis for introducing much greater complexity. Individuals will have different sets of social relationships, even within very small groups. Each person may be attached to some fellow members and not to others, or the strengths of attachment will vary. If we map the complete set of attachments within a religious group, we may find that there are *cleavages*, or lines of weak attachment linking sub-networks that are internally more strongly attached. Surveying attachments within a religious group, we can state the converse of P39 as it applies to the aggregate:

P121 Schisms in groups will be most likely along lines of social cleavage.

Def.65 *Social cleavages* are divisions of a network across which there are relatively few strong attachments.

P122 Schisms will be most likely in groups that contain marked social cleavages.

Empirical research has already shown the importance of social cleavages in facilitating fragmentation of religious groups (cf. Coleman, 1956). In her study of nineteenth-century intentional communities, Rosabeth Moss Kanter (1972) noted that even the development of relatively detached dyads within such groups constituted a threat to their integrity. White and Breiger (1975) have reanalyzed data collected in a monastery by Samuel F. Sampson. At the end of the research period, the monastery erupted and many members resigned or were expelled. Analysis showed that the disintegration went exactly along the line of greatest original social cleavage, further evidence of the importance of networks of attachment (cf. Herman, 1984).

Investment and involvement can be considered together. Persons will tend to protect their investments until they have paid off, and while they have a significant part of their resources invested, persons will be inhibited from making new investments. This inhibition stems partly from the fact that involvement leaves them with less to invest. But it also reflects the fact that new investments to achieve rewards in which the person has already invested a good deal would undesirably increase the cost of the rewards.

P123 Schisms in groups will most likely take the form of secessions which appear to preserve the investments of the individuals seceding.

P124 Schisms in groups will most likely take the form of secessions which appear not to require great new investments on the part of the individuals seceding.

The investments central to religious organizations are those made in exchange for the supernatural-based general compensators that are the essence of religion. Since the value of these compensators cannot easily be determined through empirical test, it is also difficult to test the effect of various actions that might increase or decrease the chances of eventually obtaining the great rewards for which the compensators substitute. The only available evidence may be whatever is stated in the doctrines of the religion. The doctrines provide explanations that influence the adherent's assumptions about which kinds of action, including participating in a schism, will endanger investments.

> P125 Schisms will tend to take place in the form which the tradition of religious beliefs implies will be least likely to endanger previous investments.

> P126 Schisms will tend to take place in the form which the tradition of religious beliefs implies will be most likely to facilitate the achievement of the desired rewards; that is, they will take place in accordance with the explanations in which the religious compensators are embedded.

> P127 Schisms will be most likely to take place if the tradition of religious beliefs does suggest a form schism may take without endangering previous investment, and particularly if it suggests that such a form will actually facilitate achievement of the desired general rewards.

These propositions partly explain why schismatic groups typically claim to be the purest expressions of their religious tradition. For example, sects often claim to be returning to real religion while the churches have fallen away from God's commandments. One reason for this is that such claims appear to preserve investments the members have made in religion, while a break from the original religious tradition would seem to endanger those investments.

These propositions also explain differences in recent history between Protestant and Catholic groups. Protestant tradition stresses relatively direct exchanges between the individual and God, while Catholic tradition stresses the importance of exchanges mediated through central church authority. Therefore, open schism appears less costly to the Protestant than to the Catholic, and therefore is a much more likely event in Protestant churches.

Another way of conceptualizing the different characteristics of the Catholic and various Protestant traditions is in terms of exchanges between distributors of compensators and consumers of compensators. In established churches, the clergy are professional distributors of compensators while the laity are consumers. Of course, the two roles are not absolutely separated from each other. All participants in religion are to some extent consumers, and the distributive function may be diffused to a greater or lesser degree within different religious organizations. In the Catholic church, there is only one legitimate wholesale distributor which is the central church itself. In Protestantism, on the other hand, there is much greater development of multiple competing distributors. In our earlier work, derivation P27 notes that different distributors may exist in competition with each other and will be successful in the business of distribution to the extent that they can offer the desired product at a relatively low price.

> P27 If multiple suppliers of general compensators exist, then the ability to exchange general compensators will depend upon their relative availability and perceived exchange ratios.

Consumers will switch to a new distributor (whether in schism or in recruitment to a different religious group) when they perceive they can obtain the desired rewards (including valued compensators) from the new source at relatively low cost. But different consumers may evaluate exchanges with two competing distributors quite differently. For some, distributor A may in fact provide the best deal, while for others distributor B is more attractive. This need not always be the case, of course. Often everyone in a group values one distributor above all others. Only when consumers disagree about which distributor offers a better deal, will there be a schism. The disagreement may be the result of different needs that distinguish some consumers from others, needs that are differentially satisfied by different distributors. Or the disagreement may flow from differences in perceived exchange ratios (costs) with different distributors, which in turn may come from variation in the resources held by consumers, or simply from variation in the explanations to which they have been socialized. Thus, we can derive the following:

> P128 Consumers will participate in a schism only if in so doing they can maintain exchange relationships with their most valued distributors, or can at very little cost switch to a new but similar distributor.

> P129 Consumers will participate in a schism if they perceive that by doing so they can achieve an improved exchange ratio in pursuit of rewards.

> P130 Schisms will be most likely if sets of individuals within the original religious group have markedly different exchange ratios or pursue markedly different rewards.

This last proposition reminds us that schisms are not the only changes that can take place in religious groups. If there is great consensus in the dissatisfactions of group members, they may unanimously seek particular changes in which the organization remains intact. Sometimes the result may be the firing of a minister or the convening of a doctrinal conference, rather than a schism.

So far we have merely presented some of the conditions that permit schisms. Our initial propositions will take on their full significance only after we have duscussed forces that produce schisms.

Commitment and Contradiction

In Chapter 2, three propositions about the relationship between power and religious rewards and compensators were derived from the axioms. Their initial purpose was to explain why individuals and groups within a religious organization exhibit different modes of religious commitment. But, these three propositions also describe and explain the composition of religious organizations and therefore cast light on the structure of such organizations. We now show a schismatic tendency is inherent in the composition of religious bodies, a tendency that may combine with conducive social structure, as described in the preceeding section, to produce overt fragmentation of religious organizations. First, we shall restate the three propositions.

P24 The power of an individual or group is positively associated with control of religious organizations and with gaining the rewards available from religious organizations.

P25 The power of an individual or group is negatively associated with accepting religious compensators, when the desired reward exists.

P26 Regardless of power, persons and groups tend to accept religious compensators, when desired rewards do not exist.

Proposition 24 lets us recognize two things about the composition of religious bodies. Within religious bodies rewards will go disproportionately to the more powerful, and thus unequal division of rewards is the result of ongoing competition. Since we conceive of both power and the proportion of rewards as continuous variables, religious bodies are not simply dichotomized into haves and have-nots, but contain many levels of power and degree of rewards. Therefore, deprivation in terms of both power and rewards can be relative as well as absolute, a point that assumes importance later on.

Proposition 25 allows us to see that the salience of compensators (for which a reward exists) varies inversely to power and to the gaining of rewards within religious bodies. Thus, by combining those two propositions we see that com-compensators of this type are most important to those with least control over religious bodies. Proposition 130 immediately above was based on an analysis of relations between consumers and distributors, and showed that differences such as indicated by P24 and P25 could lead to schism. But for the moment let us consider the consequences for a religious group that is at least momentarily intact. Propositions 24 and 25 imply that an internal contradiction is inherent in the composition of religious bodies – that the seeds of schism are inevitably built in. We may put this more formally:

> P131 The potential for group conflict over the distribution of rewards and the emphasis on compensators is present in all religious bodies.

Proposition 26 permits an answer to the question of why this potential for conflict often can be muted sufficiently so that schism does not occur. Since there are desires for which no reward exists, all members, regardless of their power, have a common need for compensators of this type. This shared need implies a basis for consensus and for the maintenance of a source of such compensators (i.e. the religious body). This common stake in obtaining compensators for which no reward is available also implies that religious bodies will place greatest emphasis on supplying such compensators.

Since it is our aim to construct a theory that will hold for all religious organizations in all societies we must now note that propositions 24, 25 and 131 are subject to considerable variation across religious organizations and especially across societies. Some of this variation is explained by propositions in our earlier discussion of social structure, although some, such as P121 and P122, will later be shown in turn to be influenced by propositions to be developed below. But an important source of variation is also found in A7 from which P24 and P25 are derived. That is, both propositions depend upon the existence of stratification within religious organizations – upon the unequal distribution of power among members. Should all members of a religious organization be equal in terms of their power, then proposition 24 and 25 would lead to the prediction that all members will display the same mix of rewards and compensators in their pattern of religious commitment. However, Axiom 7 tells us that this will never be the case – it asserts the universality of an unequal distribution of power among persons or groups in any society. Nevertheless, Axiom 7 is compatible with all degrees of stratification other than zero. This means that we can deduce from the theory that

> P132 The greater the degree of power inequality in a religious organization the greater will be the potential for group conflict over the distribution of rewards and the emphasis on compensators.

Now we can see why it is that church-sect theory has been the domain primarily of sociologists rather than of anthropologists. In small, simple societies there is minimal stratification. To the extent that power inequalities are small, the tendency towards religious conflict and schism will be correspondingly small. Sect movements will be rare or absent in such societies. Furthermore, since religion is not the property of a highly differentiated and formally organized social enterprise in simple societies, it will be difficult if not impossible to tell a sect movement from a rebellion or the fissioning of a whole society. That is, hunter-gatherers, for example, cannot split their church without also splitting their society, for the church and the society are not distinct. Therefore, because they have focused on simple societies anthropologists have not had occasion to study sect movements to any great degree.

This is not to suggest that anthropologists have ignored the role of religion in the power-struggles that do occur in simpler societies. They frequently report observations fully compatible with propositions 24 and 25. Leach (1954), for example, makes much of the way headmen among the Kachin of highland Burma manipulate religion to sustain their political power – that is, their control of religion permits them to exchange compensators for rewards, as outlined in our theory. And it is because of the particular salience of compensators for scarce rewards among the Kachin rank-and-file that they are subject to such manipulation. Indeed, as Spiro (1966:106) pointed out, it is "only because Kachins do believe . . . [that it is] possible to manipulate this belief for political ends."

In fact, numerous ethnographies report the presence of high-tension religious groups within relatively simple societies, although few of them can be described as sects because they did not come into being through fission of an existing religious organization. As we have pointed out, high-tension religious bodies may also take the form of cults which are organized around acts of cultural innovation. The absence of a monolithic church in such societies both permits the emergence of many novel groups, and also leaves the powerful less able to monopolize rewards from religious organizations. High-tension groups will therefore tend to emerge as the creations of several unchurched individuals, rather than in schisms. A good example is the proliferation of secret societies in Kwakiutl society. This tribe of the Northwest Coast is well known for its extreme concern with status, expressed in the remarkable potlatch ritual in which property is ostentatiously consumed in the assertion of personal honor. Lowie (1937:133) has called the Kwakiutl "caste-ridden," and Boas (1966:360) reported that extreme status tensions existed even within individual families. The development of high-tension cults like the Kwakiutl secret societies will be analyzed in the next chapter.

It is when societies become complex, highly stratified, and marked by relatively coherent religious organizations that religious schism becomes common, as our theory in fact predicts. In the great agrarian societies of both present and past, sect movements have abounded. Indeed, modern histories of medieval Europe suggest that sect formation absorbed much of the available social energy in those societies (Cohn, 1961). Proposition 132 also would suggest that the development of welfare states may dampen sect formation, other things being equal.

Thus far we have accounted for certain characteristic features of religious organizations purely on the basis of conclusions about their composition. Already we can see the threat of impending schism is inherent in the different interest groups that make up religious bodies. But why cannot members of religious groups simply agree to disagree and pursue different goals within the same group? To some extent, of course, the doctrines and practices of any religion are a single standard that all members are supposed to follow, although any particular set of religious norms will not serve all equally. But to understand the contradiction inherent in any religious group we need to derive a few more relevant propositions. We need to demonstrate that humans seek a positive evaluation of themselves and their resources.

This statement is a very basic assumption of all the social sciences – that individuals desire self-respect, self-esteem, self-confidence – in short, that people need to value themselves. Evidence on this point has come from many sources. In a study of mentally retarded persons, Robert B. Edgerton (1967) found that even those with subnormal mental powers thought in terms of self-worth and were dedicated to seeking some basis for pride and a sense of competence.

To a great extent, humans see themselves as sources of rewards, as if we were our own exchange partners, and as collections of means to rewards. We may evaluate our minds as the sum total of the explanations contained therein, and assess our personal worth in terms of the power we have in exchanges and of the resources that give us that power. This can be understood best through the following chain of deductions.

Humans seek valuable explanations that appear to lead to great rewards. Most explanations tell the individuals what to do to gain the reward, including many explanations that tell what to give to exchange partners to earn the reward (A4, Def.9, P74). The only exceptions are those highly general supernatural explanations that explicitly seek to escape this aspect of the human condition, for example the belief that God loves all his children, regardless of their actions. Thus, explanations that people ever attempt to use include the person himself in the formula. He is supposed to do and to give, before he can get. Obviously, the predicted success of an explanation will depend upon the person's estimate of how able he is to do things and of what resources he has to give in exchanges. The better he views himself and his resources, the greater the number of explanations will seem plausible instructions and the wider the range of rewards they seem capable of providing.

It is important to point out the great uncertainty an individual has in evaluating himself. Since the individual is a term in essentially all the explanations he uses, as a reward or indeed as an explanation he must view himself as quite general. Since the individual typically will expend great costs to avoid losing himself in death, by definition he views himself as a general reward of great value, at least to himself. Since he plays such a central role in all his explanations, his self-evaluation must surely be itself an explanation of great generality. Recall the following proposition:

> P13 The more valued or general a reward, the more difficult will be evaluation of explanations about how to obtain it.

From this logic and from P66 and P74 it follows that:

> P133 It is very difficult for individuals to achieve accurate evaluations of themselves.

> P134 Every person seeks a positive self-evaluation.

> > Def.66 An individual's *self-evaluation* is that person's determination of how valuable a reward he constitutes as an exchange partner.

> P135 Persons desire a positive evaluation of the rewards they possess, including the explanations and the power-giving resources they possess.

By P133, an individual has some freedom in how highly he may evaluate himself. Under favorable conditions, he may evaluate himself at the high end of this optional range, thus increasing the perceived value of this explanation and his likely future rewards. This increase constitutes a reward, itself, and therefore will be sought. Unfortunately, as every human experiences from time to time, the uncertainty in self-evaluation also places us at risk whenever a series of actions fails and a desired reward elludes us. At these times, our self-evaluation may be shaken, and we cannot be sure that we do not actually stand near the bottom end of the range of optional self-evaluation. As P66 and P74 imply, a person often must rely upon other human beings to provide him with a stable and favorable self-evaluation. From this it follows that anything that devalues a person or his rewards represents a perceived cost, and such costs may often appear in social exchanges. This kind of loss will be avoided unless significantly greater rewards accompany it. We may summarize:

> P136 Explanations that imply positive evaluations of a person and the rewards the person possesses are themselves rewards, while explanations that imply negative evaluations are costs.

Naturally this proposition is modified or limited by any other rewards or costs that are entailed by a given explanation. But P58 has a very straightforward and unambiguous application to the antagonism between rewards and corresponding compensators. To see how, we must first recall four earlier propositions. P18 through P21. Proposition 18 says humans prefer rewards to compensators and will attempt to exchange compensators for rewards. However, it will be impossible to obtain rewards rather than compensators when: (1) a reward does not exist; (2) a compensator is mistaken for a reward; (3) one lacks the power to obtain the desired reward.

Let us consider relations between persons who possess a scarce reward and persons who lack the power to obtain it and have settled for the corresponding compensator. The reward is embedded in an explanation that identifies the reward as indeed the desired reward. But the compensator is also embedded in an explanation that identifies the compensator as the reward. These two explanations are antagonistic. Each denies the value of the other, so by P136:

> P137 Persons who possess a scarce reward will avoid explanations that identify the corresponding compensator as the real reward.

> P138 Persons who possess a compensator for a scarce reward will avoid explanations that identify the corresponding reward as indeed the true reward.

Furthermore, it is important to point out the tension between the person who lacks the power to obtain a scarce reward and the reward itself. By P18, the person will seek the reward, perhaps occasionally expending costs to obtain it, and yet the result is failure, lost investment without return. By P9 and P57, we can conclude that

> P139 Contact with a scarce reward or with persons who possess the scarce reward constitutes a cost for persons who desire the reward yet lack the power to obtain it.

Propositions 137 through 139 seem a bit bland, as stated, but they explain what is often very intense hostility between a deviant religious group and the surrounding sociocultural environment. It has been suggested that we need a *frustration-aggression* proposition to explain the hostility of the deviant group, perhaps expressed as an axiom (Bannan, 1965; cf. Dollard *et al.*, 1939; Homans, 1974). But psychological research on human responses to frustration suggests that aggression is not the only possible outcome, a fact which to us suggests that it should not be enshrined in an axiom but made the contingent result of a string of derivations.

Proposition 136 states that negative evaluations of a person and the rewards that person possesses are costs, while earlier propositions state that certain types of exchange, such as those which take place under coercion, also involve net costs. These costs may be great, and thus stimulate powerful negative evaluations. It may be agonizing to interact with a sociocultural environment which reviles one and inflicts numerous gratuitous costs on one. That the result may be an intense negative evaluation of the surrounding society, tantamount to raging hatred, is not surprising. Thus, while we consider it an interesting question whether frustration necessarily breeds aggression, we see no need to invoke such a proposition here, and certainly no need to state it as an axiom.

Propositions 137 and 138 show that for each kind of person, those with rewards and those who have accepted the corresponding compensators, the explanation accepted by the other represents a cost which is to be avoided. Consider transvaluational doctrines, for example. In defense of religious compensators they deny that a wealthy person's riches are really valuable, a message that the wealthy person would not want to accept. On the other hand, persons who have accepted a compensator corresponding to wealth, perhaps the belief that their austere virtue grants them a favored place in the eyes of the Lord, will not enjoy contemplating the riches of the wealthy.

Indeed, P139 suggests that consumers of compensators will suffer more than will consumers of rewards in interactions between them. The powerful do not want to be made to take seriously the compensators that correspond to their rewards, but they are happy to be reminded that some other persons have fewer rewards than they. The compensator-consumer will tend to develop a negative evaluation of persons who possess the scarce rewards, manifested subjectively in anger, resentment and disgust. This asymmetry in the degree of antagonism between holders of rewards and holders of compensators is basically explained by P18 and P139. But P137 and P138 show that the antagonism will go both ways.

From this argument it follows that relationships between consumers of compensators and consumers of the corresponding rewards will be costly, and unless exchange with each other is highly rewarding in some other way, such relationships will not be maintained. Of course, this is not meant to apply when rewards and compensators that do not correspond to each other are exchanged. Thus we can say:

> P140 Consumers of scarce rewards and consumers of the corresponding compensators tend to avoid relationships with each other.

A glance back at P121 and P122 immediately suggests that P140 means that religious groups containing both consumers of scarce rewards and consumers of the corresponding compensators will be groups with marked social cleavages, and therefore groups that are especially free to split. Several lines of deduction from our original premises converge on the derivation that such groups will be likely to experience schism. A further reinforcement of the split between the two categories of members is seen in their patterns of behavior. Every different explanation requires somewhat different behavior in pursuit of the desired reward, as was indicated in Def.8, Def.9, Def.10, and P5. Therefore,

> P141 Consumers of scarce rewards and consumers of the corresponding compensators will advocate and follow distinctly different patterns of behavior.

Earlier, we defined different kinds of religious group. We laid especial stress on the distinction between the *church* and the *sect*. We endorsed Benton Johnson's conceptualization and explained that churches and sects can be distinguished along a single dimension of tension with the surrounding sociocultural environment. To this point in our discussion, we have apparently been defining *sect* in two ways: (1) a high-tension schismatic group, and (2) a schismatic group that emphasizes compensators for scarce rewards. Now we can show that these two definitions are really the same, that emphasis on compensators for scarce rewards causes tension, and in the case of groups that began in relatively low tension, can be the source of increased tension.

> P142 Tension with the surrounding sociocultural environment is equivalent to subcultural deviance, marked by difference, antagonism, and separation.

Five propositions derived above, P134 through P138, imply that religious groups with a preponderant involvement in compensators for scarce rewards will be high tension groups. In an empirical essay, "Sectarian Tension," we were careful to take the extra step of demonstrating that persons who possess many scarce rewards can be identified with the standard sociocultural environment. We have shown *antagonism* (P137–P139), *separation* (P140) and *difference* (P141) in a way that made it clear which side of the cleavage was in high tension with the environment and which was in low tension.

But another line of deduction can anchor the dimension even more strongly. Proposition 50 states that social organizations come into being as social enterprises that specialize in providing rewards. Proposition 9 explains that powerful persons, those with resources that permit them control over their exchange ratios, will tend to monopolize scarce rewards. Because social organizations provide rewards and are limited in number, they themselves are scarce rewards, and they too will tend to be monopolized by the powerful. Because they dominate the sources of rewards, the powerful will be able to dominate the system of exchanges that distributes most of these rewards. Thus they will define the sociocultural environment. As we will explain later in discussing church movements, such people may not be able to set norms in relatively insolated groups such as detached ethnic subcultures. Whether they can dominate a given religious group depends on its exact composition and its relations with the larger society. But it is rewards rather than compensators that define the sociocultural environment.

> P143 To the extent that religious groups are involved with compensators for scarce rewards, they are in tension with the sociocultural environment.

Other kinds of high-tension groups may exist, some relatively uninvolved in such compensators. One example that has little to do with our theory is criminal groups. Another more relevant example is the oppressed ethnic minority. To the extent that such groups suffer serious deprivations because of the antagonism of the larger society, then they also will become involved in compensators for scarce rewards. We can now derive propositions about the emergence of schismatic religious groups, beginning with those that seek increased tension.

Sect Formation

Although not all high-tension groups are necessarily deeply involved in compensators for scarce rewards, the state of high tension leaves a group relatively free to generate and exchange compensators, as the above discussion suggests. If they are already cut off from scarce rewards, from close relations with the powerful, and from the control that such rewards and relationships would enforce, groups can adopt compensators at relatively low cost. Therefore, it follows that:

> P144 The higher the tension of a religious group, the greater the number and perceived value of the compensators it can provide for scarce rewards.

Proposition 143 and the entire discussion in the preceeding section also imply the following:

> P145 In any religious body, the less powerful will tend to prefer relatively higher tension with the external society.

> P146 In any religious body, the more powerful will tend to prefer relatively lower tension with the external society.

Proposition 145 derives immediately from P15, P25, P143 and P144. Proposition 146 can be derived from the same logical chain, but has two other derivations as well. First, recall that P20 stated it was impossible to obtain a reward if a compensator is mistaken for the reward. Thus, otherwise powerful individuals will lose power to the extent that they accept the compensator-oriented explanations offered in a high-tension group. Those who do not fully accept the compensators will be more able to discover the true rewards, and thus will gain relatively greater power than those persons with significant resources yet who accept the compensator explanations fully. Thus there will be a tendency for those with potential power to realize that power more successfully by adopting and promulgating reward-oriented explanations, thus moving their group toward lower tension.

The remaining derivation of P146 examines relations between relatively powerful members of a religious group and outsiders who are also relatively powerful. To the extent that the group members are in high tension, the outsiders will find relations with them somewhat costly, by P137, P139 and P140. This means that members of the group will have to pay a greater price to outsiders in order to make them willing to carry on exchanges. Members can improve their exchange ratio with outsiders by moving to lower tension. This line of thought not only gives us a strong alternative derivation of P146, but also demonstrates that:

> P147 The lower the tension of a religious group, the greater and more valuable the supply of rewards it can earn from the outside and provide to members.

Of course, if a shift to very low tension entails the complete abandonment of compensators, the church may go out of the religion business and therefore risk loss of rewards. This possibility is considered in Chapter 9. But short of this extreme, by P24 we know that rewards are likely to wind up disproportionately in the hands of the more powerful members of the group. Taken together, P144, P145, P146 and P147 summarize the conflict within a religious group. The more powerful members want to maintain a low level of tension or even reduce it, while the less powerful will want to increase tension.

There are four obvious outcomes. First, perhaps nothing will happen; opposing forces will be equal, and the group will be sufficiently cohesive to remain unified at equilibrium with respect to tension. Second, the group can split into two pieces that move in opposite directions; if the sect fragment is small with respect to the other, the larger fragment may not seem to move along the tension continuum at all. Third, the powerful may prevail and the group will move churchward; this is of course a very common pattern. Fourth, the members who are individually less powerful may be so numerous that in the aggregate they can force their will on the group and move it toward greater tension; we suspect that this is a rare outcome, unless facilitated by special circumstances, such as the mass defection of powerful members during a period of secularization.

Alternatives three and four are beyond the scope of this chapter and will be analyzed in Chapter 8 in discussions of the evolution of religious movements. For the moment we point out that P146 and P147 suggest that sects often will evolve in the churchly direction, as Niebuhr predicted, thus setting the stage for the generation of further sects through yet another schism. But here we are still analyzing the origins of sects, so we will focus on the initial phase of the second alternative. This begins with the religious groups at a lower state of tension than some members desire, when (stating the obvious to be very clear):

> P148 The lower the state of tension of a religious group the greater the demand generated among the less powerful members for more efficacious compensators.

Earlier we derived a number of propositions setting conditions within which schisms could occur, including P128 and P129, which explained that consumers of rewards or compensators might participate in a schism if they could maintain a relationship with a valued distributor or could move to a new and similar distributor at low cost with expectation of gain. Since we are talking about schism, rather than recruitment to a pre-existing rival religious group, the distributor of general compensators that seceding members will patronize must also be a member of the original group:

> P149 Demand for more efficacious compensators creates an opportunity for those with some power to increase their supply of rewards by organizing a sect movement.

The rank-and-file do not produce movements, they merely support them. All movements need leaders – persons with the capacity to organize and focus discontent, to give it direction and intent. The notion that "the times" produce the needed leadership will not do. Indeed, when we look closely at the leaders produced by "the times" we find that they have had considerable preparation for their roles. They do not come from among the least powerful. Rather, they have sufficient resources to engage in exchanges with their followers on favorable terms. They have had past experience relevant to the task of leading a new movement. More specifically, sect movements usually are led by persons with some past leadership experience in the parent body, and thus who had some status or standing in the parent body. Often sects are led by lower status members of the clergy or by laymen who have held leadership positions.

There are other reasons why these people will tend to be the ones who lead schisms. For one thing, members of the group have known them not only as fellow members, but also as distributors of general compensators. Sometimes they are the clergy of local religious groups who lead schisms away from the national church. At other times they may only have had part-time experience as distributors. It is interesting to note that those Protestant groups with the greatest number of schisms are precisely those that encourage the largest proportion of members to play the role of preacher. For another thing, the demand for more efficacious compensators bears more heavily on these people than on those of higher standing because their share of rewards is lower, so they may be well-prepared to be mass distributors of such compensators.

Furthermore, the rank-and-file demand for more efficacious compensators presents an opportunity for the moderately powerful to increase their rewards rapidly. If they can successfully lead the formation of a new sect, then they will be the individuals with most control over their exchange ratio, not only greater than the power of others in the group, but greater than they experienced before when yet more powerful individuals were able to set the terms for exchanges with them. Whatever rewards members are willing to give in return for compensators now come to them, rather than to the leaders of the former, united group. If the sect leaders were clergy in the earlier group, by leading a new sect they escape any costs they used to have to pay their superiors. Even if the new sect has little in the way of material rewards to distribute, it will have emotional rewards including status which the new leader may gain. Thus, we can conclude:

> P150 When the potential gains offset costs, some moderately powerful but relatively deprived members will lead a sect movement.

Since people seek rewards and avoid costs, the probability of sect formation can be computed by the hedonic calculus. It will be evident that some rewards always are lost by moving into a higher state of tension with the environment. At the least, the status of all positions in the sect movement will be lower than those in the original organization, which by P134, A2 and P1 represents a cost. Leaders, therefore, must anticipate offsetting these losses by the relative gain in status level they hope to achieve by leaving the parent body. It is obvious that it is more rewarding, for example, to be bishop of a large, reputable denomination than to be bishop of a small, deviant sect. But is also may be more rewarding to be bishop of a sect than an assistant pastor of a rural congregation of a large, reputable denomination.

It is important to recognize, however, that costs of increased tension may be much more serious than a decline in status. Religious deviance sometimes engenders coercive sanctions from the surrounding environment. Even in pluralistic America, some sects have been defined as sufficiently deviant to be the targets of quite severe persecution. And at other times and places, even very slight religious deviance encountered the bloodiest responses. In such an environment the tendency toward sect formation is curtailed severely because the calculation of gains minus costs comes up negative. It becomes evident, then, that to theorize about sect formation we must include an environmental variable. We may formulate this as:

P151 The greater the degree of coercion the external society imposes on religious deviance, the weaker the tendency for deviant religious organizations to form.

A coercive environment impedes the actual formation of deviant religious organizations, not the impulse to form them. If schisms themselves are prevented, the impulse may find another expression. During the era of militant sanctions imposed on overt religious deviance by the Roman Catholic Church, the forces giving rise to the sectarian impulse ran unabated, but often, instead of resulting in schism, were channelled into organizational diversification. That is, potential sect leaders formed new orders within the Catholic church rather than outside it. Among other advantages, this preserved exchanges on mutually good terms with the doctrinally specified essential distributor (in accordance with P128), the central church organization, and merely displaced lower-level distributors. Several orders enjoyed increased tension with the environment and thus more efficacious compensators, and often sustained significant doctrinal deviance, but avoided the costs of an open split.

Admittedly P151 suggests many questions. It would be desirable to work out an explanation of the conditions under which coercion is likely to be high or low. Some hints are found in our earlier discussion of the meaning of tension with the sociocultural environment, but a full analysis would require development of a fairly complete theory of the state. This would take us far beyond the scope of our current interests. We feel it is sufficient here simply to note that environments do differ – as between the Roman Empire and the Holy Roman Empire, for example – and that sect formation, one form of religious deviance, is dependent on this variation.

However, coercion is not the only impact the sociocultural environment has on the process of sect formation. We have seen that the constituency for sect formation is a function of the presence of persons in a religious body with poorly met needs for compensators, especially those for which a reward exists. When a religious body moves from higher tension to lower tension, this constituency grows, other things being equal. But this constituency also can grow if changes in the external environment increase the proportion of compensator-deprived members within a religious body. Thus, for example, if an economic depression, natural disaster, war or other dramatic social change suddenly causes considerable downward mobility or intense fears about future well-being among members of a religious organization, the proportion demanding more efficacious compensators (and thus higher tension) is increased thereby. Anything that increases the scarcity of rewards will increase the constituency for compensators. Sometimes this may be so widespread among members as to cause the religious body to move in the sectlike direction. But when this is not the case, the potential for schism is heightened. Thus we may derive the following:

> P152 If changes in the external environment result in an intensification of the need for (and the numbers in need of) efficacious compensators, the tendency toward sect formation is proportionally strengthened.

At the individual level, the intensity of need for efficacious compensators fluctuates according to changing circumstances. The death or illness of loved ones, loss of a job, divorce, disability, and even aging can intensify individual needs for efficacious compensators. Usually, these are individual rather than collective troubles and therefore are usually manifested in increased religious commitment, or even by a switch from a lower to a higher tension religious group, not by sect formation. On the other hand, purely personal troubles have sometimes prompted persons to lead sect movements or to found cults as described in Chapter 6.

When persons beset by similar problems come into communication, personal needs can become collective. We now see how economic panics, depressions, plagues, defeats in war, contacts with a technologically superior culture, civil unrest, and similar disruptions are periods of increased sect formation. Anything that heightens the pinch for more efficacious compensators, whether changes internal to the group or external, has this consequence. Like P151, this proposition is quite global since "changes" is not specified in detail. However, we are unwilling to postpone our theoretical efforts to explain religious movements until such time as a complete theory of society is available. We are forced to suggest outlines of such a theory here, in order to achieve the maximum gains in developing a theory of religion. But we have no illusions that we can provide a complete theory of human action and society in these few pages.

Given that some societies are more tolerant than others of sects in the dominant religious tradition, we can specify a very important consequence of this axis of societal variation. The proportion of the population affiliated with religious organizations is greatly determined by the degree of freedom in the market of competing organizations. When a single church has a nearly absolute monopoly through a firm alliance with a coercive state, many people will be prevented from finding the kind of religion which would best meet their needs for efficacious compensators. While some of those forming the natural constituency for a sect movement may benefit sufficiently from the ministrations of a monopolistic church to participate actively in it, many others will not. For large numbers of the non-elite, the state church is an uncomfortable, antagonistic environment where the powerful parade their advantages and the powerless find little solace for their relative deprivations. Were they free to do so, these people would be the first recruits to a new sect movement. But in its absence their religious needs are so poorly met that they may be effectively excluded from a sense of contact with God. While they would swell the ranks of a sect, they are not affiliated with the church.

It is when the religious market is free enough to offer several brands of religion, at several levels of tension with the sociocultural environment, that the greatest proportion of the population receives appropriate compensators and responds with firm religious commitment. We can state this with confidence in reference to sects, but not in reference to cults. Proposition 67 explained that the market value of any given general compensator will be low in a society that is very cosmopolitan with respect to religious culture. That is, faith and commitment may be weak when there are many competing systems of general compensators. However, when there is but one religious tradition, expressed through sects as well as through low-tension denominations, all groups agree with the same general compensators. It is about specific compensators that they disagree. Thus, religious diversity along the tension axis in a single tradition does not undercut the value of general compensators at all. Rather it strengthens the general compensators by combining them with different sets of specific compensators designed to fit the various needs of many classes in society. We may thus conclude:

> P153 In a culture with a dominant religious tradition, the emergence of sect movements increases the proportion of the population affiliated with religious organizations.

We can now briefly consider the logical opposite of sect movements, church movements, a phenomenon of some interest if of much less importance in the religious economy.

Church Movements

Thus far our theory has demonstrated why sect movements form within churches. But it has not explained the formation of church movements – splinter groups that move into lower state of tension. Admittedly such movements are rare. They are rare because usually those within a religious body who are most inclined to reduce tension have the power to do so, and hence do not need to oganize a new group. Nevertheless, under certain quite unusual circumstances church movements do occur. They do so because power and status inside the religious group may become little correlated with power and status in the surrounding environment, and because some individual members may have the attractive opportunity to engage in profitable low-tension exchanges with outsiders despite low power inside the group. Under such circumstances, those with the greatest stake in tension reduction have inadequate power within the group to bring such a reduction about.

What we have here is a classic application of the concept of marginality (Stonequist, 1937). The initial condition is that some members of a high tension, relatively isolated group begin to acquire status in the surrounding society. Often they must bend the norms of the sect in order to rise in the outer society. And, in any event, their loyality and commitment are suspect because of their "worldliness." In addition, their association with a deviant religious organization impedes their success in the surrounding society. Such persons are caught between two worlds, with stakes in both. Their membership in each makes them a marginal member of the other. Often people resolve this status dilemma by cutting their ties to one of these worlds – by defecting from the stigmatized sect and assimilating into the mainstream religious culture. Indeed, in the U.S. today large numbers of sect members do precisely that (Stark and Glock, 1968).

But for some persons the problem is not that simply solved. If sect membership also entails a very distinctive ethnic or racial marker, defection is impeded thereby, for two reasons. First, because the surrounding society will still tend to code the defector as a member of the sect. Second, because of a double bond of loyalty – not merely religious but also racial or ethnic. There is a further barrier if the high tension group does not belong to exactly the same religious tradition as the low tension religious groups in society, as has often been the case for non-Christian groups in predominately Christian societies, as P120 among other propositions explains.

For persons who would find defection very costly, the obvious course is to lower the tension of the religious group to which they belong. However, the marginals we have been describing stand to gain more from substantial tension reduction than do other members of the organization, including many of the internally powerful whose rewards come from within the group rather than from the larger society. In consequence, the marginals lack the power to achieve the degree of tension reduction they desire. In such circumstances a church movement is likely to occur. We could carry out a lengthy analyses, parallel to that we performed for sectarian schisms, but since most of the same principles apply we will content ourselves with only two new propositions:

P154 If a substancial group of marginal members develops within a sect, who have much to gain from reduced tension but who lack the power to transform the sect, they will tend to form a schismatic church movement.

P155 The tendency to form a schismatic church movement will be reduced to the extent that members desiring lower tension with the sociocultural environment are free to transfer to established low-tension groups at little cost.

Conclusion

Such a vast empirical literature supports the proposition that sects serve the relatively deprived that it is beyond our capacity to cite it here (e.g. Dynes, 1955). Our own work has often illustrated this fact within Protestantism (Glock and Stark, 1965; 1966; Stark and Glock, 1968; Bainbridge and Stark, 1980c; Stark and Bainbridge, 1985), and most of the sociological literature on schism in Western countries focuses on this tradition. Conceivably, one might argue that these studies merely document historically accidental social characteristics of competing wings within Protestantism, a tradition which may be especially prone to schism. Thus it is a fine confirmation of the theory to learn that a major schism in the Serbian Orthodox Church in America had social roots, rather than being a purely theological argument about doctrines (Vrga and Fahey, 1970). And, of course, within American Judaism one finds socio-religious divisions that parallel those so familiar in Protestantism (Liebman, 1966; Cavan, 1971).

A well-documented case of a church movement that conforms closely to our explanations is Reform Judaism (Steinberg, 1965). For centuries the Jews were a highly isolated, deviant religious body within European society. Then in the 19th century came emancipation. Jews were granted citizenship, and rules against their employment in high status positions and occupations were withdrawn. Some Jews emerged from the ghettos to seize these opportunities. But they found it impossible fully to observe the Law as defined by orthodox Jewry and succeed outside the ghetto. Traditional Jewish dress and tonsorial customs not only proclaimed the identity of Jew, but were very deviant from standards observed by gentiles. Then there was the question of kosher food – unavailable except in the ghetto. These Jews rising in the gentile world desired to remain Jews, but to do so at less cost – to reduce the tension between Judaism and its surroundings. However, having left the ghetto, initially in small numbers, they had lost status among other Jews – sometimes they had even been formally excommunicated. They lacked the influence to transform Judaism into a state of lower tension. The result was the Reform Movement. This new movement discarded the bulk of Jewish traditions as "superstition and antiquated custom" (Steinberg, 1965). In so doing, little emphasis was given compensators, while rewards were increased substantially. Tension between Reform Judaism and its surroundings was very low. In consequence, especially in the second generation (who did not wholly inherit their parents power-giving attributes), a constituency in need of stonger compensators developed within Reform Judaism. Soon the new church movement gave birth to a new sect movement, Conservative Judaism.

Perhaps the perfect example of an equal split in a religious body, resulting in both a sect movement and a church movement, is the schism which befell Pennsylvania Quakerism in 1827 (Doherty, 1967). One constituency had achieved high status and many social ties in secular society, and wanted their former sect to move rapidly toward lower tension with the sociocultural environment. Another constituency was less well off, having less wealth, lower status and fewer outside ties than the church-movement faction. These relatively-deprived people wanted to regain the higher tension of the Quaker past, and broke away in the separation of the Hicksite sect. The "Orthodox" church movement and the "Hicksite" sect movement split the Quakers roughly in half, and each shifted its degree of tension in the direction desired by its constituency. Interestingly, the Hicksites enjoyed greater average wealth than typical non-Quakers, a fact that underscores the social and relative nature of the deprivations which generate sects (cf. Mamiya, 1982).

For many readers, the previous chapters will have seemed like mere preparation for this one, in which we engaged one of the most interesting standard topic areas of the sociology of religion. Where earlier chapters laid down basic principles upon which to build a theory, then considered numerous questions about "primitive" religion, here we finally have derived major statements about religion in modern society. And, while the end of Chapter 4 seemed to leave the future of religion in serious doubt as God evolved into a distant and vague spirit of infinite scope but little use to humans, here we have seen the rebirth of intense involvment with the supernatural. Religious revival through the schismatic generation of sects is an ever-present possibility. For every religious organization contains within it different constituencies tugging toward higher or lower tension with the sociocultural environment. If the social cleavages and inequalities are great enough, a split will occur, and the high-tension group that results has the opportunity to intensify and revive the religious tradition from which it springs.

The material of this chapter has been very familiar. Each reader must have recalled examples of schisms and sects that gave empirical support to many of our derived propositions. Indeed, this chapter has served more to place the work of previous writers in a unified theoretical context than to open new vistas for analysis. One "orphan proposition" after another has been given its rightful place in a systematic, deductive theory. And all these familiar middle-range generalizations can now be understood properly as the necessary consequences of the conditions of human life, as outlined in our seven axioms and sketched more fully now through well over a hundred derived propositions.

If the reader wondered why we went on at such length about the elementary forms of religion, and the detailed circumstances of human exchange, it can now be seen that a firm basis was laid for a practically complete understanding of contemporary religion. At the beginning, when we introduced our seven axioms, the reader may have felt we were too reductionistic. By the end of the previous chapter, there may have been some contrary worry that we were too profligate in our derivations. Here in the successful explanation of a number of familiar facts and traditional hypotheses, we have attempted to display the strength of our theory. Starting from very simple beginnings, it can derive the richness of human religion, and it can do so in a way that ties all the many ideas together in a satisfying, logical structure.

Some of the propositions of this chapter are novel, and suggest empirical studies to test them. Yet the theory as a whole received a positive test by its ability to derive so many well-known facts about sects and schisms. The chapter that follows boldly enters territory that is far less well charted, and it lets us exercise the creative power of the theory to go beyond what social scientists have already learned about religion. In it we consider religious innovation and cult formation.

CHAPTER 6:
Cults: Formation of Innovative Religious Movements

In an earlier publication we delineated three compatible models of cult innovation: *the psychopathology model, the entrepreneur model*, and *the subculture-evolution model.* (Bainbridge and Stark, 1979). This chapter will go deeper than our earlier article to derive the main propositions only suggested there, and show the ways in which the models are not only compatible but naturally spring from our theory of religion. We shall emphasize religious cults – cult movements – although much of our discussion, especially the subculture-evolution model, applies as well to magical cults providing specific compensators in a context less than fully religious.

This chapter and the next seek to integrate traditional theoretical perspectives with our deductive theory of religion. Each of the three models described here reflects a perspective to be found in numerous essays and empirical reports by other authors, although only the first has been explicitly developed by social scientists. We show that each rests on the same principles of exchange and can be derived from our axioms, definitions and propositions. Together they explain one of the most important and fascinating of human phenomena, the birth of new religions, because every religion comes into being as a cult.

Anthony F.C. Wallace has estimated that at least 100,000 different religions have achieved a significant and stable following over the course of history. And, he argued, for each of these there have been "dozens of abortive efforts by untimely prophets" who failed to gain converts (Wallace, 1966:4). In an article on the geography of American cults, we examined the spatial distribution of 501 that were born and still dwell in the United States (Stark *et al.*, 1979; cf. Melton, 1978). Let us assume for a moment that the American rates of cult birth and death are representative of those over the world range of human history, and that (as some say) the total number of humans who have ever lived is 100 billon. Cults of the type counted among the 501 live on average something like a generation. They are more successful than the larger number of brief, abortive attempts to found cults, and they are less successful than the major world religions that last many generations. From these crude assumptions, we derive an estimate of over 200,000 moderately successful cults over the entire sweep of human history. Whatever the exact count of distinct faiths that have existed, it is certain that the number is huge. Nevertheless, despite the frequency of cult formation and the profound role cults sometimes play in human affairs, the birth of new religions has received almost no serious study.

One reason for this neglect may be that in comparison with long-estabished, major world faiths, newborn cults seem a pale and trivial parody. Yet, during their early days of formation the great religions were equally deviant and unimpressive. Each of them typically began with an obscure individual who had a a new religious idea, and who struggled at first to convince even a handful of others to share this faith. The subsequent transformation of such groups into great social movements seems to have diverted attention from their humble origins. But, Jesus never preached in a cathedral and Mohammed did not start off in a mosque.

Another reason cult formation has been neglected by many social scientists is the practical difficulty in conducting empirical research on the beginnings of a successful religion. How does one find a nascent cult? How does one know which ones will die before the research is completed and which will last long enough for a worthwhile research project? Given that one has found a stable cult, how does one know if it is representative of the entire species? Happily, enough social scientists have gone ahead despite these and other difficulties and carried out good empirical research. Perhaps for the first time, we know enough simple facts about many cults to theorize usefully. The authors of this book were surprised to find themselves among the very first to publish satisfactory quantitative research on cults, adequate to the point of being able to test theory.

While we cannot voyage by time machine to study the origins of the great faiths, and extant historical records are generally quite inadequate, we can inspect cult formation in today's world. Certainly we can use whatever information exists about the early days of the major religions to evaluate conclusions based on more recent evidence. But the origins of religions can best be understood through examination of contemporary cults.

One may conceive of cult formation in a two-stage process of *innovation*:

1. the *invention* of new religious ideas
2. gaining *social acceptance* of these ideas at least to the extent of creating a group devoted to them.

Put another way, the first need is to explain how and why individuals invent or discover new religious ideas. It is important to realize, however, that many (and perhaps most) persons who hit upon new religious ideas do not start new religions. So long as only one person holds a religious idea, no religion exists. Consequently, we also need to understand the process by which religious inventors are able to make their views social – to convince at least one other person to share their convictions.

This chapter keeps a tight focus on the very earliest stages in the formation of cults. Only in the next chapter will we explain much about recruitment to deviant religions. And not until Chapter 8 will we discuss how such movements succeed or fail once they have been founded. Therefore, we shall not be very specific here about the mechanisms through which conversion occurs, including the conversion of the first converts. These limits will be clarified as the chapter proceeds.

Before proceeding, we should state crucial definitions. In the previous chapter we distinguished cult movements from sect movements, and defined the former as follows:

> Def.58 A *cult movement* is a deviant religious organization with novel beliefs and practices.

Reconceptualizing slightly, and expanding the definition to include magical cults as well as fully religious ones, we can say:

> Def.67 *Cults* are social enterprises primarily engaged in the generation and exchange of novel compensators.

Recall also the following definitions:

> Def.23 *Religious organizations* are social enterprises whose primary purpose is to create, maintain, and exchange supernaturally-based general compensators.

> Def.46 Persons who specialize in producing and exchanging compensators of great generality based on supernatural assumptions are *religious specialists*.

> Def.53 Cultural specialists whose main activity is providing specific compensators are *magicians*.

Thus, we can say:

> Def.68 *Cult founders* are religious specialists or magicians who establish new organizations to create, maintain, and exchange novel compensators.

Again, we shall concentrate on founders of religious cults. It should be kept in mind that compensators range without discontinuity from specific to general. Therefore, much of what we derive is true of magicians as well as of religious specialists. The fact expressed in P97 that there is no Church of Magic does not prevent magicians from establishing temporary organizations, nor from maintaining these organizations indefinitely by transforming them into religions. The first model of cult innovation was suggested by a great body of anthropological material, much of it focused on magic more than on religion, yet many anthropologists and others have proposed some variant of this model as a theory of the origin of religion (Freud, 1927; 1930; Zweig, 1932; Devereux, 1953; Roheim, 1955; Gardner, 1957; Messing, 1958; Sargant, 1959; Levi-Strauss, 1963; Carden, 1969; La Barre, 1969; 1972; Lewis, 1971).

The Psychopathology Model

As we presented it in our earlier article, the main ideas of the psychopathology model are as follows:

1. Cults are novel cultural responses to personal and societal crisis.
2. New cults are invented by individuals suffering from certain forms of mental illness.
3. These individuals typically achieve their novel visions during psychotic episodes.
4. During such an episode, the individual invents a new package of compensators to meet his own needs.
5. The individual's illness commits him to his new vision, either because his hallucinations appear to demonstrate its truth, or because his compelling needs demand immediate satisfaction.
6. After the episode, the individual will be most likely to succeed in forming a cult around his vision if the society contains many other persons suffering from problems similar to those originally faced by the cult founder, to whose solution, therefore, they are likely to respond.
7. Therefore, such cults most often succeed during times of societal crisis, when large numbers of persons suffer from similar unresolved problems.
8. If the cult does succeed in attracting many followers, the individual founder may achieve at least a partial cure of his illness, because his self-generated compensators are legitimated by other persons, and because he

> now receives true rewards from his followers. (Bainbridge and Stark, 1979:285).

This model rests in part on the traditional psychoanalytic claim that magic and religion are mere projections of neurotic wish-fulfillment or psychotic delusions (Freud, 1927, 1930, 1946; Roheim, 1955; La Barre, 1969, 1971). In this view, cult founders and magician-healers (often called *shamans* by anthropologists) achieve their special visions during times of extreme physical stress or mental illness, then successfully provide these visions to sick individuals and disordered societies (Wallace, 1956; Messing, 1958; Levi-Strauss, 1963; Lewis, 1971). The concept of *mental illness* apparently explains how a cult founder can himself invent new compensators then treat them as if they were objectively verified rewards.

We must define "mental illness," and shall do so not only in a formal definition, but also by contrasting other kinds of mental incapacity:

Def.69 *Mental illness* is the imputed condition of any human mind that repeatedly fails to conform to the propositions of the prevailing theory of human action.

Def.70 *Ignorance* is an abnormal lack of explanations.

Def.71 *Mental deficiency* is an abnormally weak ability to store and process explanations.

These are not distinct categories of human experience, but like most of our scientifically useful concepts, describe dimensions of variation. One may be more or less ignorant depending upon how many explanations one possesses – depending, in other words, on the extent of one's knowledge. One may be more or less mentally deficient, versus intelligent, depending upon one's ability to store (remember) and process (think about) explanations.

Note that the definition of mental illness is different in form. It refers to an imputed condition. Normal members of a society compare themselves with the mentally ill and find that the latter are more likely to seem to fail to conform to their culture's theory of human action. Again, it is a matter of degree. But we have found it useful to acknowledge the current debates about the meaning of "mental illness" right in our definition – in a way that resolves current difficulties with the concept.

To say that someone is mentally ill is to attempt to explain their behavior. They do not conform, in some important way, with the prevailing theory of human action. Calling them mentally ill suspends all or part of that theory. It says, in effect, that future exchanges with this person will be most profitable if one does not expect them to conform to the prevailing theory of human action. Particular psychiatric diagnoses identify parts of the theory the individual may be expected to violate, and parts he will follow.

We do not subscribe to the extreme view that mental illness is only a label, only a judgement by other persons (Scheff, 1966). On the contrary. Explanations do differ in their objective ability to provide desired rewards. The concept of mental illness is an explanation. The problem which has confounded diagnosis is the dual instability both of the patients and of the standards of judgement. We can resolve the problems in diagnostic standards. Cultural relativists, like Ruth Benedict (1934; cf. Ackerknecht, 1943; Murphy, 1976), have pointed out that different cultures disagree in standards for mental health. Within any culture which has not achieved full coherence as a cultural system there will be competing explanations for human action that provide divergent standards of judgement. Thus, to the extent that professionals and lay people do not judge from a coherent cultural system, they will not have a fully consistent theory of human action from which to judge mental illness.

If a single, logical, powerful theory of human action could be devised, then it could serve as an objective standard against which to judge the mental health of individuals. We believe our general theory, presented in this book, approaches such an objective standard. Our theory is meant to be more than the personal opinions of two sociologists. It provides a logically consistent framework for understanding human action, and also gives a report on the principles that actually guide behavior by successful human beings. From the start, ours has followed the line of deductions that leads to the discovery of the complex, technologically-complex social world which in truth surrounds us. If people do not follow the main propositions, then they cannot participate in the creation and maintenance of human society and culture. The correct theory allows one to label correctly, because it itself is the most effective and complete cultural system. If our axioms are consistent with each other, then the seven of them are the most general explanations of human behavior. Under them are ranked, in logical sequence, the hundreds of propositions that progressively provide the specific explanations required for human thought and action in the real world. To the extent that our theory is incomplete, then we invite the reader to help us complete it. To the extent that it is complete, then mental illness objectively is the repeated failure to conform to its major propositions.

This is not the place to lay out a full theory of mental illness, but the pathological model demands at least a cursory view. If the current theories of mental illness are at all to be believed, madness has myriad sources. Among those most frequently postulated are faults in learned behavior and perception, stemming from pathogenic social exchanges perhaps in childhood. Among other postulated causes are various defects of an individual's nervous system or the chemical reactions that permit it to function. Physical causes may effect some mental functions more than others, but originate outside the propositions of our theory. But the learned disorders, the *functional disorders*, can be understood directly in terms of our theory of human action.

First, it must be noted that our propositions often concern counteracting forces. Seen too superficially, different propositions sometimes appear to make contradictory predictions about human action. But, understood properly, they really describe pressures of various magnitudes simultaneously driving persons toward different lines of action. The true prediction they make is the resultant of forces – the behavioral vector that results from the full combination of operating principles.

The most elementary example is the observation that all behavior involves costs. Action to gain a reward will be undertaken only if the expected cost is less than the expected reward. It is simultaneously true that persons seek rewards and avoid costs. To predict action in a given case, we must be able to measure both the reward and the cost to determine the net gain or loss. This familiar example establishes that the forces described by some propositions can outweigh the forces described by other propositions, without there being any implied logical contradiction between the propositions. Thus, in accordance with some propositions, individuals may be seen to violate other propositions, and be judged mentally ill, by Def.69.

Let us look at examples of how mental illness may result from the ordinary operation of the principles described in our theory, the kinds of non-organic disorder often called "functional." Consider the following two basic statements:

A2 Humans seek what they perceive to be rewards and avoid what they perceive to be costs.

P6 In pursuit of desired rewards, humans will exchange rewards with other humans.

In part, P6 is derived from A2. But notice that P6 does not say that humans will seek rewards only through exchanges with other persons. Nor does it say that all humans will continue to exchange rewards with other humans after their initial experiences in such trade. P6 rests upon the fact that humans sometimes can profit from exchanges, not from an unrealistic assertion that humans always profit. For human society to be possible, profit must often result from exchanges. But society does not need the participation of all humans. A5, A7 and the random concentrations of rewards and costs that result from the complex patterns of exchange in society give some individuals a happier experience in exchanges than others.

One can imagine many circumstances in which an individual will suffer repeated heavy losses in exchanges with others. Such a person will learn to avoid exchanges with others, in full accordance with A2. This does not violate P6, however. The individual merely fails to conform to P6 because its terms, including the steps through which it was derived, do not apply to the conditions the individual actually faces. Failure to conform to P6 is some sign of mental illness, according to the definition of this term, since any society must be based on P6 and will have some variant of it in its prevailing theories of human action. These considerations are well supported by evidence. For example, persons judged to be suffering from psychopathology do have difficulty cooperating in stable social relationships, and they also tend to come disproportionately from the least-rewarded segments of the population (Bixenstine and Douglas, 1967; Hollingshead and Redlich, 1958; Srole *et al.*, 1962).

If P6 does not describe the action of a particular individual for the relevant period in his life, then any or all of the propositions derived from P6 may not apply either. Certainly, without P6, P64 cannot be true:

> P64 In the absence of a more compelling standard, the value an individual places on a reward is set by the market value of that reward established through exchanges by other persons.

Proposition 64 may have applied earlier in the individual's life, but once he has forsworn exchanges with others, he will not be able or willing to let them evaluate rewards, including new explanations, for him. Among other things, this means that his evaluation of new explanations will be quite uncertain, unstable, and arbitrary in the absence of the most compelling objective standards. He may reject some perfectly fine rewards and accept some dubious compensators, depending on random twists and turns in the course of his life. After a while, the individual will possess a highly ideosyncratic system of explanations, indicative of extreme mental illness (Faris and Dunham, 1939; Lemert, 1967).

Thus, an individual to whom P6 does not apply will violate or fail to conform to several other propositions and is likely to be described as mentally ill. And P64 is especially important. Outsiders may believe an individual even violates A2 if the private explanations and evaluations of rewards he has adopted deviate markedly from those common in the market of exchanges participated in by his judges.

Often people impute mental illness to persons whose objective situations bring them to unusual evaluations of rewards and costs. Humans generally value their own lives – the sum total of rewards and resources possessed by the individual – because their futures promise a net profit of rewards over costs, at least in some time scale. But sometimes an individual may come to feel that the future holds only costs, or overwhelming net costs even after subtracting some rewards. Then the individual might well turn to suicide, as the only way of limiting the net costs of future actions. Other persons, whose futures promise net rewards, will be prevented by their own situations and the explanations they trust for their own futures from agreeing with the individual's explanation that suicide is the best course of action. They will impute mental illness to the individual who kills himself. Mere suicide is not enough to gain status as a martyr, but many religions count martyrs among their saints and founders, so even this gloomy kind of imputed mental illness may have a role in the early histories of new religions.

Among the most common forms of mental deviance that are capable of aiding cult innovation are those conditions in which the individual has certain pressing needs, *compulsions* if you will, that drive him to seek unavailable rewards far beyond the point where others would have given up. In accordance with P13 and P14, compulsions may lead individuals to accept compensators under circumstances when the uncompelled person would not do so.

Consider the drive for high social status. All persons might find high social status and its accompanying power (control over exchange ratio) rewarding, but many find that the costs are great measured against the slim chance they have of gaining it. But some persons, perhaps those from families that have recently lost precious status, may have learned status attainment as a prime general explanation. They may both value status more highly than most and believe they are capable of gaining it, despite a lack of the ordinary resources that provide status. After ordinary efforts at upward mobility have failed, these people with a status compulsion may be forced to invent and accept a new system of status compensators. They may, for example, claim the supremely high status of religious messiah. Their explanations will be rejected by most, and their fervor identified as mental illness. But if even a few followers accept the claim, then, paradoxically, the compulsion may succeed in gaining the desired status, at least within the new cult.

If we were framing a rigorous theory of mental illness, rather than merely taking a quick look at madness to see how it might fit into the sociology of religion, we undoubtedly would consider at length what we find the most persuasive model of hysteria, the hypothesis that it represents nothing more than a particular interaction strategy. In modern society, hysteria presents itself mainly as a medical problem, and hysterics display such apparantly physical symptoms as paralysis, mutism, .tremor, anaesthesia and blindness (White, 1964). In preindustrial societies – and still to some extent in our own society – hysteria presents itself as soul loss and spirit possession (Kiev, 1972). One can view hysteria as cases of deviant role playing. In primitive societies, the hysteric is willing to play the central role in a religious drama. In advanced societies, the hysteric is willing to play the central role in a scientific-medical drama. Both roles are fiction. The hysteric is not possessed. The hysteric is not sick. Rather, the hysteric acts in these ways because this in the only course of action that offers a chance for intensely desired rewards.

In a felicitous phrase, Ioan M. Lewis referred to these behavior patterns as "oblique redressive strategies" (Lewis, 1971:88). The hysteric is someone oppressed by the coercion of close relatives or the powerful groups in society – for example women in male-dominated societies and minority ethnic groups overpowered by an unsympathetic elite. Hysteria is an attempt to achieve a more favorable exchange ratio for people markedly low in power. A different strategy people might choose if they are the victims of unfavorable exchange ratios is to abandon the coercive relationships and seek new exchange partners. Hysteria arises when this is impossible. Unable to escape the unfavorable exchanges, unable to marshal the resources to achieve a better exchange ratio within the context of conventional exchanges, the individual turns to an oblique redressive strategy.

In hysteria the individual seeks to avoid responsibility for aggressive action, thereby escaping the costs, while demanding rewards from the previously coercive exchange partner. The possessed individual is not responsible because the alleged possessing spirit is to blame. The mentally or "physically" ill person is not responsible because a disease has struck for no reason and deprived its victim of the full capacity to behave as others wish.

A good example, discussed at length by Lewis, is that of the Sar or Zar cult of Ethiopia, Somalia, Sudan and surrounding countries. This is a possession cult in which women are seized by spirits known variously as shaytan, afreet, abless, jinn or zar. Leaders of the cult are mainly women who have come to terms with their possessing spirits and help others achieve the same happy truce with the supernatural. The first signs of possession are very general hysterical symptoms, but a professional diagnosis by a Zar leader discovers and identifies the possessing spirit. The curing ceremony is an expensive, week-long extravaganza that showers honor and wealth on the spirit, thus incidentally on its victim. The spirit demands much of what the woman wants from her husband, and at least in the form of compensators the woman gets her wishes. Once a woman has adopted the possession strategy, she can employ her spirit to get a somewhat better deal from her husband, without accepting full responsibility (costs) for her own demands. To the extent that the husband believes in spirits, wives may use the cult "to extort economic sacrifices from their husbands by threatening a relapse when their demands are ignored" (Lewis, 1971:79).

Those who have studied the Zar cult agree it is primarily an adult female activity reflecting social conditions of sex-separation, low female status, restriction of women from religious participation, an unbalanced sex ratio, marital insecurity, and relative isolation (Kennedy, 1967). As Simon Messing notes,

> Most patients are married women who feel neglected in a man's world in which they serve as hewers of wood and haulers of water, where even the Coptic Abyssinian Church discriminates against females by closing the church building to them. (Messing, 1958:1120–1121)

Again, were this an exchange theory of mental illness, we would derive many propositions about hysteria and about other "mental illness" strategies as well. It should be clear that such derivations from our axioms are quite possible. Further, it should be clear that an oblique redressive strategy can produce new compensators – new spirit exchange partners, for example, or simply the honor or being worth the attentions of a possessing supernatural being. The strategy serves not only to give the "victim" some emotional satisfaction from the drama she plays in the cult, but also increases her slight power in exchanges with her husband. Since the strategy really is rewarding under some circumstances, a few people will follow it, thereby generating and accepting new compensators. Generally a given case produces very little innovation. But some Zar sufferers become cult leaders, and there has always been the potential for a leader to transform the ceremonies somewhat, or even to start a new cult organization.

Physiologically caused mental illness, while it operates from outside the theory of action presented here, might still be made partially intelligible from our perspective. Let us emphasize that we do not want to make too much of this idea. It is little more than speculation. But perhaps specific mental illness syndromes represent biological disruption of single axioms. Either a defect in the person's nervous system (however caused) may disable an axiom, or it may add an extra axiom, or substitute a new one for an old one.

It is said that some humans have a very poor sense of the future. Despite the ability to process a respectable number of explanations and other data, they are incapable of planning for the future or even acting according to relatively short-term strategies. Among the unfortunates may be various schizophrenics, victims of prefrontal lobotomies, or others brain-damaged or senile. One could conceptualize persons with a defective time sense as people for whom the operation of Axiom 1 is irregular or absent.

The whole area of "affective disorders" (chronic depression, mania, or that classic combination of the two known as manic-depressive psychosis) may be conceptualized by the addition of a new axiom about evaluation that would apply in these cases: "Ax: Evaluation of rewards and costs is subject to a largely unpredictable external factor that may increase (mania) or decrease (depression) the evaluation of all rewards." A person whose behavior follows Axiom X may easily accept as truth any kind of compensator if he evaluates it during a period of mania.

Unlike hysteria and other functional mental disorders, organic mental illness does represent the affliction of an otherwise normal person with terrible incapacities, ungoverned emotions and incomprehensible perceptions. Real mental illness is very costly. The unpredictability of symptoms is frightening, because it renders uncertain all actions and exchanges undertaken to obtain or preserve rewards. The victim is incapacitated, in greater or lesser degree, and therefore cannot achieve goals that otherwise would be within reach. Beset by the horrible problem of mental illness, the individual seeks an explanation. Recall that explanations are statements about how and why rewards may be obtained and costs are incurred. The victim wants to know why such agonizing costs are being incurred and how to obtain the reward of health, or at least how to obtain normally desired rewards despite the illness.

In cultures that emphasize religious and magical explanations, the individual is encouraged to understand and deal with his affliction as a problem of the supernatural. In modern society, a medical explanation may be pressed upon the individual. It would be wrong to think that medical explanations are not available in preliterate societies, for indeed various physical explanations have been documented in several such groups (Edgerton, 1966). But the relative emphasis on supernatural versus natural explanations does vary by culture. In societies, like some segments of our own, which offer both kinds of explanation, the sufferer himself will tend to prefer the supernatural perspective. Until real cures are discovered, and they definitely have not been invented yet, the medical explanation says why the mentally ill must suffer, but does little to reduce the cost or provide compensating rewards. A religious explanation, on the other hand, may suggest that some of what appear to be costs are really rewards – that the hallucinations of madness are really glimpses of a marvelous alternate reality.

The religious explanation of madness may imply that the victim is honored by his illness, that he has closer contact with the supernatural than the ordinary mortal. Many societies provide respected social roles for such a person to play, including that of shaman. But industrial-secular societies may increase the person's suffering through degrading incarceration and by closing all social roles to the mad (Silverman, 1967). When the culture permits a supernatural explanation, but does not fully provide a ready-made explanation into which it fits every case, then some victims of organic mental illness will fashion their own compensator-packages and get them accepted by other individuals. Then is born a cult.

Several mental illness syndromes might be analyzed in terms of our propositions and axioms, showing many routes to cultic conviction. We can state the general conclusion with confidence:

> P156 Mentally ill persons often invent novel compensators and accept them as rewards.

To the extent that a mental disease covers many of the most important propositions, it frees the individual from a larger number of conventional explanations. Slight cases do not permit free experimentation with radical explanations. Put formally,

> P157 The more extensive a case of mental illness, the greater the number, deviance, and generality of novel explanations it may generate.

> Def. 72 A case of mental illness is *extensive* to the degree that the individual fails to conform to many propositions of the prevailing theory of human action.

This proposition says that extensive mental illness favors the invention and personal acceptance of a set of novel compensators. But if madness favors invention, the first half of innovation, it harms the gaining of social acceptance. If a compensator inventor is perceived as mentally ill, no one will accept his compensators. But, beyond that, serious mental illness means the individual will fail to conform to much of our theory of action – a theory designed to explain human success. Therefore, quite apart from the stigma of mental illness, serious mental illness renders the victim incapable of performing the tasks required in establishing any social organization, including a successful cult.

Some mentally ill persons may be able to get the advantages of madness without all the disadvantages. If a person can invent new compensators during an episode of mental illness, then enjoy renewed health while he attempts to share his new vision, he is more likely to succeed in creating a viable, distinctive cult than if he were either always sane or always insane.

P158 Chronically mentally ill persons are poor in the resources required to establish and maintain social enterprises.

Def.73 *Chronic* refers to a condition that persists unchanged for a long period of time.

P159 Successful psychopathological cult invention is more likely to result from an episode of acute mental illness than from chronic mental illness.

Def. 74 *Acute* refers to a marked condition of limited duration with a sharp beginning and ending.

If the person experiencing the vision is too easily reintegrated into normal society, however, the vision itself may be dissolved into the standard religious tradition. In Catholic countries, visions that initially seem to have little to do with doctrines of the established church have often been transformed in the public mind into apparitions of the Blessed Virgin (Carroll, 1983; 1985). If the visionary is a powerless person who is tied by stong social bonds to more conventional people, as is true for most children, the vision is especially vulnerable to such reshaping. An old religion gains a local revival and a new shrine, but no new religion is born.

The psychopathology model demands a fine balance of opposing factors. The psychopathology must be extensive but not chronic. The visionary should be moderately alienated from surrounding social life, but fully capable of entering into it. This may seem too fine a balance, but then, of course, successful cult formation is a relatively rare event. As soon as the model was proposed objections were raised to it, notably the doubt that the most effective founders of religions showed real evidence of clinical pathology (Schweitzer, 1948), and two other models of equal plausibility exist.

The Entrepreneur Model

As outlined in our earlier publications, the *entrepreneur model* presents the following ideas.

1. Cults are businesses which provide a product for their customers and receive payment in return.

2. Cults are mainly in the business of selling novel compensators, or at least freshly packaged compensators that appear new.
3. Therefore, a supply of novel compensators must be manufactured.
4. Both manufacture and sales are accomplished by entrepreneurs.
5. These entrepreneurs, like those in other businesses, are motivated by the desire for profit, which they can gain by exchanging compensators for rewards.
6. Motivation to enter the cult business is stimulated by the perception that such business can be profitable, an impression likely to be acquired through prior involvement with a successful cult.
7. Successful entrepreneurs require skills and experience, which are most easily gained through a prior career as the employee of an earlier successful cult.
8. The manufacture of salable new compensators (or compensator-packages) is most easily accomplished by assembling components of pre-existing compensator-systems into new configurations, or by the further development of successful compensator-systems.
9. Therefore, cults tend to cluster in lineages. They are linked by individual entrepreneurs who begin their careers in one cult and then leave to found their own. They bear strong "family resemblances" because they share many cultural features.
10. Ideas for completely new compensators can come from any cultural source or personal experience whatsoever, but the skillful entrepreneur experiments carefully in the development of new products and incorporates them permanently in his cult only if the market response is favorable. (Bainbridge and Stark, 1979: 288)

Despite its plausibility, this model of cult innovation has been slighted by social scientists, and only journalists have applied it with any consistency. There is much evidence that many cults are successful businesses. Considering the valuable rewards some cult founders obtain, there should be no mystery surrounding the attempt to get into this lucrative profession. Arthur L. Bell's cult Mankind United took in four million dollars in the ten years preceeding 1944 (Dohrman, 1958:41), while the Washington branch of L. Ron Hubbard's Scientology organization paid him more than $25,000 a year in the late 1950s (Cooper, 1971:109), and the couple that founded the nominally satanic Process cult personally earned $4,000 a month in 1973 (Bainbridge, 1978:168). In addition to obvious material benefits, successful cult founders also receive valuable intangible rewards, including praise, power and amusement. Many cult leaders have enjoyed almost unlimited sexual access to attractive followers (Orrmont, 1961; Carden, 1969; Jacobs, 1984).

Axiom 2 says a person will do anything for a significant net profit, counting as costs to be subtracted any recognized negative effects on other exchanges and aspects of his life. It follows that an individual will seek to found a cult when he perceives a high net reward from doing so. Considering how directly this follows, why does not every human being start a cult? Of course, if everyone sought the same career, none could make a living. There are many other ways to obtain rewards, and most people are quite incompetent to perform cultic innovation. A person needs special skills to found a successful cult. This observation is supported by all our ethnographic research inside cults, and by the historical record. But the fact also follows from our deductive system. One could derive it in several ways. Cult founders are religious specialists, practitioners of one of the earliest cultural specializations to emerge in society. Recall the definition:

> Def.33 *Cultural specialization* refers to the tendency of individuals to master parts of their culture and to engage in exchanges with others who have mastered different parts.

One masters part of a culture through specialized socialization – the accumulation of the best available explanations – which can be achieved only through extended interaction with persons who already are specialists. Several propositions noted the special powers and resources held by religious specialists in at least moderately developed societies. For example:

> P24 The power of an individual or group is positively associated with control of religious organizations and with gaining the rewards available from religious organizations.

> P86 Religious specialists can exert great influence over their exchange ratios with others, and thus over the exchange ratios experienced by others.

The power of a religious specialist rests on certain resources he possesses. Among them are personal attributes, such as intelligence for example, that may be possessed by persons without any religious training. Other resources include some that the priest of a conventional church enjoys but that a cult founder does not, such as strong relationships with valuable exchange partners in the state, provided by the church's alliance with the secular elite. But for religion especially, many of the resources are cultural in the form of explanations that confer power. Some are supernatural compensators, but other explanations are basic skills of social interaction: how to preach, how to comfort, how to organize assistants, and so on. Such power-giving attributes are rare. Recall these statements:

A7 Individual and social attributes which determine power are unequally distributed among persons and groups in any society.

P9 Rewards that exist in limited supply will tend to be monopolized by powerful persons and groups, thereby becoming relatively unavailable to others.

P13 The more valued or general a reward, the more difficult will be evaluation of explanations about how to obtain it.

A7 merely notes that some individuals will be better provided with the resources to carry out successful social exchanges in founding and maintaining a cult. Some people, but A7 does not say which ones, will be better able to sell compensators in exchange for rewards they desire. Therefore, some people, and not others, will become religious specialists. The resources capable of conferring this advantage are themselves rewards, and by P9 they will tend to be monopolized by powerful persons and groups. Proposition 9 applies not only to material rewards but also to explanations. Religious organizations are notorious for maintaining trade secrets, both secret or arcane doctrines and other valuable information.

Proposition 13 was a crucial step in our derivation of the fact that people often accept compensators instead of direct rewards, but many other facts derive from P13 as well. For one thing, P13 implies something about transmission of skills. Suppose we interviewed people at random, asking what makes a successful cult founder. They would offer a dazzling array of alternative theories about how to succeed at this endeavor. Success promises attainment of a whole series of highly valued rewards, everything from honor to money to gratification of animal pleasures to social power. Therefore, P13 says, evaluating explanations about how to succeed in founding a cult will be very difficult. Successful religious organizations already have good evaluations, so the best place to acquire well-evaluated explanations about running a religious enterprise is inside a successful religious organization. Good instructions for founding a cult, as opposed to merely running a church, are most readily acquired inside a successful, recently-founded religious organization. Therefore, these things will be learned better, the more closely the would-be cult founder works with already-skilled religious specialists.

P160 The skills required for successful operation of a religious organization are best acquired by intimate participation in a successful existing religious organization.

Def. 75 *Skills* are valuable explanations that enable an individual who possesses them to solve immediate practical problems.

P161 The skills required for successful establishment of a new cult are best acquired by intimate participation in a successful, recently-founded cult.

P162 Entrepreneurs who found cults tend to have first served an apprenticeship working closely with the leaders of a successful earlier cult.

Def. 76 *Entrepreneurs* are persons who start and promote new enterprises in order to obtain rewards through profitable exchanges.

Def. 77 *Apprenticeship* is an exchange relationship between a skilled person and an unskilled person that allows the latter to learn the skills of the former.

Proposition 162 is an important proposition for our theory of cult innovation and has other derivations beyond the one suggested above based on transmission of skills. The founder of a new cult not only needs to be able to do the job, he also must want to do it. That is, he must have reason to accept the rather general explanation that he can obtain valuable rewards at reasonable cost by founding a new cult and offering novel compensators in exchange for rewards. Since persons have difficulty evaluating explanations that promise general and valuable rewards, as P13 states, this explanation, too, is difficult to evaluate independently. Therefore it will be gained by entrepreneurs from repeated exchanges with successful cult leaders. Proposition 162 could be derived from this reasoning. Both trains of logic, the original derivation and this parallel one, permit us to deduce general propositions about the emergence of entrepreneurial cults. The greater the number of successful cults existing in a society, the greater the number of individuals who are serving the necessary apprenticeship. That means more people with the necessary skills and desire to found cults.

P163 The greater the number of successful cults in a society, the greater the number of entrepreneurs who will seek to found still more cults.

If a person is able to found a cult and wants to found a cult, there remains one more issue he must face before proceeding to practice cultic entrepreneurship. He must find some warrant for fashioning and selling a new compensator package. How can he tell others that his compensators really offer great rewards, yet unlike the psychopathological founder be fully aware of the origins of these compensators? There are two possibilities, not entirely mutually exclusive.

P164 Religious engineering may be undertaken either in order to practice deception or in the belief that the product constitutes a real value.

Def.78 *Religious engineering* is the conscious design of compensator packages and other elements of culture for use in cults.

Def.79 *Deception* is any interaction strategy that intentionally leads other people to accept explanations which one privately rejects.

Deception requires special interaction skills, and may be most successful when the cult founder is able to avoid intimate, enduring exchange relationships with his followers. Magical cults are a particularly common field for deception, because the exchanges tend to be of short duration (Glick and Newsom, 1974; cf. MacDougall, 1958). True, there is more chance for clients to disconfirm magical specific compensators empirically, but the magician may be more able than a religious priest to conceal from clients the fact that he does not trust in his own compensators.

Honest entrepreneurs need a source of personal confidence in their compensators, and the most likely place to find it is in the positive evaluations performed by valued exchange partners, as P64 predicts. It is a short step from P64 and similar propositions to the following.

P165 To the extent that a cult founder has had exchange partners who were satisfied members of a similar cult, he will tend to accept their favorable evaluation of the kind of compensators he offers.

P166 To the extent that a cult founder has been the satisfied member of a similar cult in the past, he will already personally value the kind of compensators he offers.

P167 To the extent that a cult founder has exchange partners who are satisfied followers, he will tend to accept their favorable evaluations of the compensators he gives them.

P168 Honest entrepreneurial cult founders will tend to have been deeply involved in a cult similar to the one they themselves found.

Def.80 *Honesty* is the interaction strategy of offering only those explanations to others which one personally accepts.

Notice that P168, derived from P166, gives further support to the observation that P162 applies to a large proportion of entrepreneurial cults. Of course, cult founding, in the terms discussed here, still involves a measure of real innovation, not just appropriation of an earlier cult's compensators. One warrant the honest cult founder may find for innovating, and one that may actually help business for any cult innovator, is the concept of progress. A culture that values invention in other spheres of culture will accept the general explanation which we might call a doctrine of progress – the belief that rewards (including true explanations) may readily be gained through human inventiveness.

P169 Honest religious engineering is most likely within a culture that trusts in a doctrine of cultural progress.

Def.81 *Progress* is the gradual improvement in the human ability to achieve desired rewards.

P170 Overt religious engineering will be most rewarded in a culture that trusts in a doctrine of cultural progress.

We must ask where entrepreneurial cult innovators find the material or inspirations to invent new compensators and other elements of culture. In principle, we can find no limit to the variety of sources from which an inventor draws ideas. Certainly, there may be some advantage in using relatively obscure sources, both to achieve a more novel result and to avoid trying to sell compensators already discredited in many people's eyes. The amount of innovating may be more predictable. Proposition 157 says that psychologically normal entrepreneurs may be in a poor position to innovate radically. Indeed, from P157 it follows that honest entrepreneurial cult founders will innovate in relatively modest ways, retaining the bulk of the culture of the earlier cult in which they participated.

P171 Honest entrepreneurial cult founders tend to innovate in specific explanations while preserving the more general explanations they gained in prior experience with other cults.

The dishonest entrepreneur is more free to innovate, at least in the appearance of the compensator packages he offers. But he is discouraged from innovating by the very success of any earlier cult from which his own derives. He will want to duplicate the success of the earlier cult, and has three alternatives with respect to initial innovation. The first strategy, discussed in the previous chapter, is not to innovate but to found a sect of the earlier cult, providing its compensators in a more pure form. The second strategy is to retain all apparently valuable parts of the first cult, and innovate in superficial symbolisms, such as in names of things. The third strategy is not open to all cult founders: to combine the most successful aspects of two or more earlier cults, thus winding up with a product distinctly different from them (Bainbridge, 1985a).

P172 Entrepreneurs with prior experience in a single cult will innovate only slightly when founding a new cult.

P173 Entrepreneurs who innovate greatly in founding a new cult are apt to have had prior experience with two or more successful cults.

P174 The invention of religious culture is easier to the extent that the inventor is able to use elements and sub-systems from existing religious systems.

Proposition 167 suggests a source of support for progressive innovation after the cult has been established. Whether honest or not, the cult founder may offer continual slight innovations to his followers. Depending upon a favorable response, he not only will incorporate these innovations in a gradually developing compensator package but also will be encouraged to continue innovating in the customer-approved direction. Thus, innovation may not stop with the founding of a cult. Some psychopathological founders may be cured of their madness and cease having visions, others will experience repeated episodes of psychopathology, but still others will turn into entrepreneurs and practice religious engineering to improve their cults.

P175 Entrepreneurial cult leaders tend to continue innovating after founding their cults, adding to their systems whatever compensators appeal to their followers.

The entrepreneur model says that cults tend to cluster in lineages – families of related cults. This certainly is true for cults that come into being through entrepreneurship. Proposition 162 says entrepreneurs serve apprenticeships in earlier cults, while such propositions as P168, P171 and P174 suggest that the new cult will be similar in many respects to its "parent." Proposition 173 even introduces the cultic equivalent of sexual reproduction, at least in a functional or metaphoric sense. A highly innovative entrepreneur is one who has participated in two or more cults and brings cultural material from each together in creating their offspring.

The concept of clustering in lineages says slightly more than that cults beget cults. It also hints that there is some structure to the progress of cult generations, that there are groupings of various sizes, and not just a uniform pattern of each cult giving birth to a standard number of younger cults. This is because some cults are more successful than others – their explanations about religious engineering and organizational maintenance are especially good. Such propositions as P160 and P161 show that a successful cult tends to give birth to other cults sharing the secrets of success. Augmented by P163, they prove that a successful cult will engender a family cluster, not only directly through its own offspring, but indirectly through their fertility. Proposition 175, among other propositions, indicates that the grandchildren of a cult will be different even from its children, although some family resemblances may still be visible after several generations.

P176 Cults founded by entrepreneurs cluster in lineages, sharing transmitted cultural similarities.

P177 Cultural similarities between cults in a lineage tend to be greater the more direct the historical connection between the cults.

To conclude this section, we must consider the costs an entrepreneur faces in founding his own cult. First of all, the fact that entrepreneurs learn their craft in existing cults means they do not have to move from low tension with the sociocultural environment to costly high tension. As participants in earlier cults they are already at high tension.

P178 Founding a new cult generally does not require an entrepreneur to increase his tension with the surounding sociocultural environment.

This fact provides yet another reason why entrepreneurial cult founders first participate in earlier cults. Most people would face higher costs in attempting to found a cult because they would have to accept higher tension. Propositions at several points in this book identify the societies in which deviant religions of various kinds are most likely to emerge. But one such observation should be made here. Entrepreneurial cult innovation depends more directly on rational evaluation of the opportunity to gain net rewards than does psychopathological cult innovation. The mentally ill person may have his vision and try to share it with others regardless of how hostile the surrounding society or the state are to cults. The profit-seeking entrepreneur is less likely to take such a risk.

P179 The proportion of cults founded by entrepreneurs, compared to those founded by the mentally ill, will be greater the less the costs imposed by the society upon participation in cults.

In our article originally presenting the three models we said they were compatible rather than being competing theories of cult innovation. So far, this chapter has shown that both the psychopathology model and the entrepreneur model can be derived from our general theory of religion. Each is an exchange model, and they share many elements. They diverge in the motivations of cult founders.

The psychopathology model suggests that compensators can serve as rewards for the innovator. Perhaps they provide a boost to self esteem. Perhaps they provide a coherent and satisfactory explanation for the abnormal activity itself, for sensations and thoughts that exact great costs from the individual unless or until they are coded successfully in terms of an explanation. From this perspective only an outside observer can distinguish between rewards and compensators. For the individual experiencing hallucinations or pathological emotional states, anything that gives relief is rewarding, be it a wonder drug or the attribution and organization of these phenomena into a religious experience.

Furthermore, if the psychopathology is "cured" by the invention of a compensator system, the victim is not merely relieved, but possesses a potentially exchangeable commodity.

At this point the psychopathology and entrepreneur models become the same. Despite the different sources of their compensators, each model predicts that religious innovators must find exchange partners or no cult is born. The psychopathology model suggests that only through exchange, only by getting others to ratify the worth of the compensator system, can religious inventors such as shamans validate their own inventions and re-enter the world of the sane. In fact, until someone else "buys" the product, only the continuing pressures of the psychopathology can sustain a shaman's faith that the new compensators are genuine. Madmen such as the "Three Christs of Ypsilanti" (Rokeach, 1981) may sustain their solitary faiths indefinitely. But we hardly call such unfortunates either sane or cult founders.

It is the recognition that religious innovation depends upon exchange that dissolves "the paradox that man is capable of producing a world that he then experiences as something other than a human product" (Berger and Luckmann, 1966:61). There is no longer a paradox when we realize that the "man" who does this is at least two people: a producer and a consumer of culture. These are different roles. The consumer has no basis for experiencing the production as merely a human product. The producer, on the other hand, is ratified in the belief that it is not merely a human product because others will exchange rewards in order to obtain the compensators in question.

Finally, it should be clear that key concepts of these models are continuous variables, rather than mutually exclusive "ideal types." Madness exists in varying degrees and for various durations. Consequently, the occasional madman may invent his best compensators in episodes of delerium, then perfect and sell them in periods of cool, calculating entrepreneurship. Honesty, too, exists in varying degress. While honesty and deception are alternative interaction strategies, there is nothing to prevent people from employing one or the other under different circumstances. Thus, while some cult founders may be described with a small subset of our propositions, others fit many models within our theory, some models more closely at one point in their careers, and others best when circumstances change. These ideas bring us to the final model of cult innovation.

The Subculture-Evolution Model

In many ways, the third of our models is an extension of the first two. But instead of one producer and several consumers of compensators, it postulates a group of persons, each of whom plays either role in different exchanges with his fellows. Each produces a small part of the compensator package, while simultaneously being a consumer of others' productions.

1. Cults are the expression of novel social systems, usually small in size but composed of at least a few intimately interacting individuals.
2. These cultic social systems are most likely to emerge in populations already deeply involved in the occult milieu, but cult evolution may also begin in entirely secular settings.
3. Cults are the result of sidetracked or failed collective attempts to obtain scarce or nonexistent rewards.
4. The evolution begins when a group of persons commits itself to the attainment of certain rewards.
5. In working together to obtain these rewards, members begin exchanging other rewards as well, such as affect.
6. As they progressively come to experience failure in achieving their original goals, they will gradually generate and exchange compensators as well.
7. If the intragroup exchange of rewards and compensators becomes sufficiently intense, the group will become relatively encapsulated, in the extreme case undergoing complete social implosion.
8. Once separated to some degree from external control, the evolving cult develops and consolidates a novel culture, energized by the need to facilitate the exchange of rewards and compensators, and inspired by essentially accidental factors.
9. The end point of successful cult evolution is a novel religious culture embodied in a distinct social group which must now cope with the problem of extracting resources (including new members) from the surrounding environment. (Bainbridge and Stark, 1979:291).

Our final model is the most eclectic of all, drawing on so many sources that few social scientists seem aware of its potential. Albert K. Cohen developed a similar model to describe the formation of delinquent subcultures (Cohen, 1955), and Bainbridge has shown the strengths of this approach in understanding how several groups evolved toward religion (Bainbridge, 1976, 1978). Frankly, all social theorists including ourselves prefer simple models that go once through a short series of steps and then are done. Repeated iteration of the same steps, as required by this model, feels complicated. But once one understands what the model is meant to accomplish, the repeated steps become quite clear.

This model describes how people can progressively commit each other to a set of compensators they simultaneously construct. Thus, it sketches *mutual conversion* that assembles a compensator system while accomplishing a *social implosion* that results in a cohesive, closed group broken away from the rest of society. Therefore, this model has much in common with our analysis of schism, presented in the previous chapter, and with our analysis of recruitment to religious movements, presented in the following chapter.

The intragroup processes described by the subculture-evolution model can be seen as multiple repetitions of the other two models, building a compensator system in steps so tiny that they may not even be noticed by participants. However, the model does not necessarily assume that members of the group share any significant level of psychopathology nor that they consciously fabricate compensators in pursuit of great rewards through exchanges. Each action that builds the compensator system may be so minor that exceptional mental conditions or motivations are not required. Each member may contribute so little to the final result that it seems to each an objective discovery, given him by the other members. Of course, the group may contain individual members who rise out of the mass and play special roles akin to the shaman or entrepreneur. If this is true in great degree, the case demands use of all three models for its full analysis.

Much of our general theory rests on observations about human inadequacies. Axiom 4 tells us that the human mind is finite, limited in the information it can store and process. Axiom 5 tells us that rewards are limited in supply, while A6 notes that even those rewards humans do achieve often are consumed. Axiom 7 says that attributes which determine power are unequally distributed, and the sum of all these axioms is that the human condition is one of strife, limitations, confusion and tragedy. Propositions 10, 11, 12 and 13 underscore the difficulty of the human predicament by demonstrating how uncertain are human explanations, that failure to solve problems is a constant possibility, and that misplaced confidence abounds.

Human action would be impossible without a measure of faith and optimism, without the willingness to act despite uncertainty. To err is human, we remind ourselves, and to be human one must continually risk and often commit error. In exchanges of any but the most instantaneous kind, humans promise to deliver rewards to each other. But all human promises rest on explanations of how the promise might be fulfilled, and sometimes these explanations fail. So, even with the most honest motives and the greatest power to gain and provide rewards:

P180 Parties to an exchange sometimes are unable to provide their exchange partner with the reward they have promised to give.

The alternatives for the person who fails are few. He can flee the situation and leave his partner short-changed. He can admit his failure and promise to secure some other reward for his partner, balancing the books in some other way than that originally agreed. But if he is committed to the exchange relationship and his partner is determined to gain the reward originally desired, the result may be a continuation of the attempt to secure that reward. Proposition 14 and P15 indicate the possibility that the debtor may offer his partner a compensator instead of the reward.

To give a mundane example, instead of paying an agreed sum of money, he may offer a stock certificate of uncertain but alleged greater value. But this chapter has emphasized the inhibitions that limit an individual's ability to generate compensators of great significance. Honest sane persons are more likely to offer compensators of modest dimensions. This may most often happen when they are able to provide part of the agreed reward, and add a weak compensator to make up the slim difference. To give another mundane example, a real estate salesman who promises to locate a tract of ten acres may only be able to find one nine acres in size. He may stress the quality of the land as compensation for the slightly lower quantity. Since quality is hard to measure, his exchange partner may accept the explanations and be satisfied with the nine acres.

P181 When a party to an exchange falls just short of providing the reward expected by his exchange partner, he is apt to offer a compensator in addition to whatever reward he is able to provide.

This proposition may seem a minor point applying to very few economic exchanges, but we think in fact it applies quite frequently, especially when the exchange involves relatively intangible rewards. As the poet Catullus said, one may count kisses. But the strength of love accompaying each kiss is beyond precise measurement. As the same poet discovered, disappointments and self-justifications are among the most common psychological phenomena. Proposition 181 is especially salient when an exchange is but one of a long series aiming at a distant reward. Each single exchange is meant to achieve only a tiny part of that reward – a small step toward it – perhaps to increase slightly the resources one has that will be needed to secure it. Progress toward the ultimate goal may be difficult to measure, and the inflation of apparent progress through minor compensator-explanations may easily take place.

For example, suppose a group member is sent to give a speach to an unfamiliar crowd, promoting the group's cause. He will be able to report back factually that he spoke, but may slightly overestimate the favorable response to give the impression that fully successful promotion was achieved. Proposition 32 suggests we should consider cases in which a long series of exchanges is directed toward a highly-valued distant goal. The greater the value of a reward, the greater the costs people will expend to achieve it. Therefore,

P182 The greater the value and difficulty of a reward to which a group has committed itself, the longer the series of exchanges in which the members will engage in pursuit of that reward.

Def.82 When a group *commits itself*, its members agree to carry out the actions and exchanges required to obtain a specified reward.

Each exchange has the potential to introduce compensators, as P181 says, and a series of exchanges permits the aggregation of tiny fragments into a significantly greater compensator than any one exchange could accomplish. Repeated exchanges in pursuit of an elusive reward may generate a collection of compatible compensators and then link them through more general explanations constituting general compensators. We do not say the process is simply additive, because exchanges may produce incompatible little compensators. But the function is very likely to be one with an upward slope.

P183 The longer the series of imperfect exchanges in which a group engages, the greater the number and generality of compensators they will generate.

Def.83 An *imperfect* exchange is one that is somewhat rewarding but fails to provide the full desired reward for one or both parties.

The rewards actually exchanged in imperfect exchanges may include whatever persons have to give each other, including affect and various other benefits having nothing to do with the original agreement. Persons who frequently exchange with each other tend to seek a variety of rewards in their meetings, and to become valued exchange partners. Indeed, one of the factors maintaining a group's commitment to distant goals is the member's commitment to each other. If the members value each other for a number and range of previously exchanged rewards, they are more apt to exert themselves in satisfying each others' desires for the reward to which the group has committed itself. As P117 implies,

> P184 The more the members of a group value each other, the greater costs they will expend to provide valued rewards for each other.

To the extent that exchange partners value each other, they value other persons less and tend to have a higher proportion of their exchanges with each other. By P184, to the extent that they value each other they will persist in seeking the agreed goal. Therefore, by P182 and P183, they will tend to go further in the generation of compensators. Furthermore, P63 and P65 say individuals often accept the evaluations of others, communicated through exchanges, while P66 and P67 note that the perceived value of compensators will be greater the more unanimous one's exchange partners are in endorsing it. On a slightly more abstract level, P38 says that social cleavages tend to produce cultural cleavages. Therefore, the processes we are talking about will most readily produce compensators when all the exchange partners participate. This means not only that participants will constitute a rather autonomous group, but also that members of it will be in constant, immediate interaction with one another so that sub-groups do not form to slow and divert development of a shared compensator system.

> P185 The more socially closed a group, the more readily it can generate and sustain compensators through exchanges among members.

> P186 The more thoroughly interconnected a group, the more readily it can generate and sustain compensators through exchanges among members.

If the process of compensator generation goes on for a long time, the result will be a somewhat novel system of compensators. As the desired reward continues to elude group members, they will be forced to discover ever more general explanations. Indeed, a highly closed group of members who value each other are very likely progressively to commit themselves to obtain all the rewards which members intensely desire. Thus they will develop great, multiple, overlapping commitments. Several processes of compensator-generation will take place superimposed, in pursuit of several distant, valued rewards. The group will begin to produce and accept novel compensators of the most general kind, and will qualify as a religious cult. The group may be other things as well. For example, primitive bands of hunter-gatherers are families, economic units and political units; each one also is a religious cult.

P187 Given sufficient time, groups that commit themselves to highly valued but unobtainable rewards tend to become religious cults.

How far a group evolves does depend upon time. While we are not prepared to suggest formulas to calculate the velocity of cultural change, the concepts of *speed* and *cultural distance covered* have real meaning. A group that begins its journey with a supernatural orientation, or at least with some compensators relevant to its quest, yet persists in seeking its reward, does not have as much ground to cover as a group that begins at a more remote distance from cult status.

P188 The greater the number and generality of compensators a group possesses at the beginning of incremental compensator-generation, the greater the number and generality it will possess at the end.

Def.84 *Incremental compensator-generation* is a process in which compensators are collectively invented and developed through a series of small steps constisting of exchanges.

Note that this does not mean the process is especially likely to begin in all types of groups that do possess compensators. Rather, it says that the more religious the participants are at the beginning, if the process takes place, the more likely it is that a religious cult will be the result. In fact, members of strong, stable, existing religious groups may be far less likely to experience this process. They may already possess efficacious compensators that prevent them from seeking unobtainable rewards. But if they do commit themselves to attaining the unattainable, a religious cult will result.

One of the most likely starting points for a religious cult is in a magical cult. In our own society, the greatest number of magical cults is found in the subculture of psychotherapies and human potential groups. Magic provides specific compensators for specific rewards, and it risks disconfirmation, as P91 notes. For several interconnected reasons, magical cults tend to evolve into religious cults. For one thing, according to P99, magicians are less powerful than religious specialists, and therefore can increase their rewards by entering religion. Conversely, by P93, over time religious specialists tend to reduce the amount of magic they supply. Magicians cannot require others to engage in long-term and stable patterns of exchange, as P96 states, but this does not keep them from trying. Some magical cults do rest on exchange relationships that persist for a few years. Some magical cults link numbers of persons with shared, difficult goals. While each participant in some may already be a magician, each may also want the kind of reward promised by the magic. Under these circumstances, incremental compensator-generation is very likely.

P189 Magical cults tend to evolve into religious cults if participants have long-term relationships with each other.

Earlier we noted that the conditions of a closed, highly-interconnected group make participants rely upon each other for a wide variety of rewards, and thus come to value each other. To the extent that they are in pursuit of a common goal and come to feel (rightly or wrongly) that they are progressively achieving that goal, they will come to value each other more and more. Propositions including P67, P139 through P144, P185 and P186 show that a group undergoing this process will tend to close and that the intensity of ingroup relations will increase.

P190 The members of a group engaged in incremental compensator-generation will become exchange partners of increasing value to each other.

P191 A group engaged in incremental compensator-generation will experience social implosion.

Def.85 In a *social implosion*, part of a relatively open social network becomes markedly more closed.

The extreme result of social implosion is a cohesive group completely cut off from relations with outsiders. Naturally, a number of factors can limit implosion, including all those that limit schism, as outlined in the previous chapter. Indeed, implosion is a kind of schism, except that it represents secession from society in general rather than merely from a religious organization.

Since the aim of a group going through these processes of compensator-generation and implosion is the attainment of real rewards, it winds up possessing a number of novel specific compensators, explanations not accepted by the surrounding society. Such a group may eventually halt compensator generation and begin accommodating itself to society – a topic for Chapter 8. But, initially at least, a thorough course of evolution such as we describe will lead to a state of high subcultural deviance.

> P192 An unchecked process of incremental compensator-generation will result in a high-tension cult based in a thoroughly-closed social group.

What more can be said about the kinds of groups most likely to complete this evolution? We did say they would be highly interconnected. This means each member will have a strong social relationship with a high proportion of other members. But any individual can sustain relationships with a limited number of other persons. Therefore, a highly interconnected group must be small.

> P193 Groups that become cults through incremental compensator-generation tend to be small enough for each member to have a relationship with every other member.

Religious cults can emerge from very large magical cults, such as the Psychoanalytic movement. But in these cases, the original group is very loosely organized as P96, P97 and P98 state. Therefore, there is ample room for small groups to close and implode within the loose structure of the large network of the magical cult (Brown, 1967; Rieff, 1968; Fodor, 1971). This certainly is akin to schism. But if there is a true group at the beginning, it is small.

Among the groups most saturated with schism and free to undertake this evolution into a religious cult are certain religious sects. Some of the more extreme small "sects" of past decades were really cults, because in their escape from conventional Christian organizations they engaged in considerable innovation. Such groups as the Appalachian snake handler churches interpret traditional scriptures in such a novel way that they might just as well have made up their own Bible.

Sects are particularly vulnerable to this evolution because they emphasize specific compensators and in their tension with the sociocultural environment would seek to change the conditions of society or of members' lives within society. Thus, sect members may often commit themselves collectively to real but unobtainable rewards. The process is further more likely if societal influences do not pull the sect back toward traditional compensators. If a sect is small, it is free to implode and detach from external inhibitions. If society does not punish religious innovation, or if the sect is already in extreme conflict with the society, then the costs of innovation may be slight.

P194 To the extent that a society does not punish religious innovation, small sects tend to evolve into cults.

P195 The higher the tension of a small sect, the more likely it is to evolve into a cult.

These final propositions of the subculture-evolution model, like P179 before, bring us to the question of societal conditions that either stimulate or retard cult innovation. It is with this topic that we will close this chapter.

Innovation and Market Conditions

Throughout this book we emphasize that religion arises out of and is maintained by exchange processes, and we treat the surrounding social and cultural environment as a market influencing such exchanges. Exchange holds the key to the manner in which new compensator systems are made social. It follows that conditions in the social and cultural marketplace determine whether, and the extent to which, novel compensators can be exchanged. Drawing upon propositions already developed in previous chapters, let us now begin to characterize this marketplace. Recall from Chapter 5:

P151 The greater the degree of coercion the external society imposes on religious deviance, the weaker the tendency for deviant religious organizations to form.

By definition, religious cults are deviant. Thus the degree to which novel compensators will be exchangeable for rewards depends upon the costs imposed on such exchanges. Societies differ greatly in the degree to which they coerce religious deviance. In contemporary America, for example, the marketplace is crowded with distinctive brands of compensators, both religious and secular, some of which are very novel. Correspondingly, little coercion is used against such deviance, although it is not absent. We have found that the degree of coercion varies markedly even from one part of the country to another (Bainbridge and Stark, 1980a).

Some societies have imposed much greater coercion than even in the most illiberal part of the United States, and attempts to market novel compensators have sometimes drawn the death penalty. In such a circumstance, it will be relatively difficult to found cults, except perhaps in remote backwaters beyond the reach of coercive forces. Indeed, in the more coercive climate that prevailed in nineteenth century America the Mormons were forced to flee to the unsettled West following the murder of Joseph Smith in Nauvoo, Illinois, to which they had originally removed to avoid persecution.

It must not be supposed that coercion will prevent religious invention. Rather, the strains and tensions of repressive societies may produce much religious invention of the kind depicted by the psychopathological model and subcultural model, though not (as P179 notes) by the entrepreneur model. But it will be much harder to transform such inventions into social movements.

We shall not discuss here why social environments vary in this fashion, although other chapters take up this question. We shall employ coercion as a variable in our theory even if we must take its values as empirical givens.

A second important aspect of the market environment on cult formation can be identified by a slight adaption of P152, also found in Chapter 5:

> P152 If changes in the external environment result in an intensification of the need for (and the numbers in need of) efficacious compensators, the tendency toward sect formation is proportionally strengthened.

> P196 If changes in the external environment result in an intensification of the need for (and the numbers in need of) efficacious compensators, the tendency toward cult formation is proportionally stregthened.

Because they are in a state of relatively high tension, cults, like sects, can provide more efficacious compensators than can bodies in a state of lower tension. Therefore, other things being equal, the larger the market for strong compensators, the larger the market for novel varieties of strong compensators.

This deduction is very significant because it captures the essence of the tradition of theory concerning "revitalization movements" and "crisis cults" cited near the beginning of this chapter in the psychopathology model. If the availability of rewards declines because of crises such as war, famine, natural disasters, economic depressions, and the like, the market for compensators expands correspondingly. Furthermore, P196 as stated need not be limited to times when great events occur. It is stated in proportional language so that small increments (or decrements) in need will be reflected proportionally in the rate of cult formation.

Furthermore, P196 can deal with other ways in which social change influences the market for cults. Culture tends to be designed to fit the social and physical conditions around it. Thus compensator systems tend to deal with rewards that have an established pattern of unavailability. As a result, social change can make some compensators irrelevant and worthless by making corresponding rewards more available. If science discovered the secret of eternal life, one could expect severe damage to compensator systems in which life beyond death was the central element.

By the same token, social change can place demands upon compensators for which they are ill-designed. For example, contact with a technologically superior society may create intense needs for which no existing compensators were designed. Such a market demand is likely to generate suppliers. Thus many societies that came in contact with the technologically advanced West found an intense need to find a protection against firearms. No direct means (rewards) were known to them, nor did they already possess compensators developed for that purpose. And from the Boxers in China to the Ghost Shirt Dancers of the Great Plains, such compensators quickly appeared in the form of magical invulnerability to bullets (Wilson, 1975a). That these cults were short-lived merely establishes that when compensators are made subject to the appropriate empirical test, often they are found wanting. It is worth stating our observation about change as a formal proposition.

> P197 When cultural change or other factors produce new needs and new conditions of life for numbers of people, the rate of cult formation will increase proportionally.

This discussion introduces again the fact that compensators compete within a social and cultural marketplace. Proposition 27 already stated that if multiple suppliers of general compensators exist, then the ability to exchange general compensators will depend upon their relative availability and perceived exchange ratios. Here we can say,

> P198 The ability to exchange novel compensators depends upon the relative efficacy, availability and cost of competing compensators.

We have already seen that the state of the economy of rewards determines the need (or market) for compensators. But which compensators will be exchangeable (and for what level of rewards) is determined by market competition. Thus the ability of a religious inventor to gain adherents depends upon how well the established religions are meeting the demand.

A major conclusion in previous chapters is that all religious organizations contain the seeds of internal schism. Indeed, we will show in Chapter 8 that large religious organizations always will tend to be in a state of relatively low tension, and growing religious organizations will be tending toward lower tension. Therefore, as P131 hints,

> P199 The religious organizations that encompass the majority of persons in any society will always contain a significant minority who desire more efficacious compensators than are available from these organizations.

Such persons provide the constituency for sect movements. But, at any given moment, many such persons will not be involved in a sect movement. Since cults are high tension religious groups they (like sects) are able to provide highly efficacious compensators and therefore have a comparative advantage over more churchly organizations in that respect.

> P200 Potential cult converts always exist within more conventional religious organizations.

Our deductions thus far tell us something about what people have to gain by accepting novel compensators. However, we must not lose sight of the fact that in so doing people engage in deviant behavior and therefore may incur costs, considerable costs in repressive societies, but some costs even in the most liberal societies yet known. Therefore, to press this analysis further we must examine variations in the costs and benefits of deviance, or, more fundamentally, the basis of social control.

This line of analysis was already introduced in Chapter 5 where we analyzed factors that inhibit or permit participation in schisms. We shall carry it through to a number of important insights in Chapter 7. In concise form, for present purposes, we can say that exchange behavior governs stakes in conformity. Since people vary in power, rewards, socialisation, and in the number and quality of their relationships, the following is true.

> P201 In all societies and all organizations, people vary in the degree to which they have stakes in conformity.

> Def. 86 *Stakes in conformity* consist of attachments, investments, involvements, and beliefs.

Stakes in conformity can be thought of as those things at risk (which represent potential losses) when a person deviates, or fails to conform. They also tell us that persons with low stakes in conformity may incur minimal costs by deviating, and may, in turn, have much to gain from it.

P202 Persons with low stakes in conformity are relatively deprived in terms of rewards, compensators, and self-esteem.

P203 Persons with low stakes in conformity are relatively free to deviate.

P204 Persons with low stakes in conformity tend to have less favorable evaluations of conventional explanations than do persons with higher stakes in conformity.

People continually attempt to evaluate explanations, that is, to judge them in terms of their success in gaining rewards. For persons with low stakes in conformity, conventional explanations tend to be evaluated negatively because they have not worked satisfactorily for these persons and because exchange partners are not urging acceptance of them. For persons who are failing to gain an average level of rewards, two choices are possible: to blame the explanations they have followed, or to blame themselves. Proposition 134 tells us that people seek a positive evaluation of themselves. Therefore, people will tend to externalize blame and thus to become disaffected from conventional explanations if they are relatively deprived of rewards. Furthermore, compensators are easier to come by than are desired but scarce rewards. Thus those with low stakes in conformity will be especially suspectible to new compensators that hold the potential of giving more satisfaction than those they already have tried and found wanting. In the following chapter we shall examine how factors like these determine which persons will join cults that have already come into existence. Here we note that brand-new compensators can most readily become the seeds of new cults among those with low stakes in conformity.

P205 Persons with low stakes in conformity have relatively much to gain and little to lose by creating novel compensators.

P206 Persons with low stakes in conformity have relatively much to gain and little to lose by accepting novel compensators.

P207 In any society, a significant supply of potential cult founders exists.

P208 In any society, a significant supply of potential followers for utterly new cults exists.

Conclusion

In many respects, this chapter provides a general theory of deviant behavior, especially the generation of deviant subcultures, not of religious deviance alone. And the concept of *stakes in conformity* is a way which our criminologist colleague, Travis Hirschi (1969), likes to conceptualize commitment, and its obverse, freedom to deviate. Of course, the supply of people in society with low stakes in conformity will vary, in accordance with several of our propositions. And the propositions which conclude the above section permit us again to see that the three models are indeed compatible.

The *psychopathology model* deals primarily with individual responses to low stakes in conformity: how a person both is pressed to deviate and is very free to do so if he lacks stakes in conformity and suffers from the consequent threat to self-esteem. Such people tend to be social atoms. Their lack of attachments to others means they may initiate deviant lines of action without attracting much attention or promoting interference. Their investments appear to have gone for naught. Their lack of involvements gives them time and energy to deviate. Indeed time may hang heavily upon them. Their beliefs have been corroded by negative evaluation and by their efforts to retain self-esteem. We do not wish to enter any further than we did at the beginning of this chapter into the maze of specific psychodynamic models. But it should be noted that low stakes in conformity can be the result of personality disorders – forms of deviance that impede the development and maintenance of attachments, investments, involvements and beliefs. Conversely, personality disorders may be the result of low stakes in conformity: isolation from social life can undercut the ability of persons to maintain normal thoughts and actions (Faris and Dunham, 1939). In either case, the creation of efficacious compensators may permit such persons to solve their problems, if they can successfully exchange their compensators for rewards. That is, successful exchanges of compensators for rewards builds stakes in conformity while acceptance of new compensators may have the same effect.

The *subculture-evolution model* also is captured by these propositions. The primary consequence of a social implosion is to reduce greatly the group's stakes in conformity to its environment and thus to the conventional moral order. Thus, while people may become involved in the process that leads to a social implosion because they already have low stakes in conformity, this need not be the case. The social implosion itself will have this effect as it greatly reduces attachments, investments, involvements (and therefore beliefs) in the conventional world. Conversely, a social implosion greatly increases stakes in conformity to the group. For it is here that member attachments, investments, involvements, and beliefs are now lodged.

The compatibility of the *entrepreneur model* with the final propositions of this chapter is obvious. Persons with low stakes in conformity have much to gain and little to lose by attempting to purvey novel compensators, for a potential market awaits them. However, low stakes in conformity are more important for entrepreneurs who practice deception than for those who practice honesty. Indeed, honesty is sustained through social attachments, so we would expect the dishonest entrepreneur to be especially low in such stakes, while the honest entrepreneur may not be. However, the honest entrepreneur began his career in an earlier deviant cult, and thus probably had his honesty sustained by social bonds within the cultic deviant subculture. He, like the member of the socially imploded cult, had low stakes in conformity to the conventional world, but higher stakes with respect to his cultic fellows.

Our concluding propositions about cult innovation take us away from the first flash of invention to that point at which the new compensators are made social. The next chapter will spell out the specific mechanisms by which cult founders, whether individuals or small imploded groups, attract exchange partners.

CHAPTER 7:
Affiliation with Sects and Cults

This chapter asks why people sometimes join high-tension religious groups. We will see that the basic principles at work already have been suggested in earlier chapters, but it is worth stating them in the precise forms that best explain the development of deviant affiliations. This chapter could be very short, if it merely reminded us of the basic principles and then stated the obvious conclusion. But, as in the previous chapter, we have taken on the added task of integrating our derivations with the key statements of earlier, classic perspectives such as Strain Theory, Control Theory, and Differential Association Theory. In so doing, we fulfill the earlier perspectives by placing them in a larger deductive framework that salvages their proven power to explain while jettisoning the occasional excesses that have brought some of them into serious question among social scientists. We must begin by debunking and explaining a myth.

The study of religious ritual and symbolism is intrinsically important, but we must not be misled into thinking it is the same thing as the scientific explanation of religion. Since religious concepts are first and foremost compensators, they may contradict reality more often than they describe it. Consider the concept of *charisma*, for example. Weber noted that one way in which leadership was legitimated was through the claim that the leader possessed special powers; in the religious context the leader would be imagined to have supernatural abilities or at least direct contact with supernatural beings. Certainly, a strategy of legitimation can increase the leader's power over his followers, if the followers believe in it (Wallis, 1982). But Weber does not say that the leader is able to influence his followers because he actually has superhuman power (cf. Haley, 1980). Yet, some incautious contemporary writers seem to use the concept of charisma as a primary explanation of an individual's power, rather than as a mode of legitimation of that power.

While *charisma*, as a concept, alerts us to the fascinating questions of how individuals attract followers and how they legitimate their leadership, it does little to explain the capacity to lead. The notion of religious *conversion* can be equally misleading, if seriously used as an explanation for behavior. Both notions come directly from religious thought, and both are saturated with magical connotations. *Charisma* is unscientific because it implies that the charismatic person actually possesses superhuman powers to lead and pursuade. *Conversion* is unscientific because it suggests a radical, perhaps supernatural transformation in the nature of a person who is converted. The notion of conversion assumes that an individual really changes in some basic sense when he joins a new religious group, and it typically hints that this change is accomplished rapidly through either divine intervention or an autogenic spiritual metamorphosis.

Instead of *conversion*, we need a more neutral term that will not infuse our theory with the wrong connotations. We have considered *recruitment*, and will use this term in some contexts, but the verb "recruiting" puts the locus of action in the group that tries to draw in new members. "Joining" places the locus of action in the new member. We need a term that gives equal roles to the new member and to the group (Long and Hadden, 1983). In the absence of a really stunning linguistic inspiration, we have chosen the verb *affiliate* and the other words derived from it. Members of a group *affiliate* with each other. Membership is *affiliation*. The two-sided process of recruiting-joining is *affiliating*. These words do not prematurely specify what changes might or might not take place inside the individual, and simply point to the plain facts that changes in group membership are important to explain and easy to measure.

Before we look at affiliating, a comment about the meaning of *conversion* is in order. We must explain why the idea of conversion, in one form or another, is so widespread. If it is a false and misleading concept, why have people in such a variety of religious traditions come to believe in it? Simply put, the answer is that conversion is a very basic compensator, likely to be invented again and again and put to the service of unmet human desires. Recall the following three propositions from Chapter 5:

P134 Every person seeks a positive self-evaluation.

P135 Persons desire a positive evaluation of the rewards they possess, including the explanations and the power-giving resources they possess.

P136 Explanations that imply positive evaluations of a person and the rewards the person possesses are themselves rewards, while explanations that imply negative evaluations are costs.

Persons who possess little are often powerless to increase their store of scarce rewards; and those who are evaluated negatively by others are likely to suffer from negative self-evaluations. In Chapter 4, P64 noted: in the absence of a more compelling standard, the value an individual places on a reward is set by the market value of that reward established through exchanges by other persons. Chapter 3 also noted that persons come to be evaluated as rewards by their exchange partners. Thus, a person may have two primary sources of self-evaluation:

(1) direct evaluation by the person of his own ability to secure rewards
(2) evaluation of the person by others who seek rewards from him in exchanges

Since many rewards are scarce and unequally distributed among humans, some people will acquire relatively negative self-evaluations. Proposition 134 states that such a person will seek a more positive self-evaluation, but the scarcity of rewards capable of helping many people accomplish this disposes them to accept compensators that will give them the feeling of taking effective action, quite apart from any real changes in their ability to secure the desired rewards. If the person can be given a new explanation that asserts the person is now of a new and better nature than formerly, then compensation is accomplished. The idea of *conversion* is just such an explanation. It invalidates old evaluations and substitutes a new and positive evaluation. It identifies the act of joining a religious group as a transmutation of the neophyte (Snow and Machalek, 1983; 1984). Therefore, we can state:

P209 Persons with a relatively negative self-evaluation are most likely to conceptualize religious affiliating as conversion.

Def.87 *Conversion* is affiliation of a person to a new religious group, conceptualized as a positive transformation of the nature and value of a person.

Note that this proposition does not say that persons with negative self-conceptions of themselves are more likely to join religious groups than other people. This may or may not be so. Rather, P209 merely states that if such people affiliate they will tend to conceptualize affiliation as conversion. It also follows that a person whose exchange partners have relatively negative self-evaluations will also think in terms of conversion, regardless of his own personal level of self-esteem, because the exchange partners will communicate their explanation to him. Therefore:

P210 Persons who belong to social groups with relatively negative self-evaluations are most likely to conceptualize religious affiliating as conversion, even if they themselves have positive self-evaluations.

We can also look at conversion from the point of view of old members of the religious group to which the neophyte is recruited. They want the new recruit to be a valuable exchange partner, but cannot be certain that he will be. Especially if P209 has already impelled them to accept the notion of conversion, they may also use the compensating effect of this conceptualization to make them feel that the new recruit is of great value, and therefore well worth the effort of recruiting, despite whatever inferior characteristics he used to have. This will especially be true if the person did not look like a reward of high value, to start with. Thus both from an extension of P209, and from this line of thought parallel to P209, we can derive:

> P211 Groups that recruit persons who possess and constitute rewards of relatively low value will tend to conceptualize affiliating as conversion.

Numerous religious groups carry out initiation rituals that are supposed to accomplish conversion. Anthropologists have noted that these rituals, whether brief or protracted, are frequently carried out in three stages. In many preliterate societies, such religious rituals are simultaneously puberty ceremonies accomplishing a symbolic transformation of children into adults (van Gennep, 1960; Eliade, 1958, 1971). Van Gennep calls the three stages: *separation, transition*, and *incorporation*. In *separation*, the old identity of the person is stripped away, while *incorporation* gives him a new identity with new group membership. The *transition* stage serves to insulate the other two stages and is a period of limbo that presumably affirms that separation has been completed successfully and lays the basis for incorporation. In religious terms, the ritual separates the individual from the profane world and incorporates him in the sacred realm. Van Gennep says, "So great is the incompatibility between the profane and the sacred worlds that a man cannot pass from one to the other without going through an intermediate stage" (Van Gennep, 1960:1). Eliade adopts the common religious view that conversion is akin to resurrection:

> It is impossible to attain to a higher mode of being, it is impossible to participate in a new irruption of sanctity into the world or into history, except by dying to profane, unenlightened existence and being reborn to a new, regenerated life. (Eliade, 1958:118)

Our theory does not assume that any means are sufficient to allow a mere mortal to attain that higher mode of being, but what is in question is not the right means to accomplish a sacred reward but the likely explanations that will be accepted as compensators for this reward. Death and rebirth lose some of their symbolic power unless separated by a period in which the person is imagined to be dead. For Eliade, the intermediate stage is an embryonic state similar to that before a person's original birth, a temporary return to Chaos, a formless condition that permits radical reformation (Eliade, 1971:119). In its symbolic intent, "initiatory death abolishes Creation and History and delivers us from all failures and 'sins.' It delivers us from the ravages inseparable from the human condition." (1971:157) Since these "ravages" are "inseparable from the human condition," so long as we in fact remain human beings, these rituals cannot provide true personal transmutation. They can only give us the compensator of alleged conversion.

No particular compensator is universally found in all human culture, as far as we know. Because they are not firmly tied to empirical reality, religious explanations show great variation across societies, even when they attempt to serve universal needs. The fact that many religious groups thrive without tripartite initiation rituals does not render the pattern uninteresting. The basic concept is so simple that it must have been reinvented many times. Some T-group practitioners similarly conceptualize personal change in three stages: *unfreezing* the person's attitudes, *changing* them, and then *refreezing* so that the changes will last (Schein and Bennis, 1965: Chapter 15). We leave to others the interesting task of deriving propostions about when different varieties of the conversion concept are most likely to be accepted, and give these examples merely to show something of the scope of this common compensator.

The fact that conversion is not essential to religious affiliating, whether lightning conversion by the hand of God or an elaborate series of rituals in three steps, is most simply demonstrated by the fact that many groups fail to employ this concept. Perhaps more interesting is the fact that some religious groups offer repeated conversion experiences, possibly to reinforce their compensatory power and revive hope in the face of some measure of continuing disappointment. Apparently, many of the conversions that take place in Protestant revivals, such as the Billy Graham "crusades," are ritual experiences repeated numerous times by the same individuals (Weldon T. Johnson, 1971; Altheide and John M. Johnson, 1977). In cults such as Scientology and the various Rosicrucian organisations, a cumulative series of conversion rituals is provided, each supposed to mark one step toward total self-transmutation. Thus, it is essential to separate conversion, a highly variable compensator, form the social regularities of religious affiliation.

The Lofland-Stark Model

Our discussion of affiliation will be guided by the model of this process proposed in 1965 by John Lofland and Rodney Stark (Lofland and Stark, 1965; Lofland, 1966). This model serves our present purposes especially well because it is eclectic, incorporating ideas representative of several different and potentially competing theoretical perspectives. Therefore, it will help show the connections between our current deductive theory and a broad spectrum of earlier work. The model contains elements of every line of thought we want to develop here. Indeed, this chapter is a direct outgrowth of the 1965 model.

Originally, Lofland and Stark described the model as "a theory of conversion to a deviant perspective." We have already indicated reasons for preferring the analytically more fruitful term *affiliation* instead of *conversion*. Later we will consider the ramifications of the phrase "deviant perspective," but it should alert us that the model is meant to apply to high-tension religious groups, rather than those of low tension, although parts of it might have wider application. The 1965 model tries to explain how a person could become the "deployable agent" of a cult, meaning a committed member who will contribute significantly to the group and may be used to recruit more neophytes. The model was meant to be taken as a series of steps, each effective only if the previous steps had been completed, but now we prefer to treat it as a collection of attractive ideas rather than as a compelling unified whole (cf. Richardson and Stewart, 1977; Bainbridge, 1978; Richardson, Stewart and Simmonds, 1979; Snow and Phillips, 1980; Stark and Bainbridge, 1985). The 1965 model states that the following sequence of steps leads to an individual joining the "D.P." cult, the first American cell of the group known today as the Moonies.

For conversion a person must:

1. Experience enduring, acutely felt tensions
2. Within a religious problem-solving perspective,
3. Which leads him to define himself as a religious seeker;
4. Encountering the D.P. at a turning point in his life,
5. Wherein an affective bond is formed (or pre-exists) with one or more converts;
6. Where extra-cult attachments are absent or neutralized;
7. And, where, if he is to become a deployable agent, he is exposed to intensive interaction. (Lofland and Stark, 1965:874)

Here, Lofland and Stark assembled a number of themes that run throughout the literature on "religous conversion," and this chapter will expand on these themes within the context of our general theory. But the reader might feel the theory of religion presented in this book demands a radical simplification of the 1965 model. Why can't we dispense with all the steps except the first? "Enduring, acutely felt tensions" sounds like the unmet human desires that give rise to compensators. Haven't we shown that religion is simply a matter of compensators? Can we not reduce the model to the following terse statement, and be done with all complexity?

> "Enduring, acutely felt tensions impell a person to seek compensators by joining a new religious organization."

The shortcomings of this radical simplification will become progressively clearer as we develop the arguments of this chapter. But this is a good point to stress as forcefully as we can that our theory of religion is not a simple deprivation theory. In Chapter 2 we explained that all human beings (not just the relatively deprived) desire rewards they cannot achieve, and are impelled to accept compensators. But this fact does not immediately give rise to religion. Chapters 3 and 4 showed in some detail the intricate and myriad steps in human interaction required to create religious institutions, while Chapter 6 added information about the development of new religious culture.

Compensators, which are responses to deprivation, are important in our theory. But even more basic are the features of exchanges between humans. The laws of exchange permit compensators to be generated and distributed through religious organizations, but these laws set their own terms for recruitment to religious organizations, just as they do for religious schism. Specific deprivations play a role in determining these processes, but they cannot operate in a social vacuum, and affiliation takes place without specific deprivations in some cases.

To understand how the terms of the 1965 model fit together, we will introduce a simple typology of theories proposed by Travis Hirschi. Like all rough typologies, this one is primarily of heuristic value, but our subsequent discussion will incorporate the key ideas into our general theory of human action. Hirschi outlined three "fundamental perspectives on delinquency and deviant behavior," three general approaches that were popular in the sociology of deviance at the time he wrote. The three do not exhaust all possible perspectives but do offer a wide range of ideas on the same level of theoretical abstraction. Their relevance here is that each may contribute something to the explanation of religious deviance – participation in high-tension religious groups. Hirschi summarized the tenets of the three perspectives:

> According to *strain* or motivational theories, legitimate desires that conformity cannot satisfy force a person into deviance. According to *control* or bond theories, a person is free to commit delinquent acts because his ties to the conventional order have somehow been broken. According to *cultural deviance* theories, the deviant conforms to a set of standards not accepted by a larger or more powerful society. (Hirschi, 1969:3)

The chief utility of the list for present purposes is the fact that different steps in the 1965 model can be classified under different headings in Hirschi's typology, then compared with other theoretical statements under the same headings. The first step, "tension," suggests *strain* theory. The second step, "religious perspective," suggests religious cultural influences and therefore may be linked to *cultural deviance* theory. The third step is the resultant of the first two; "religious seekership" is a pattern of behavior that results from strain within a particular cultural orientation. The fourth step, "turning point," is a nexus concept that unites the three preceding steps with the three that follow, and therefore hints at more than one type of theory. The three concluding steps describe the loss of social bonds with outsiders and the gain of social bonds with members of the cult, and therefore describes a transformation in *social control*. We shall now examine these matters more closely, beginning with the first step in the model.

Tension, Deprivation and Strain

Many theories of deviance and of social movements may be placed in the broad category of *tension-strain* perspectives. We hyphenate this term advisedly. *Tension*, as used in the Lofland-Stark model, is a psychological concept, referring to a state of unhappiness on the part of an individual. *Strain*, as identified by Hirschi, is a condition of contradiction in the sociocultural environment surrounding the individual. Presumably, strain can produce tension, so this distinction blurs in particular cases. But the distinction is important, both because classical theorists have stressed one side or the other in their statements, and because the two halves of the term play different roles in our theory. Another familiar word, falling somewhere between tension and strain, is *deprivation*.

Years ago, Glock and Stark presented a tension-deprivation-strain theory of affiliation to various kinds of religious organizations, postulating that different needs drove people to join different types of movement. But their theory was not simply a tension model. It contained the seeds of our exchange theory, stating that even powerful motivations would not lead to affiliation unless social relations among the deprived and between them and potential movement leaders were also conducive:

> We suggest that a necessary precondition for the rise of any organized social movement, whether it be religious or secular, is a situation of felt deprivation. However, while a necessary condition, deprivation is not, in itself, a sufficient condition. Also required are the additional conditions that the deprivation be shared, that no alternative institutional arrangements for its resolution are perceived, and that a leadership emerge with an innovating idea for building a movement out of the existing deprivation. (Glock and Stark, 1965:249)

Many standard works in the social sciences present similar views, including some cited in our discussion of the *psychopathology model* of cult formation (Chapter 6). Other examples could be cited by the dozens. Hans Toch states the thesis broadly and simply:

> A social movement represents an effort by a large number of people to solve collectively a problem that they feel they have in common. (Toch, 1965:5)

Much of the effort lavished by tension-strain theorists in elaborating their theories has been spent on the question of how people come to feel they have a problem that requires an unusual solution. What is deprivation? For a century, social theorists have argued that deprivation was not merely physical pain or objective poverty, but represented a relative gap between what a person has and what he intensely desires (Davies, 1962). As Ted Gurr puts it:

> Relative deprivation is defined as a perceived discrepancy between men's value expectations and their value capabilities. Value expectations are the goods and conditions of life to which people believe they are rightfully entitled. Value capabilities are the goods and conditions they think they are capable of attaining or maintaining, given the social means available to them. (Gurr, 1970:13)

When John Lofland defined the term *tension* from the 1965 model, he suggested that people who joined the Doomsday cult suffered from a kind of deprivation: "This tension is best characterized as a felt discrepancy between some imaginary, ideal state of affairs and the circumstances in which they actually saw themselves" (Lofland, 1966:7).

Both Gurr and Lofland point to a tension between two images in a person's mind, to an evaluation of rewards in hand (or costs) compared with those desired or expected. Gurr focuses on persons who feel they cannot attain the goods and conditions to which they are rightfully entitled. Approximately, this translates into our theory as a perceived state of coercion. A person gets what he "deserves" when he receives the market value in return for costs he expends in exchanges. The "deprived" person does not get the full market value for what he gives in exchanges, and it is a sense of market value which gives rise to an estimate of what one is rightfully entitled to. Recall Def.38 from Chapter 3:

> Def.38 *Coercion* is the interaction strategy of threatening to inflict great costs on others, thereby imposing on them exchange ratios which are below market value.

In contrast, Lofland's formulation does not refer to a standard of what one rightfully deserves. It merely states that the individual desires a better state of affairs than he currently enjoys – desires not deserves. Lofland implies that the individual believes he might possibly attain the desired state, and this belief may be strengthened or even generated by contact with a movement. We can translate both Gurr and Lofland into the language of our theory, the better to compare them:

Gurr: *Relative deprivation* refers to the perception that one is the victim of coercive exchange relationships.

Lofland: *Tension* refers to strong, unmet desires.

Lofland's formulation is much simpler in substance than Gurr's, not merely more direct in language. But it is not that Lofland has missed something or that Gurr saw more deeply into the problem. Rather, they sought to explain significantly different kinds of behavior. Gurr wanted to explain political rebellion, while Lofland was interested in religious cults. We will examine the simpler concept first.

Tension

How can Lofland's *tension*, which we identify simply as strong, unmet desire, impell a person to deviance? Surely, all human action is performed in pursuit of desired rewards. Perhaps the answer is found in yet another question: why do people refrain from committing deviant acts?

The only relevant way that deviant behavior differs from conventional behavior is that it tends to be punished. Deviant behavior entails greater cost than conventional behavior. In our discussion of the social bond, in Chapter 5, we identified some of the costs a person must risk if he defects from one religious group to join another. Other costs may be inflicted by secular exchange partners on a person who joins a high-tension religious group. A person who accepts such costs must expect a net reward in all his exchanges, so he must be seeking a valued reward to satisfy great desires.

Desire is equivalent to the willingness to expend costs to obtain a reward. Great desire is the willingness to expend costs of great value. Most people do not join costly high-tension religious groups. From this fact we can deduce that unusually great desire (tension) must motivate joining. Biographies of the early Moonies, used by Lofland and Stark to illustrate their model, show ample evidence of tension.

But is it true that joining a deviant religious group necessarily entails very great costs? Not always. In fact, there are three conditions that can reduce the costs significantly. First, societies vary greatly in how much they punish religious deviance. Second, individuals already at a high-tension point on the religious spectrum may suffer relatively little cost in moving to slightly higher tension, even though the point they reach might entail a very costly leap for someone initially at low tension. Third, high-tension groups can reduce the cost of joining by masking their deviance, by dissembling in one way or another, perhaps by organizing themselves as secret societies so that the new recruit's secular exchange partners may fail to inflict punishment for his new affiliation because they are ignorant of it. All three factors are socially patterned, but now we will examine only the first.

Later we will explain factors that might provide positive motivation bringing those with only average levels of desire to join high-tension groups. Assume, for now, that such factors exist. In societies that inflict little, if any, punishment on those who engage in religious deviance, "acutely felt tensions," the first step in the 1965 model, fades in significance, and these other factors take over. In such non-coercive societies we may still be able to explain affiliation with minority religious organizations, but we may not be able to distinguish new recruits from non-recruits merely in terms of predisposing level of need. But at the other extreme, when a society inflicts great costs on religious deviance, "acutely felt tensions" become crucial. In coercive societies, tension is a necessary condition. In completely non-coercive societies (if any exist), tension is unimportant. And in societies of medium coercion (such as ours), tension becomes a contributory factor.

Chapter 6 pointed out the seeming paradox that increased societal coercion can stimulate deviant religious groups at the same time that it inhibits them:

> P196 If changes in the external environment result in an intensification of the need for (and the numbers in need of) efficacious compensators, the tendency toward cult formation is proportionally strengthened.

One likely cause of an intensified need for efficacious compensators, whether through sects or cults, is the development of a repressive state. If the elite exercise their monopoly over the cultural means of coercion in most vital spheres of life, but avoid applying great coercion against deviant religious groups, then the scene is set for massive growth of high-tension religious groups recruiting persons who experience especially "acutely felt tensions." Recall one of our propositions from Chapter 5:

> P151 The greater the degree of coercion the external society imposes on religious deviance, the weaker the tendency for deviant religious organizations to form.

The parallel propositions concerning individual affiliation are:

> P212 The greater the degree of coercion the external society imposes on religious deviance, the greater the probable cost experienced by an individual who joins a deviant religious organization.

> P213 The greater the degree of coercion the external society imposes on religious deviance, the greater the value of desired reward required to bring an individual to join a deviant religious organization.

> P214 The greater the degree of coercion the external society imposes on religious deviance, the more restricted the range of persons likely to join deviant religious organizations.

Our own society imposes very little coercion on religious deviance; less and less all the time. The reasons will be explained in Chapter 9, but the immediate cause is the lack of a dominant established church allied to the state. Since all religious groups are minority religions, it is in the interest of each to support norms of tolerance. In Western European nations, competing political ideologies have had somewhat the same effect as the competing religious bodies in the United States. But this is a topic for Chapter 9. For present purposes, we need merely note the disestablishment of religion in modern societies and the concomitant decrease in coercion inflicted on religious deviance. The above propositions immediately lead to the prediction that the number and variety of radical religious groups (cults) are relatively great in modern society, while the intensity of tension required to motivate a person to join is less than in more traditional societies. Disestablishment of the churches is a progressive process, expressed as much in weakening of informal ties between the state and church, as well as in the more obvious abrogation of laws. Therefore, as Chapter 9 will explore, we must expect a continuing paganization of religious life, a general trend masked in the short term by shifts in fashion and the publicity given various forms of religion.

Deprivation

Earlier we translated Gurr's concept of *relative deprivation* as the perception that one is the victim of coercive exchange relationships. There has been much confusion over the concept of *relative deprivation* in the sociological literature, mainly centered on the standards of reward human beings use in assessing whether they are deprived. In a sense, the question is purely empirical. We should investigate which standards human beings actually use, under what conditions and in what proportion, then incorporate the findings in our theory. Much social scientific research has shown that individuals frequently use one or both of two standards: the level of reward achieved by other persons, especially people in similar circumstances, and the level of reward the individual previously experienced and came to feel was to be expected in the future.

For present purposes, our theory conceives of both of these standards in terms of market value, the median reward usually received in similar exchanges for a given cost. Individuals can come to believe that X is the market value in exchanges of type E in at least three main ways: (1) they can observe the rewards they, themselves, usually received in E exchanges; (2) they can observe the rewards that others typically receive in E exchanges, or (3) they may receive from others certain explanations about E exchanges that communicate a notion of the market value, whether correct or not. Sometimes, radical movements can arouse great feelings of indignation and outrageous demands by giving recruits unrealistically high notions of the market value. However, here we shall not worry about the correctness of beliefs about market value but, rather, focus on the consequences of such beliefs, correct or not.

But consider the person currently suffering in actual coercive exchange relationships. A restoration to market value in the exchanges would be a valuable reward for this person. Definition 39 noted that the victim of a coercive exchange loses in the exchange. Therefore, an end to the coercion would produce a gain in rewards, and thus constitute a reward itself. The person who merely thinks that his rewards are held down by coercion below market value, will behave in the same manner as the person who correctly knows this to be true. Thus, the following proposition will describe behavior by those who perceive themselves to be on the losing end of coercive relationships, as well as being the natural course of action for those who actually do suffer:

P215 The victim in a coercive exchange relationship will seek means to remove the coercion.

Recall that social resources, the cultural means of coercion, are the major source of coercive power. Recall also that the state is the monopoly of the cultural means of coercion by a clearly differentiated group of specialists. Definition 43 defined the *repressive state* as one in which this monopoly does result in significant coercion inflicted on some numbers of non-elite members of the society. As we have seen again and again, when individuals cannot obtain rewards by themselves, they turn to other people who may provide the rewards through exchanges. In Chapter 3, we expanded our discussion of social relationships, emphasizing that they can constitue very valuable rewards conferring power on those who have them. Therefore, if a number of people who wish to escape coercion come into contact with each other, they may initiate mutual exchanges directed toward assembling a counter-force capable of resisting or overturning the monopoly of the coercive elite.

P216 People who perceive themselves to be victims of a repressive state will seek to organize their own cultural means of coercion against the state.

Def.88 The organization of cultural means of coercion against the state is called *political rebellion*.

All this is quite familiar thinking. We have merely translated a small portion of Gurr's logic into our own language. A proper deductive theory of politics developed from our core theory would require a book as large as this, paralleling it in many respects. For our current purposes, it is important to emphasize that the logical social response to relative deprivation is political rather than religious. Thus, by itself, relative deprivation will seldom cause many prople to join religious movements. Rather than accepting religious compensators to offset the coercion they suffer, they will seek the political means to achieve a rewarding end to the coercion.

As explained in Chapter 2, however, there are circumstances in which persons will accept compensators instead of rewards. Propostions 19 through 21 explained that it is impossible to obtain a reward rather than a compensator: (1) when the reward does not exist; (2) when the compensator is mistaken for the reward; and (3) when one lacks the power to obtain the reward.

The reward of escape from coercion does, logically, exist, so the first point does not apply here. The question of when people mistake a compensator for the corresponding reward is taken up elsewhere in this chapter and book, so we will pass the second point by. The third point deserves comment. It is sometimes impossible to organize a counter-force to defeat, or at least combat, state repression. Proposition 216 leaves open the possibility that the state will be so powerful that the non-elite will manifestly fail to organize a political rebellion. Or, they may fail in an episode of rebellion and be thrown back into an even more abject condition than before. Then the victims will be most likely to accept the compensators provided by some religious movement as the best substitute available. The religion may provide alternate explanations about how the state will be overthrown, or it may merely offer compensators that promise the desired rewards in some other context, such as an afterlife.

> P217 Victims of a repressive state will tend to join high-tension religious movements if the state is sufficiently powerful to suppress political rebellion.

Note that this proposition identified social conditions under which one version of deprivation will explain the affiliation of some people to high-tension religious groups. It does not say that this is the only reason people will join these groups, nor does it say anything about affiliation in societies that lack a repressive state. One important kind of high-tension religious group that is almost fully explained by P217 is the *millenarian movement*.

P218 Victims of a repressive state will tend to affiliate with millenarian religious movements if the state is sufficiently powerful to suppress political rebellion.

Def.89 A *millenarian* religious movement is one in which the participants believe that supernatural intervention will soon effect a radical transformation of the conditions of life.

Here, the conditions of life that members hope will be transformed radically are relations between themselves and the elite that currently monopolizes the cultural means of coercion. They hope a savior will come, providing the resources they lack to overcome the elite. Proposition 218 may not explain every single millenarian movement, because a few may be responses to disastrous natural conditions. However, we suspect that these non-political millenarian movements, if any truly exist, merely transfer to different problems supernatural explanations originally designed for and sustained by political tensions. Many if not all of the millenarian movements described by historians appear to be the nearest thing to a political movement available to participants (Cohn, 1961; Hobsbawm, 1959).

Many contemporary writers paint a tragic picture when they describe millenarian movements or other religious movements that substitute for political action. But there is good reason to believe that political movements also are often doomed to failure, and may frequently cause great human misery on the road to failure. In the first decades of the twentieth century, millenarian, nationalist, and communist movements developed in Vietnam. The millenarian movements are said to have been supported by ill-educated primitive rebels (Wolf, 1969), while the Communists and the Nationalist Party, who staged bloody and unsuccessful insurrections in 1929 and 1930, are said to have been created by "modern" middle-class citizens. By 1972, the national war of liberation had succeeded in driving first the French and then the Americans out of Vietnam, at great cost, and the international-socialist ideological ties of the ruling party had been disrupted and reformed into simple nationalist alliances. The net effect has been the creation of a highly capable but exceedingly aggressive state at constant war with its neighbors. A millenarian movement might have been incapable of organizing effective political opposition to the colonial powers, but it might not have led to the degree of suffering actually experienced by the Vietnamese.

In the end, the decline of French colonialism was a world-wide process that gave independence to nations like Senegal that did not fight, as well as to Algeria and Vietnam that did. Thus, the millenarian movement might well have "achieved" just as much success as the "modern, political" movement that in fact swept to power. Before we can dismiss compensator-based supernatural movements, we must examine the real cost and typical benefits of the alternative political movements. When the real engine of history is inexorable demographic, economic, and technological change, superficially potent political movements may not, in fact, have anything to recommend them over apparently impotent religious movements.

Of course, one of the false assumptions of some political movements is the belief that deprived persons constitute a coherent class sharing a single set of common deprivations. But society is complex, so even coercion may concentrate in certain exchanges, and not in others, patterned complexly and experienced quite differently by various persons. Earlier, we noted the Glock and Stark hypothesis that persons with different unmet desires might be attracted to different kinds of religious movement. Religious movements that provide specific compensators are likely to specialize in pursuit of market advantages and to focus their energies on sustaining those compensators especially desired by the original members, a phenomenon to be discussed in the following chapter. Our discussions in Chapter 5 and Chapter 6 about sects and cults were based on distinctions in compensators provided by types of groups.

Consider sects, first. In Chapter 5, we showed the importance of power differentials among persons in producing sect movements. One way of summarizing the argument is in the following proposition:

> P219 Persons who desire limited rewards that exist, but who lack the social power to obtain them, will tend to affiliate with sects, to the extent that their society possesses a dominant religious tradition supported by the elite.

The last phrase of this proposition points out that sects take on significance only within a powerful religious tradition. The sect breaks away from the church, claiming that it represents the pure or revived religious tradition in contrast to the allegedly decadent church. The ideology of a sect can provide especially strong compensators for low social status and the feeling of political powerlessness. Not only does it assert that sect members are of high moral and spiritual quality, but it specifically undercuts the claims to status of the churchly elite. A cult could not undercut as effectively the claims to status of the churches because its ideology is concerned with alien symbols and assumptions that are irrelevant to the popular supernatural explanations of the tradition supported by the churches.

But what happens in societies where there is no single dominant church or religious tradition? This may be the case in conglomerate cosmopolitan societies like early Imperial Rome, or in highly secularized modern communities such as found in some parts of the American Pacific region today. Without a dominant tradition, the elite do not use a single stable set of religious symbols and explanations to express and help support their status. Instead, various more-or-less independent secular institutions perform these function for them. When low-power individuals seek compensators vis-a-vis the rewards possessed by the leaders of these secular institutions, they will find no particular advantages in a sect. The sect is in rebellion against a church that is irrelevant to such an individual's needs. Rather, such persons may be attracted to religious and magical movements that are in *specific tension* with the given high-status secular institution.

Of course, if there remains even only a faint remembrance of a religious tradition, one now abandoned by the elite, then sects in that tradition can attract recruits, for these sects will serve as counter-cultures directly accusing the elite of having abandoned the old faith. In a society such as ours, in which social networks of religious traditionalists often interweave with networks of free thinkers, one must predict a mixed outcome. But for people who have no sense of a definite religious tradition which can channel rebellion, specific compensators are best provided by cults.

For one thing, cults find it easier to specialize in compensating for particular relative deprivations, because they can be precisely designed as supernatural attacks on particular elite institutions. Thus, an individual suffering a particular set of resentments against the elite can find the right cult to give maximum compensation for the particular specific deprivations which cause misery to the individual. At the same time, differently designed cults will attract different segments of the relatively deprived. The high differentiation of conglomerate, cosmopolitan, and contemporary secular societies thus encourages differentiation in religion – a fact which stimulates cults.

But perhaps more important, in rapidly changing cultures, counter-cultures oriented against specific non-religious institutions must also change. They must aim their rhetorical guns at a set of moving targets. Under such conditions one must expect the continuous production of novel religious cultures, and this will result in a fluid tangle of cults. When no established church exists, high tension religious organizations cannot share a set of dominant religious explanations. Therefore, cults will be common.

P220 Persons who desire limited rewards that exist, but who lack the social power to obtain them. will tend to affiliate with cults, to

> the extent that their society does not posses a dominant religious tradition supported by the elite.

Our own society is a mixed case. In many communities and families, traditional religion remains a powerful force with which only sects can compete. But the more cosmopolitan sectors of our society are best attacked by cults. Therefore, the prevalence of cults and their proportion in the total mix of religious and magical groups vary geographically. Several of our most successful empirical studies have documented this fact, in one cultural context after another. Cults proliferated where the churches were weak in America in the 1920s (Stark and Bainbridge, 1981b), and in America around 1970 (Stark and Bainbridge, 1980b); Bainbridge and Stark, 1980a). We found the same to be true for contemporary Canada (Bainbridge and Stark, 1982), Western Europe (Stark, 1985), and Latin America (Stark, forthcoming).

A good contemporary example of a state-connected institution that confers great status and power is education. Many people fail in school, drop out of college, or are unable to complete professional training programs. These people become likely recruits for cults organized in opposition to the standard educational institutions. Some have achieved Bachelor's, Master's and even Doctor's degrees in *Psychorientology* from Jose Silva's Mind Control cult. Others have attended Rose-Croix University of San Jose, California, a college run by the AMORC Rosicrucian Order. Students in the occult can receive various strings of impressive initials to append after their names, indicating achievement of various obscure "degrees." At one time, Scientology offered Bachelor and Doctor degrees (Hubbard, 1954:12), and this world-wide cult currently provides compensatory military status, in its Sea Org, as well as educational status (Smith, 1968; Malko, 1970; Evans, 1973; Wallis, 1976). Cults potentially can mimic any institution of standard society, and today they function as extremely diverse and often oppositional countercultures (Tiryakian, 1972; Yinger, 1977; Richardson, 1978; Robbins, *et al.*, 1978).

We have discussed tension-deprivation stemming from unmet desires for scarce rewards monopolized by the powerful members of society. In our original explanation of low-tension religious organizations we also discussed the general compensators, such as widespread belief in an afterlife, that serves the needs all people have for universally unavailable rewards. But there is another category of compensators – those that attempt to satisfy desires for rewards that no one can obtain but which only certain people want. A cure for cancer does not exist today. Happily, only a minority of people are attacked by this dread disease. It strikes the mighty as well as the powerless. While the rich may afford more and better medical care than the poor, no amount of wealth or power can provide a reliable cure. Thousands of cancer sufferers each year turn to quack doctors providing essentially magical cures, just as members of prescientific societies would consult the aid of a shaman. We can state the general proposition:

> P221 Persons who desire specific but nonexistent rewards will tend to become customers of client cults.

Notice that we did not say they become members of client cults. They may retain their membership in the Presbyterian Church at the same time that they visit the local Krebiozen clinic or their neighborhood psychoanalyst. In the next chapter we will discuss the evolution of client cults into cult movements, a topic we mentioned earlier. It sometimes happens that the clients of a client cult are swept along and transformed into members when the organization evolves into a movement. We know of many cult movements that maintain client services as front organizations facilitating recruitment to the sponsoring movement. Examples include Scientology and Transcendental Meditation. But the desires identified in P221 do not, in themselves, attract people to cult movements. Recall that there is no church of magic.

We should also point out that client cults can exist alongside and even embedded within conventional sects and even churches. Individuals who "have the healing gift" may practice their alleged cures even inside a church, but are usually not acting as church officers in doing so. Fundamentalist faith healers are usually independent practitioners, and (as discussed in Chapter 4) they do not bring the standard religious explanations into discredit when they fail to cure. Faith healers are, strictly speaking, cult practitioners because, in a narrow but important sense, their healing gift is a new revelation. This man has it, but not another. "Oral Roberts can heal by laying on of hands," is a very elementary but definite article of faith, a terse but deviant credo. Thus, with great specificity that need not touch the wider body of church doctrine, the identification of one individual as a healer is a novel piece of culture, a non-standard explanation. The independent faith healer is practicing a client cult, even if he and his clients abjure the name.

We have just seen that relative deprivation and specific unmet desires have an effect on recruitment to religious movements. We will soon see that they are facilitating (but neither sufficient nor even necessary) conditions for affiliating. But before continuing on in examination of the steps in the Lofland-Stark model, we must show the link to Hirschi's concept of *strain theory*.

Strain

A leading source of ideas in the strain theory tradition is Neil Smelser's *Theory of Collective Behavior*. Smelser says "the central defining characteristic of an episode of collective behavior is a belief envisioning the reconstruction of some component of social action" (Smelser, 1962:11; cf. Parsons and Shils, 1962). In our terms, a belief that guides human action (including collective action) is an *explanation*. Smelser is interested in *generalized beliefs*, as he calls them, beliefs that "restructure an ambiguous situation in a short-circuited way" (Smelser, 1962:82). By "short-circuited" Smelser means "a *compressed* way of attacking problems" (Smelser, 1962:71), one faught with error and false hope and therefore one kind of compensator. While Smelser's system is ornate, and based in structural-functionalist logic quite alien to our basic assumptions, we can translate valuable parts of his system.

The "components of social action" described by Smelser are elements of the culture possessed by the society in question. For example, the first component mentioned by Smelser is the values of the society (Smelser, 1962:25). We have spoken of value as a characteristic of a reward, as judged in terms of human desires, but we have not defined the values of a culture. Smelser defines the term as follows:

> Values are the major premises of the social order; they set the bearings of society toward general kinds of ends and legitimize these ends by a particular view of man, nature, and society. (Smelser, 1962:35)

In our terms, a societal value is a very general explanation that plays a major role in the culture of a society. It seems to us that this is an exact translation of Smelser's definition into our terms. But Smelser, and many other social theorists, assume that "values" have numerous qualities which we find debatable. Therefore, we shall not incorporate the concept into our deductive system. Most importantly, Smelser assumes that a "social order" exists and that the "components of social action" form a unified system. Smelser's book contains many charts of structural analysis showing hierarchies of cultural elements, arranged from the most general to the most specific. The most general elements are "societal values."

Smelser's analysis is clearly of what we have called a *cultural system*. At the apex are the prime explanations of the system, under which ranks of more and more specific explanations are arranged. When a person or group experiences strain, it is because some relatively specific explanations have failed. The "short-circuiting" response Smelser identifies is the attempt to reconstitute the cultural system on an excessively high level, seeking a quick solution to strain by introducing a new general explanation. This discussion of Smelser may seem rather abstract. Rather than to make it clearer by a detailed and lengthy examination of Smelser's system, we shall accomplish a better and quicker clarification by looking at a simpler and more familiar version of strain theory – Merton's model of anomie.

In Merton's model, the 28 factors listed in Smelser's master table are reduced to just two: *values* and *norms*. Sometimes the values are called *goals*, and the norms are seen as *means* for achieving the goals. Merton himself sometimes mixes the pairs of terms. He specifically says that each is a type of "element of the cultural structure" (Merton, 1968:187). The values "are the things 'worth striving for'" but they are not simply "the biological drives of man." Thus, the values identify very general rewards that are believed to serve ultimate human desires, as the general reward of wealth serves the basic desires for food, drink, warmth and entertainment. A *value*, as Merton uses the term, is not the reward itself but the statement that such-and-such is a reward and a means to other rewards. He says these are "culturally defined goals, purposes and interests, held out as legitimate objectives for all or for diversely located members of the society."

As Merton and Smelser point out, values are too vague (too general) to instruct people in what they should do in specific situations. People need more specific explanations, such as norms:

> A second element of the cultural structure defines, regulates and controls the acceptable modes of reaching out for these goals. Every social group invariably couples its cultural objectives with regulations, rooted in the mores or institutions, of allowable procedures for moving toward these objectives. (Merton, 1968:187)

In principle, the norms should serve the values. People who act in accordance with the norms should be able to achieve the values. To give a Mertonian example, Americans who get a good education and then work hard at their jobs may be able to achieve the "American Dream." Of course, we do not believe that the "values" are either ultimate or arbitrary, but represent cultural solutions to the problem of fulfilling innate human needs – general explanations for achieving myriads of widely desired rewards. The relatively specific explanations of a cultural system are supposed to support the more general explanations of the cultural system. But, Merton feels, people often fail to achieve the American Dream because the norms (means) are not "effectively integrated" with the values (goals). This is the condition Smelser calls "structural strain" and is a major source of anomie, according to Merton. What, then, is this strain?

Strain is a flaw in the cultural system. While some writers refer to this as strain in the social structure of a society, by "social structure" they mean the pattern of norms that govern social relations, including those clusters of norms they call "institutions." Thus they refer to aspects of the culture that govern what we here call social structure – regular patterns of social relations – rather than to social structure itself. Strain is a flaw in a cultural system, because it is a lack of integration where integration is supposed to be found. In our terminology, cultural systems are integrated sets of explanations. Now we can give a formal definition of strain.

Def.90 *Structural strain* is a lack of integration or a contradiction between elements of a cultural system that people feel should be intimately connected and mutually supporting.

We can follow Merton a few steps further, adapting the most fruitful of his ideas for use in our theory. Many students misunderstand Merton's most famous article and think that structural strain is identical with anomie. Rather, strain is a major source of anomie, according to Merton, but the possibility is left open that some anomie has other sources.

Def.91 *Anomie* is the state of being without effective rules for living.

Anomie is a lack of good explanations for achieving the most important human goals. It might come, as in Merton's model, from a lack of integration between norms and values, or it could come (for example) from a simple absence of norms. Anomie is the link between "strain" and "tension," because tension is a subjective consequence of anomie. Strain-generated anomie has been blamed for many kinds of deviance, including participation in high-tension religious groups. Unfortunately for the strain theorists, numerous recent studies have failed to find expected evidence for a relationship between deviance and presumed indicators of strain such as low social class (Hirschi, 1969; Tittle, *et al.*, 1978; cf. Hindelang *et al.*, 1979). Our theory agrees that structural strain can exist and can provide the motivating force behind a variety of deviant actions, but it suggests that strain simply is much rarer than Merton and other strain theorists assumed. We have no reason to believe, for example, that social stratification has anything to do with cultural strain in Western nations, whose cultures endorse stratification, but stratification could conceivably produce strain in nations like the Soviet Union where official ideology opposes stratification.

We have just explained that structural strain is a rather special kind of problem, not equivalent to the general class of social problems. It is an attribute of an imperfect cultural system, recalling that:

> Def.31 Explanations form a *cultural system* if they are parts of a greater explanation that includes them.

Strain theorists, including Merton and Smelser, tend to assume that each society possesses a unified culture, that is, a cultural system. There is no reason to believe that this is ever the case, certainly not for complex, cosmopolitan societies (Bainbridge and Stark, 1981a). Instead, as we showed earlier:

> P39 Any culture contains a number of cultural systems.

Real human societies are not organized around a small number of very general prime explanations. They possess many unconnected explanations, as well as numerous more-or-less coherent structures of explanations. As we have shown at length, societies are large and relatively bounded complexes of social relationships. Nothing about societies ensures that a single set of rules will emerge to govern exchanges or to guide individual action. Least of all will this occur in large, complex, cosmopolitan societies! Thus, we have no reason to believe, and every reason to doubt, that real human societies will possess neat sets of values and norms. Since they are not cultural systems, the cultures of human societies will not be susceptible to structural strain, or to what we would prefer to call *cultural strain*. Of course, the culture may contain many poor explanations that cause people to want better substitutes. But this produces tension directly, not tension caused by strain.

Within a culture, there may exist numerous lesser cultural systems, for which strain is quite possible. As we noted in Chapter 3:

> P36 The explanations of a religion are a cultural system.

Therefore, strain is quite possible within a religious tradition. The processes through which it develops are the subject of the next section.

Religious Problem-Solving-Perspective

While the Lofland-Stark model begins with tension, a psychological state that may energize affiliation with a cult or sect, it is not sufficient to say that strong desires drive persons to join deviant religious organizations. People have other options. The 1965 model noted that tension alone could not force the people Lofland and Stark studied to join the "D.P." cult (Moonies):

> Because people have a number of conventional and readily available alternative definitions for, and means of coping with, their problems, there were, in the end, very few converts to the D.P. An alternative solution is a perspective or rhetoric defining the nature and sources of problems in living and offering some program for their resolution. Many such alternative solutions exist in modern society. Briefly, three particular genres of solution are relevant here: *the psychiatric, the political* and *the religious*. In the first, the origin of problems is typically traced to the psyche, and manipulation of the self is advocated as a solution. Political solutions, mainly radical, locate the sources of problems in the social structure and advocate reorganization of the system as a solution. The religious perspective tends to see both sources and solutions as emanating from an unseen and, in principle, unseeable realm. (Lofland and Stark, 1965:867)

Each of these three problem-solving perspectives constitutes a general explanation that might be at the heart of a cultural system shared by a number of individuals within a society. The psychiatric explanation for human problems suggests sub-explanations that help a person find means to transform himself. The political explanation for human problems suggests sub-explanations that guide people in organizing collectively to transform society. The religious explanation for human problems suggests that a person seek aid in establishing a new and better relationship between himself and the supernatural.

In the Lofland-Stark model, a person possessing a religious problem-solving perspective would normally remain faithful to the religious denomination in which he was raised. Typically, the person was instructed in religious explanations by his family and their church, and would be satisfied with their religious beliefs. He is unlikely to quit his church and join a cult. Recall the following proposition:

P120 When a person believes in a particular explanation, the person is unlikely to invest in competing explanations in which the person does not believe.

Def.64 *Belief* is positive evaluation of an explanation.

Explanations are rewards, and the loss of an explanation represents a cost. Individuals seek to preserve the rewards they possess, and therefore will cling to explanations that they have evaluated positively. We made this point in Chapter 5 when discussing religious schism.

P126 Schisms will tend to take place in the form which the tradition of religious beliefs implies will be most likely to facilitate the achievement of the desired rewards; that is, they will take place in accordance with the explanations in which the religious compensators are embedded.

This proposition can be extended to explain individual defection from a conventional denomination to a high tension religious movement. If a person has learned that religion offers contentment but has experienced acutely felt tension for a long time, he might seem to have cause to jettison his religious faith. But, again, religion is a cultural system. He can feel that his misery devalues some specific explanations within the system, but leaves the key general explanations unshaken. That is, he will continue to hope that religion will afford him contentment, but will decide that the specific form of religion given him was not the right kind. The individual faces cultural strain, and seeks to resolve it by replacing the specific explanation with one that will better serve the general explanation. Formally put:

P222 If a single explanation in a cultural system fails, people tend to seek another to replace it, without disturbing the rest of the system.

P223 When explanations in a cultural system fail, people will seek the most modest revision of it that will apparently repair the damage.

P224 A person who is convinced that religion will provide great rewards, yet has failed to receive these rewards from one religious organization, will tend to seek another religious organization with distinctly different specific explanations.

Sects can recruit defectors from churchly denominations if they can give some evidence that the domination did not really fulfill the terms of its own scriptures. The sect may credibly explain that it, unlike the denomination, can produce the promised rewards through correct application of the general explanations in the religious tradition.

Lofland and Stark described a cult that offered significantly novel specific explanations, which therefore had not been discredited, within a cultural system unified by familiar general explanations. These included belief in God and a rather unimaginative reinterpretation of the Bible. The degree of novelty required of a substitute religious explanation depends on what experiences a person may have had that disconfirmed traditional explanations.

Smelser assumed that people quickly discard explanations of intermediate generality, and short-circuit immediately to the general explanations. He gave only the most anecdotal and unsystematically acquired evidence on this point. What may look like short-curcuiting to the casual and distant observer may in fact be a complex, long process of progressive disconfirmation and experimentation with alternative explanations of medium generality. There is no warrant for Smelser's assertion, which is in direct disagreement with P222 and P223. Of course, people may discard formerly valued general explanations, but only, we suggest, if a snowballing disconfirmation has outweighed the original evaluation or if social processes unrelated to disconfirmation come to dominate. Continued failure can cause disconfirmation to spread like an infection through a cultural system:

P225 When two or more explanations fail, and are connected by a single explanation more general than they, participants in the cultural system will tend to seek a substitute for the more general explanation, and this tendency will be greater the larger the proportional value of explanations under it that have failed.

P226 Failure of numerous lower-level explanations in a cultural system tends to be communicated upward until the failure compounds to disconfirm much of the system.

P227 Persons who have experienced great misery and continued failure in obtaining rewards and effective compensators from religion will be more apt than others to accept radical religious explanations.

This last proposition, only slightly different from P224 which has smaller scope, brings us back to the tension-deprivation orientation. However, we have not yet discussed the limitations of the concept of problem-solving perspective.

Modern society possesses a very large number of popular general explanations. Some, like the psychiatric or political, may commit unhappy people to lines of action that preclude affiliation with a religious movement. But others, not the religious alone, may prepare an individual to accept cultic ideas. For example, the widespread (but often challenged) belief that all problems have technological solutions may encourage some people to try spiritual technologies like Scientology and est.

The three problem-solving perspectives named by Lofland and Stark are general explanations sustained by particular cultural specialties. Many other general explanations float through our culture, unattached to formal organizations but capable of forming the keystone in personal systems of explanation adopted by diversely located individuals. For example, innumerable scholarly essays and amateur speculations have centered on a logical pair of alternate problem-solving perspectives: *control* versus *liberation* (Bainbridge, 1978:24). These can be given many names: *Apollonian* and *Dionysian* (Nietzsche, 1872; Benedict, 1934), *tough-minded* and *tender-minded* (James, 1963), *obsessive* and *hysteric* (Freud, 1924), *control* and *cathartic* (Wallace, 1959).

According to the control perspective, personal problems are best solved through precision of thought and action under a regime of self-control. According to the liberation perspective, personal problems are best solved by freeing oneself from inhibitions and social restrictions in pursuit of self-expression. These two perspectives are based on competing general explanations that are not embedded in particular societal institutions, but may be diffused throughout the culture and adopted because of a variety of individual experiences. The two sound suspiciously like the unideal "ideal types" we have criticized, and indeed they are. Here we are not concerned with the question of whether they have scientific utility. Rather we simply note that human beings in many times and places have adopted one or the other as a valued general explanation.

An individual who accepts the liberation perspective, and who suffers enduring acutely felt tensions, will be open to recruitment appeals from an organization that itself claims to employ the liberation perspective. This observation leaves quite open the question of whether the individual will seek help from psychiatry, politics or religion. He may be entirely indifferent about this. Perhaps he will accept the first liberation appeal that comes his way. Only chance may determine whether he then participates in psychiatry, politics or religion. He may enter liberative Pschoanalysis, a radical "freedom" political party, or an antinomian religious movement. Perhaps there are many different general explanations that guide human behavior, that are irrelevant to accepting or rejecting religion, but that significantly influence the style of religious organization that can recruit an individual.

We are not suggesting that all human beings have general explanations that can be called problem-solving perspectives. When we discussed the emergence of cultural specialties, in Chapter 3, we showed that it is usually very difficult to assemble explanations into an effective cultural system (cf. Bibby, 1983). People very much want general explanations, but competing claims of alternatives are practically impossible to evaluate independently. Recall the following propositions from Chapter 2 and Chapter 4:

P13 The more valued or general a reward, the more difficult will be evaluation of explanations about how to obtain it.

P67 The more cosmopolitan a society with respect to religious culture, the lower the market value of any given general compensator.

These facts place many citizens of cosmopolitan societies in a quandry. They want general explanations, but cannot find satisfactory ones. They are ready to accept general compensators, but so many are offered they cannot trust any given one. They may not be religious seekers, but are open to a forceful appeal if it comes their way. Many writers on religion have identified this situation as a "crisis of meaning" that encourages people to accept explanations from divers sources, including new religions (Eister, 1972).

Religious Seekers at Turning Points

The 1965 model saw religious seekership as a state of mind as well as a pattern of behavior. The religious seeker actively hunts for new religious affiliation, for compensators to replace the discredited specific explanations of his former church. The prospective Moonies studied by Lofland and Stark were on quests for a religious solution to their tension.

> . . . each came to define himself as a religious seeker, a person searching for some satisfactory system of religious meaning to interpret and resolve his discontent, and each had taken some action to achieve this end. (Lofland and Stark, 1965:868)

In formulating our current theory, we realized that persons may affiliate with cults and sects without a prior state of active searching. Also, Stark had long ago noted that some persons are chronic seekers, unwilling or unable to commit themselves to any religious group for more than a few weeks. These facts need to be explained.

Concurrent with religious seekership, the prospective Moonies had reached turning points in their lives:

> That is, each had come to a moment when old lines of action were complete, had failed or been disrupted, or were about to be so, and when they faced the opportunity (or necessity), and possibly the burden, of doing something different with their lives. (Lofland and Stark, 1965:870)

To some extent, this concept overlaps that of religious seekership. A person whose religion has failed him and seeks a new affiliation is at a religious turning point. Lofland and Stark listed other "lines of action," particularly life careers, that may come to turning points. A person leaves school, moves to a new town, sees children grow up and leave home, fails in business, or experiences some other life transition. The early Moonies had generally experienced changes that were also disasters, but turning points are frequently reached by happier routes: graduation as well as flunking out, neolocal marriage as well as divorce, promotion as well as termination, retirement as well as unemployment, recovery of health as well as onset of disease. It has long been known that geographical mobility promotes new religious affiliation, in the most simple case because the new town lacks a church of the former denomination (Roberts, 1968; Flora, 1973; Hadaway, 1978:325–326). Therefore, unlike religious seekership, turning point does not necessarily imply abnormally high tension. A turning point requires a person to seek new rewards, but does not indicate a person has failed to find them through habitual means.

The sourced of religious seekership were covered in the previous section, but it is important to note that seekership does not necessarily follow from failure during membership in a religious group. Seekership is an intermediate stage that begins when commitment to one religious affiliation collapses and ends when a new commitment is established. Thus it is rather like the transition stage in many initiation rituals described by van Gennep (1960). Similarly, it becomes entangled in religious ideology and may be used as a compensator. Our arguments about the myth of conversion, at he beginning of this chapter, could easily be extended to show why people might like to conceive of new recruits as religious seekers who have just ended their quest in ultimate success. New members frequently testify that "conversion" constituted a turning point in their lives, and will retrospectively reconstruct their autobiographies to make "conversion" the necessary outcome of a personal odyssey of turning points strung like beads on the thread of seekership.

Testimonials are exchanges in which a person tells a dramatic story in return for the attention and approval of his audience. A neophyte is typically rewarded for giving a glowing testimonial of his previous unhappiness, divinely inspired seekership, and joyful conversion because such a story rewards the group by raising the market value of its compensators. Therefore, these stories are frequently exaggerated while persons with very different affiliation histories may keep silent altogether. The alternatives to seekership are a smooth transition from one affiliation to another or recruitment from a contented state of no religious affiliation.

In its cleanest version, the 1965 model assumes that the individual enters seekership before achieving contact with the cult. This is most likely, of course, when cults are rare and socially segregated so that few people normally have contact with them unless they are on an active search for religious novelty. Recall that Lofland and Stark had to hunt for a long time before they could find a new cult, while just a half dozen years later the West Coast was teeming with novel religious movements. In cosmopolitan societies, cults may proliferate, and many people will have friends or other associates who belong to minority religious groups. Under these circumstances, when current religious affiliation begins to fail a person's needs, he can shift quickly and easily to a new affiliation, without necessarily even articulating a sense of dissatisfaction. This is most likely if both groups profess norms of religious tolerance and do not punish a person who spends some time with the other.

We can also look at this in terms of the amount of increase in the degree of tension with the surrounding socio-cultural environment and in terms of the degree of coercion inflicted on religious deviance.

P228 When a person transfers from one religious affiliation to another, the tendency for him to pass through a stage of religious seekership is greater the greater the increment in tension with the sociocultural environment entailed by the transfer.

Def.92 *Religious seekership* is the state of a person unsatisfied with currently available religious affiliation and carrying out exchanges in search of more satisfying affiliation.

P229 When a person transfers from one religious affiliation to another, the tendency for him to pass through a stage of religious seekership is less the more cosmopolitan the society in which he lives.

To be a religious seeker, a person must accept the very general explanation that great rewards can be gained through participation in religion, but he must be dissatisfied with the compensators (and rewards) offered by past affiliations. Remember that the person really wants only rewards, but accepts compensators as possible paths to reward. Explanations promising relatively specific rewards are more susceptible to test than explanations offering general compensators. Therefore, persons with acute needs for scarce specific rewards, and who already accept the general explanations provided by religion, are more likely than others to experience disillusionment with one religious affiliation, to seek another, and subsequently to become disillusioned with that one and seek further.

P230 Persons with acute unmet needs for relatively specific rewards are more likely than other people to become religious seekers.

P231 Persons with acute unmet needs for scarce or nonexistent relatively specific rewards are more likely than other people to become chronic religious seekers.

During several episodes of field research, both authors of this volume have observed many chronic seekers who go from one religious movement to another, never settling with one group. The more rapidly a person rushes from group to group, the more obviously he is a religious seeker, and we were mainly impressed by those who stayed no more than a few days in their latest affiliation. Careful observation over time, however, revealed that some people stick with a new group for as long as several months, or even a year, before seeking further. To their dismay, the Shakers had to contend with thousands of seekers and temporary exploiters over many years (Whitworth, 1975; Bainbridge, 1982, 1984a). The length of a cycle of attraction and disillusionment may be determined by several factors. The following section of this chapter will show that affiliation for a significant period is likely to solidify into permanent membership as powerful social bonds are developed with other people in the group. The fact remains, however, that people with very specific desires may not suffer disillusionment until after some time as members, and therefore a large portion of the apparent membership of religious movements at any moment may consist of slow seekers who will not remain indefinitely.

One factor in the cycle of chronic seekership is the short-term flow of unusual social rewards that frequently marks the early stages of recruitment of an individual by a movement. The newcomer is often treated as a person of great value, as a great reward for which members are willing to expend significant costs. Even high-status members of a sect or cult often lavish great personal attention on the newcomer. Many times, we have seen chronic seekers given center stage in group meetings, inundated with solicitations and professions of love. Temporarily, the newcomer has a very favorable exchange ratio, but the group cannot continue this expensive series of exchanges indefinitely. Some newcomers turn out to offer the group significant rewards on a continuing basis, thereby maintaining the rewards they receive in return at a fairly high level. But newcomers who turn out to be low value members will experience a precipitous decline in exchange ratio and rewards. This may drive them to leave the group and experience another rush of rewards in brief affiliation with another group.

> P232 Religious seekers who are of less value to groups they contact than they initially appear will tend to become chronic seekers.

This process is encouraged if the seeker has experienced cycles already, and has thereby learned that an increase in exchange ratio can be obtained temporarily by switching to a new movement. Some persons may wander from group to group at first simply because the compensators offered by them are not satisfactory solutions for strong specific needs. After a couple of cycles, however, they may learn about the process we have just described and become confirmed in their seekership in perpetual search for the rush of rewards many groups lavish on new or prospective members.

> P233 Religious seekers who have already experienced a number of cycles of affiliation and disaffiliation are apt to continue in chronic seekership.

A further justification for this proposition comes from the fact that continued disillusionment tends to devalue even the general explanations upon which the quest is based, and therefore the person will be less and less willing to make the costly investment that may be required to become a committed member of a movement.

Yet another factor encourages chronic seekership. Defection from a low-tension church to a high-tension cult or sect is inhibited by the costs of going to higher tension. But a person who has already joined one high-tension group, but who has perhaps not established valued ties to group members, can shift to another without any further increase in tension. Taken together, the considerations above predict a high level of chronic seekership among persons receiving specific compensators at the high-tension level. The force that might prevent someone in a high-tension group from becoming a chronic seeker is the power of the social bond. But, bonds aside, we can state the following principles:

P234 Chronic religious seekership is most common around high-tension religious groups.

P235 A chronic seeker tends to stay at about the same level of tension, while going from group to group.

Note that chronic seekership cannot simply be operationalized as frequent shifts in nominal affiliation. Persons at the low-tension end of the spectrum, in religiously pluralist and cosmopolitan societies, may experience little cost in drifting from one denomination to another, moved by random shifts in their secular affiliations rather than by seekership.

The Lofland-Stark model says that new affiliations are especially likely at a turning point in the person's life. In compressed form, this restates several propositions we gave in our discussion of religious schism in Chapter 5. Recall the four concepts we introduced then:

Def.61 *Attachment* is positive evaluation of an exchange partner.

Def.62 *Investments* are costs expended in an exchange which have not yet yielded their full potential of desired rewards.

Def.63 *Involvement* is that proportion of one's total resources that one invests in an exchange.

Def.64 *Belief* is positive evaluation of an explanation.

It follows from the discussion in Chapter 5 that a person is less apt to leave a religious organization the more strongly he is attached to its members, the greater his current investment in the group, the more fully he is involved in its projects, and the more he believes in its explanations. Similarly, to the extent that a person has these bonds to institutions or social groups that are not religious, he would still risk something if he joined a high-tension movement. Turning points are moments when one or more of these aspects of the social bond are unusually weak, and therefore mark a new condition of greater freedom to join a religious movement.

P236 Persons are more likely to join religious movements at turning points in their lives.

Def.93 A *turning point* is a period of markedly decreased attachment, investment, involvement and belief, taken singly or in any combination.

Of course, this proposition is merely a special case of the general principles enunciated in Chapter 5. Some persons are always low on these four measures, or remain low for an extended period of time that cannot be called a point. Just above, we discussed the tendency toward chronic seekership, or religiously-oriented people who need but never find certain specific rewards or compensators. They are not at turning points, except perhaps in the beginning. Instead they are in protracted slumps that might stretch out to become chronic misery. Some people, however, may be caught in chronic cycles of commitment and collapse in the non-religious aspects of their lives. For example, chronically unstable romantic relationships, caused by anything from personal pathology to the annual cycle of a boarding school far from home, may leave a person without a partner every few months. Intermittent employment, whether from repeated failure or from seasonal agricultural work, may again and again leave a person with nothing to do. These people live lives marked by turning point after turning point. In societies where many sects and cults are available, this intermittently explosive lifestyle may lead to a sequence of short-term affiliations with religious movements, or at least oscillations in participation in a single group over time.

P237 People who repeatedly experience turning points in their lives are more likely than other people to become chronic religious seekers.

To this point, the chapter has stressed motivation and the explanantions that guide people in seeking rewards and in accepting compensators. The discussion has mainly focused on psychology and culture, with sociological forces implied and sometimes mentioned but not given their proper central role. Indeed, without the power of social relationships, the people attracted to religious movements might all become chronic religious seekers, wandering lost in a world of confusion.

We now turn to the three concluding steps in the 1965 model, reconceptualized in terms of the social exchanges out of which any religious organization is built and through which true affiliation takes place.

The three concluding steps of the Lofland-Stark model describe the development of strong social ties linking the neophyte with members of the religious movement, weakening of ties to outsiders, and the imposition of social control through intensive interaction. It is social exchange that fulfills the process of affiliation begun with the earlier steps. Each of the steps described to this point facilitates recruitment to a high-tension religious group, but is neither necessary nor sufficient. We have explained some of the social conditions that deactivate or amplify the effect of each of these factors. Now we complete the model with the one, essential factor: the social bond (Noyes, 1870; Stark and Bainbridge, 1980a; Snow and Phillips, 1980; Snow *et al.*, 1980; Rochford, 1982).

P65 The value an individual places on a general compensator is set through exchanges with other persons.

This statement was limited to general compensators only because specific compensators can often be disconfirmed through practical test by an individual. A positive evaluation of a specific compensator, as a rule, will also come through exchanges with other persons. Recall also:

P66 When there is disagreement over the value of an explanation, the individual will tend to set a value that is a direct averaging function of the values set by others and communicated to him through exchanges, weighted by the value placed on such exchanges with each partner.

This proposition is reminiscent of the classic Theory of Differential Association (Sutherland and Cressey, 1974), but is not identical either with the original statement of the theory nor the interesting recent restatment of it in terms of learning theory (Burgess and Akers, 1966; cf. Scott, 1971). We cannot interrupt our derivations here to examine deviance theories in detail, so a few words must suffice.

Differential Association implies that individuals are influenced by the intensity, frequency, and other attributes of the messages they receive from others. The learning theory version is straightforwardly behavioristic, asserting that people will accept those messages for which they are directly rewarded. Both these positions seem reasonable to us, and both may contribute to the learning of doctrine by persons who are already members of a deviant religious movement. Our proposition points out that individuals may be influenced to believe without either frequent stimulation by the doctrinal message or direct social reinforcement for professing belief. Proposition 66 does say that persons in search of a scarce reward, and faced with alternative compensators, will tend to accept the particular compensator offered by exchange partners who have previously provided valuable rewards. This means that even highly motivated, first-time religious seekers will be unlikely to accept a compensator for their acute desire unless it is offered by people with whom they have already enjoyed rewarding exchanges.

P238 Religious seekers will not accept new compensators, and be willing to expend costs over time to maintain them, until they experience repeated rewarding exchanges with other persons who already accept the compensators.

In accordance with the general explanation that guides the seeker's quest, the person will tend to invest some time and energy investigating a new compensator-package that promises to meet his needs. But the person is a religious seeker only because another compensator-package failed him earlier. Therefore, he will already be convinced that religious groups can fail him, and will not persist in dealings with a new group forever, unless it promptly provides him with social or other rewards that make members valuable to him. Only after the people in the group have proven their worth can their influence prove the worth of the compensators they offer.

Neophytes do not merely accept the specific compensators that soothe their own special needs. They also come to accept other aspects of the belief structure. There are two reasons for this. First of all, we have shown that religious beliefs tend to be organized in a cultural system. In an intellectual structure of this kind, specific compensators are linked to general explanations, and through them to the other specific compensators. Each belief either supports or depends upon the others. There may not be strict logical connections binding the separate beliefs together, but at the very least there is an assertion that the explanations do fit together. Although propositions given earlier in this chapter showed that people tend to preserve as much of a cultural system as possible when any segment of it is disconfirmed, that defense is not accomplished without cost. Even the hint of potential disconfirmation of one part of a system announces the risk that other parts will fall as well.

P239 Persons who believe in some parts of a strict cultural system will tend to believe in the other parts as well, although they will be prepared to expend the greatest costs for those parts of the system that directly meet their personal needs.

The second reason why individuals tend to accept more of a religion than just the compensators that particularly meet their own needs is that a religious organization is a structure of exchanges involving people with needs for other compensators. Suppose the person we are considering has very low self-esteem (but good health) and receives a boost in subjective worth from the religious group. Suppose that other members suffer chronic ill health and derive great comfort from aspects of doctrine and ritual focused on curing or hope of perfect health in a future Heaven. The unhealthy members will reward the man who has low self-esteem for supporting the value of faith healing, and he will come to believe in it even though he might never have wanted this benefit for himself. In Chapter 4, we explained that disagreement reduces the value of a compensator, a fact derived from P66 quoted immediately above. Consider the following we stated then:

P67 The more cosmopolitan a society with respect to religious culture, the lower the market value of any given general compensator.

This is true because the value of the compensator is supported through social exchanges, and the more nearly unanimous a person's exchange partners are, the more secure in his evaluation he will be. This principle applies to any social system, no matter how large or small. Therefore, individuals who have need of compensators will tend to reward unanimity and fail to reward or even punish people with views that would upset the system.

P240 Members of a religious organization tend to reward others who support the beliefs of the religion and tend to punish or break off relations with those who oppose the beliefs.

P241 Newcomers to a religious organization will be influenced through exchanges to accept the entire system of beliefs of the religion.

These principles are universal, but the degree of their power varies across religious groups. Low-tension denominations may have very few specific compensators in their system, and their general compensators may be associated with only the vaguest explanations. Today, members of Episcopalian churches may get by with only the most indistinct faith in God, and need not have any clarity in their definition of God. There is not much to argue about between such denominations. Thus, at this high level of abstraction, we may not really be dealing with cosmopolitan religious culture. There is wide consensus in our society over the most general compensators, like the existence of God – and the propositions concerning dissensus do not apply. At the other extreme are high-tension religious groups that adhere to doctrines of great specificity that support a system of numerous specific compensators. Thus, P241 applies only weakly to low-tension religious organizations, but applies with a vengeance to high-tension groups.

P242 Within a religious group, pressures toward doctrinal conformity are greater the higher the tension of the group.

This is true because compensators highly valued by many members are easily threatened by competing compensators and other explanations. Of course, they are threatened not only by discordant messages from within the group, but also from outside. This threat is all the greater for small high-tension groups surrounded by non-believers. There is an extra cost added to exchanges with persons who do not accept the compensator-package. Exchanges with outsiders that lack solid profitability to outweigh this increased cost, are likely to be terminated. This is especially true of relationships based on pure sociability – outside friendships. New members will acquire friendships within the group to offset friendships forsworn with outsiders, and perhaps they can even recruit their friends to the group. Relationships with a familial or economic basis may not be given up as easily, because special rewards are exchanged in them that confer continuing competitive advantage. Thus we can derive one of the attributes of a high-tension religious group, clannishness (Dynes, 1957; Balswick *et al.*, 1970; Bainbridge and Stark, 1980c).

P243 Members of high-tension religious groups tend to have a high proportion of their social relationships with other members, this tendency being limited primarily by the inability of members to give each other all commonly available desired rewards.

This fact has implications for recruitment of new members, which we mainly examine in the following chapter. Now we must backtrack, and summarize the argument to this point.

We have shown that the unmet desires that drive religious seekers and prepare them to accept specific compensators are not sufficient to result in new religious convictions. The development of valued new social relations with members – the affiliation process – is essential. But, beyond this, persons who are not driven actively to seek new religious compensators will also be brought to accept them if they happen to become members of the social group that constitutes the membership of the religious body. There is, of course, a spectrum of possible degrees of seekership running from the religiously indifferent to the religiously desperate. These differences in motivation may produce very different patterns of behavior – the confirmed seeker seeks. But the seeker does not find faith, nor does the non-seeker serendipitously discover it, unless new beliefs are supported through valuable social relationships.

For the person who does not become an active seeker, yet who ultimately develops a new religious affiliation, two patterns of religious career are possible. Either the person develops a new set of valued social relationships with persons sharing membership in a particular group. Or the person's habitual exchange partners may themselves transfer to a new religious affiliation, bring new influences to bear on him, and draw him along with them. Of course, these two possibilities may combine in any proportion, but we can most easily conceive of them separately. In the first case, as we determined earlier, a religious person weak in religious affiliation is a good candidate for recruitment. But the principle goes beyond this. Persons low in social relationships are not just low in religious affiliation, but also low in rewarding social exchanges altogether. Therefore, they are open to new relationships, among which may be some that press new religious affiliation on them.

> P244 Persons low in social relationships are more likely than others to become members of a new religious group.

This proposition includes people who are not guided by a religious problem-solving perspective and who may not have suffered tension of great scope or duration. The principle applies with special strength to high-tension religious groups, because someone low in social relationships has less to lose in moving to high tension. We state P244 without describing the kind of religious organization involved, because it does apply to transfer from one group to another at constant tension, and to transfers that involve some decrease in tension, as well as to movement to higher tension. The other principles are also familiar, if more complex:

> P245 When a person's most rewarding exchange partners transfer to a new religious affiliation, the person is likely to transfer with them.

P246 Expanding religious movements will gain much of their new membership by chains of recruitment spreading through preexisting networks of social relationships.

Further implications of P246 will be examined in the following chapter. For now, we can note that these networks of social relationships may include kinship structures, friendships, and less personal economic ties. These propositions say nothing about the personal set of compensator needs of the recruit, but do imply something about the balance of needs for compensators of people around him. We must explain why a person's exchange partners gain new affiliation before we can explain the new influences that come to bear on the individual.

P247 A person whose valued exchange partners include many who lack the power to obtain scarce rewards is apt to become a member of a high-tension religious movement, under the influence of his partners, quite apart from the person's own power to obtain scarce rewards.

This proposition is an extension of P245 and P65. The sequence is as follows: in general, persons who lack the power to obtain scarce rewards are open to accepting religious compensators. Appropriate compensators are best distributed by high-tension groups. Therefore, a goodly proportion of such people will join high-tension groups. They will influence their exchange partners, including those of somewhat greater power, to join the groups as well. Powerful recruits to a new religious movement are likely to take over leadership positions or find other reasons to remain as committed members, even though they did not begin as religious seekers. We are not saying that high-tension groups are particularly able to recruit powerful neophytes. Far from it. But some such folk may be recruited, even if the bulk of new members are of a different kind.

In a cosmopolitan society which inflicts few if any punishments for experimentation with novel religious alternatives, cults may recruit with special success among the relatively advantaged members of society. Of course many categories of person in the powerful classes still suffer various deprivations (cf. Simon and Gagnon, 1976). Sometimes they seek rewards, such as health or beauty, which their social power cannot give them. Also, many individuals within the elite are individually weak in power. They may achieve very favorable exchange ratios in their dealings with members of other classes, but in exchanges with many other members of the elite, they lose. Such persons suffering special deprivations, while enjoying the general power of their class in society, may be open to systems of compensators which most of their fellow elite would reject. The success of a magician like Rasputin with the Czarina has been repeated many thousands of times over throughout history.

While some members of the elite may be so estranged from their fellows that they affiliate with a sect, more likely they will be open to a cult-like manifestation of the established church, or to a full-fledged cult if the society permits them near its heart. A sect accuses the elite and offers specific compensators that undercut the exact rewards the elite possesses as a class. But an innovative cult is not oriented in opposition to the state church. It can offer a set of compensators outside the political antagonisms which divide the elite from other citizens, and focus instead on providing compensators for particular sets of citizens with a shared set of desires that wish to add something to the power of the elite while preserving it. Thus there may be an easily-reached constituency for novel religion, but not for a high-tension sect, among advantage members of the society.

But another reason for the possible success of cults among the elite rests on the fact that novel cults represent cultural innovation, a special case of a more general process of invention and diffusion. To spread rapidly beyond their social origins, cults must transmit novel religious explanations through extended social networks. This implies diffusion through the network of the advantaged, for two reasons.

First of all, the advantaged are generally more able to create and maintain wide-ranging extended social networks than are the deprived. Since networks are composed of interlocking exchange relationships, a network will be more extensive, including more kinds of exchanges for more valued rewards, if its members possess the power to obtain many rewards. Enjoying more different kinds of exchange relationship, through which a wider selection of rewards is obtained, members of the elite may have exceedingly wide social networks. No doubt, many factors may shape social networks. But in cosmopolitan societies the elite will tend to possess networks that are more open and more extensive than those possessed by the lower classes (cf. Whyte, 1943; Bott, 1955; Young and Willmott, 1957, 1973; Gans, 1962a, 1962b; Granovetter, 1973; Milgram, 1977).

Secondly, in a cosmopolitan society, one in which the elite accepts and supports cultural pluralism and thus encourages cultural novelty, the elite will believe in the general explanation that new explanations are valuable. This means they will accept a doctrine of progress, which by P120 means low resistance to religious "progress." Now, all members of the society may share this belief to some extent. But the elite are the ones with relatively more power – thus with both the surplus resources to experiment with new explanations and, through such institutions as higher education, the power to obtain potentially valuable new explanations before others do, in the same manner that they can obtain other rewards.

While sects may reject progress in hearkening back to their old religious tradition, cults plausibly can claim to represent progress. Sects, which do not require transmission of new culture, may be able to invade a particular local community of relatively deprived persons rapidly through the missionary work of an effective leader. Cults, however, do require transmission of new culture, and often the market is prepared for acceptance of one cult organization by the general explanations diffused earlier from similar cult organizations. Thus, in our own society, Psychoanalysis may have promulgated general explanations which made success easier for General Semantics and Scientology, because these later cults did not have to educate prospective recruits to the idea that depth psychology could provide techniques for self improvement. So, cults will find growth easier through the same social channels which most readily transmit other innovations. Thus, cults may spread more readily through the extensive, progress-oriented social network of a cosmopolitan elite (cf. Katz and Lazarsfeld, 1955; Katz, 1960; Rogers, 1960). When the conditions are as describe, cults will be more able than sects to recruit among the advantaged, while sects will garner the relatively-deprived. Stated as propositions, this argument becomes:

P248 The social networks of advantaged persons tend to be more extensive than those of the relatively deprived.

P249 New culture not exclusively oriented toward a particular non-elite subgroup in society tends to spread more rapidly through networks of the advantaged than of the relatively deprived.

P250 In cosmopolitan societies which possess a doctrine of progress, cults not designed to appeal to particular deprived groups spread more rapidly among advantaged members of society.

Certainly, these propositions are based on complex, long chains of logic extending back through many prior derivations, and one might raise numerous hypothetical counter-examples and other objections. For example, one might argue that today novel deviant culture spreads most rapidly among the relatively-deprived because the mass media transmit culture without the necessity of an extended social network. But earlier derivations showed that cults, and other religious organizations, do depend primarily upon network transmission. And, as noted above, contemporary empirical studies do support our conclusion that the elite, in cosmopolitan societies, is a fertile ground for cult recruitment.

Conclusion

This chapter has developed our exchange theory of religion to explain basic principles motivating and channeling affiliation with high-tension religious organizations. We based our analysis in the Lofland-Stark "model of conversion to a deviant perspective," an influential, eclectic model now twenty years old and the historical starting point for our own deliberations. As we went through the steps of the model, we criticized and adapted elements of other classical perspectives. The result is not only empirically sound (Stark and Bainbridge, 1985), supported by available evidence, but also merits consideration by social scientists because it draws together the main ideas of other perspectives, thus fulfilling the work of earlier theorists as well as modifying it.

We showed that the tension-deprivation-strain theories explain much, but not everything, about affiliation to high-tension religious movements. We showed some of the social factors that either amplify or deactivate the effects of tension, deprivation and strain. We saw that individual socialization to cultural patterns had important and sometimes complex effects. But the key factor, always necessary and occasionally sufficient, is the differential development of social relationships with outsiders and group members.

The next chapter will introduce more propositions about affiliation with high-tension religious movements, in a discussion of the alternative developmental tracks that such movements can take.

CHAPTER 8:
EVOLUTION OF RELIGIOUS MOVEMENTS

This chapter outlines the factors determining the fate of a new religious movement. Will it prosper, or will it die? Will it remain at high tension with the sociocultural environment, or will it gradually reduce its tension until it becomes a conventional denomination? These are the classic questions. Indeed, for present purposes, tension is again the most salient variable. Where first we discussed sects and cults separately, here as in the previous chapter we consider them together, and the characteristic they share is tension, which is synonymous with subcultural religious deviance:

Def.57 A *sect movement* is a deviant religious organization with traditional beliefs and practices.

Def.58 A *cult movement* is a deviant religious organization with novel beliefs and practices.

The analysis here is firmly based in our analyses of schism, innovation, and recruitment, discussed in the three preceding chapters. If a religious movement develops significant internal differences in members' ability to obtain personal rewards vesus the need for compensators, schism is its likely fate. Our analysis of innovation showed not only that client cults can evolve into high-tension cult movements, but also that small sects can become cults and that cultic innovation can continue with great consequence long after a cult's formation. The conditions of recruitment are also in great measure the conditions for growth of a movement, because biological fertility is not sufficient to support the rapid growth needed to establish a new movement as a permanent fixture of the society, and high levels of recruitment are usually needed to offset defection (cf. Stark and Roberts, 1982).

An important earlier proposition was P131, which stated that the potential for group conflict over the distribution of rewards and the emphasis on compensators is present in all religious bodies. Members dispute among themselves over the future course of the group. Some are more inclined toward maintaining or increasing the tension of the group; others want tension reduced. In following sections we will examine the consequences of this internal contradiction in great detail, beyond what was said in the chapter on schism. But let us begin by restating some main points from that earlier discussion, observations that apply to the evolution of high-tension groups as well as to their birth:

P145 In any religious body, the less powerful will tend to prefer relatively higher tension with the external society.

P146 In any religious body, the more powerful will tend to prefer relatively lower tension with the external society.

P147 The lower the tension of a religious group, the greater and more valuable the supply of rewards it can earn from the outside and provide to members.

P148 The lower the state of tension of a religious group, the greater the demand generated among the less powerful members for more efficacious compensators.

While there are differences of need and power within any group, factions and categories of members vary in how large and distinct they are. In these respects, the internal structure of a group will greatly determine its future history. Thus, the pressures toward higher or lower tension depend in great measure upon the character of members recruited, especially the degree of their diversity and the distribution of power and rewards among them.

Diversity

It would be simplistic to assume that high-tension religious groups are born having members who are identical to each other in power and needs. Proposition 200 said that in all societies and all organizations, people vary in the degree to which they have stakes in conformity. This means that the costs of religious deviance differ among members of high-tension groups. But, of course, power and rewards vary also. Our analyses both of schism and innovation gave an important role to leaders, whether formal or informal, and leaders constitute a relatively powerful elite within any society or social group. To the extent that a new religious group is a self-contained society, it is bound to illustrate axiom 7, which states that individual and social attributes which determine power are unequally distributed among persons and groups in any society.

Hypothetically, it is possible to skim off from a society a thin stratum of people with virtually identical rewards and needs. But if this category begins to interact as a group, somewhat removed from whatever factors made them so uniform in the first place, it has the quality of society and it will develop its own inequalities in accordance with Axiom 7. No religious group is completely homogeneous in membership, and even those most fiercely dedicated to norms of equality display marked inequality (Nordhoff, 1875; Della Fave and Hillery, 1980). Much of this chapter derives the course of evolution of a high-tension religious group from the fact of inquality, and this section notes that groups begin with a measure of heterogeneity, while other sections note the further development of salient differences among members.

Although high-tension religious groups tend to recruit persons who experience extreme relative deprivation within the larger society, some less-deprived persons also join, as it were by mistake. Proposition 247 states that social bonds can draw in the less-deprived along with their more-deprived exchange partners:

> P247 A person whose valued exchange partners include many who lack the power to obtain scarce rewards is apt to become a member of a high-tension religious movement, under the influence of his partners, quite apart from the person's own power to obtain scarce rewards.

Furthermore, human action is guided by individuals' perceptions of reality, not by the objective facts. People who feel they are deprived and feel they lack the power to obtain rewards, comparing themselves with the circumstances they imagine other people enjoy, will be drawn toward high-tension groups. Proposition 133 notes it is very difficult for individuals to achieve accurate evaluations of themselves. Therefore, some among those who join high-tension cults and sects are mistaken that they lack the power to obtain scarce rewards. Unless their lack of confidence is so extreme as to incapacitate them in social exchanges, they will act more successfully than others in their new congregation. Their actual power will contribute to diversity within the group, despite their illusions of powerlessness. Thus we can say:

> P251 Individual and social attributes which determine power are unequally distributed among participants in any new religious group at the time of its formation.

However, religious groups differ in how narrow or how broad is this distribution of power among the members. Smaller, higher-tension groups generally will have narrower distributions than will larger, established denominations. One factor significant in determining the breadth of distribution is the degree of coercion imposed by the social environment. Proposition 212 and 213 explained that individuals must endure greater costs and therefore must be in search of greater rewards in joining a high-tension group when the society imposes great penalties on religious deviance. From this, we derived the following proposition:

P214 The greater the degree of coercion the external society imposes on religious deviance, the more restricted the range of persons likely to join deviant religious organizations.

For a deviant religious group to reduce (or increase) its tension after formation, it must have or develop a constituency desiring a different level of tension from that desired at the birth of the organization. True, the fortunes of all members may shift in unison, bringing the entire group to a different level of reward and consequent willingness to accept specific compensators. But as our chapter on schism showed (and we shall here further demonstrate), it is often the tug-of-war between factions that moves a religious group toward lower or higher tension. Below we will analyze the impact of random external influences and the emergence of a second generation of members, but alongside these factors the degree of inquality within a religious group is decisive for tension reduction. Very narrow distributions of power fail to impell change of any kind. Very high differences in power precipitate schism, as P130 noted, when schism is possible under other terms of our earlier analysis. At middle distributions, the more powerful desire less tension and have exchange relationships with other members of sufficient mutual benefit to move the group toward lower tension. Therefore:

P252 High-tension religious groups with very narrow distributions of power among members are unlikely to decrease in tension.

P253 High-tension religious groups with medium distributions of power among members tend to move toward lower tension.

P254 High-tension religious groups with broad distributions of power among members are likely to undergo schism.

This last case, of course, results in two or more schismatically-formed groups to which P252 and P253 may apply. The resultant groups will tend to have narrower distributions than the original group – permitting one (a church movement) to reduce tension, and one (a sect movement) to maintain high tension. Since the shape of the power distribution is partly determined by the degree of coercion imposed upon religious deviance, the likely course of high-tension groups also depends upon the degree of coercion:

> P255 High-tension religious groups formed in societies which impose great coercion on religious deviance are unlikely to decrease in tension.

This observation also is supported by a consideration of the entire range of relations between high-tension groups and their social environment. A hostile environment means more hostility returned, a greater separation between the deviant religious and outsiders, and pressures toward greater cultural differences. Thus, if there is any room for change at all, high-tension groups formed in such societies will tend to increase in tension shortly after formation, and will enjoy little opportunity to decrease tension later on. The isolation and quality of membership in high-tension groups are discussed in the following sections which stress that at levels of tension less than the most extreme there are many sources of diversity in the group's membership, and several mechanisms that translate diversity into tension reduction.

Social Isolation

In their pursuit of specific compensators, and often possessing an intensity of dedication to general compensators unusual in low-tension groups, sects and cults are pressed to become or remain at rather high tension with the sociocultural environment. As earlier chapters showed, this means there is a strong tendency for them to be socially closed groups that experience a measure of social implosion at the time of their formation.

> Def.27 A portion of a network is *closed* to the extent that a high proportion of members' relationships are with other members.

Def.85 In a *social implosion*, part of a relatively open social network becomes markedly more closed.

P138 Persons who possess a compensator for a scarce reward will avoid explanations that identify the corresponding reward as indeed the true reward.

P185 The more socially closed a group, the more readily it can generate and sustain compensators through exchanges among members.

P186 The more thoroughly interconnected a group, the more readily it can generate and sustain compensators through exchanges among members.

P219 Persons who desire limited rewards that exist, but who lack the social power to obtain them, will tend to affiliate with sects, to the extent that their society possesses a dominant religious tradition supported by the elite.

P220 Persons who desire limited rewards that exist, but who lack the social power to obtain them, will tend to affiliate with cults, to the extent that their society does not possess a dominant religious tradition supported by the elite.

P240 Members of a religious organization tend to reward others who support the beliefs of the religion and tend to punish or break off relations with those who oppose the beliefs.

P242 Within a religious group, pressures toward doctrinal conformity are greater the higher the tension of the group.

P243 Members of high-tension religious groups tend to have a high proportion of their social relationships with other members, this tendency being limited primarily by the inability of members to give each other all commonly available desired rewards.

Most of these propositions apply equally both to sects and to cults. Propositions 219 and 220 identify a tendency for some societies to produce more sects than cults, and for other societies to produce more cults than sects. In societies possessing a dominant religious tradition, cults will be rare and those that come into being will be in quite high tension. Societies lacking a dominant religious tradition not only have more cults but also are less likely to punish religious deviance of either kind. In societies of the latter type, many of our propositions about tension reduction (derived both above and below) have less force. Since cults are more common in less coercive societies, and since cults as innovative groups by difinition are prepared to adapt even by abandonment of basic principles, the typical cult may be in a better position to reduce its tension than is the typical sect. Indeed, a great body of recent evidence on the characteristics of persons recruited to cults suggests that in cult-prone areas of Western Society the most successful cults seem to act like relatively low-tension groups, attracting persons who hold favored positions in society rather than being severely deprived (Wilson, 1961; Nelson, 1972; Church of Scientology, 1978; Nordquist, 1978; Wuthnow, 1978; Barker, 1981; Volinn, 1982, Stark and Bainbridge, 1985). These points should be kept in mind as we examine principles that apply to both kinds of religious movement.

The tendency for a new high-tension group to retreat from social relations with outsiders is encouraged by the personal histories of people it recruits. Proposition 122 noted that schisms will be most likely in groups that contain marked social cleavages, and P121 says the formation of a new sect will tend to take place along these cleavages. Therefore, a newly-formed sect will start with relatively few social bonds linking members with outsiders. To the extent that a cult is formed partly through schism, it also will begin life in some measure of social isolation. Of course, cults that form through incremental compensator-generation tend to be small, relatively closed and interconnected, and to experience social implosion. Cults founded by individuals, whether they be psychopaths or entrepreneurs, come into being according to the laws of recruitment to a deviant religious organization, as the founder gathers converts to his new creed. The realities of recruitment to high-tension sects and cults will favor social isolation.

Recall that those most willing to accept specific compensators are the relatively deprived among the citizens of a society. These unfortunates include many who lack valued exchange partners who might provide rewards possessed by other citizens. Such people are low in attachments, as well as in other aspects of the social bond to conventional society. The majority of them who do happen to have considerable attachments are tied to others of negligible resources, entire families and groups cut off from the channels of reward distribution in the society. Thus, many recruits will be unattached to the larger social structure, whether as isolated individuals or as members of small closed groups. Seen more formally, those who join high-tension religious groups – who thereby commit religious deviance – tend to be persons with low stakes in conformity. Recall:

Def.86 *Stakes in conformity* consist of attachments, investments, involvements, and beliefs.

P202 Persons with low stakes in conformity are relatively deprived in terms of rewards, compensators, and self-esteem.

P203 Persons with low stakes in conformity are relatively free to deviate.

The following obvious conclusions are hardly more than restatements of main conclusions of the chapters on sects and cults:

P256 At formation, sects and cults tend to have relatively deprived members.

P257 At formation, sects and cults tend to have members with low stakes in conformity.

P258 At formation, sects and cults tend to have members with weak attachments to outsiders.

P259 At formation, sects and cults tend to be closed social groups.

One should not forget the crucial role that high tension and the need for specific, intense compensators play in this. As P144 stated, the higher the tension of a religious group, the greater the number and perceived value of the compensators it can provide for scarce rewards. Those with high levels of reward have high stakes in conformity. Therefore, the movement of an individual or group toward higher tension is permitted by low stakes in conformity and encouraged by the deprivations associated with low stakes. This means that church movements will show the opposite tendency from cult or sect movements. Rather than being born in social isolation as closed groups experiencing social implosion, they will emerge as groups with many attachments – indeed, increasing attachments – to the conventional society and often to its elite (Steinberg, 1965; Doherty, 1967).

P260 At formation, church movements tend to have few relatively deprived members.

P261 At formation, church movements tend to have members with strong attachments to outsiders.

P262 At formation, church movements tend to be open social groups, blending into the larger social network that surrounds them.

This means that the character of each kind of group tends to intensify shortly after formation. High-tension groups move to somewhat higher tension, low-tension groups to somewhat lower tension, in the initial phase after birth. Such evolution is treated at length throughout this chapter, but here we must concentrate on one aspect of increased tension – the tendency toward social isolation. In the previous chapter, we already summarized main points about the level of attachments persons bring with them when they join religious movements of the high-tension varieties. New recruits tend to be low in attachments, whether this is a recent condition or a chronic lack of exchange partners.

P236 Persons are more likely to join religious movements at turning points in their lives.

Def.93 A *turning point* is a period of markedly decreased attachment, investment, involvement and belief, taken singly or in any combination.

P244 Persons low in social relationships are more likely than others to become members of a new religious group.

Thus, many propositions show that high-tension religious groups are born in isolation, and that they tend to stay relatively closed with few attachments to outsiders and few other stakes in conformity to the wishes of the surrounding society. These facts of social structure are underscored by the very fact of tension between the powerful members of society who possess rewards and the deprived minority who constitute the members of any new sect or cult and who accept the competing compensators.

Proposition 24 said that the power of an individual or group is positively associated with control of religious organizations and with gaining the rewards available from religious organizations. Therefore, as leadership emerges in a high-tension group, it will tend to concentrate the rewards (including social power) in its own hands. As Chapter 5 explained, the members of a religious group who possess rewards will seek lower tension with the sociocultural environment. But the movement was created to fulfill needs for more efficacious compensators and therefore for higher tension, needs undoubtedly still felt for a considerable time by the bulk of the membership.

This presents the leadership with a dilemma, particularly because the new religious organization is prey to defections or devastating further schisms if the initial enthusiasms of members are too seriously disappointed. The powerful must balance the gains of increasing the value of their own rewards via reduced tension against the loss of rewards via the failure of the organization to survive and to prosper. In the early days of a new movement, the potential losses from tension-reduction outweigh the gains, except of course for those born as church movements which are not our main concern here. In the interests of growth and survival, tension will be kept high. But this too, has serious consequences.

P263 If a new religious group keeps tension high and relies heavily on compensators to attract and keep converts, the powerlessness of converts will be maximized.

P264 If a new religious group keeps tension high and relies heavily on compensators to attract and keep converts, the outside attachments of converts will be minimized.

As we have seen repeatedly, it will be people for whom compensators have the greatest salience who are drawn to high-tension bodies on the basis of their more efficacious compensators. This means that recruits will be lacking in those individual and group attributes which give power. In contemporary America, for example, members of high-tension sects will be heavily over-recruited from among low-income, low-IQ, uneducated, female, older, non-white, handicapped, neurotic, and otherwise less powerful persons. For cults, the situation has been somewhat more complex, and the systematic empirical studies required to reveal exactly why have not yet been completed. Certainly, there have been innovative religious groups that served the seriously deprived (Cantril, 1941). But, as we noted earlier, cults often seem able to recruit from favored rather than from deprived segments of the population. One reason for this was explained in our chapter on affiliation. As P250 noted, novel religious culture may often spread most readily along the networks of communication that transmit other kinds of new culture, that is the social network of elite opinion leaders.

Thus, when the costs inflicted by the surrounding sociocultural environment are low, cults have an advantage that compensates to some extent for the remaining tension they experience. And, of course, the many sects in American society at present may be more attractive to those deprived in culture as well as in scarce rewards, thus giving cults what may be overpowering competition among the relatively deprived. At the contemporary stage of religious evolution, therefore, cults suffer a limitation in recruitment pool which may be a blessing in disguise if it reduces their likelihood of recruiting less-powerful and lower-status members.

But most sects and many cults do recruit especially among the relatively deprived. To the extent that such over-recruitment is perceived by outsiders, the status of the group (and the value of its rewards) will decline correspondingly, thus causing an even greater reliance on compensators for conversion and the maintenance of commitment. Since recruits will tend to be without attachments to outsiders, as well as being power-deprived and the low-status victims of prejudice, few outsiders will have personal reasons for moderating negative sanctions inflicted upon the movement.

> P265 High recruitment of powerless members will decrease the group's ability to avert or resist sanctions.

This is simply to acknowledge that the backing of some very powerful, high status, or well-attached members can provide protection to deviant groups. The lack or scarcity of such members makes for vulnerability. Indeed, deviant groups may suffer as much from a lack of knowledgeable and talented members, able to employ legal recourses and effective public relations tactics, as from lack of members with powerful statuses in the external environment.

> P266 Keeping tension high tends to maximize the extent to which the sect or cult is subjected to sanctions by the external society.

Reliance upon compensators for growth, of course, entails external costs. The greater the degree of tension (or deviance), the more (and more severe) sanctions will be imposed on the group. As has been pointed out, societies vary in the extent to which they impose such sanctions, and the degree to which naked coercion will be employed. Thus, the costs of high tension are much less in situations of maximum religious liberty. This is one reason why the United States has enjoyed a high level of sect and cult formation, despite many non-religious alternatives for persons who experience strong deprivations. But, even in our own society, stigma does attach to membership in a deviant religious body and will be expressed at least in such informal sanctions as social distance.

Born in anguish and enthusiasm, cults and sects immediately enter an extended period of organizational crisis, in which many factors press them toward even greater rebellion against the surrounding society at the same time that leaders and some other members seek a rapprochement to achieve increased conventional rewards. On every side, forces strip away the bonds with conventional society, and not the least among them is the outsiders' antagonism that expresses itself in sanctions and completes the separation indicative of tension:

P267 The more severe the sanctions imposed on a new religious movement, the more it will tend to become isolated from the social environment.

Coping with Isolation

Religious isolation, which implies closure of the group, really represents the full complement of characteristics that make up increased tension: subcultural deviance marked by difference, antagonism, and separation. Furthermore, such a group faced with severe external sanctions has very few resources for dealing with them. One alternative is simply to disband or to accept defeat by reaffiliating with a lower-tension group. But, if the cult or sect is to be sustained in the face of serious outside pressure, the most common strategy is to escape sanctions by limiting exposure to them. Thus the Mormons adopted the tactic of physically fleeing their hostile environment. So did various other groups such as the Amish, the Hutterites and the Boers. This is a response to isolation by creating more complete isolation.

Other groups have not made a physical retreat but have responded by constructing an alternative social structure within close physical proximity to the larger society. Thus, in many West Coast cities it is possible to find a miniature Mormon society wherein Mormons can live with little contact to non-Mormons. Indeed, the extent to which high tension religious groups in urban America manage to limit contact with outsiders is one of the true revelations of both ethnographic and quantiative studies of these groups (cf. Balswick and Faulkner, 1970; Quinley, 1974; Bainbridge and Stark, 1980c, 1981b; Welch, 1981).

In addition, cults and sects sometimes adopt the strategy of the secret underground. Members avoid sanctions by keeping secret their affiliation with outsiders, but only divulge their membership under controlled circumstances to those whom they judge to be potential converts. Christianity, in its early days in Rome, operated partly as an underground. The underground strategy may be a very effective one, especially for groups which otherwise would have become isolated. For the underground strategy makes it possible for a deviant movement to recruit because members continue to interact with outsiders. Indeed, we suspect that the underground strategy has many payoffs, not the least of which is the excitement, self-importance and exclusivity of being in a secret society. Furthermore, in highly coercive environments, only sects and cults adopting the underground strategy may be able to persist and grow.

A parallel example from deviant political movements is instructive. In his classic study of the Communist Party, Selznick (1960) shows why only secret "combat parties" can succeed in political opposition under repressive regimes, and that therefore such parties are the only available organization for political protest. Our earlier discussion of millenarian movements is relevant here to explain conditions under which "combat parties" might take on a religious character.

Groups sometimes alternate among these forms of isolation and may use mixtures of various strategies. For example, the Mormons successfully withdrew from contact with non-Mormons by settling in the desert of Utah where they created a separate society within which they are the religious institution. From this base, they sent out missionaries and also have established "colonies" that exhibit a fairly high degree of isolation within a non-Mormon environment. Another example is the many "front organizations" established today by highly deviant cult movements, producing a double or multiple tiered social structure. Client cult services are given at acceptably low tension to outsiders, while the cult movements lurk sometimes secretly behind these services, recruiting unsuspecting neophytes toward membership in the cult itself and therefore to higher tension (Bainbridge and Stark, 1980a; 1980b; Bainbridge and Jackson, 1981).

Whatever strategies are available, high tension does carry with it the threat of isolation. And that in turn has serious implications for growth. Recall P246 which states that expanding religious movements will gain much of their new membership by chains of recruitment spreading through pre-existing networks of social relationships. Isolated, high-tension movements cannot easily enter such networks of family and friendship ties. Therefore:

> P268 To the extent that a group is isolated, it will have great difficulty growing through recruitment.

Some highly isolated groups may grow through exceptionally high fertility. One example is the Hutterites, said to produce an average of 10.4 children per adult woman (Pratt, 1969). But for most high-tension groups, success must be achieved through more than just high fertility. Isolated groups are unable to spread their message at all effectively because they are prevented from much interaction with potential recruits. As all prophets know, one does not spread the word by preaching to the converted, and for a thoroughly isolated group such preaching is all that is possible. Today, almost anyone with a little money has access to the mass media, but such "disembodied appeals" as radio advertizing, magazine stories and wall posters are notably ineffective compared to recruitment through personal ties (Lofland, 1966; Shupe, 1976; Stark and Bainbridge, 1980a; Snow, *et al.*, 1980; Rochford, 1982).

True, groups may recruit individuals who do not have any other social ties – social isolates. Indeed, it is often easier to recruit such individuals because they lack stakes in conformity that might restrain them, as noted above. But, of course, such isolates do not provide access to social networks through which the group can grow. A few social isolates may be ordinary, somewhat talented persons who happen temporarily to be at turning points. But many will be persons who are isolated because they have great difficulty forming relationships. Perhaps they have few rewards to offer other persons – this type abounds in high-tension religious groups – or perhaps they have learned patterns of behavior that repell other persons. In either case, chronic social isolates make very poor recruits. If one does succeed in recruiting such a person, he will be almost valueless in recruiting still other new members. In fact the social resources he requires, such as personal attention, will reduce the supply available for recruitment. A new group made up originally of fairly effective members may be smothered by a social layer of these isolates, and be rendered incapable of further growth because of the low quality of initial recruits.

P269 A high proportion of recruits to isolated religious groups are chronic social isolates.

Def.94 *Chronic social isolates* are persons who lack the resources to attract and hold exchange partners.

P270 Isolated religious groups which initially recruit primarily chronic social isolates will subsequently find it almost impossible to grow through recruitment.

Furthermore, as P234 explained in the previous chapter, religious groups such as those we are discussing are attractive places for chronic seekers to visit. During their sojourn, chronic seekers consume social resources, but by definition never become committed members. After a while, they move on, having merely wasted the group's time and energy.

The disadvantages experienced by high-tension groups that try to recruit despite severe isolation are so great as to be tragic. Anyone who has studied an extreme sect or cult – and anyone who has been an active member of one –

can tell of vast social resources wasted in the deeply disappointing effort to recruit new members from the outside. Leaders, especially, are conscious of all the time and effort they expend in the often fruitless search for valuable new followers. No wonder many small sects and cults simply quit, and gradually fade away until death and defection have claimed all their members. And the temptation to reduce tension and isolation in the hunt for recruits is often irresistable.

Successful cults and sects – ones that grow and prosper – cannot rely exclusively on compensators to hold and attract new members, nor can they seek maximum tension in order to make their compensators of maximum efficiency. For this course results in isolation and the frustrating of hopes for recruitment. Thus the costs of tension combine with the shortage of rewards in the newly-formed cult or sect to create a delicate contradiction. How this contradiction is balanced out determines the future of the movement.

In our judgment, most sects and cult movements move into too high a state of early tension and become isolated. In consequence, they fail to grow and become merely another footnote in the history of religious movements (Stark and Bainbridge, 1981a). They may utilize their isolation to impede defection to such a degree that they live on for centuries, for example the Amish and Hutterites (Peters, 1965; Hostetler, 1968, 1974; Keim, 1975). But as permanently isolated groups they are living fossils. It is clear that such movements have no significant role to play in the making of future religious history.

What we are arguing is that isolation substantially is irreversable. Once a group is fully stigmatized as "weird" and is walled off from interaction, rarely can it recover respectability. Any later effort to reduce tension probably will result only in rapid defection of the least deprived followers, especially second-generation members who have no recollection of the gains experienced at the time of formation, with no gain for the group's leaders to offset this loss. It appears that once a group is isolated, the leaders have little to gain, and many intra-group rewards to lose, by attempting to re-enter the host environment.

Of course, one can identify rare circumstances which circumvent the forces behind these observations. The Mormons were able to set up their own society – with the generation of great material wealth as well as a complete social structure – then they negotiated peace terms with outsiders as Utah became a state progressively more integrated into the nation's economy and culture. Also, individual cult and sect leaders may occasionally gain such great material wealth in their work that they can abide the loss of psychic and material income occasioned by tension reduction. Further, the isolation we describe applies to groups which start with very high initial tension, while some sects and cults may be born at more moderate levels of tension where these effects are considerably weaker. But for the majority of sects and cults, formation is a time of very high tension, and isolation dooms the organization to linger or die still at high tension.

Random Factors

The fate of a religious organization depends in great measure upon the fates of its individual members. Large churches that draw members from great, stable segments of the population may themselves show firm stability because the nature and needs of the membership remain constant over the span of generations. But religious movements, born in the lightning of innovation or the thunder of schism, struggle to satisfy persons who either live in radically changing circumstances, or who seek such revolution. What are the consequences for new religious movements of the unstable fates of their members?

Before we can answer, we should demonstrate more fully that the movement's constituencies will often experience significant personal change. Consider the fate of any human being who possesses net rewards R at time T. What will be his net rewards at time T + 1? We cannot know for sure. True, it is often safe to predict that the immediate future will be like the present. Furthermore, one may safely predict that in the distant future the person will be dead and possess no earthly rewards at all. But what about all the moments that lie between the extreme of Now and the End of Time? Definition 2 reminds us that the future is greatly indeterminate.

> Def.2 The *future* consists of the universe of conditions which can be influenced but not known.

Another way to express Definition 2 is to say that the very nature of time precludes the discovery of explanations to secure all rewards or to explain all costs. Axiom 5 tells us that some desired rewards are limited in supply, including some that simply do not exist. Explanations – statements about how the future may be influenced – are rewards many of which cannot be attained. If man could achieve all desired explanations, he could use them to achieve all rewards of other kinds. And this is impossible. So both by contemplation of Definition 2 and by considering the relationship between explanations and scarce rewards we can show that many desired explanations cannot be found.

To predict perfectly the future course of an individual's life we should have to know a great sector of the unknowable future and to specify several nonexistent explanations about how rewards and costs of all kinds might come to him. For example, to predict with absolute perfection the course of a year of his life, we would have to have perfect knowledge of all objects and phenomena for a radius of one light year at the beginning of the period. Or – to specify the variations in the net rewards a person possesses, we should have to have such good explanations that if he possessed them he could escape the limitations of mortal life. For one thing, each individual's fate is influenced by the desires, actions and power of other human beings. Proposition 180 reminds us that persons sometimes fail to deliver on their promises, causing losses that their exchange partners could hardly have predicted.

It is fashionable to attribute events beyond our understanding to "random factors," a conceptualization perhaps only slightly superior to the alternate theory that they are expressions of the supernatural (cf. Stewman, 1975; Singer and Spilerman, 1976). For present purposes, we can summarize human ignorance and derive from it useful propositions, as follows:

P271 Much of the time, it is impossible to predict the future course of an individual's fortune.

P272 The change in a person's net rewards from one time to another is greatly determined by random factors.

Def.95 *Random* refers to the unknown and unknowable among natural causes.

P273 In any category of people, the fate of any one individual will be an imperfect predictor of the fate of another.

P274 In any category of people initially at the same reward level, in future some will possess more than others.

Proposition 274 is reminiscent of axiom 7, upon which so much of our theory has been based:

A7 Individual and social attributes which determine power are unequally distributed among persons and groups in any society.

We do not mean to derive A7 from proposition P274, although the two statements certainly overlap. Axiom 7 is not merely a comment on human ignorance, but also reflects the fact that the physical universe is not homogeneous. We made this point back in Chapter 3, when we derived the division of labor on both the level of individuals and the level of groups (P46). And the inhomogeneity of the universe extends through time as well as across space. Objects in space are not at rest, but in dynamic movement, possessing various velocities. They do not move in straight lines, but in infinitely complex curved trajectories, under the influences of other bodies whose spatial distribution and movements are also complex. By their very nature, organisms and the ecological systems they inhabit are heterogeneous and ever-changing. In addition to the factors of social power and random events, the heterogeneity of the environment gives humans unequal access to rewards, and from superior access to some rewards comes the power to obtain still other rewards.

Proposition 274 adds to Axiom 7 by showing that inequality is not merely a feature of whole societies – differences in power among persons and groups in society – but that inequality emerges within all groups (Mayhew and Levinger, 1976). Thus it supports P251 which stated this was true of newly-formed religious groups, and proves that this diversity will not vanish after formation. If there were a moment in group G when all members possessed equal rewards, a moment T + X after the time of formation T, then P274 says there will be inequality again at T + X + 1. For a hypothetical group of infinite duration there might conceivably be an infinite number of points $T + X_n$ when members were equal, but (since the conditions required to specifiy each moment are essentially infinite) for each of these potential moments of equality there will be an infinite number of moments of inequality, and inequality dominates the history of the group. Of course, no group can achieve infinite duration, and the odds against ever passing through a moment of perfect equality are so great that such an event may not yet have occurred in the history of the world.

A kind of inequality necessarily occurs within the life of each single individual, because the individual's momentary store of rewards is constantly changing. His power and satisfaction sometimes rise and sometimes fall, in ways very difficult to anticipate even approximately. These basic facts of existence have significance for the histories of religious movements through the processes we call *evaporation* and *regression.*

Social Evaporation

Persons join high-tension religious groups in pursuit of rewards, especially scarce rewards which do exist. Random factors and the uneven distribution of rewards within a group cause some members actually to receive scarce rewards in greater supply than they had formerly. Other members stay at about the same level of rewards as before, and typically some lose. In our chapters on schism and recruitment, particularly in P224, we noted that persons experiencing great deprivation within a religious group will tend to drop out, whether into a new group, into seekership, or into despair. Thus, those for whom fate and the machinations of power actually reduce the supply of rewards after they join a religious group, will tend to leave.

Consider what happens to a group whose total sum of rewards remains constant while this sorting-out process occurs and some persons rise in fortune and others fall. Those who rise will attribute at least part of their success to the explanations that encouraged them to anticipate rewards from the religion in the first place. That is, they will evaluate their new religious affiliation very highly, based on their own personal experience. Those who stay at the same level of reward will at least have compensators to comfort them, and seeing improvement in others may feel they are about to gain in the same ways. But those who lose, leave.

The net effect is an increase in the average level of rewards of those who remain with the group. This is a process very similar to the familiar physical process of evaporative cooling, such as the chill of alcohol evaporating on human skin. As a volatile liquid evaporates, the faster-moving (hotter) molecules escape, leaving the cooler molecules behind. Or, put differently, those molecules near the surface with sufficiently great momentary energy depart, reducing the average energy of those which remain. If the evaporation progresses rapidly enough, there is a perceived cooling of the unevaporated liquid. Of course, measurement of the temperature of the unevaporated liquid neglects the energy carried by the escaped molecules, and there is no reduction in the total energy of all the molecules from the liquid.

With religious groups, it is the dissatisfied who depart, leaving behind those who are more satisfied. Thus, there is an apparent increase in satisfaction of the group, even if the total satisfaction of those who originally formed it remains constant. But the composition of the group really changes as some become the carriers of dissatisfaction and depart.

P275 Social evaporation increases the average level of reward of members of a group.

Def.96 *Social evaporation* is the process in which members of a group whose fortunes decline defect from it, leaving behind those members whose fortunes rise or remain constant.

P276 A moderate rate of social evaporation increases the commitment of members who remain in the group.

This last proposition is true not only because many of those who remain have experienced increases in reward which convince them that the religious faith is valuable, but also because people evaluate their explanations in terms of the experience of their exchange partners. In social evaporation, those likely to express negative sentiments break off ties with group members, and so do not communicate their dissatisfaction to them. Many of those who remain are highly satisfied, and communicate this positive evaluation to the others who remain.

Evidence for the importance of social evaporation as a phenomenon guiding human action can be found immediately outside the realm of religion, in that wide adjacent field known variously as psychiatry, psychotherapy, and the human potential movement. Some among a cohort of patients experience improvements in fortune, even if entirely for random reasons, during treatment with a psychotherapist, while others will decline. Patients whose fortunes improve greatly will be defined as "cured" and thank their therapists for the great help apparently rendered. Those whose fortunes fall rapidly will drop out of treatment early and not even be counted as full cases to be considered failures. Thus, social evaporation may give therapists a false sense of success with their treatment approach (Eysenck, 1965; Rachman, 1971; cf. May, 1971).

In religion, there probably are two events equivalent to cure. First, some members of a high-tension congregation may become solid, stable citizens possessing a secure source of scarce rewards. For them the sect or cult now functions as a church, beloved for the help it apparently gave in the past, but no longer needed for its specific compensators. Second, members may be seen as achieving ultimate cure at death (if they happen to die pious), when they are said to "have gone to their reward." Those who die in failure and disaffiliation may have been lost from sight by the group years before.

The apparent successes of religion, which really are caused by social evaporating, can have either of two opposing consequences, depending on the structure of social relations surrounding the religious organization. First, if the group is in extremely high tension to begin with, the increased average commitment resulting from evaporations may lead to increased separation of the group from the world as members seek all rewards from the religion, encouraged by the apparent value of increasing commitment. Second, at less extreme levels of tension, it is important that social evaporation does mean at least a significant proportion of members really have more rewards. These fortunate folk will have higher exchange ratios now with outsiders, and may find more opportunities for profit in exchanges with outsiders. If such exchanges are open to them, either because the environment is highly favorable or because the religious group is not at such high tension that its social network is closed, then the more fortunate members will seek to increase worldly rewards and therefore do decrease their reliance on the specific compensators provided by the religious group.

In the first instance, the group will implode still further, increasing in tension with the sociocultural environment and withdrawing from exchanges with outsiders within the limits set by economic survival. In the second instance, there will develop a significant category of persons within the cult or sect who want lower tension with the sociocultural environment. If these more successful people prevail, the group will be pulled churchward by them, reducing its tension and isolation. If these people are not sufficiently powerful to move the group, then there is the potential for a schismatic church movement led by them. Note, however, that social evaporation increases the ability of those who desire lower tension to move the group churchward, because those most-deprived folk who most want high tension have defected from the group. We can state these observations as formal propositions.

P277 The higher the tension of a religious group, the more strongly will social evaporation tend initially to increase the tension of the group.

P278 The lower the tension of a religious group, the more strongly will social evaporation tend to decrease the tension of the group.

P279 Social evaporation increases the ability of powerful members of a religious group to move it toward lower tension.

P280 Social evaporation reduces the pressures toward formation of church movements and sect movements.

When is evaporation most likely? Whenever individuals are most free to defect from any religious group. It is least likely when the secular social network is highly closed and members of the religious group must rely upon each other for many of life's necessities. Thus, it is not surprising that social evaporation was not sufficiently vigorous to prevent the development of a church movement within Judaism, an ethnic group as well as religious tradition, and Reform Judaism was born (Steinberg, 1965). Evaporation is most common in mobile, relatively secular societies such as described in the following chapter.

Obviously, extreme levels of social evaporation represent lethal explosion of a religious movement. But moderate levels may contribute to the success of an organization, if recruitment and fertility maintain or increase the group's size.

P281 Moderate levels of social evaporation contribute to the success of a religious movement.

Regression Toward the Mean

Despite all the random, unpredictable factors that impact on human life, there seems to be a measure of gross stability in the fortunes of large groups. While some individuals rise and others fall, the average level of reward holds fairly constant. Of course, one can note many significant mass changes in history, from the the swift costs of war to the slow expansion of total human population. We do not mean to say that everything changes on the individual level yet remains the same on the societal level. Many tribes, from Britons to Tasmanians, would remind us that their societies once knew happier days. And there are new things under the sun. But the fortunes of the entire species have varied within discernable limits.

Moreover, the random shifts in individual fortune cannot take the person to any conceivable level of reward, but tend to operate only within certain limits. While cultural change and other factors can increase or decrease gradually the total rewards possessed by a large society, one can for present purposes ignore such large-scale trends and see that individual fortune tends to be dynamic within a static population pattern. When some gain, generally others lose. (Here, of course, we are talking about fate and levels of reward, and in no way mean to contradict P2.) In the absence of complicating factors, one can make at least approximate predictions for the fates of many anonymous persons who happen initially to have much more or much less than the typical level of reward.

If one wants to think in statistical terms, one may say that cases with extreme values tend to regress toward the mean. Suppose we survey the population's wealth at one point in time and identify some individuals who are very rich. A later survey will tend to find that these same individuals have lost ground in comparison to others. Similarly, persons very poor at the outset of the study will be less poor later on. Of course, there are various strategies elite groups may use to hold or even increase their power, but in the long run their power erodes none-the-less. Sometimes the phenomenon is masked by processes like evaporation. The Caesars who ruled Fourth Century Rome were little related by blood to the Caesars who established the Empire. At the top end of the power scale, this phenomenon is sometimes called "circulation of the elites." But there is an equal circulation at the bottom end of the scale, as well.

Note we say this regression happens in societies that do have typical limits both in the extremes of individual fortune and of the mass fate of society itself, conditions which do normally apply, but not always. Note that we say it happens in societies. The fact that people interact and exchange rewards, even if indirectly, binds them to the over-all fate of the social system and provides a background of stability against which they act out their erratic personal fates.

If individuals' fates rise and fall in ways that cannot be predicted exactly, yet the over-all distribution of power is roughly constant, then those at the extremes must tend to move toward the average, while some near the average move toward the extremes. This can be stated more precisely:

> P282 Individuals with extreme levels of reward at one point in time will tend to be nearer the average for the society at a subsequent point in time.

> Def.97 The process of random events operating within a constant population distribution, which brings extreme cases back toward the average for the population, is called *regression*.

Since this proposition describes a general, statistical tendency and cannot specify the particular changes in fortune of any given individual, it does not violate Def.2. We are not prepared to translate this "average" into technical statistical terms. Whether it is the arithmetic mean, geometric mean, median or mode presumably depends upon the shape of distribution of rewards in the society. If a nation really contains multiple societies, two endogamous castes for example, then regression may operate separately in each subsociety. The Spartan regresses up or down toward the Spartan average; the Helot regresses toward the Helot average.

This principle of regression has great consequences for high-tension religious movements. Because they are high in tension, they tend to recruit persons with exceptional needs – often people with extraordinary deprivations. As time passes, some of these unfortunates may experience even further declines in net reward, but because P282 is true, the typical highly-deprived person will gain in fortune as he regresses toward the average level of reward in his society. Thus, cults and sects that begin with a deprived membership will tend to see their congregations improve in fortune over the years after formation – other things being equal – even without any evaporation of dissatisfied members. As they become less deprived, the members will have less need of compensators and will tend to reduce the tension of their religious organization.

P283 Individuals who join religious groups at times of extreme personal deprivation will tend to be less deprived at a later point in time.

P284 High-tension religious groups will be drawn by regression toward lower tension with the sociocultural environment.

We must stress five limitations to this last proposition. First, it is possible that the regression will operate so slowly that its impact on the tension of the group will be weak, and most members may fall into the decline of old age and die before experiencing a marked time of greater fortune. Second, the regression of individual members may be offset by rapid recruitment of new members who are highly deprived; thus the movement toward lower tension may be blocked if the group continues to serve the needs of suffering newcomers. Third, those who regress most rapidly and completely may escape the group through defection to an existing low-tension group. Fourth, the forces leading to regression may not operate if the group secedes from the larger society and thus from the stabilizing pattern in which regression can occur, so the highest-tension groups which become socially isolated may not experience any tension reduction. Finally, of course, P284 describes one force acting on religious organizations, a pressure toward tension reduction which can be countered by other forces.

Regression, like evaporation, can serve as a potent commitment mechanism. Consider a number of persons who join a high-tension religious group at times of great deprivation. While some will languish in misery, most will experience random improvement in their fortunes and will most likely attribute this gain to the religion. The advantage of regression over evaporation is that a higher proportion of original members experience satisfactory improvement, and that it is thus more able to build a growing religious movement, rather than merely to hold some portion of recruits who happen to join.

Again, the field of psychotherapy can provide empirical examples. Persons seek help at low times in their lives, not when they are supremely happy. If exceptionally low times tend to be followed by average and high times (even for no reason at all), many clients of emotional and spiritual healers will experience improvement during treatment and come to value it (cf. Brownsberger, 1965; McConaghy and Lovibond, 1967; McCleary *et al.*, 1979).

To have much influence on the larger society, and indeed to survive for long, new sects and cults must grow soon after they are born. There can be no doubt that most high-tension groups begin very small. Sometimes, it is true, great political events and ethnic migrations can produce large religious groups through schism. Episcopalians are almost Anglicans, but not quite. The American Civil War divided many conventional denominations into Northern and Southern halves. With the defeat of the South, the Southern denominations became, for a time, higher-tension than their Northern counterparts. But the purely religious, internal causes of schism we have discussed, and the processes of cultic innovation, produce high-tension groups that are small.

When a group splits, there is always the question of which piece is a continuation of the old group, and which is the splinter group. The rule of thumb widely used is which group retains the property. Generally speaking, it is the larger group which does so, because it has the greater power, and it is the smaller group which must obtain new buildings and other needed facilities for pursuing its activities. Furthermore, a new group must develop a new social structure, and typically secedes before this process is far toward completion. New cults are born in small groups and the friendship networks of their founders. The chief exception to the rule that sects and cults are smaller than their parent organizations is when the parent itself is so small that an objectively small faction within it can be the majority. In these cases, as well, the resultant sect or cult is small.

> P285 Sects and cults start out relatively small, smaller then their parent groups and considerably smaller then the dominant religious groups in the society.

Cults that develop around the ministry of a single individual cannot even come into being unless they grow – unless they gain at least a second or third member. Of course, groups that come into being through schism may exist for a time and then die out never having grown at all. The earliest stages of a cult, a time of growth, is also a time when rewards available within the group increase. New people bring new resources, and the very fact of their recruitment adds to the power of the group. The earliest stages of sects, too, tend to be times of increased reward.

In the beginning any new organization is an empty structure. Its positions all are open and must be filled. While one must wait for vacancies in order to move up in an on-going organization (White, 1970), an organization just being formed is vacant. Even the sect founded by low-level leaders of the parent church will offer nominally higher statuses for its clergy. In consequence, the formation of a new organization provides maximum availability of high status positions, and this is, of course, a common reason why people start new organizations – a tendency that is particularly marked in business. A leadership that gains in reward is more able to share some of its rewards with other members, so there may be a net gain in rewards for all members at the time of formation.

The foundation of a sect or cult is also a time of increased generation and exchange of compensators. It is a time of new hope and commitment to religious explanations. Not only religious specialists but also ordinary members of the group will continually exchange compensators for such rewards as they have to give each other, both material and psychic. Among the rewards available to any group is *positive affect*. Proposition 134 noted that every person seeks a positive self-evaluation. Proposition 135 added that persons desire a positive evaluation of the rewards they possess, including their explanations and their power-giving resources. Positive affect is the expression of favorable evaluations of one's fellows, of the organization, and of common purposes and beliefs. Thus, the positive affect of others is rewarding, especially if it is directed at the group and its explanations. In the case of love, positive affect is directed at a person, because an exchange partner values him or her and expresses the willingness to expend costs to maintain the relationship and thus to satisfy the person. All these forms of positive affect will be exchanged in the early enthusiasm of a new religious organization, and together they constitute an inextricable mixture of manifold rewards and compensators.

P286 The period of initial organizational formation is a time of high availability of statuses in a new sect or cult.

P287 The period of initial organizational formation is a time of high exchange of compensators in a new sect or cult.

P288 The period of initial organizational formation is a time of high exchange of positive affect in a new sect or cult.

Def.98 *Affect* is the intense expression of evaluations.

P289 The period of initial organizational formation is a time of high availability of rewards in a new sect or cult.

Obviously, rapid growth can sustain high availability of rewards. It provides more statuses for leaders as branch churches and other organizations must be established to serve a great influx of members. While the nature of compensators may not change after formation, growth can sustain the group's faith in them. New members bring new positive affect with them to replace any decline in affect from older members. But growth not only can maintain the happy situation that may prevail at the birth of a movement; it also may be caused by that enthusiasm.

Our lengthy analyses of religious commitment, early in this book, and of the emergence of religion, and of recruitment to religious organizations, all stress the exchange of compensators including religious explanations. For one to be converted to a new religion, it is not enough that one come into contact with members and develop exchange relationships with them. It is necessary also that they communicate rather uniform, highly positive evaluations of their religion. This is particularly likely at the very birth of a religious organization. Isolation may starve recruitment, but enthusiasm nourishes it.

> P290 Unless a new religious organization is too isolated socially, the period immediately following formation will be a time of rapid recruitment of new members.

This propostion suggests that there is a crucial cut-off point in degree of isolation. New organizations slightly too isolated, will become fully encapsulated, become confirmed in their high tension, and fail to grow or change. Organizations that are born in slightly less social isolation will be able to grow rapidly and at least have the opportunity to evolve in response to success.

The life history of a new sect or cult tends to be determined early, at the time of its formation and in the first few years of operation. One reason for this is expressed in an old aphorism that may be read falsely as a tautology: Nothing succeeds like success. In the context of our general theory of religion, these four words take on a richer meaning. People come to religion seeking rewards and accepting compensators. But nothing proves the worth of a compensator package like a liberal admixture of rewards. If many individual members gain after joining, perhaps for reasons described above, and if the movement rapidly recruits many new members, the whole operation will seem a success. The still unredeemed compensators will look like good investments because rewards and growth are manifest in so many other areas.

The aura of success will communicate itself to the newcomers. They find the successful little sect or cult a powerhouse of human enthusiasm. Not only does the organization enjoy rewards, but it shares them with neophytes. Especially when rapid recruitment itself is a source of success and enthusiasm for the group, potential recruits will be showered with attention and hope. This, in turn, gives the already successful group a competitive advantage against its less successful rivals who experience a corresponding depression and drop in recruitment as the successful group defeats them in the market place.

Thus, out of all the new sects and cults struggling to recruit at a given moment, a few will tend to beat out the others, increasing an initially often quite slim advantage, as success breeds on success. The tendency of high-tension groups to become socially isolated is increased by failure in competition against more vigorous rival groups. Not only does isolation come from lessened rewards from interacting with the environment, and from concomitant increase in private compensators, but isolation may serve the leadership of such a group because it protects them from raiding.

Aggressive religious groups frequently seek to raid other groups, recruiting their less-attached members. For example, John Lofland (1966) noted that the earliest branch of the Moonies in America sent members into conventional churches, pretending to have no untoward motives but really trying to steal converts. Several of our propositions suggest this may sometimes be a reasonable tactic for groups that have a competitive advantage. For one thing, they can be sure that the membership of other sects or cults, especially those that share considerable culture with the raiding group, will be persons who already have religious problem-solving perspectives and who share some general explanations making them fit prey for the raider.

But if a group is at a competitive disadvantage, the members sent out to raid may themselves be recruited away by more successful groups they encounter. It is not uncommon for an expanding sect or cult to gobble up the greater portion of weaker groups' memberships. Of course, this typically means that the leaders of these other groups are suddenly out of work, and the aware leader of a less competitive group may seek to avoid this possibility through isolation and similar strategies.

P291 The initial characteristics and earliest achievements of a new religious movement tend to set the pattern for its future history.

P292 Religous movements which already are growing at a rapid rate tend to benefit from the tactic of raiding the memberships of other religious groups.

P293 Religious movements which fail to grow rapidly can increase the possibility of suvival through social isolation.

P294 In a religious market, a few high-tension religious organizations will grow rapidly, while most will decline.

P295 In a religious market, a few high-tension religious organizations will become prosperous and will move toward lower tension.

P296 In a religious market, the majority of high-tension religious organizations will not prosper and will remain at high tension.

The Course of Rewards and Revival

We have noted that the time of formation of a religious movement is one of great rewards, and that growth can sustain this high level of reward, while a failure to grow brings on a crisis that may lead to the death of the movement if its members are not sufficiently isolated from alternative commitments. We also have seen that random phenomena like evaporation and regression can increase the average net rewards of members without membership itself actually producing any benefits. But membership can produce benefits, adding to the total power of the group, thus increasing members' satisfaction and dedication.

For persons who were accidental social isolates, religion can provide exchange partners. Some persons moderately deficient in the skills and other resources needed to develop relationships are given the opportunity to build relationships with each other. Perhaps they gain interpersonal skills through simple practice and through guided group activities. Perhaps they now operate in a less demanding market of relationships. Perhaps the shared compensators reduce debilitating social anxieties. In any case, these people now have more rewarding social contacts, facilitated originally by the exchange of compensators and positive affect, but sustained later by the many valuable rewards humans can give each other. To cite the most powerful example, churches are well-known places of marriage courtship, and many a couple married in the church began their relationship at a "church social" and developed it in various other activities that strengthen the organization, including rituals and church projects.

If persons who join deviant religious groups have low stakes in conformity, persons who remain in any religious group develop stakes which bring them to conform. A major factor leading to instability and failure in one's private life is disaffiliation from other people – the loss of social bonds capable of restraining the individual from violating societal norms. Those who violate norms often are punished, and the punishment frequently means a less rewarding life. Further, an individual cut off from social interaction does not receive the information (explanations) necessary to guide him toward success in material as well as social terms. These considerations suggest that all religious groups, if they persist, may bring their members into line and make them more successful conformists.

This is true even for many groups that begin in extreme deviance. For example, the Process cult attempted to follow the disruptive dictates of Satan but found that intragroup harmony and economic success quickly demanded more sober behavior (Bainbridge, 1978). The cult submerged the Satanic aspects of its doctrine, and produced a dutiful membership, quite ready to meet the demands of the larger society when required. But one would expect that the ability of a religious group to transform its members into persons successful in secular life depends on how closely the church is integrated into the channels of that success. An isolated, high-tension group may demand the basic values of reliability and sobriety, but it is too disconnected from the secular order to transmit more subtle societal norms or practical information about the economic system.

One then would conclude that there are two levels at which a religious organization can tailor its members for success in society. First, it requires basic interactive compètence from members and teaches them primary skills of social interaction necessary in any mutually-rewarding group. It is not surprising that the Commandments of religions state many particular norms for proper interaction among humans, in addition to any norms they promulgate about relations with the supernatural. Second, it can engage in direct socialization to the norms and explanations favored by the surrounding society. Any persisting group may achieve the former. The latter requires the group to possess connections with secular society precluded by the highest levels of tension.

> P297 Religious organizations socialize their members to the general norms required for successful human interaction.

> P298 Religious organizations, except those at the highest tension, socialize their members to the specific norms required for success in the society.

Together, these two propositions repeat in forms most useful for present purposes a truth derived way back in P80: "Religious specialists promulgate norms, said to come from the gods, that increase the total rewards possessed by the clients as a group." One might raise an apparent counter-example in arguing against P298 – the Mormons. They were in extremely high tension when they fled to Utah, yet the Mormons are famous for their success in secular affairs.

But in fact, the Mormons fit this proposition quite well. In Utah they set up their own independent economic base – their own society – and thus were intimately connected with (and indeed possessed) the secular institutions which made sure their religion would promulgate norms designed to ensure material as well as social success.

The limited economic base of such completely agrarian sects as the Hutterites does not permit the same explosion into national prominence enjoyed by the Mormons, but surely these radical Anabaptists have become highly successful farmers. Both Mormons and Hutterites promulgated norms supporting successful life, because both were tied to complete economies. High-tension sects that dwell entirely within the economies of the larger society, yet are isolated from key economic institutions, are far less able to tailor their norms for material success.

We certainly do not mean to embrace the Functionalist fallacy that culture always solves human problems in the best possible ways. On the contrary, our theory is based upon the limitations of human strength and understanding. Many new religious organizations have fatal flaws in their doctrines and practices. For example, however useful it may be as a compensator, the doctrine that only God can heal sickness can produce an unnecessarily high death rate in religious groups that reject the better aspects of modern medicine in favor of their compensators. Religious communities that practice total celibacy, like the nearly extinct Shakers, may gain millenarian compensators from this practice but lose the ability to grow or even survive without massive rates of recruitment (Bainbridge, 1982, 1984a).

But among those religious groups with somewhat dysfunctional cultures at the time of formation are many that can learn and adapt. Proposition 41 said, "The greater the number and the diversity of exchanges that have occurred over time, the more complex and apparently rewarding the culture will become." This was meant to apply in the first instance to the totality of human culture – to entire societies and to the species as a whole – but it also applies to any moderately adaptive subculture with reasonably effective means for evaluating and changing its explanations. From this it follows that religious organizations will tend to adapt so as to maximize the rewards gained by their members. Proposition 80 has already stated this in societal terms, but the point must be made with respect to high-tension groups principally composed of persons with low levels of initial reward.

P299 Relatively high-tension religious groups, except those at the highest tension, tend over time to increase the rewards received by their members.

This point must be seen in the light of all our derivations about schism, defection, and recruitment to other religious organizations. While increasing reward actually caused by the religion strengthens commitment, human memory is short and the lure of even greater success in the secular society and in lower-tension religious groups is especially appealing to the members with greatest resources (rewards) within the sect or cult. Again, we must remember that there is a contradiction within any religious group, as some members press for increased tension and others for decreased tension. At the time of most rapid recruitment of deprived persons, the pressure toward high tension may be irresistable. But for groups that are neither socially isolated, nor inundated by deprived recruits, actual religion-caused improvement of members' fortunes (as well as the statistical processes of evaporation and regression) will move the group towards greater rewards and hence toward lower tension. If we consider "successful" a movement which has grown significantly since birth, and call "stable" any group which has achieved secure membership undisturbed by current waves of deprived recruits or by massive defection among the most fortunate, then we can state the general proposition:

> P300 Successful, stable sects and cults tend to move toward lower tension.

This is a very important traditional conclusion in church-sect theory (Niebuhr, 1929), and has often found support in empirical studies (e.g., Alston and Aguirre, 1979; Aguirre and Alston, 1980). The arguments above show not only that several mechanisms contribute to tension reduction, but also that very common conditions can block such churchward evolution. If a group is highly isolated, it will stay in high tension. If a group continues to recruit numbers of persons who want high tension, it will tend to serve their need. Once these numerous cases are removed, we are probably left with a small minority of sects and cults which achieve significant long-term growth and become moderate and low tension denominations. Despite their small numbers, these groups are among the most important for the sociologist of religion, because they are the influential new organizations whose emergence constitutes the main events of religious history.

Some among the great residue of groups that remain at high tension achieve a different kind of success. They may live and spice up religious communion for a long time. If the period of organizational formation was one of great reward stimulated by great enthusiasm for the group's compensators, then later episodes of *revival* can restimulate enthusiasm and initiate a new flow of rewards (especially affect) among members (Bibby and Brinkerhoff, 1974). Revivals are like contained schisms, in which the need for more efficacious compensators reasserts itself without organizational rupture. They are episodes of increased affect flow, and therefore present somewhat elevated levels of reward for participants. Every religious group experiences revival to some extent, although the higher tension groups are more apt to stage overt revivals of many kinds on several levels.

Among the most familiar forms of revival are regular religious holidays, appointed times of rededication and enthusiasm. Each religious holiday will tend to emphasize a sector of the religion's compensators, to have its own doctrinal emphasis, and to have its own forms of worship and celebration. Consider Christmas. Some portions of the Bible are read and preached, but not others. The emphasis is on family values and love of children, in the theology as well as in the practice. The birth of Christ represents the greatest gift from God to man since Adam. One could well predict that such a holiday would become a time of human gift-giving, rendering concrete the rewards exchanged for compensators. Interestingly, a very few high-tension groups de-emphasize gift-giving at Christmas for more religious and compensator-oriented concerns, and those churches with many holidays find a variety of excuses for these regularized days of revival. One would suggest that low-tension groups (especially state churches of whatever tradition) are more likely to regulate revival, and therefore to have a greater number of holidays.

Leaders of religious groups, like other professionals, continually plan future work and evaluate past work. Thus, they often are brought to feel their church needs a boost, a project, a focus of renewed activity. Any minister, or anyone who has ever worked around a church, knows this. There is, of course, the greatest array of projects a church may undertake outside the appointed structure of holidays. Every new project has an element of revival. For example, a social-service program to feed the hungry or tend the ill can become simultaneously a good work, a recruiting campaign, and a ritual of increased involvement for old members. But we generally restrict the term *revival* to activities of a special religious character, designed to arouse the supernatural feelings of members and to achieve renewed commitment.

Propositions 209, 210 and 211 explained that high-tension religious groups tend to conceptualize the affiliating of new members as *conversion*, conceptualized as a positive transformation of the nature and value of the person recruited. Whenever things are going poorly, when members feel bad about the lack of religious progress in the group and in their own personal lives, the high-tension religious body will tend to resort to revival. For the same reasons that recruitment was conceived by these groups as conversion, revival will be conceived as *re-conversion*. In revival episodes, individuals will be stimulated to relive the conversion experience, with its crucial sense of greatly increased self-worth and religiosity. Empirical research has shown repeatedly that the persons who "come forward for Christ" in revival meetings are not new recruits, but old members experiencing renewed dedication and revived positive affect for their accustomed compensators (W. Johnson, 1971; Altheide and Johnson, 1977). These people are "born again" – again and again.

Especially at the higher-tension end of the spectrum, revivals may be the business of professional revivalists, religious specialists who travel around the country staging public meetings where an intense but artfully-contrived performance elicits greatly increased affect, including hope and rededication. If the traveling evangelist can convince local church leaders he is not a raider seeking to kidnap their congregations, he may get them to carry out valuable advance work, advertising the revival meetings, bringing out the flock, and even hiring the hall. In return, the evangelist revives religious hopes, distributing familiar compensators and extremely positive evaluations of them, inspiring renewed participation in the local church. These meetings must be episodic, perhaps coming every couple of years. The hopes they raise can never be fulfilled on this earth, so it is necessary to have a satisfactory means for ending the revival without sharp disappointment. The evangelist's departure accomplishes this, leaving participants in the calmer care of their accustomed pastors. But the hopes must be raised periodically, as daily life drains enthusiasm from the chronically deprived in the congregations.

Cults have their own form of revival: *re-innovation*. When things begin to drag and the promises of the faith face disappointment, the cult leader frequently innovates in searching for a solution to the momentary problem. We saw this in earlier chapters. New dispensations are the business of cults, and revival typically takes the form of secondary new dispensations – new procedures, rituals, prophecies, and ancillary doctrines. Highly magical religious cults, like Scientology, produce new magic almost regularly, new levels of spiritual technology coming out every year.

While many recent cults have experimented with outside cultic evangelists, this practice is very dangerous for them. The traveling sectarian evangelist can present a familiar product quickly to local sect members, achieve a good revival, and depart before establishing strong social ties that could recruit people away to his banner. And this evangelist's banner will bear the same symbols as the local sects, leaving them in a good position to garner the enthusiasm aroused by his performance. However, the cult evangelists must have a somewhat new and different doctrine or practice, which takes time to share, which stands outside the normal cultural range of the local cult, and which gives him several advantages if he wants to raid. Of course, the larger cults with many branches send their own circuit riders around to local organizations, avoiding this problem.

Ths solution we have seen many smaller cults adopt is inviting traveling revivalists who were involved in audience cults, or the mildest magical cults, not in the socially more powerful cult movements. For example, they may hold weekly lecture sessions in which their audiences will listen one week to a UFO expert, to an astrologer the next, and to an aura-reader after that. The lecturers make some money without being able to raid, while the cult gets a small dose of revival, perhaps not very effective in maintaining members' commitment, but at least stimulating a measure of very generalized hope and enthusiasm.

P301 To remain successful, long after formation, religious groups rely greatly upon the tactic of revival.

Def.99 *Revival* is the staging of episodes of increased religious affect to sustain compensators.

Tranformation

To conclude this chapter, we shall consider a few other consequences of the principles stated earlier. In order to grow a group must avoid being greatly isolated from its surroundings. This means that compensators alone will not be adequate to sustain growth, for maximum efficacy of compensators cannot be achieved without causing the sect or cult to be isolated. Thus, even though we have deduced above that compensators will play a greater role in attracting and holding members to high-tension movements than to more churchlike groups, to avoid isolation while still growing, a movement must continue to provide a substantial flow of rewards. But we have already suggested above that the time of formation is an episode of increased reward, so the flow of rewards will decline after this, unless a very high level of recruitment is achieved.

To pursue this apparent dilemma we must pause and give closer attention to the concept of rewards. We have already seen that a religious group can increase its stock of rewards by reducing tension with the sociocultural environment – a key factor in transforming successful movements into churches. But rapid tension reduction is seldom an option during the early years of a sect or cult. Although we have seen above that these groups must keep their degree of tension below the threshhold above which they become isolated, they cannot drop rapidly below their initial tension level. Propositions like P299, charting the growth of rewards for members of a successful group, describe processes that take considerable time. To drop tension prematurely would cost the group too much in terms of its very reason for existence: specific, efficacious compensators. This is a cost that can be paid in the long run (at the cost eventually of losing a new sect movement), but in the early years of a high-tension group's life, when its fate is being determined, it cannot increase the supply of rewards by greatly reducing tension. Indeed, the core on which it was formed is tension.

However, if we examine rewards more carefully, we see that some rewards can be increased without tension reduction. At issue here is social control, broadly conceived. The movement seeks to give converts and potential converts a stake in conformity – something to gain by joining, something to lose by leaving. We have distinguished four kinds of stakes in conformity: attachment, investment, involvement, and belief. The last of these has been treated above in consideration of revivals.

Attachments often manifest themselves in exchanges of affect among persons. Quite simply, people risk the loss of affect from others if they commit acts of deviance which makes it too costly for others to exchange affect with them. It is pertinent to our analysis that affect is also the cheapest of all rewards – everyone has a considerable amount of it to give. Hence sects and cults can increase stakes in conformity – increase their supply of rewards – by devising means to heighten the flow of affect among members and towards potential members. The tactic of revival is one example. That sects often succeed in this strategy is reflected in the widespread observation about the "coolness" of social relations in churches and the "warmth" of such relations in sects. Contemporary cults possess a remarkable collection of interpersonal activities, including supposedly psychotherapeutic exercises that really function to create and sustain affective bonds (Bainbridge, 1978). High tension helps to supply increased affect because the boundary between "them" and "us" is intense and visible.

A second class of stakes in conformity we called *investments*. These are status and material rewards, both realized and potential. The greater the amount of status and possessions a person stands to sacrifice through deviance (those rewards currently enjoyed and those likely to be gained), the greater the cost of deviance from the group's norms. We are surprised when a banker commits a petty theft, because the costs risked appear prohibitive, but we see no contradiction when a derelict does so. High-tension religious bodies increase the level of investments members and potential members have in membership. For example, they often can increase the level of material rewards received by members in the secular economy by engaging in *favoritism*, a specific tactic not covered by previous discussions. Members can patronize one another in business, hire and promote one another, use collective resources to finance one another in new economic ventures, and the like. They can vote as a bloc. The early Christians often bought the freedom of slaves who converted. Furthermore, the early church engaged in massive welfare programs, thus offering obvious material stakes in membership (Johnson, 1979). Observation of successful cults and sects ought to reveal many such tactics to increase the material pay-offs of membership.

When an organization grows, it offers more functionary roles, but this proliferation of valued statuses also can occur by design. Thus cults and sects can increase the flow of status rewards, which particulary constitute investments because status is always a mixture of achieved rewards and the compensator of anticipated future rewards, by creating an elaborate internal status system whereby a high proportion of members can benefit. Human inventiveness is such that a great many duties and responsibilities can be manufactured to give substance to these "superfluous" roles. In principle, all members could hold functionary roles and aspire to rise frequently in an endless system of ranks. For example, all Jehovah's Witnesses are members of the clergy, and all Scientologists occupy elevated positions in an endless status hierarchy said to begin above the conventional statuses of outsiders. In creating many new functionary roles, it is not necessary that they be highly decorative, ceremonial, or have other trappings which might be called "high church." All that is required is that these roles be distinct and that they be made plausible by having definite rights and duties attached to them.

Finally, we consider those stakes in conformity which, following Hirschi (1969), we call *involvements*. These are anything that absorbs a person's time or interest, thereby incapacitating him from committing deviant acts. Juveniles busy making model airplanes, for example, will not be busy stealing cars. Among these involvements are pleasures – activities which people find it enjoyable to pursue without any intention of using them to obtain other rewards. Analytically, little actually is known about the psychic functions of play and entertainment (cf. Huizinga, 1950; Winnicott, 1971). Social science has paid vastly more concern to the material and the affective. Yet it is clear that people treat play and entertainment as rewards – they will pay costs to gain them. Organizations that effectively provide such rewards thereby build a person's stake in that organization. There is no reason why sects and cults are at a competitive disadvantage with churches in offering such pleasures to members. On the contrary, we suspect that successful sects and cults will offer a much wider range of play and entertainment rewards – pleasures – than will churches, that such high-tension movements will seek to dominate all aspects of their members' lives, including their use of leisure.

Thus, reviewing familiar deductions from the present perspective, we can say:

> P302 If they are to grow, religious movements must find means to expand the supply of attachments, investments, and pleasures available through membership.

> P303 If they are to grow, religious movements must increase stakes in conformity to the movement.

We have pointed out that most high-tension religious movements do not grow. Most exceed the tension threshhold and become isolated. But some manage the delicate balance of tension needed for success. They not only persist, they grow. As growth is achieved, many new contingencies arise that transform groups from higher to lower tension with their surroundings. The extreme case makes the point. If most members of a society join a religious movement, the movement becomes one with the society and can hardly be in tension with it. This was the course rapidly traced by Lutheranism in many German states and principalities. Or, in an earlier time, Christianity rose from a despised religious underground to the Church Triumphant through growth. But the case can be made also for less total success stories. As a movement grows, it becomes statistically less deviant. It is much harder to stigmatize convincingly that which is common. Admittedly, rapid growth may cause a crisis by causing anxiety in the prevailing religious instutions. But when this does not lead to successful repression, the mere fact of substantial size will lead to accommodation and the reduction of tension in the long run.

Examples can be found in any society. Morioka (1975) reports on Sōka Gakkai, a Buddhist sect that emerged in Japan following World War II. From about 1950 to 1970, this sect grew from a handful of adherents to a major religious body with several million members. At the beginning, Sōka Gakkai violently denounced other Japanese religions. For example, it demanded that members not engage in ceremonies at their local Shinto shrine, although Japanese traditionally have held plural religious affiliations combining a second faith with Shinto. Sōka Gakkai was thus in a very high state of tension with its surroundings. However, in 1972 after a little more than twenty years of rapid growth, the sect began to soften its stance toward other faiths and formally declared the acceptability of cooperating with other religions to attack social evils. The movement toward becoming a church had begun.

As growth reduces tension, the value of rewards provided by the religious movement increases and pressure toward further tension reduction occurs. The value of some rewards available from religious organizations is set by the external society. The less deviant the group, the more valuable the status rewards of membership and office in a religious body. Growth, by reducing tension, makes the value of further tension reduction apparent. Because growth makes the rewards given by a religious movement more valuable, growth makes it more likely that members will be attracted and held for whom specific compensators are less salient. Put another way, through growth the constituency favoring high tension becomes weaker.

At this point we must reconsider what it means to be lacking in attributes that confer power. Initially, sects and cults are heavily recruited from such persons – those with physical, psychological, achieved, or ascribed characteristics that diminish power. It will be clear that only a few such characteristics, under very special circumstances, will be strictly hereditary. Thus, for example, low IQ parents have many children with higher IQ (Jencks, 1972; McCall, 1977; Scarr and Weinberg, 1978). Neurotic parents do not generate only neurotic children (Pollin, *et al.*, 1969; Kay, 1978). Sickly parents occasionally have healthy children. In consequence, the offspring of a group overselected for powerlessness will not fully inherit this incapacity and will, on average, be more powerful. Thus it can be seen that:

> P304 As the membership of a sect or cult shifts from a converted to a socialized base, the compensator-oriented constituency will shrink relative to the reward-oriented constituency.

Unless the tension chosen by their parents is so great as to deny them opportunities to learn ordinary skills, not only are the capabilities of the new generation significantly different from those of the older generation, but so, too, is their past experience with religion. Conventional religious explanations have not been discredited in their personal experience, a factor that P204, P224 and P227 made significant for joining high-tension movements. Furthermore, P304 is entirely in line with our discussion of regression, the principle here applying across generations. This proposition certainly is a very old generalization about the basis for the shift from sect to church. The children do not inherit all the failings and disappointments of their elders, and will be more reward-oriented. This, of course, may not apply to sects or cults which become highly isolated, for then the stigma of membership may in-and-of-itself constitute a severe, inherited deprivation. But we are speaking here of growing movements on the road to success. For them, the second generation adds to the constituency in favor of reduced tension (Stark and Bainbridge, 1985).

Obviously, this does not apply if there is no second generation. Hence, by strict norms of sexual abstinence the Shakers never faced a second generation problem, nor do Roman Catholic orders. It is significant that in the case of Sōka Gakkai, the substantial reduction of tension occurred not merely after more then twenty years of sustained growth, but also after the passage of one generation (Morioka, 1975).

Growth and concomitant tension reduction have not, of course, swept the world clear of high tension religious groups. Rather, tension reduction prepares the process to start all over again.

> P305 Movement of a high-tension religious body toward lower tension creates both a cadre and a constituency for a new sect movement.

Conclusion

While growth leads to tension reduction, and many other stated principles support this evolution, the acquisition of new rewards is not infinite and their distribution through the membership is not even. Those leaders with the poorest prospects for increased rewards, and with the least supply of scarce rewards, are in the closest contact with a constituency who desire greater tension. This loops our theory back to the process of sect formation already discussed. And it is this loop that permits the theory to deal with the circular process of the birth of sects, their eventual transformation into churches (if they remain viable), and the subsequent generation of new sects, whereupon the cycle repeats. The following chapter explains that the society-wide tension reduction known as *secularization* has the same effect on a larger scale, promoting the emergence not only of sects but also of cults.

CHAPTER 9
Secularization, Revival and Experimentation

Many social theorists would want this book to conclude with an analysis of the impending death of religion. But the story does not end that way. Our seven axioms were meant to describe the enduring conditions of human existence. From them we derived the emergence and development of religion. Nothing in the axioms causes our theory to self-destruct in the year 2000, nor does any part of our theory predict an end to religion so long as humans desire rewards they cannot have and pursue lines of action guided by anything less than complete knowledge. Until that day when our axioms are overturned and humans become gods, people will continue to postulate gods capable of providing those rewards they cannot obtain for themselves.

Secularization is the dominant trend affecting religion in contemporary industrial societies, and scholars often assume this means not only the decline but the fall of all religion (Wallace, 1966; Wilson, 1979). In this chapter we will explain that secularization means the transformation of religion, not its destruction. We do not deny that profound challenges confront the traditional religious denominations. Indeed, we will explain that these challenges are probably too powerful for the traditional low-tension organizations to resist. But religion is far greater than just the low-tension denominations. It also includes high-tension sects and cults. When secularization erodes the power of respectable denominations, it leaves the market for general compensators first to the familiar intensity of sects and then to the novel innovation of cults.

While this chapter will not describe the end of religion, it will bring our theory to closure. New propositions are introduced here, but in the main they complete earlier lines of argument and act as capstones bridging intellectual structures built in preceding chapters. In *The Future of Religion* an analysis of secularization was offered in less systematic form but supported by ample empirical evidence and extended by many middle-range theoretical comments. Here we shall explain the conditions of contemporary religious life and attempt to use the lens of deductive logic to see some distance into the future.

The chief causes of secularization are to be found outside religion itself. As the years pass, humans invent, evaluate and preserve increasingly effective explanations which successfully offer rewards. According to Definition 81, *progress* is the gradual improvement in the human ability to achieve desired rewards. As we shall see shortly, progress has a direct corrosive effect on religion. Suppliers of rewards drive traditional religious organizations out of the business of providing the most specific compensators. But progress has a great indirect effect as well. Religion primarily deals in very general compensators. Therefore the chief foes of religion will be alternate cultural systems that not only provide many rewards beyond religion's scope but also offer competing general explanations – whether these general explanations be true rewards or merely nonreligious compensators. True, only religion can offer the most general compensators which require supernatural explanations. But other cultural systems can offer many relatively general explanations that promise large collections of specific rewards.

Both observation of recent history and analysis within our axiomatic theoretical system reveal that there are primarily two types of cultural system that rise in advanced societies to compete with each other and with religion: *politics* and *science*. Each of these words suggests diffuse clusters of concepts, too vague for proper theorizing, so we choose to define them narrowly:

> Def.100 *Politics* is the cultural specialty dedicated to negotiation of power relationships among groups in society.

> Def.101 *Science* is the cultural specialty dedicated to invention and systematic evaluation of explanations.

Definition 33 said the term *cultural specialization* refers to the tendency of individuals to master parts of their culture and to engage in exchanges with others who have mastered different parts. But a cultural specialization is not necessarily a true cultural system. As Definition 31 presented the concept, explanations form a cultural system if they are parts of a greater explanation that includes them. Cultural specializations may draw on a variety of explanations which do not fit together. We explained that religion tends to emerge early in society, to evolve more rapidly than other parts of culture into a true cultural system, and finally to express itself in aggressive social organizations which specialize in providing general compensators.

P47 Cultural specialties evolve into cultural systems, dependent upon the discovery of explanations that prove valuable in uniting the relevant subexplanations.

P48 Cultural specialties tend to be divided along lines which divide cultural systems.

P49 A cultural specialty dedicated to providing general compensators based on supernatural assumptions tends to evolve into a cultural system, thus becoming a religion.

P70 Religion will be among the very first cultural specialties to emerge in the development of societies.

Recall why religion emerges early. It does not have to wait until progress discovers objectively correct explanations before it can unite its subexplanations into a cultural system. Nor does it even need to wait for systematically evaluated explanations of middle rank. It can forge ahead because by definition it deals in general compensators. The only factor holding back the development of religion is the time it takes for the society to reach the level of size and complexity sufficient to support any formal organizations specializing in providing rewards or apparent rewards (compensators). Politics and science must emerge more slowly.

Political specialists begin to emerge almost as soon as the development of the state. However, political specialists are not just powerful persons. Professional politicians are not simply members of the political elite, and some primitive elites may not include any such specialists. Recall Def.42 which says that those who monopolize the use of coercion are the political elite. To monopolize is not to negotiate. Politicians – political specialists – achieve personal rewards in exchange for channeling power to groups and individuals. Like priests and scientists they offer a service with various apparent rewards in exchange for other rewards.

Negotiation of power implies that power is somewhat fluid and transferrable – that the society contains more than a single, monolithic elite. Thus, political specialists tend to emerge after a society has become complex and somewhat cosmopolitan. Of course, one may find some politicians even in preliterate societies of moderate size. But then one will find them working only part-time, resolving disputes between factions, lineages and tribes, without developed bureaucratic administrative organizations. And of course the emergence of political specialists is not yet the development of political cultural systems. These come considerably later.

Politics deals with demonstrable effects. Either the taxes get collected, or they do not. Either the *Populares* prevail over the *Optimates*, or they do not. There may be some magic in politics, to be sure, but empirical tests of the value of political explanations are continually made. Specific political explanations are readily susceptible to disconfirmation. Further, as a pure specialty politics does not have recourse to supernatural explanations in building a cultural system. Ideas like the divine right of kings are not strictly political but religio-political. We are concerned in this chapter with politics as it can exist separate from religion, because we want to see the two compete in the secularizing process. The fact that politicians traditionally drew on religion to cap their political theories with general explanations shows that politicians were unable to find efficacious, distinctively political, general explanations. Reliance on religion to complete a political ideology proves that the politics has not yet itself evolved into a cultural system.

> P306 Politics will emerge as a cultural system after religion has already done so.

What about the relationship between politics and science? Were this an essay on modern times, rather than a narrow discussion of the competition religion faces in highly developed societies, we might invest much time in delineating the relationships between the two. One point needs to be stressed. Politics can get along with a considerable load of compensators, while science by definition labors incessantly to discard compensators in favor of rewards. Political ideologies may be more susceptible to empirical disconfirmation than are religious ideologies, but science is more susceptible than either.

Science is a search for general explanations, as well as for specific explanations (Russell, 1962). Whatever the personal failings of individual scientists and whatever social conditions may halt or distort scientific progress, the systematic evaluation of explanations is its chief dedication. Although individual scientists and schools of science will continually propose theories purporting to consolidate fields of knowledge under general explanations, the profession will subject them to close scrutiny. Subfields of science may achieve system status, but the whole of science will not achieve full status as a cultural system until after a very long, arduous struggle to find good explanations that stand the test of systematic evaluation. Therefore, science lags behind politics because the latter is able to satisfy itself in part with general compensators.

For example, Marxism as a political doctrine achieved something like system status a century ago with its founder's concepts of stages of economic development and classes. We suggest that these and other traditional Marxist ideas are really compensators. They qualify as such because they were adopted by Marxist parties before the social sciences had evolved to the point where any important explanations could be systematically evaluated, let alone these particular sweeping ideas. There may be much truth to Marxist ideas, or there may not. They became the faith of vast political movements and states before their truth could be evaluated.

Science, like politics, drew upon religion for general explanations before it could develop its own. Several respected scientists and historians have argued that seventeenth century science was assisted by the view that Nature must be intelligible because it was created by a rational, good God (Westfall, 1958; Whitehead, 1967; Merton, 1970). The technology of the time had succeeded in creating machines of some complexity, notably clocks (White, 1962; Cipolla, 1977), and scientists took ideas from both technology and religion to produce the fruitful if compensator-laden explanation that Nature was a mechanism created by a supernatural God and open to human understanding and control through scientific research.

The distinctively scientific general explanation is mathematics. It surprises some lay people to learn that mathematics is still in rapid evolution. Whether twentieth-century group theory or some other approach equally removed from the ordinary experiences of daily life will ultimately achieve full coherence for a unified scientific cultural system, we cannot say. Despite frequent setbacks when old theories are discarded or transcended, the thrust of scientific evolution is in that direction. Parts of science are unified and well-understood, including parts with great relevance for religion. But not yet the whole of science.

P307 Science will emerge as a cultural system after politics has already done so.

P308 Cultural progress permits the development of cultural systems specializing in each major kind of reward that people publically exchange.

P309 As a society achieves a high level of cultural progress, its politics and science will evolve into cultural systems of great scope.

Now we must examine the consequences of the above proposition for religious systems that were already in existence before politics and science approached system status.

Disconfirmation of Religious Culture

Religious traditions that evolved and consolidated before politics and science had developed far tend to contain many explanations vulnerable to disconfirmation by science and competition from politics. We may view these endangered religious explanations as falling into two rough categories: (1) specific compensators for desired rewards which do exist, and (2) other explanations supporting the cultural system. First, we shall consider specific compensators. Religion tends to retain some specific compensators regardless of how old the tradition or how low-tension the group. This can be explained by Chapter 5 and Chapter 8 which show the competition between churches and sects. It is a rare church willing to surrender the community to a rival sect. It is a rare religious specialist unmoved by his customers' desires for specific rewards. But even before the emergence of politics and science as cultural systems, there are strong pressures toward differentiation of religion from magic. Earlier we explained that religious specialists will tend to build a cultural system of great generality and to reduce the amount of magic they offer to escape the disconfirmations suffered by magicians. Recall the following propositions:

P14 In the absence of a desired reward, explanations often will be accepted which posit attainment of the reward in the distant future or in some other nonverifiable context.

P18 Humans prefer rewards to compensators and attempt to exchange compensators for rewards.

P93 Religious specialists will, over time, tend to reduce the amount of magic they supply.

Proposition 14, of course, first introduced compensators into our theoretical system. Proposition 18 noted that people will abandon compensators for the corresponding reward when it is made available to them. Proposition 93 rests on the fact that specific compensators often can be disconfirmed whether or not the desired reward can be obtained by other means. If the reward is cure of a disease, for example, the person may die or linger in chronic illness for many years. Such outcomes disprove magical compensators that promised cure. Religious specialists are well advised to withdraw to a significant extent from the magic business. But there is a great market for compensators to satisfy desires for scarce rewards, and many specific compensators are not readily disconfirmable at a given level of cultural development. What upsets the integration of such specific compensators as can be integrated with religion is cultural progress both in evaluating explanations and in providing rewards.

P310 Cultural progress reduces the market for magic.

P311 Cultural progress promotes the abandonment of magic by religion.

Three earlier propositions charted what would happen when religious specialists perfect their systems of compensators under the pressure of cultural progress:

P58 People will not exchange with the gods when a cheaper or more effective alternative is known and available.

P61 As societies become older, larger and more cosmopolitan they will worship fewer gods of greater scope.

P106 If a religion evolves until it has but one god of infinite scope, it can no longer provide supernatural specific compensators as part of its cultural system, and it will have little to offer most people.

These observations must be tempered with the awareness developed in Chapters 5 and 6 that pressures continue in advanced societies for the formation of high-tension sects and cults, religious organizations cut off from central political and scientific elites. Proposition 242 noted that, within a religious group, pressures toward doctrinal conformity are greater the higher the tension of the group. Thus, sects particularly may resist erosion from secular progress. We shall examine the role of high-tension religion later. Now we mean to focus on low-tension churches and on entire religious traditions as represented by churches. As we have explained, the main assault on religion's more specific compensators is two-pronged: from politics and from science.

P312 The evolution of politics and science into cultural systems of great scope will promote the transformation of low-tension religion into a cultural specialty providing compensators of only the greatest generality.

The more magic a religion offers, the greater its likely number of gods and demigods and the greater need for priests to mediate with them on behalf of parishioners. This was explained in Chapters 3 and 4. Conversely, the less magic the less need for various spirits and saints to accomplish various jobs for humanity or for demons and devils to inflict various costs from which other supernatural beings can save us. If evil gods are not used to explain the costs humans suffer, then one good god of infinite scope will suffice to explain the meaning of life and offer some hope for the great reward after death. Belief in the existence of one or more evil gods offers specific compensators. The evil of this Satan or Ahriman reveals itself in human afflictions, and it logically follows that these can be alleviated by moving closer to a good God. Conversely, if people have been convinced to abandon supernatural magic altogether, they will have no use for the concept of an evil deity. Their religion will shrink to a Deist conception of a good God whose purposes for mankind must themselves be good. This has happened in low-tension religious groups in our own society, especially for clergy who, as educated religious specialists, must be particularly aware of the implications of tenets of faith.

While a God of infinite scope may still wish humans to be good, he has lost most of his bargaining power with his congregations. A good God solely responsible for creating and ordering the world would not punish humans with total damnation for minor transgressions. He provides no specific rewards that might be withheld. There is little he can demand of his congregations beyond the prevailing secular standards of decent behavior. Thus, the ability of religious specialists to demand rewards on behalf of the gods suddenly shrinks just at the point when one God achieves a full monopoly over the powers of Heaven.

An infinite God who made all the universe for his own divine purposes has little reason to intervene in human affairs. Of course science long ago promoted the idea that the world was a mechanism set up by God that does not require continual repair. If God is a watchmaker, He would not make a cheap watch constantly in need of tinkering (Westfall, 1958). Other factors, including pressure from competing cultural systems, accelerate the evolution of a single God into a distant creator no longer requiring much from his believers. But the seeds of this evolution are found in religion itself, seeds free to sprout once religion is severed from magic. If God is single, powerful, and good, he will give us all good things in his own time, regardless of what we given him in return.

P313 Belief in a single good god of infinite scope renders unnecessary the exchange of rewards to obtain religious compensators.

P314 Belief in a single good god of infinite scope severely reduces the ability of religious organizations and specialists to get others to give them rewards in exchange for compensators.

P315 It is impossible to sustain powerful religious organizations based on belief in a single good god of infinite scope.

When we say "impossible to sustain," we do not mean that on one day Episcopalianism decided God was good, great and unchallenged by other supernatural beings – and on the next day the church went broke and retired from the world. Rather, we describe gradual processes, stimulated by general cultural progress in a variety of ways. Some of these factors were present in Classical society and caused erosion of religion among elites. Today and in the future, more factors operate with greater strength for more people – and widespread secularization takes place.

P316 Cultural progress eventually curtails the ability of low-tension religious groups to provide compensators in exchange for valued rewards.

But we said there were two ways in which progress tended to disconfirm religious explanations. Not all of the empirical claims of religion are solely designed to support specific compensators. Some help hold the cultural systems together, while others are accidental appropriations from secular culture. Especially since progress gave priests the tool of writing, religions consolidate in particular cultural contexts and commit themselves to many of the assumptions of their age. The major religious texts of the world, even the highly historical and worldly Old Testament, are not as extensively burdened as they might be by empirically false claims about the physical or social worlds. Yet it must at some time strike every intelligent person that these books show far less prophecy of cultural progress than a real God could have provided his priests. Surely God knew it was a round world that he created, that there were continents on the other side of it, and that man developed over ages of biological evolution. For all the prophecies of messiahs and armageddons, it is hard to discern in the ancient texts much prophecy of science and invention. And, certainly one does find much at variance with modern science and political theory in traditional religious doctrines.

As cultural progress leaves far behind the conditions under which a religion consolidated, more and more explanations within its system fail or are rendered superfluous. What is the result? First of all, people do treat religions as cultural systems:

> P239 Persons who believe in some parts of a strict cultural system will tend to believe in the other parts as well, although they will be prepared to expend the greatest costs for those parts of the system that directly meet their personal needs.

This means that disconfirmation of any part of a religious system is somewhat costly for believers, even if it is other aspects of the religion that primarily sustain their commitment. The struggle to defend a cultural system will be painful, and it is merciful that the erosion of traditional religion has taken place over several centuries rather than impacting catastrophically on any one generation (cf. Abelson, 1959).

The following propositions from Chapter 7 describe the losing battle with creeping disconfirmation:

> P222 If a single explanation in a cultural system fails, people tend to seek another to replace it, without disturbing the rest of the system.

> P223 When explanations in a cultural system fail, people will seek the most modest revision of it that will apparently repair the damage.

> P225 When two or more explanations fail, and are connected by a single explanation more general than they, participants in the cultural system will tend to seek a substitute for the more general explanation, and this tendency will be greater the larger the proportional value of explanations under it that have failed.

> P226 Failure of numerous lower-level explanations in a cultural system tends to be communicated upward until the failure compounds to disconfirm much of the system.

The repairs to a system noted by P222, P223 and P225 can insidiously erode the system from within, in ways not intended. For example, what might happen if the Bible says the world was created in six days but geology and paleontology estimate a period of six billion years? One simple repair is to say that the Bible really means "six periods of time" not six literal days. This risks the possibility that scientists will arrive at a sequence of five or seven periods instead of six. But worse than that, the repair to the system not only turns "days" into "periods" but introduces the tacit new explanation that the Bible contains metaphor as well as fact. At first, this will seem a clever tactic as other conflicts can be resolved by recourse to metaphoric interpretations of scripture. But it furthers the retreat of religion from the world and toward only the most abstract general compensators.

P317 As cultural progress reaches a high level, low-tension religion will accommodate its explanations to science, politics and any other successfully evolving secular cultural systems.

Def.102 *Secular* refers to any parts of society and culture that are substantially free of supernatural assumptions.

Pluralism

The erosion of the power of religion is promoted by pluralism – the existence of two or more low-tension religious groups existing in a measure of harmony with each other. Actually, we may view pluralism as an intermediate stage in secularization. When a single religious organization achieves monopoly through an alliance with the state, it has every reason and the power to suppress alternative religious organizations. But once a religion's power has been eroded slightly it is no longer able to suppress competitors. History tells of many circumstances in which multiple religions came to coexist within a single society. Most cases probably can be assigned to one of two rough categories. First, the processes of sect development described in Chapter 5 and Chapter 8 can produce schismatic splinters of the core religious organization that evolve into competing low-tension denominations. This has happened in Europe and North America. Second, the geographic expansion of a state can absorb several unrelated religious traditions along with the populations that adhere to them. This happened in India and Classical Rome. Unless organizational unification or strict social separation of the constituencies can defuse doctrinal disputes, the result will be weakened power of religion.

Propositions derived earlier describe the effects of time, size and complexity in producing cosmopolitan societies. The factors already mentioned in this chapter ensure that religious cosmopolitanism is highly likely in advanced societies. We can review the earlier propositions with this in mind:

P39 Any culture contains a number of cultural systems.

P42 As a society grows and endures, it will come to have a progressively more complex culture.

P52 The more cosmopolitan societies become, the more complex their cultures.

Def.36 *Cosmopolitan* refers to the existence of plural cultures within a society.

What happens to the power of religion under these circumstances? We have seen that competing cultural systems like politics and science undercut the ability of religious specialists to demand rewards in exchange for their compensators. We have already shown that the same is true when religions compete with each other in an open market.

P67 The more cosmopolitan a society with respect to religious culture, the lower the market value of any given general compensator.

This is because people usually rely on the testimony of other persons in evaluating general compensators. If one's associates disagree, one will be forced to conclude that the proffered compensators are uncertain in value, perhaps not very valuable at all. Proposition 67 affects an individual to the extent that his primary social relationships are not encapsulated within a monolithic group of believers, but are spread out across a range of affiliations and private opinions. Durkheim long ago noted this effect (Durkheim, 1933). In Chapter 3 and elsewhere we saw several lines of derivation for the division of labor, each reinforcing the others. Some of our conclusions about this process may be summarized from the perspective of the individual rather than from that of the society:

P318 Cultural progress multiplies cultural specialties.

P319 Cultural progress increases the number and reduces the average scope of exchange relationships for most individuals.

The multiplication of cultural specialties reflects increasing complexity as well as as size, and is already expressed in a different way through the concept of a *cosmopolitan culture*. It is worth pointing out that individual human beings are required to staff each of these specialties, and that the specialists in each field will be under the influence of different explanations, both specific and general. One can then imagine two alternate ways the professions in society might be organized, each with great consequences for religion. If each cultural specialty is a distinct subculture (an endogenous caste or hereditary guild), then each might be expected to develop its own brand of religion, under the influence of the special needs and perspectives of the specialty. At the other extreme, one can imagine completely random assignment of persons to specialties, with family and friendship ties completely crosscutting the specialties. Then there will be the greatest possible flow of explanations and evaluations, tending to dissolve any particular ideology. Over time, we suspect, historical development will transform the first case into something like the second.

A factor that contributes to erosion of religious commitment in cosmopolitan societies is mobility – both social and geographic mobility. The exegencies of moving from one social stratum to another, within the same community, are more subtle than but similar to those of geographic mobility. Therefore, for the sake of concision, we shall focus on the impact on religious affiliation of geographic mobility (Wuthnow and Christiano, 1979; Bainbridge and Stark, 1981c, 1982; Stark and Bainbridge, 1985; Kevin Welch, 1983; Michael Welch and Baltzell, 1984; Stump, 1984a, 1984b).

In societies that are not yet cosmopolitan, individuals generally live out their lives within a single social group comprised of family and clan members, or at most are exchanged in marriage to another social group tied culturally as well as socially to their family of origin. Thus, one is surrounded by a closed, cohesive primary group. Whether or not the religious specialty has emerged yet, there will be a slurry of more-or-less fluid forms of magic. But if religion has fully developed, it is religion of a single kind, and in large but simple agrarian cultures, it will be a monopolistic church. Under these social conditions, geographic mobility may take the form of migrations of whole societies who take their religion with them unweakened. Individual mobility may be very costly under these circumstances because a mobile individual must gain admittance to a new, alien, closed, cohesive primary group in order to survive.

Surrounded by stable, primary relationships, one is under great pressure to accept the prevailing religion, no matter what one's current personal needs for compensators might be. As P240 explained, members of a religious organization tend to punish or break off relations with those who oppose the belief. Therefore, the member of a tribe or simple agricultural community will be under strong social pressures to conform to the religion shared by its citizens. Further, the individual will have been socialized to this single religion, accepting its explanations along with other explanations of the culture during the most formative years. Individual geographic mobility, if it does take place, may often incorporate the person in a new social group with the same familiar religion. As the person establishes ties to new people, he re-establishes ties to the religion. If the individual moves into a community with an alien religion, he must accommodate himself to their wishes and adopt the new faith, or live in constant tension with his sociocultural environment, unsupported by fellow sectarians.

In cosmopolitan societies, on the other hand, individual geographic mobility is much easier, as P319 implies. Because most relationships are narrow in scope and relatively low in value, it is easy to establish each of them. A newcomer does not have to become the committed member of a closed, cohesive primary group in order to survive. Cosmopolitanism generally means cities, locations of high population density and cultural diversity. The newcomer enters town, exchanges some wealth for lodging among tolerant strangers, and seeks employment. Soon, he has established a number of weak social ties – to people at work, to others where he lives, and to habitues of any place of recreation he frequents. Most likely, he will establish these secular relationships first. He must first see to his needs for specific rewards, mainly economic but also social, before worrying about longer-term needs for general rewards and compensators.

Of course, if there is but one dominant religion in his society, he may re-establish affiliation eventually. A church in his new neighborhood with a vigorous outreach program may contact him as soon as he comes to town and recruit him right away (Kunz and Brinkerhoff, 1970). Some geographically mobile individuals may be religious seekers who quickly establish ties to a new congregation. Other special factors we cannot now imagine may secure the religious affiliation of geographically mobile individuals. But in the absence of some such force, the geographically mobile individual is especially prey to disaffiliation from religion.

In cosmopolitan, religiously pluralist societies the newcomer has a good chance of establishing social ties to a number of other persons without respect to their religious affiliations. He passes daily through several social worlds – workplace, residence, recreations – and may establish friendships with several individuals who do not even share the weakest social relationships with each other. He will enter an open, heterogeneous, only weakly interconnected network. Depending on the mix of religious affiliations in the population, and their distribution across sectors of the society, he has a good chance of developing relationships to people with a variety of religious affiliations including some who are not tied to a religious organization at all. Unless chance permits an accidental consensus of religious affiliation among the new friends, the individual will not be drawn into any particular congregation, and thus will drift without membership in a religion. This does not mean he has lost all trace of this original religious socialization. Nor will he never feel the need for general explanations about life nor be a potential customer for general compensators. He has not suddenly become a secular rationalist free of all superstition. Rather, he has become a social atom in an extended, religiously diverse social network that fails to provide him with the influence and fellowship of a congregation. He may be more open now to political or scientific ideological appeals and hence become psychologically irreligious. But it is first of all his affiliation which has been lost, not his faith or his needs.

P320 The more cosmopolitan a society, the more common is individual social and geographic mobility.

Def.103 *Mobility* is movement from one material and social environment to another.

P321 In cosmopolitan societies, social and geographic mobility tends to sever the ties of religious affiliation.

P322 Cosmopolitan societies tend to have rates of religious affiliation significantly lower than the maximum permitted by other characteristics of the societies.

We can now end this section with a very general proposition, one that could have been stated earlier because it is supported by the arguments of previous sections as well as the one completed here. We held this key proposition for this point in our deductions so the reader could see that it follows from several lines of derivation that describe parallel and mutually supporting historical evolutions. They are threads in a single rope of great strength supporting *secularization*, defined in terms of the strength of religious organizations (Gerharz, 1970).

P323 A high level of cultural progress produces secularization.

Def.104 *Secularization* is the progressive loss of power by religious organizations.

Suppression of Religion

To this point we have discussed the competition between religion and other cultural systems as a polite struggle for men's minds and social relationships. There is a vicious side to the game, unfortunately. When it held an effective alliance with the state, religion was quick to suppress its rival, science, and to work on behalf of traditional elites to retard the development of politics as an independent specialty. Proposition 84 noted that religious specialists who enjoy a monopoly in the field of religion will tend to support the state, while Proposition 85 explained that they will also work to limit the state's repressiveness over its citizens. These are functions that secular political specialists would like to serve. Only after religion has been ousted from its alliance with the state can political specialists take full control of power negotiations in the society.

The topics of this chapter are historical processes that take place at certain levels of cultural development and not at others. We might ask in which order the various struggles between cultural specialties will take place. Propositions 306 and 307 define the order of emergence of the three main cultural systems. Specialists in each will see and achieve alliances with the state about as soon as they can, so the alliances will take place in the same order as the specialties achieve system status.

> P324 Cultural specialties become cultural systems and forge their alliances with the state in the following order: religion, politics, science.

These alliances are not necessarily total. Britain and other countries that kept ancient traditions while industrializing may be the best examples of societies in which the state has balancing alliances with all three systems, although as in America the role of religion has become largely ceremonial. Many developing countries show vivid contests among all three, because each cultural system offers itself as the means to channel explosive demographic, technological and economic changes. The Soviet Union and its allies show how far politics can go in suppressing religion. Certainly, the former alliance between religion and the state has been abolished in these societies, but even with the support of the state, a monolithic political party has not yet succeeded in eradicating human hopes for the supernatural. Even in the Soviet Union, the party and its state find some use for religion as a tool to manage social strain (London and Poltoratzky, 1957; Glezer, 1976; Mihajlov, 1976; Beeson, 1977; Ellis, 1978; Kowalewski, 1980a, 1980b).

To see how the systems compete, a few more words about politics are in order. First, we must repeat a caveat that might well be embossed on every page of this book: When we define a word, that is what we want it to mean, and nothing else. A word like *politics* could be used to express several different concepts. We have no quarrel with readers who wish to employ "politics" concepts different from that given in our definition. But we need to distinguish these concepts from each other. Let us agree on a different name for each different concept that any of us wishes to use, and we can converse with sufficient clarity for good theorizing. But if we use a technical word in ways other than that given in its definition, chaos will result.

Many readers might wish to use the word *politics* for any processes of power adjustment, including an individual's strategies for amassing personal power. We have defined *politics* narrowly as the cultural specialty dedicated to negotiation of power relationships among groups in society. Thus, the mere existence of an elite does not prove the existence of politics in this sense. Politics arises as a cultural specialty when the society develops competing subgroups, each with some power, and needs formalized means for negotiation among them. The evolution of politics into a cultural system requires more than this. There must be a variety of kinds of situation negotiated, each with appropriate explanations organized in a conceptual hierarchy with general explanations uniting the parts.

As in religion, the most general explanations are apt to be compensators. Much twentieth-century political theory explains that political ideologies will tend to serve the interests of competing groups (Mannheim, 1936; Habermas, 1978). The general explanations of each will encourage action the effect of which will be to promote the interests of its constituency. Therefore, as in religion there will tend to be competing political faiths serving different segments and strata of society. We might call competing political ideologies, sustained by groups of supportive specialists and adherents, political *parties*.

However, parties vary so much in character in our changing world that in the absence of a fully-developed theory of politics we hesitate to set firm definitions. The two major parties in the United States are hardly more than election-coalitions with an uncertain degree of ideological disagreement. Neither the Democrats nor Republicans can be said to possess true political cultural systems. Not so the one party in the Soviet Union. Whatever its subterranean factions, it is as monolithic as any state church ever was, possessing a true cultural system capped by a few relatively general compensators – "revolution," "dictatorship of the proletariat," "inexorable course of history," and "dialectical materialism." Without pausing for a full analysis, we should note that most principles relating to the development, schism and competing of religious organizations apply also to political organizations.

Proposition 72 noted that in in socially complex and cosmopolitan societies, a religious organization can achieve an effective monopoly only through an alliance with the state. We also explained that religious specialists seek such a monopoly. The same principles apply to politics, once it has fully emerged, and for the same reasons. Only through a monopoly can a particular political organization freeze out competition, and only through coercion provided by the state can it achieve such monopoly. Thus, parallel to P71, and P72, we can say:

> P325 Once political specialists have emerged in a society, they will tend to combine in organizations seeking a political monopoly.

> P326 In socially complex and cosmopolitan societies, a political organization can achieve an effective monopoly only through an alliance with the state.

This alliance is only an intermediate stage. Through it, a political organization may achieve monopoly. Then, the successful organization tends to supplant other elites until it is the state. Recall our definition: The *state* is the monopoly of the cultural means of coercion by a clearly differentiated group of specialists. These specialists need not be modern politicians with coherent political ideologies. They may be a military caste. Frequently, the primitive state consists of a dynasty backed by lesser nobles all controlling military units. Political activity may be a part-time job for some of them whenever the claims to power and other rewards need to be negotiated between groups.

When full-time political specialists first appear, professional negotiators of power, they may be lackies or associates of the traditional elites. If political specialists form a number of political organizations, many may overtly oppose the traditional elites while others may collaborate with them. Opposition political groups are much more likely to develop general ideologies and qualify as true cultural systems, because groups collaborating with traditional elites will have to accept a variety of explanations (including religious compensators) favored by those established elites.

If a "right-wing" party originally friendly to the elite does achieve system status and gain a monopoly, it will tend to supplant or absorb the old elite, as was the case for Nazism. If a "left-wing" or other revolutionary party achieves political monopoly, it will cast out old elites and install itself as the state. Thus, an alliance can only be partial or temporary. The full force of political monopoly is felt when a political organization becomes the monopoly of the cultural means of coercion.

Religion, too, may seek to consume the state. In a few cases, such as the Byzantine Empire, the chief of state may also claim to be head of church. But religion is in the compensator business, primarily, while the state is a structure of power and the rewards it garners. Therefore, however secure the alliance, religion will always draw or be driven somewhat apart from the state. True theocracy is unstable. Politics deals in exactly the commodity out of which the state is built: secular power.

P327 A political organization can sustain an effective monopoly only if it becomes the state.

P328 In socially complex and cosmopolitan societies, a political organization can achieve an effective monopoly by replacing the state.

P329 A political organization with an effective monopoly becomes the state.

What kind of state will this monopoly produce? Since the political ideologies of which we speak are well-developed cultural systems, there will be an orthodox belief to which people can be bound. Any changes in the ideology or social structure of the state threaten the leadership because they expose cleavages along which lines of dispute and factional competition can arise. Traditional religion, like alternative political ideologies, will threaten not benefit the new elite, and will be suppressed. To the extent that the political ideology fails to provide all desired rewards, there may develop loosely-organized forms of magic outside the party, but any strong counter-organizations will be broken up. The political specialists and their immediate exchange partners will constitute a New Class (Djilas, 1974) which, in economically and technically advanced societies, may be able to achieve unprecedented control over other facets of society. A repressive state is the result.

P330 A state consisting of a political monopoly is a repressive state.

As is our habit, we earlier defined a repressive state in terms of contingencies of exchange: A *repressive state* exists when the political elite use their monopoly of the cultural means of coercion to impose below-market exchange ratios on non-elite members of the society. Repression is limited by cleavages within the elite, by competing yet cooperating elites who cannot defeat each other or agree in all particulars about how to exploit non-elites. When elites compete, they tend to distribute rewards to non-elites in return for support against the other elites.

A single, monolithic elite, unrestrained by religion or other independent sources of power, will go far in draining other groups of resources which it turns to its own purposes. This does not mean that all elites are hedonistic, as the Roman aristocracy became. Factors of elite society may limit the expenditure of rewards on personal enjoyment. This is the case today with the Soviet Union. True, supreme leaders tend to have summer dachas and fleets of elegant foreign automobiles. But far more of that nation's resources are expended in collective purposes of the elite, such as military strength, than in extravagant personal pleasures.

Among the institutions the repressive state dominates are religion and science. In modern societies with fully developed political cultural systems, only special circumstances give a repressive state good reason to permit religion, let alone support it. While they cannot completely destroy religion, they are well advised to suppress it as far as practical to prevent it from becoming a successful rival. This threat does not vanish with time because as the years pass the political system's compensators will become disconfirmed, one by one. At first, the Revolution holds nearly as much promise as Heaven. But the Revolution comes, while Heaven remains hidden behind the veil of death, and soon all may see that politics failed to bring utopia. The great generality and supernatural support of religious explanations renders them fit competitors for politics when its more magical compensators are proven false.

As the state, a political system may find itself seeking an alliance with religion, but this is a dangerous course because religion will seek to limit the power of the state, opening a crack where counter-elites may grow. We do not describe a stable relationship between the repressive, political state and religion, but one of great instability in which religion may occasionally seem a resource to a beleaguered elite, but is also ultimately a mortal threat.

Science stands in an ambivalent relation to politics, just as it does to religion. Bereft of its compensators, religion is nothing. Bereft of its compensators, politics is the naked application of power for personal or group gain. Science erodes compensators. To be sure, many things masquerade as science. But as we have defined it, science is the pursuit of good explanations objectively evaluated. The standard of evaluation is the real ability of explanations to provide humanly desired rewards, including understanding. To gain effective explanations, science seeks general explanations that can efficiently unite and strengthen specific scientific discoveries and every-day observations.

We have no Pollyanna notion that the explanations of science provide only rewards and never costs. We know that one man's fission is another man's poison. But science does not tell us we should melt our cities with atomic explosives. It tells us how to create such explosions and also reports the effect they might have on human populations. Physical science increased the human ability to achieve desired rewards; it did not ensure that humans would use the new means for general enrichment.

Some hope remains that the social sciences will provide effective explanations for how to create just and peaceful societies able to make use of advanced physical technology for human benefit, not harm. However, in proposing and evaluating ideas for social improvement, the social sciences run afoul of both religion and politics. To the extent that science provides explanations about human conduct, it invades territory as dear to politics as to religion.

The highly-politicized twentieth century might be seen as the era of greatest perversion of the social sciences amid unchecked promotion of the physical sciences. It is said that the only science completely outlawed in Nazi Germany was sociology (Schoenbaum, 1966). Anthropology and political science were debased beyond recognition. Even some physical sciences with sociopolitical implications were seized by political ideologies. Genetics suffered not only under the Nazis but also under Stalin (Medvedev, 1971).

Repressive states need advanced technology to compete with other states, no matter how saturated with compensators their social ideology (Viereck, 1965). But the cultural system of science is organized by general explanations that encourage the invention and testing of hypotheses in all fields. Thus, in the Soviet Union one of the main sources of dissent is the ranks of creative scientists who often may be tempted to apply their professional norms to taboo aspects of Soviet culture (Medvedev and Medvedev, 1971). One strategy that the Soviet state uses to extract benefits from science while limiting its danger is the geographical and social isolation of science. For decades, science towns have been built apart from the rest of society, and leaders of major scientific programs are kept anonymous to prevent their gaining public support or independent bases of power (Bainbridge, 1976).

While modern political monopolies may want to suppress religion, they absolutely need to control science. If they can, they will establish unequal alliances with science, extracting benefits while restricting free scientific inquiry. Some repressive states many choose to import their science, rather than risk the disruption caused by native scientists. Among these repressive states may be some where religion remains strong. For repressive states that are political organizations guided by fully developed cultural systems:

> P331 A state consisting of a political monopoly will seek to repress religion.

P332 A state consisting of a political monopoly will seek an alliance with science in which it is the dominant party.

Surely politics is different from religion, although some of the same sociological principles do apply to organizations within these cultural specialties. But science is markedly different from either religion or politics. The factors operating to produce monopolistic organizations seem much weaker in science. For politics, as for religion, one motive of monopoly is to protect compensators from disconfirmation. In the long run, true science disconfirms compensators, even though individual scientists and schools of thought may invent compensators in the search for new explanations. Furthermore, except for instructional purposes, the work of science need not be repeated from generation to generation. Completed scientific investigations tend, sooner or later, to become public knowledge. Discovery of good explanations does not confer stable power on scientists because they quickly loose possession of their own creations. Science, it has frequently been remarked, is democratic in many respects. Whatever the shortcomings of this view of science, we find it difficult to see how science can produce monopolistic social organizations in contemporary society, unless these are created for its own purposes by the state.

As science moves closer to cultural system status, its relationship to politics may change in two ways with different consequences. First, if subfields and fields within science succeed in finding general explanations to unite their subexplanations and observations, then those branches of research become less valuable. Their work is done, so their costs need no longer be borne. However unlikely an end to scientific progress may seem to many readers, achievement of good general explanations does largely complete the task of science in a given area – by definition. There will remain the lesser tasks of filling in specific gaps, perhaps a less imaginative job to be completed by technicians. Pretend, purely for example, that Einstein had answered all major questions in his branch of theoretical physics. Then no repressive state need ever suffer the political liberalism of an Einstein because it can find his discoveries in old scientific journals rather than only in the creativity of a great and free mind.

Our second point about science is what might happen if it were to achieve general system status. If it became a unified, positively evaluated set of principles about all aspects of human existence, then it might attain monopoly over the means of coercion and become the state. This is the dream – and nightmare – of many writers. Dictators today sometimes claim they rule on behalf of science, but the reality is otherwise. We modestly withdraw from the threshold of this vast and engaging topic, noting only that if science were to achieve cultural system status on the general level, it would severely undercut all religion and ideological politics. The reader may consult utopian and dystopian authors for further insights about the quality of rule by science.

We shall conclude this section, as we did the last, with a summary proposition that could have been stated earlier but speaks with special force here:

> P333 When they become cultural systems of great scope, politics and science will severely limit the power of religion.

Secularization and Revival

To this point in the chapter we have painted pictures of bleak, constricted futures for religion. This is so because we have concentrated on the destructive effects of secularism as the clearest way of introducing the concept. Now we can begin to examine the ways secularization can actually stimulate the growth of religions of certain kinds. We shall retreat for a time from consideration of those unhappy societies dominated by secular repressive states and return to consideration of more open, liberal societies as they experience loss of power by traditionally influential churches.

Earlier we mentioned that the fates of low-tension and high-tension religious groups are different at the stage when churchly power begins to weaken. Indeed, the slow collapse of the churches gives sects a new market to exploit. As Chapter 5 showed, the natural constituency for sect movements is the ubiquitous category of persons who suffer relative deprivation of one kind or another and are prevented from controlling low-tension denominations by those more fortunate than they who wield power in churches and secular institutions. The pressures toward schism produce high-tension sects which then can recruit anyone socially free to switch affiliations and desirous of efficacious compensators. Earlier in this chapter we derived the following proposition:

> P316 Cultural progress eventually curtails the ability of low-tension religious groups to provide compensators in exchange for valued rewards.

This does not happen because congregations unanimously reject compensators offered by their religious specialists. On the contrary, the forces of cultural change operate much more strongly on elites within the churches than on rank-and-file members. The religious specialists are trained in contemporary theology and make it a matter of status within their own profession to keep up-to-date on controversies and trends of religious and secular ideology. Powerful lay members of their congregations tend to be tied to the more advanced sectors of the larger culture, and thus will also be influenced first by widespread secularization. Rank-and-file members of the congregation will tend to become dissatisfied by the brand of religion offered them. They want rewards, and their ministers have become unwilling to provide even the corresponding compensators (Hadden, 1969; Stark *et al.*, 1971). Ordinary members generally have not yet joined the elites in acceptance of secular ideologies – and may never do so since the driving cultural specialties, politics and science, are occupations for tiny minorities which come to constitute elites.

The dissatisfied parishioners will tend to be locked into their current religious affiliations by the same forces that generally retard recruitment to high-tension groups as described in Chapter 7. But the very cosmopolitanism of secularizing societies gives people greater freedom to switch affiliations. Individuals who are mobile can switch at "turning points." Other individuals in cosmopolitan societies may develop exchange relationships with persons in more satisfactory denominations, and gradually shift over without much notice from other exchange partners. Since may religious groups in modern society have high intermarriage rates, individuals may switch to a more satisfying religious affiliation at this juncture in their lives (Greeley, 1981), as well as at other turning points. As Chapter 5 explained, the tendency will be for people to switch to other religious groups in the tradition in which they were socialized. At this stage in secularization, therefore, sects have an advantage over cults.

> P334 When cultural progress curtails the ability of low-tension religious groups to provide compensators, sects will increase their share of the compensator market and recruit numbers of people they could not gain previously.

Among those most liable to recruitment, paradoxically, are those who have already made the transition to complete disaffiliation from religion. Many educated participants in low-tension denominations will simply drift away from religion altogether when it ceases to offer efficacious compensators. They may receive shallow indoctrination in the corrosive myths of secularism, fail to gain anything distinctive from church participation, and lapse into lifestyles that are not actively atheistic but which simply make no room for religion. However, the need for scarce and unavailable rewards continues. For some people, professional activity in science, politics or associated fields may reward continuing secularism (cf. Faia, 1976). But for others, probably the majority, there is a lingering familiarity with a particular tradition of supernatural belief that can be exploited by a high-tension religious group if it can offer fellowship and efficacious compensators at a vulnerable time in the person's life.

This process of disaffiliation from an unrewarding low-tension group, a period of no affiliation, then recruitment to a high-tension group often spans two generations. The offspring of a lapsed low-tension church member joins a sect undeterred by any personal memory of dissatisfaction with religion. It is the higher-tension denominations and sects that will recruit, because low-tension groups cease aggressive proselytizing when they lose faith.

> P335 In secular societies, persons without any religious affiliation and without strong stakes in conformity to political or scientific ideologies will be especially likely to join high-tension religious groups.

Naturally, all of the principles of affiliation outlined in Chapter 7 apply here. Recall the following:

> P236 Persons are more likely to join religious movements at turning points in their lives.

> > Def.93 A *turning point* is a period of markedly decreased attachment, investment, involvement and belief, taken singly or in any combination.

> P244 Persons low in social relationships are more likely than others to become members of a new religious group.

Recall also P320, which noted that cosmopolitan societies have high rates of individual social and geographic mobility. Such mobility produces turning points and temporarily cuts the mobile individual off from restraining social bonds. This not only produces lower rates of religious affiliation, as noted by P322, but also permits more people to be recruited to new religious affiliations, whatever the level of tension of the new group. Furthermore, in cosmopolitan societies a high proportion of an individual's associates may not be members of his own denomination, so even if he is not mobile he will be held in his original church by fewer ties and drawn toward others by more ties.

> P336 Cosmopolitan societies tend to have high rates of denominational switching.

When people are free to switch denominations easily, they are more able to gain the kind of religion they personally want. In Chapter 5 we noted that the emergence of sects in a society with a single religious tradition will lead to a very high rate of religious affiliation. Here we note that secularization brings factors which increase affiliation as well as factors which reduce it. While we cannot yet specify the mathematical functions that would describe precisely the contrary trends, we can confidently observe that secularization is self-limiting. The level of affiliation in a cosmopolitan society may be lower than in a culturally-monolithic society with tolerance for sects. But it may be high compared with societies that prescribe religious diversity. Thus, despite P67 and P322:

> P337 Cosmopolitan societies have substantial rates of religious affiliation.

True, many features of cosmopolitanism erode religion, but we must recognize that an open market does permit people to seek satisfaction, however corrosive of absolute commitment it may be. We must emphasize that secularization does not end the human need for religion. The axioms in Chapter 2 from which we derived the existence of religion were stated as true for all human societies.

> P338 Cultural progress cannot eliminate the need for highly general compensators or for every specific compensator.

The decline in power of low-tension churches, the ease of denominational switching, and the continuing human desire for unavailable rewards means that one striking consequence of secularization is a flowering of religion, not its demise. Secularization produces an era of religious revival and experimentation (Bell, 1971, 1980).

For a time in the experience of any community, the traditional religious ideologies retain some force, even as organizations decay. The sects remain strong even after the liberal churches lose power. By the principles of Chapter 5, new sects emerge out of the wreckage, and by Chapter 7, individuals are more readily recruited to sects. Far from promoting ecumenism, secularization promotes sectarianism.

> P339 In the short run, secularization stimulates the development of sect movements.

P340 In the short run, secularization stimulates recruitment to sect movements.

We must note a limitation on the development and growth of sects, however. Recall that sects especially provide specific compensators, notably compensators for scarce rewards that do exist. They offer members compensation for the wealth, power and status jealously guarded by elites in the society. But radical political movements can also serve this function. Secularizing societies that contain one or more high-tension political movements will experience less growth of religious sects because potential members are siphoned off by the hope of gaining the specific rewards through political action. Indeed, the ability of radical political parties to provide efficacious compensators, especially for status deprivations, is notable.

P341 The existence in a secularizing society of one or more viable high-tension political organizations inhibits the growth of religious sects.

We should not ignore the role, at least as played over the short term, of enduring cultural traditions. Protestant nations have long known sectarianism and been forced to accommodate themselves to it. Catholic nations have not. Just as radical parties draw recruits away from sects, so too sects draw recruits away from radical political parties. Therefore, we might expect cultures that encourage religious sects to experience less political radicalism, holding constant the intensity of needs for scarce rewards.

Germany would be an interesting case for study. Before the Nazis sought to link politics to their own brand of magic, Germany experienced the greatest social strains and produced the most bewildering array of political parties and radical social movements. It is hard to know what level of sect formation and recruitment to expect for Germany in the 1920s, with the tradition of religious pluralism and extreme social strains. But after World War II we see an utterly different situation in many respects. Religious traditions remained, but strain and serious factionalism were reduced to near absolute minima in a context of far advanced secularization. And in Germany, the growth of religious sects, spawned within or introduced from without, has been marked (Hutten, 1964; Stark and Bainbridge, 1985).

The German case reminds us that international conditions, as much as the conditions within a society or community, determine contemporary history. Cultural progress brings an ever-larger number of people at ever-greater distances into the category with whom any individual may have an exchange relationship.

Cultural progress permits powerful states to exert their power against even the most distant other states. Far from deflating our propositions about high-tension religion, these changes give them greater potential scope. There are no limits to the number of persons who can experience relative deprivation and seek collectively a high-tension solution to their problems. In Germany this led to National Socialism, a political sect with strong mystical overtones and the tendency to manufacture almost religious compensators.

Every proposition we have derived concerning sects, except for one or two that include size as a variable, may apply to groups as large as nations. Unless acting as agents for a superpower, radical groups that seize control of nations and experience great *antagonism* toward outsiders will also display other characteristics of the high-tension sect, including *separation* and *difference*. Ideologies promulgated by other nations, especially those broadcast by the superpowers, may draw forth angry sentiments from nationalists of whatever political stripe. There will be a tendency for independent revolutionary parties to seek their own national ideologies, perhaps a local brand of socialism but perhaps also a blend of socialism and a revitalized native religion.

The reader will have the benefit of months or years of added history which we do not possess as we write this book. We, however good our theory, are not prophets. Yet today the world seems fairly bursting forth with religious or religiously-tinged nationalist movements, especially in the Islamic tradition. In the absence of international coercion, some radical movements may seize power in the name of traditional religion, where it has not been discredited by alliances with foreign oppressors or exploitative native elites. To achieve the cultural difference that marks high-tension movements, they will be encouraged to avoid the ideologies of Thomas Jefferson or Karl Marx and seek local creeds that can be adapted to serve the revolution. And local religions may provide not only suitable ideology but sometimes also highly trained cadres – the religious specialists.

> P342 To the extent that available political ideologies have been discredited by association with national enemies, popular and nationalist revolutions will tend to revive or create religious organizations in alliance with the state that are in high tension vis-a-vis other states.

Hitlerian Paganism represented the creation of a new national cult, bearing dim resemblances to pre-Christian German traditions, but containing so many innovations that it cannot properly be seen simply as re-establishment of a millennia-dead church. Whatever the future may hold for Iran – and the reader knows some of this future – recent establishment of Shiite religion as the dominant cultural force guiding the state represents what outsiders might properly call establishment of a sect.

Here the definition of sect must be recalled. Certainly the dominant religious organizations in a society are not deviant with respect to that society's norms, whether they be Nazi or Shiite. But from the perspective of the surrounding world, both are deviant if in different degree. From the perspective of the Moslem world as a whole, the Shiite branch is relatively high in tension, a minority with more intense practices and deviant beliefs – different – compared to those followed by more numerous Sunni. The sectlike Southern Baptist denomination might recognize in the loose, charismatic Shiite authority structure its own sectarian tendencies. Yet as a "sect" that dominates an entire society, the Shiite faith is the local "church." This current example shows what many others might underscore: secularization may give religious sects great international importance and place them in positions of unaccustomed power.

We cannot pursue these geographical ruminations further here. Let them remind us that sects can be significant on a large stage, not just in personal dramas of private religion. The forms of revival stimulated by secularization are not trivial.

Secularization and Innovation

The advantages enjoyed by sects over churches in the early stages of widespread secularization do not last forever. While low-tension denominations lose power, higher-tension groups resist erosion by ignoring intellectual trends in the surrounding sociocultural environment and by drawing strength from constituencies somewhat outside the cultural mainstream. As we noted in the previous chapter, there are tendencies for sects and sect members to move toward lower tension. By this means, the high rates of social and geographic mobility in cosmopolitan societies will to some extent replenish the reservoir of believers near the society's centers of power. But as secularization advances, the zone of weakness spreads to include more and more of the formerly dominant religious tradition.

Partly, this diffusion of secularization is promoted by the continuing growth of politics, science and other competing systems. Art and the mass media, especially popular fiction, provide compensators in the vicarious experience of rewards. Development of social service organizations supplants some of religion's former power to alleviate or compensate suffering. Public recreations provide a social life once found principally within a church congregation. As these trends continue, particularly the spreading systematization of politics and science, more and more people come to be included in the secularized portions of society.

The cultural developments in politics, science and elsewhere discredit traditional religious beliefs first for some segments of society, then for others. The wavefront of social awareness of these developments and acceptance of their implications spreads from the low-tension end of the religious spectrum through the middle range toward the high-tension end. Sects at the extreme in tension will be well-isolated from this influence and may resist it indefinitely, so long as they can survive without much contact with the larger society and without recuiting many new members from it. Such sects must be small, and therefore will not represent the main trend in future religion. And it is the old religious tradition as a whole that is threatened by secularization, not just single organizations within it. We have noted that the development of competing cultural systems discredits religion, but we must here emphasize that the victim is primarily the traditional religion.

Science and politics do not disconfirm all compensators that might be postulated, but have a tendency to disconfirm the most popular specific compensators of the traditional religion. Since these compensators were invented to give apparent satisfaction to enduring needs of the society, science and politics will also address themselves to these needs, either providing the long-sought rewards or at least offering competing compensators. Furthermore, as we explained earlier, when a religion is first consolidated, its prophets do not achieve fully radical insights but instead incorporate many conventional aspects of the ambient culture. Thus they will place in their holy writings various popular notions that will be overturned by scientific and political developments. To summarize our earlier arguments in a form useful for present purposes:

> P343 Cultural progress tends to disconfirm traditional systems of compensators.

This proposition specifies that it is the traditional compensators that are most vulnerable to disconfirmation by cultural progress. Other compensators may exist that progress has not yet touched. Most importantly, it is not difficult to invent brand new compensators designed to harmonize with the most recent political and scientific developments. Despite the corrosive effect of secularization on the main religious tradition, existing cults may not be touched. New cults may easily be invented to avoid the archaic and primitive notions of the world and crude explanations offered by ancient religions. Thus, cults have a special advantage once secularization has progressed far enough to discredit the society's religious tradition.

Secularization, as we have noted, does not remove the need for compensators. Some specific compensators may be rendered obsolete, but progress also may produce new problems – whether new threats that must be faced or new opportunities that will draw forth human desire. While P310 correctly noted that cultural progress reduces the market for magic, because by definition progress means an increased ability to achieve rewards and less need for compensators, this happy effect does not touch human life evenly. As great old needs are satisfied, some perhaps lesser new needs are generated. Some market for magic is constant, and the overall reduction is somewhat offset by shifts in the particular needs. Further, as religion retreats further and further from specific compensators, there is more rapid decline in traditional satisfaction of needs for magic that outpaces the decline in need itself.

Thus, secularization stimulates the growth of cults – cults of many kinds, both merely magical and fully religious. Some earlier propositions foreshadowed this observation. Keep in mind that secularization means loss of power by religious organizations, the concomitant decline of coercion on behalf of the religious tradition, progressive discrediting of traditional religious explanations, and the abandonment by standard churches of much of the magic they previously offered communicants. These conditions stimulate cults, for the following reasons among others:

P94 To the extent that a demand for magic continues after religious specialists have ceased providing it, others will specialize in providing it.

P151 The greater the degree of coercion the external society imposes on religious deviance, the weaker the tendency for deviant religious organizations to form.

P194 To the extent that a society does not punish religious innovation, small sects tend to evolve into cults.

P220 Persons who desire limited rewards that exist, but who lack the social power to obtain them, will tend to affiliate with cults, to the extent that their society does not possess a dominant religious tradition supported by the state.

Proposition 94 predicts the proliferation of magical cult services as secularization progresses, and of course these client cults will frequently pretend to be branches of science or politics when it is no longer culturally necessary to invoke religious symbolism. Proposition 151 says that as religious coercion goes down, the cost of religious deviance declines also, so more cults will be free to emerge. A repressive state can achieve some gains in suppressing cults, if it chooses to, but one advantage of cults as a type of operation is that they can innovate to escape the definitions used by the state in deciding when to apply punishment. The flowering of pseudoscientific cults in the Soviet Union is a fact that illustrates this advantage cults have over the more readily categorized churches and sects.

Proposition 194 shows that sects in secular society are especially free to evolve into cults, and we might add that when the wavefront of disconfirmation reaches a sect it may react to this challenge by innovating and gaining the advantages of cult status. Proposition 220 states in another way that the erosion of a religious tradition gives an advantage to cults or sects. Part of the logic behind the derivation of this proposition was the observation that sects stand in opposition to churches, high-tension versus low in a single tradition, and when the elite stops supporting the church the deprived will lose the churches as a target of their resentment. Sect members assert their superiority over the elite by denegrating their churches; when the elite become secularized the sects lose the advantage of opposition to the churches. Cults may now arise to attack directly whatever symbols the elite has freshly adopted to express its power and prestige.

Two other propositions derive increased rates of cult formation and recruitment from the fact of social change and its reflection in an ideology of progress, conditions inextricably bound with secularization.

P170 Overt religious engineering will be most rewarded in a culture that trusts in a doctrine of cultural progress.

P197 When cultural change or other factors produce new needs and new conditions of life for numbers of people, the rate of cult formation will increase proportionally.

Granting that a variety of factors may sustain sects for a long time after secularization, still it appears that cults will enjoy progressively greater advantages over sects in ever larger segments of the population. At least for many generations, the effect of secularization is not the destruction of religion. Rather, secularization first disestablishes and demotes the low-tension denominations, while giving freer reign to the sects. Then, the sects lose to the benefit of the cults.

P344 In the long run, cultural progress stimulates the emergence of cult movements.

Conclusion

We have finished our long series of deductions with a proposition, among many, which shows that secularization is a self-limiting process. As we explained in our companion volume, *The Future of Religion*, secularization is not a new phenomenon. Rather, the processes that erode commitments to a particular set of supernatural assumptions are found in every society, even the most simple. Magic designed to cure disease or to command the forces of wind and weather can be seen to fail even if scientific theories of biology and meteorology are lacking. Thus, systems of general compensators that also incorporate specific compensators are open to partial disconfirmation long before the birth of science as a cultural specialty. Of course, this only opens the market to new systems of compensators and encourages religion to get out of the magic business.

But people desire many scarce and nonexistent specific rewards, so there is always a market for specific compensators, Religions that abandon specific compensators, perhaps as their theologians postulate a single god of infinite scope, not only encourage independent magicians but also the emergence of high-tension sects and cults which are brave enough to offer specific compensators. The fact that large societies consist of many different groups of people with different needs and different levels of power means that religions will suffer internal divisions often leading to schisms. Organizations in lower tension with the sociocultural environment will tend to be more secular, and the movement of a successful sect toward lower tension will entail an appreciable secularization of the formerly high-tension group. Thus, tension reduction is a form of secularization, but it inevitably leads to schism as those desiring more efficacious specific compensators demand religious revival.

The advancement of politics and science toward the status of cultural specialties and ultimately cultural systems offers religion serious competition, especially as they provide middle-range compensators in the form of promises that life will be vastly better after the revolution and that research can banish the terrors of human mortality. To the extent that a particular religious tradition has based its general compensators in a vulnerable mythology about the workings of society and of the cosmos, the rise of politics and science will greatly discredit its faith.

But the ultimate source of religion is the fact that humans greatly desire rewards which are not to be found in this material world of scarcity, frustration and death. Neither politics nor science gives any convincing promise of freeing our species from its dire limitations any time soon. And in our analyses of complex cosmopolitan societies we found many factors favoring religion, as well as a few working against it.

Religious affiliation is encouraged by a free market of faiths, as found in the United States and other non-repressive industrial nations. Those citizens who wish high-tension sectarian religion can easily find it, while those who wish only a vague generalized sense of hope and fellowship, as offered by low-tension denominations, have several to choose from. Religious innovation has reached a high level of cult productivity, in recent decades. Not only does this provide an alluring range of intense spiritual experiences for chronic seekers and persons afflicted by special deprivations, but it also satisfies the desire for strong but progressive religion among some of the elite. Perhaps even more important, religious innovation occasionally produces powerful new traditions, capable of adapting with great success to the new conditions of contemporary society, notably Mormonism (Stark, 1984b).

Secular trends that do not directly concern religion frequently impact indirectly in ways which both promote and alter religion. Geographic mobility encourages denominational switching, even to radical alternatives, as much as it encourages disaffiliation. While science has undercut some old beliefs, it also, surprisingly, creates the raw material for new myths. In Scientology we find but one of many examples of outer-space religion, and a strange Occidental form of Taoism is currently organizing itself around the discoveries of quantum physics (Capra, 1975; Zukav, 1979). Thus, the shape of religion to come will be the result of many opposing forces.

We wish we could end this last deductive chapter with a grand formula, permitting prediction of future rates of affiliation with religious organizations. Clearly, many of our propositions would stand as terms in that equation. But at this early stage in the science of religion, we cannot specify the multipliers and exponents which could give the formula a definite form and solution. It seems to us that the factors encouraging the growth of religion are of similar magnitude to those pressing to reduce religion. And, with the core-theory statements of Chapter 2 in mind, we must predict that religion will continue to be of great significance in human society. The characteristics of religions will change, and we think future changes will be great, but religion will continue undiminished.

In the final chapter, we shall briefly consider what we have achieved in this book, and suggest future directions for the science of religion and for religion itself.

CHAPTER 10:
A Social Science of Religion

We frankly admit our optimism about the future of social theory. We believe sociology is a science and therefore that it will be possible to formulate sociological theories that share logical form and scope with theories produced by the natural sciences. Rather than enter into futile epistemological disputes with the many social scientists who deny this view, we offer this book instead. Here is an example of what we claim can be done. Maybe it's crude. Maybe it has many breakdowns in logic. Maybe we have selected too few or poorly formulated axioms. Maybe some of our concepts are muddy. But the book does not settle for parading and pondering a metaphor or two nor does it substitute classification for explanation. Whatever else it may be, this is a deductive theoretical system.

We think one measure of the value of this theory is that so much of the best prior work of the field was deduced so easily. But we take equal reassurance from the fact that the theory is rooted in a few very obvious principles about how people act and interact. It seems likely that these propositions are understood, in some form, by all normal adults. We have merely attempted to render them explicit and systematic and then show how much complexity arises from them. For this reason, our first task in this chapter will be to provide a brief overview of our journey from axioms to large scale social phenomena. Then we will discuss various matters concerning the future of our theory. What do we hope and expect, what are appropriate and inappropriate ways to move forward from here?

The first chapter of the book was programmatic; the theoretical labor begins in Chapter 2 where we introduced our seven axioms and enough definitions to show that we could derive empirically testable propositions about religion. By the end of the chapter we have explained the motive behind religious behavior and have shown that different social classes tend to have different religious motives and hence to prefer different religious emphases.

All humans share the desire for very general rewards, such as everlasting life, which seem unavailable to anyone this side of paradise. Such unfulfilled desires serve as a universal motive for religion. In addition, the powerful want religion to support their position of privilege and their superior level of rewards, while the powerless want forms of religion more saturated with specific compensators and in tension with the sociocultural environment dominated by the powerful. While Chapter 2 could postulate the existence of religious organizations designed to meet these desires, it could not yet really derive it. That task required the extended evolutionary analyses of the third and fourth chapters.

Chapter 3 began with a close look at social exchange and the ways in which larger social structures are built around relationships linking individuals. This was necessary before we could consider the emergence of religious organizations, because we needed to derive the possibility of organizations of any kind and to provide an outline of the society that surrounds religion. Despite our ambitions for the theory of religion, we are reluctant to claim too much for our efforts in other areas. Yet we could not progress very far in our deliberations without a serious attempt to sketch, if not to delineate fully, theories of society, the state, cultural evolution, and even, in later chapters, of human deviance. We hope the reader has forgiven us for occasional simplifications in these subsidiary theories and we regard them instead as opportunities there are to develop parallel deductive theories of other important facets of social life.

The emergence of religion as a cultural specialty, encouraged by the ever greater division of labor in society, gives us the familiar role distinction between clergy and laity – between those who create and distribute supernaturally-based general compensators and those who merely consume them. Once priests are in business, then formal doctrines consolidate and evolve as large social organizations come into being to provide a uniform religion to the citizens of a society.

In Chapter 4 we follow the processes of evolution beyond the initial stages to see the pressure toward rigid organization of religion and the attempt of particular religious organizations to seek a monopoly. This they cannot achieve, unless their society has developed a core of powerful people and institutions constituting a state, for it is only in collaboration with the state that a church can effectively freeze its competition out of the market, ultimately adding fire and the sword to the gentler weapon of the word. Without coercion, the natural condition of the religious market is one of numerous competing faiths and organizations. But for the greater part of recorded history, societies have been guided by dominant religions that have achieved near monopolies through serving the needs of the state and receiving coercive support in return.

Of course, the relations between even an established church and the state are uneasy, and we saw that in many ways even a state religion serves the society as a whole. Uneasy also are the relations between religion and magic. While religious organizations may wish to offer specific compensators when demanded by their customers, this is risky business since magic is prone to disconfirmation. Thus major religious organizations tend to minimize the amount of magic they offer, but the competition from individual magicians and from high-tension religions providing specific compensators is a constant problem. Our third and fourth chapters outlined the evolution of the gods, carried forth by the evolution of religious organizations and by the rationalizing theological work of organized religious specialists. This brought our considerations of religion up to modern times.

In Chapter 5 we again considered general sociological principles – developing further a theory of social bonds – in preparation for an understanding of religious schism. Our second chapter had already identified the motive for schism, the fact that antagonistic constituencies exist, the more powerful members seeking low-tension religion and the less powerful members seeking high-tension religion. In Chapter 5 we saw how these motivations operate through social structure to rip apart some religious organizations, producing sect movements and church movements. Tension with the sociocultural environment, such as experienced by a sect, was shown to be equivalent to subcultural deviance, and we were able to specify many of the conditions that would generate and shape such deviance. Perhaps the main accomplishment of the fifth chapter was that it placed important traditional observations of the sociology of religion in a deductive theoretical context. Surely the birth of sects has been a standard topic of research for a long time, and here we have carefully connected it to a general theory of human action and society.

If the fifth chapter cast old questions in a new light, the sixth chapter raised new questions – or at least questions which have not previously been given their rightful significance in the sociology of religion. How does religious innovation occur? How can people invent new systems of general compensators and then invest their faith in them? Drawing on earlier work that identified three compatible models of cult formation, we were able to derive many propositions stating the conditions under which new religions will emerge. Where the fifth chapter for the first time placed much existing research in a firm theoretical context, Chapter 6 laid the conceptual basis for much future research. Now that we have a formal, logical structure of theory-derived hypotheses about cults, we can know what to study about these novel and exotic religious groups.

Once sects and cults have been born, to succeed they must recruit new members. Chapter 7 fits together the best previous models of affiliation to high-tension religious organizations. Thus it provides a comprehensive explanation of why and how people join sects and cults, modelling exactly the results of published empirical research in a formal, deductive theory. Affiliation is not a simple process, as the old Lofland-Stark model already acknowledged, but it mirrors in many respects the processes of exchange with create sects and cults, and indeed which brought religion into being in the first place.

Throughout our derivations, the two key components are always motives and exchanges. People desire certain kinds of scarce or nonexistent rewards, and they seek them through exchanges with other humans. To become the member of a new religion is to gain social bonds with the group which sustains it, and faith in a doctrine comes from faith in the people who already subscribe to it.

The principles derived in the fifth, sixth and seventh chapters make it possible for Chapter 8 to chart the processes of growth, change and decline that shape the histories of religious movements. Among the most important factors is the collective fate of the individuals who form a sect or cult, and prosperity, perhaps caused by nothing more subtle than regression toward the societal mean, will result in a lowering of tension. Conditions that favor or impede recruitment to the movement are described as well, as are some strategies of revival.

For those successful groups which do grow. and whose membership tends to lose the deprived status which may have given birth to the movement, tension reduction is the main thrust of evolution, and reduction in tension with the sociocultural environment works against the interests of a constituency within the group who wish more efficacious specific compensators. The result will be schism or innovation, and the process repeats itself in the formation of a new religious movement.

In Chapter 9 we considered the competition religion experiences from politics and science, as these evolve into powerful cultural systems promoted by cultural specialists. Where many writers see an unstoppable secularizing trend moving toward the extinction of religion, our deductions from general principles of human needs and exchanges forces us to see a complex struggle in which religion changes but does not die. Religious specialists in low-tension denominations accept the corrosive skepticism of political and scientific intellectual elites, and their churches lose the capacity to serve the needs of their congregations. The liberal wings of entire religious traditions may be dissolved into the cauldron of secularism. But secularization is ultimately self-limiting, and the responses from religion are revival and innovation. Sects and cults will fill the market gaps created by the decline of the liberal denominations.

It seems to us that our axioms do correctly describe human nature and the conditions of human existence. From them we derived the emergence of religion, and from them we derived basic features of the secular society which some think is prepared to overcome religion. Yet nowhere on the horizon of human progress do we see any prospect that the secular exchange of rewards, on which society is based, can ever eliminate the existential basics which sustain religion.

However healthy science makes us, we cannot live forever. However wealthy technology makes us, relative deprivations will always exist.

The purpose of this book has been to outline a theory that models the real world experienced by humans and that derives the main facts of religion from that model. A deductive theory is a cultural system, composed of many specific explanations united by more general explanations. The most general in our system are the axioms, while some propositions are at an intermediate level of generality, and others are derived from them and are very specific. Thus our theory's propositions concerning cultural systems should apply to the theory itself.

In particular, we think P222 and P223 offer good advice on how to respond to any well-conducted research that produces findings contradicting some of our specific propositions. Those propositions say: "If a single explanation in a cultural system fails, people tend to seek another to replace it, without disturbing the system. When explanations in a cultural system fail, people will seek the most modest revision of it that will apparently repair the damage."

To some readers this may sound like a license to fiddle with our system so that no research could ever defeat us. If one has a "great man" model of social theory, then one might well complain that such minor adjustments of a theory are nothing but self-serving rhetorical tricks to blunt the thrust of an aggressive opponent. But we don't think of sociology as a gladiatorial contest in which the egos of great men battle to the death. Nor do we view adjustment of a theory in response to partial disconfirmation as the equivalent of throwing sand in the eyes of our critics. Instead, we like to think of social science as a cooperative enterprise in which both good new thinking and well-collected new evidence are helpful feedback that permit us – all of us together – to get closer and closer to the truth, achieving models of human reality that fit better and better.

But how can inductive findings adjust a deductive theory? How can facts oozing up from below improve a tight system of deductions assembled down from above? There are two mutually-reinforcing answers, each requiring a lengthy exposition and offering a more precise picture of what theory building is all about.

First of all, this is an exercise in modelling. A deductive scientific system does not spring into being as a perfect, inspired thought. Instead it grows through several stages of progressive approximation. We did not in fact begin with our seven axioms, and then spin out our system in one grand, monodirectional derivation. And by *axiom* we certainly do not mean "self-evident truth." To be sure, we expect that the reader will assent to our seven most general statements on the basis of his or her life's experience as a human being. They do describe the world we live in. But it is neither self-evidence nor direct experience which recommend these statements to us, but rather their capacity to explain so many other statements about the world.

There is a sense in which our seven axioms were derived from our propositions, rather than the other way around as presented logically here. We began with a body of observations about religion supplemented with scientific findings and personal experiences concerning the social world in general, and we were guided as well by existing social theories of all kinds. In constructing our system, we first worked to reduce a large collection of specific conclusions to a smaller number of general principles, then sought to derive and test still other propositions from the general principles. Which of our hundreds of propostions we began with, and which were later derived from the emerging system, does not matter. That was the result of mere accident in the way our thinking developed.

But the general process is a sound one, and mirrors the way geometry, physics and other empirically-based mathematical fields were first developed. One can conceive of the process as having two aspects, carried on simultaneously or in alternating phases: *discovery* and *simplification*. Discovery involves the construction of new statements which seem to describe reality. Simplification involves the hunt for more general statements which can bring together several lower-level statements, thereby explaining them.

Both of these have two faces: *empirical* and *theoretical*. On the empirical level, discovery means exploratory research that hunts for new facts, and simplification involves hypothesis-testing to see if a statement fits a set of particular phenomena. On the theoretical level, discovery involves deducing new propositions from accepted general statements, while simplification involves the quest for new general statements that will summarize several more specific statements.

If one wishes a thorough and detailed meta-theory of this book, a logical epistemology of how we propose to proceed, it can be found within the theory itself. Epistemologically, our theory is in great measure reflexive, a quality prized by some popular philosophers of logic (Hofstadter, 1979). This is the case because the book is greatly about cultural systems, and our theory is itself a cultural system. Indeed, throughout we have followed a maxim that may be taken as a general explanation on how to achieve a rewarding science: *Thou shalt build a deductive theory*.

To be sure, we fully understand that competing general explanations exist, each urging that social science go in a different direction. We think the ultimate test is the utility of each approach (James, 1963). Nagel (1961:12–13) has explained that the rules of science are validated by their performance under test, the same criterion which is used to evaluate the most specific hypotheses. The approach used in this book is the same one which has proven itself in the physical sciences and thus promises to achieve equal gains in the social sciences (Braithwaite, 1953; Nagel, 1961; Homans, 1967). We like the deductive approach both because it provides maximum conceptual coherence and because it works. That is, it suits the human mind and it fits reality.

But this does not mean our theory must be perfect to be valuable. Consider the historical development of celestial mechanics, the oldest of the exact sciences. Many ancient civilizations collected observations of the movement of the sun, moon and planets, assembling these data into systems as best they could without efficacious general explanations. The Ptolemaic system developed by the classical world was based on the simple general premise that celestial motions must be circular, but a very complex set of cycles and epicycles was required to fit the observations even approximately. Copernicus argued for a heliocentric rather than geocentric model. Then, guided by very fine sets of astronomical observations, Kepler provided explanations that solidified the case for the modern view of the solar system. Guided by some general assumptions about the world which no longer seem tenable, Kepler developed laws that mathematically describe the movements of the planets with great precision (Ronan, 1971; Wilson, 1972).

Stripped of their original mystical justifications, Kepler's laws are what we have called "orphan propositions" and what Nagel has called "experimental laws." One may use them to predict or control phenomena, and one may derive more specific propositions from them. But one cannot explain the orphan propositions themselves. They have no logical relationships to parent propositions from which they might be derived. It was Newton who explained Kepler's laws through mathematical derivation from more general propositions. And Newton's principles explained far more, as good general explanations should.

The system developed from the work of Kepler and Newton did a better job of predicting the movements of the planets than any previous theory (cf. Kuhn, 1959). But there continued to be discrepancies, for example in the movement of the planet Uranus. Sustained through their great computational labors by faith in the explanations, Leverrier and Adams separately deduced the existence of a previously undiscovered large planet, and their predictions were fulfilled when Neptune was found (Grosser, 1979). Thus, data which might have caused rejection of a deductive system led instead to a new discovery and confirmation of the system. But then, discrepancies in the movements of Uranus and Neptune led to prediction of a ninth planet.

As it turns out, however, the discovery of Pluto was entirely the result of dogged determination in hunting the skies, not of mathematical prediction, and Pluto is far too tiny a body to influence the greater planets appreciably (Tombaugh and Moore, 1980). Suggestions of an undiscovered tenth planet continue to be published, but if a sufficienty massive planet exists, it should already have been seen. However, astronomers are not about to abandon celestial mechanics because of the discrepancies of orbits in the outer solar system. They tend to blame observational errors, the effect of gas jets on comets, or exotic objects like black holes. True, discrepancies in the orbit of the planet Mercury, closest to the sun, seem best explained if one shifts from Newton to Einstein and applies some principles of relativity. But the limitations of the classical system of Kepler and Newton do not in any way invalidate it, and the Apollo moon flights followed navigational computations carried out entirely in the classical system.

Note that each step in the history of celestial mechanics involved an improvement in the existing cultural system, often a harmonizing addition but sometimes the replacement of an old proposition. But however general the proposition that was abandoned, there was never a complete abandonment of the old system. It may have been a "revolution" for Copernicus to make the sun stand still – although again today it moves. But the conceptual change was not so great that the principle of circular motion of the planets was abandoned. When Kepler replaced the circle by the ellipse, he expanded the notion of orbit to include all the conic sections but did not switch to an entirely different kind of curve. Galileo was right to consider the highest duty of empirical science to be saving the observations – fidelity to the facts of the world we wish to understand – but over this history of celestial mechanics considerable portions of the older theoretical systems have been saved as well.

This brings us, finally, to the second reason why it is possible to adjust our axiomatic system in response to empirical evidence. The fact is that our method of derivation is not fully rigorous and formal. We have done as much as we could, as well as we were able. But immense gaps remain, for example, when we speak of *exchange ratio* we really do not refer to a particular form of computation of rewards over costs in an exchange, but merely suggest that some such calculus is possible. A more complete statement of our theory would have to supply such missing specifications. Definition 14 says that exchange ratio "is a person's net rewards over costs in an exchange." This can be interpreted as a simple function expressing net rate of return on an investment. Net rewards can be calculated by subtracting the cost invested from the total rewards returned in the exchange. Exchange ratio can then be calculated by dividing net rewards by the cost invested. While this is a reasonable definition, it might be that the human nervous system, in evaluating exchange ratio, uses non-linear scales, as it does in measuring the loudness of sounds for example. So the real function may be far more complex than implied by our definition.

We are entirely in favor of quantitative specification of the hedonic calculus, which has been proposed for the better part of two centuries as more metaphor than precise formula (Herrnstein, 1971). It is not our job here to state the exact mathematical functions which shape human exchange, but rather to derive the major features of religion from analysis of general principles. Terms such as "exchange ratio" are meant to convey an approximate image of the kind of function we have in mind, while other work is required to complete the final specifications.

In the most preliminary way, we have considered the possibility that the theory sketched here might be formalized through symbols and manipulation laws like those of symbolic logic (Quine, 1959; cf. Maris, 1970; Kunkel and Nagasawa, 1973). Ultimately, we need a meta-logic which can handle the fact that different human actors themselves follow somewhat different explanations and disagree about both values and facts. But we think it would be premature to attempt one now. This book explores difficult territory which must be charted more precisely through future works of modification and testing. We applaud the attempts to formalize sociological arguments which have begun to appear in the journals, but we are daunted by the fact that even rather simple formulations seem replete with technical errors (cf. Kunkel and Nagasawa, 1973; Greene, 1974; Nagasawa and Kunkel, 1974).

Certainly, it would be great progress even to achieve the formal structure of Euclid, as represented in contemporary plane geometry textbooks, even before trying to algebraize this theory as Euclid was in analytic geometry. Classic textbook deductions are carried forth in two columns of numbered statements. On the left are assertions, the last of which is the thing to be proven. On the right are justificiations for each of the assertions, many of them being propositions (theorems) proven earlier in the book. Plane geometry texts also use illustrations to help the reader understand the proof, and this same function for a theory of religion could be fulfilled by a brief summary of empirical studies on the question.

It would be a vast labor, requiring more years than the two of us have left, to achieve such a classical formal structure for this book. And we suspect that our theory needs many revisions before it is ready for such formalization. But whether our book provides the template or merely the inspiration for a theory of religion formalized in this way, we feel the collective effort of a generation of social scientists of religion would be well spent in creation of one.

We are well aware of the major developments in mathematical epistemology that have taken place since Euclid, and know that the task we begin here has natural limitations. For example, we know that any rich deductive system is inherently incomplete – that many truths which can be stated in the system can nevertheless not be derived from its axioms (Nagel and Newman, 1958; Kline, 1980). But this does not disturb us. To explain much about religion is a worthwhile accomplishment.

And that brings us to our final topic. Does religion have a future? Will our theory become no more than an intellectual oddity because its primary subject matter has disappeared? We think not. Indeed, our theory generates propositions that would seem to make religion a permanent part of the human scene.

There are some "ifs," of course. If we destroy all life on the planet, religion will vanish too. If a tyrannical state finds means for truly effective mind control, it might banish even private contemplation of the gods. If we find a solution to all existential problems – if we become eternal beings, living in a world without worry or want – then too religion might vanish. Or would it? One could argue that such a world could only exist if religious compensators were redeemed at face value. Call it the Resurrection or what you will, in such a world humans would have become supernatural, one and all.

In any event, these "ifs" do not compel alterations in the form and focus of our theory. Rather, variations in the kind and quality of religious organizations and movements, the ebb and flow of faith and enthusiasms, the birth and death of gods, these are the stuff that will command our attention. To say how and why these phenomena occur is the mission of the social science of religion. Here is our best effort at some answers.

APPENDIX

For the easy reference of the reader, we have listed the axioms, definitions and propositions, in the order in which they were derived in the text.

Axioms:

A1 Human perception and action take place through time, from the past into the future.

A2 Humans seek what they perceive to be rewards and avoid what they perceive to be costs.

A3 Rewards vary in kind, value, and generality.

A4 Human action is directed by a complex but finite information-processing system that functions to identify problems and attempt solutions to them.

A5 Some desired rewards are limited in supply, including some that simply do not exist.

A6 Most rewards sought by humans are destroyed when they are used.

A7 Individual and social attributes which determine power are unequally distributed among persons and groups in any society.

Definitions:

Def.1 The *past* consists of the universe of conditions which can be known but not influenced.

Def.2 The *future* consists of the universe of conditions which can be influenced but not known.

Def.3 *Rewards* are anything humans will incur costs to obtain.

Def.4 *Costs* are whatever humans attempt to avoid.

Def.5 Reward A is more *valuable* than reward B if a person will usually exchange B for A.

Def.6 Rewards are *general* to the extent that they include other (less general) rewards.

Def.7 The *mind* is the set of human functions that directs the action of a person.

Def.8 Human *problems* are recurrent situations that require investments (costs) of particular kinds to obtain rewards.

Def.9 To *solve* a problem means to imagine possible means of achieving the desired reward, to select the one with the greatest likelihood of success in the light of available information, and to direct action along the chosen line until the reward has been achieved.

Def.10 *Explanations* are statements about how and why rewards may be obtained and costs are incurred.

Def.11 A *limited* supply means that not everyone can have as much of a reward as they desire.

Def.12 Rewards that *do not exist* cannot be obtained by any person or group.

Def.13 *Consumables* are rewards which are destroyed when they are used.

Def.14 *Exchange ratio* is a person's net rewards over costs in an exchange.

Def.15 *Power* is the degree of control over one's exchange ratio.

Def.16 *Evaluation* is the determination of the value of any reward, including explanations.

Def.17 The *value* of a reward is equivalent to the maximum cost a person would pay to obtain the reward.

Def.18 *Compensators* are postulations of reward according to explanations that are not readily susceptable to unambiguous evaluation.

Def.19 Compensators which substitute for single, specific rewards are called *specific compensators*.

Def.20 Compensators which substitute for a cluster of many rewards and for rewards of great scope and value are called *general compensators*.

Def.21 *Supernatural* refers to forces beyond or outside nature which can suspend, alter, or ignore physical forces.

Def.22 *Religion* refers to systems of general compensators based on supernatural assumptions.

Def.23 *Religious organizations* are social enterprises whose primary purpose is to create, maintain, and exchange supernaturally-based general compensators.

Def.24 *Socialization* is the accumulation of explanations over time through exchanges with other persons.

Def.25 A *relationship* exists between two persons if, after a series of exchanges, they have come to value each other as exchange partners and will seek more interaction in the future.

Def.26 *Society* is the structure of social exchanges.

Def.27 A portion of a network is *closed* to the extent that a high proportion of members' relationships are with other members.

Def.28 A portion of a network is *open* to the extent that a high proportion of members' relationships are with persons who are not members.

Def.29 A *society* is a closed structure of social relations.

Def.30 *Culture* is the total complex of explanations exchanged by humans.

Def.31 Explanations form a *cultural system* if they are parts of a greater explanation that includes them.

Def.32 *Complexity* of culture refers to the number, scope and detail of explanations, and the amount of technology.

Def.33 *Cultural specialization* refers to the tendency of individuals to master parts of their culture and to engage in exchanges with others who have mastered different parts.

Def.34 *Differentiation* refers to cultural specialization at the level of groups rather than at the level of individuals.

Def.35 *Social organizations* are collective enterprises that specialize in providing some particular kinds of rewards.

Def.36 *Cosmopolitan* refers to the existence of plural cultures within a society.

Def.37 A *class* is a set of persons, of all ages and both sexes, with a relatively similar degree of control over their exchange ratio with other sets.

Def.38 *Coercion* is the interaction strategy of threatening to inflict great costs on others, thereby imposing on them exchange ratios which are below market value.

Def.39 A *coercive exchange* is one in which one party, with full knowledge, has a lower net supply of rewards after the exchange begins than before.

Def.40 *Cultural means of coercion* refers to knowledge, capacities, and technologies that can inflict unbearable costs on the human organism.

Def.41 The *state* is the monopoly of the cultural means of coercion by a clearly differentiated group of specialists.

Def.42 Those who monopolize the use of coercion are the *political elite*.

Def.43 A *repressive state* exists when the political elite use their monopoly on the cultural means of coercion to impose below market exchange ratios on non-elite members of the society.

Def.44 *Gods* are supernatural beings having the attributes of consciousness and desire.

Def.45 The *scope of the gods* refers to the diversity of their powers and interests and to the range of their influence.

Def.46 Persons who specialize in producing and exchanging compensators of great generality based on supernatural assumptions are *religious specialists*.

Def.47 An *alliance* is a continuing relationship between persons or groups, in which each contributes to the power the other enjoys in exchanges with third parties.

Def.48 An *exchange partner* is someone who participates in exchanges vis-a-vis a given other person.

Def.49 An *intermediary* is a person who receives rewards in exchanges with one party in order to provide them to another party through other exchanges.

Def.50 *Norms* are the rules governing what behavior is expected or prohibited in various circumstances. Thus, they are equivalent to culturally shared explanations that govern the terms of exchanges.

Def.51 An *elite* is a group with great control over its exchange ratio.

Def.52 *Magic* refers to specific compensators that promise to provide desired rewards without regard for evidence concerning the designated means.

Def.53 Cultural specialists whose main activity is providing specific compensators are *magicians*.

Def.54 *Rationality* is marked by constistent goal-oriented activity.

Def.55 *Good* and *evil* refer to the intentions of the gods in their exchanges with humans. *Good* consists of the intention to allow humans to profit from exchanges. *Evil* consists of the intention to inflict coercive exchanges or deceptions upon humans, leading to losses for the humans.

Def.56 A *church* is a conventional religious organization.

Def.57 A *sect movement* is a deviant religious organization with traditional beliefs and practices.

Def.58 A *cult movement* is a deviant religious organization with novel beliefs and practices.

Def.59 *Deviance* is departure from the norms of a culture in such a way as to incur the imposition of extraordinary costs from those who maintain the culture.

Def.60 A *schism* is the division of the social structure of an organization into two or more independent parts.

Def.61 *Attachment* is positive evaluation of an exchange partner.

Def.62 *Investments* are costs expended in an exchange which have not yet yielded their full potential of desired rewards.

Def.63 *Involvement* is that proportion of one's total resources that one invests in an exchange.

Def.64 *Belief* is positive evaluation of an explanation.

Def.65 *Social cleavages* are divisions of a network across which there are relatively few strong attachments.

Def.66 An individual's *self-evaluation* is that person's determination of how valuable a reward he constitutes as an exchange partner.

Def.67 *Cults* are social enterprises primarily engaged in the generation and exchange of novel compensators.

Def.68 *Cult founders* are religious specialists or magicians who establish new organizations to create, maintain and exchange novel compensators.

Def.69 *Mental Illness* is the imputed condition of any human mind that repeatedly fails to conform to the propositions of the prevailing theory of human action.

Def.70 *Ignorance* is an abnormal lack of explanations.

Def.71 *Mental deficiency* is an abnormally weak ability to store and process explanations.

Def.72 A case of mental illness is *extensive* to the degree that the individual fails to conform to many propositions of the prevailing theory of human action.

Def.73 *Chronic* refers to a condition that persists unchanged for a long period of time.

Def.74 *Acute* refers to a marked condition of limited duration with a sharp beginning and ending.

Def.75 *Skills* are valuable explanations that enable an individual who possesses them to solve immediate practical problems.

Def.76 *Entrepreneurs* are persons who start and promote new enterprises in order to obtain rewards through profitable exchanges.

Def.77 *Apprenticeship* is an exchange relationship between a skilled person and an unskilled person that allows the latter to learn the skills of the former.

Def.78 *Religious engineering* is the conscious design of compensator packages and other elements of culture for use in cults.

Def.79 *Deception* is any interaction strategy that intentionally leads other people to accept explanations which one privately rejects.

Def.80 *Honesty* is the interaction strategy of offering only those explanations to others which one personally accepts.

Def.81 *Progress* is the gradual improvement in the human ability to achieve desired rewards.

Def.82 When a group *commits itself*, its members agree to carry out the actions and exchanges required to obtain a specified reward.

Def.83 An *imperfect* exchange is one that is somewhat rewarding but fails to provide the full desired reward for one or both parties.

Def.84 *Incremental compensator-generation* is a process in which compensators are collectively invented and developed through a series of small steps consisting of exchanges.

Def.85 In a *social implosion*, part of a relatively open social network becomes markedly more closed.

Def.86 *Stakes in conformity* consist of attachments, investments, involvements and beliefs.

Def.87 *Conversion* is affiliation of a person to a new religious group, conceptualized as a positive transformation of the nature and value of a person.

Def.88 The organization of cultural means of coercion against the state is called *political rebellion*.

Def.89 A *millenarian* religious movement is one in which the participants believe that supernatural intervention will soon effect a radical transformation of the conditions of life.

Def.90 *Structural strain* is a lack of integration or a contradiction between elements of a cultural system that people feel should be intimately connected and mutually supporting.

Def.91 *Anomie* is the state of being without effective rules for living.

Def.92 *Religious seekership* is the state of a person unsatisfied with currently available religious affiliation and carrying out exchanges in search of more satisfying affiliation.

Def.93 A *turning point* is a period of markedly decreased attachment, investment, involvement and belief, taken singly or in any combination.

Def.94 *Chronic social isolates* are persons who lack the resources to attract and hold exchange partners.

Def.95 *Random* refers to the unknown and unknowable among natural causes.

Def.96 *Social evaporation* is the process in which members of a group whose fortunes decline defect from it, leaving behind those members whose fortunes rise or remain constant.

Def.97 The process of random events operating within a constant population distribution, which brings extreme cases back toward the average for the population, is called *regression*.

Def.98 *Affect* is the intense expression of evaluations.

Def.99 *Revival* is the staging of episodes of increased religious affect to sustain compensators.

Def.100 *Politics* is the cultural specialty dedicated to negotiation of power relationships among groups in society.

Def.101 *Science* is the cultural specialty dedicated to invention and systematic evaluation of explanations.

Def.102 *Secular* refers to any parts of society and culture that are substantially free of supernatural assumptions.

Def.103 *Mobility* is movement from one material and social environment to another.

Def.104 *Secularization* is the progressive loss of power by religious organizations.

Propositions:

P1 Rewards and costs are complementary: a lost or forgone reward equals a cost, and an avoided cost equals a reward.

P2 Sometimes rewards can be obtained at costs less than the cost equivalent to forgoing the reward.

P3 In solving problems, the human mind must seek explanations.

P4 Explanations are rewards of some level of generality.

P5 Explanations vary in the costs and time they require for the desired reward to be obtained.

P6 In pursuit of desired rewards, humans will exchange rewards with other humans.

P7 Humans seek high exchange ratios.

P8 Exchange ratios vary among persons and groups in any society.

P9 Rewards that exist in limited supply will tend to be monopolized by powerful persons and groups, thereby becoming relatively unavailable to others.

P10 Explanations can be evaluated correctly only by reference to their known ability to facilitate the attainment of the desired reward.

P11 It is impossible to know for certain that a given reward does not exist.

P12 When a desired reward is relatively unavailable, explanations that promise to provide it are costly and difficult to evaluate correctly.

P13 The more valued or general a reward, the more difficult will be evaluation of explanations about how to obtain it.

P14 In the absence of a desired reward, explanations often will be accepted which posit attainment of the reward in the distant future or in some other non-verifiable context.

P15 Compensators are treated by humans as if they were rewards.

P16 For any reward or cluster of rewards, one or more compensators may be invented.

P17 Compensators vary according to the generality, value and kind of the rewards for which they substitute.

P18 Humans prefer rewards to compensators and attempt to exchange compensators for rewards.

P19 It is impossible to obtain a reward rather than a compensator when the reward does not exist.

P20 It is impossible to obtain a reward rather than a compensator when the compensator is mistaken for the reward.

P21 It is impossible to obtain a reward rather than a compensator when one lacks the power to obtain the reward.

P22 The most general compensators can be supported only by supernatural explanations.

P23 As social enterprises, religious organizations tend to provide some rewards as well as compensators.

P24 The power of an individual or group is positively associated with control of religious organizations and with gaining the rewards available from religious organizations.

P25 The power of an individual or group is negatively associated with accepting religious compensators, when the desired reward exists.

P26 Regardless of power, persons and groups tend to accept religious compensators, when desired rewards do not exist.

P27 If multiple suppliers of general compensators exist, then the ability to exchange general compensators will depend upon their relative availability and perceived exchange ratios.

P28 All patterns of human perception and action are conditioned by socialization.

P29 Individuals will favor exchanges with certain exchange partners rather than with others, depending upon the particular rewards desired and upon the perceived exchange ratio that is experienced with different partners.

P30 To satisfy desires for consumable rewards, humans will engage repeatedly in exchanges in which they seek the same reward.

P31 Humans tend to develop persistent exchange relationships with particular other individuals and groups.

P32 Relationships with some other human beings are rewards of high value.

P33 Humans tend to develop several relationships with other human beings, differing in value and in the particular rewards exchanged.

P34 To the extent that a social network is closed, its members will tend to occupy and hold a particular, bounded area of land.

P35 Human culture occurs through the accumulation and transmission of explanations over time.

P36 The explanations of a religion are a cultural system.

P37 A culture is created by a society and consists of whatever explanations are accepted by the members of the society.

P38 Social cleavages tend to produce cultural cleavages.

P39 Any culture contains a number of cultural systems.

P40 Humans retain that culture which appears more rewarding.

P41 The greater the number and the diversity of exchanges that have occured over time, the more complex and apparently rewarding the culture will become.

P42 As a society grows and endures, it will come to have a progressively more complex culture.

P43 The more complex the culture, the less of it that can be mastered by any given individual.

P44 To the extent that its culture is complex, adult members of a society must exchange culture.

P45 The more complex the culture, the greater the degree of cultural specialization.

P46 Given some degree of cultural specialization, the larger societies become, the greater their degree of differentiation.

P47 Cultural specialties evolve into cultural systems, dependent upon the discovery of explanations that prove valuable in uniting the relevant subexplanations.

P48 Cultural specialties tend to be divided along lines which divide cultural systems.

P49 A cultural specialty dedicated to providing general compensators based on supernatural assumptions tends to evolve into a cultural system, thus becoming a religion.

P50 Social organizations emerge in human society.

P51 Religious organizations emerge in human society.

P52 The more cosmopolitan societies become, the more complex their cultures.

P53 Some cultural specialties will produce greater power than will others.

P54 Cultural specialization and differentiation will increase stratification in societies to the degree that classes will emerge.

P55 The growth, duration and differentiation of societies leads to the emergence of the state.

P56 Humans will tend to conceptualize supernatural sources of rewards and costs as gods.

P57 The gods tend to enjoy high exchange ratios.

P58 People will not exchange with the gods when a cheaper or more efficient alternative is known and available.

P59 The more complex the culture, the greater the scope of the gods.

P60 The older, larger and more cosmopolitan societies become, the greater the scope of their gods.

P61 As societies become older, larger and more cosmopolitan they will worship fewer gods of greater scope.

P62 No human being can personally evaluate all the explanations he uses, including verifiable ones.

P63 The value an individual places on an explanation is often set by the values placed on it by others and communicated to him through exchanges.

P64 In the absence of a more compelling standard, the value an individual places on a reward is set by the market value of that reward established through exchanges by other persons.

P65 The value an individual places on a general compensator is set through exchanges with other persons.

P66 When there is disagreement over the value of an explanation, the individual will tend to set a value that is a direct averaging function of the values set by others and communicated to him through exchanges, weighted by the value placed on such exchanges with each partner.

P67 The more cosmopolitan a society with respect to religious culture, the lower the market value of any given general compensator.

P68 The more complex the culture, the more likely that persons will specialize in producing and exchanging compensators of great generality based on supernatural assumptions.

P69 The older, larger and more cosmopolitan societies become, the more likely they will be to contain religious specialists.

P70 Religion will be among the very first cultural specialties to emerge in the development of societies.

P71 Once religious specialists have emerged in a society, they will tend to combine in organizations seeking a religious monopoly.

P72 In socially complex and cosmopolitan societies, a religious organization can achieve an effective monopoly only through an alliance with the state.

P73 The emergence of the state in a society will tend to be followed by the emergence of a single dominant religious organization, to the extent that the state is repressive.

P74 When an individual finds he cannot obtain a desired reward by himself, he will tend to seek an exchange partner who can provide it to him.

P75 Religious specialists act as intermediaries between their clients and the alleged sources of the desired general rewards – the gods.

P76 Religious specialists direct others to offer material, psychic and behavioral rewards to the gods.
P77 By defining behavioral rewards desired by the gods, religious specialists can influence norms.
P78 Religious specialists promulgate norms, said to come from the gods, that increase the rewards flowing to the religious specialists.
P79 Religious specialists promulgate norms, said to come from the gods, that increase the ability of their clients to reward the religious specialists.
P80 Religious specialists promulgate norms, said to come from the gods, that increase the total rewards possessed by the clients as a group.
P81 It is the nature of the supernatural that the gods are not observed to take physical possession of material rewards exchanged with them.
P82 Religious specialists act as receivers for the gods and partly define what material rewards they receive.
P83 Religious specialists share in the psychic rewards offered to the gods, for example: deference, honor and adoration.
P84 In socially complex and cosmopolitan societies, a dominant religious organization will promulgate norms, said to come from the gods, that increase rewards flowing to the state.
P85 Religious specialists promulgate norms, said to come from the gods, that limit the repressiveness of the state.
P86 Religious specialists can exert great influence over their exchange ratios with others, and thus over the exchange ratios experienced by others.
P87 Religious specialists constitute an elite.
P88 Religious organizations and positions are controlled by the powerful.
P89 Explanations in pursuit of very general compensators require individuals to exchange with the gods on a continuing basis.
P90 Religious elites can implicate others in long-term stable patterns of exchange.
P91 Magic is more vulnerable than religion to disconfirmation.
P92 It is not in the interest of religious specialists to risk disconfirmation of the compensators they supply.
P93 Religious specialists will, over time, tend to reduce the amount of magic they supply.
P94 To the extent that a demand for magic continues after religious specialists have ceased providing it, others will specialize in providing it.
P95 The roles of religious specialist and magician will tend to be differentiated, as will religious and magical culture generally.
P96 Magicians cannot require others to engage in long-term, stable patterns of exchange.

P97 In the absence of long-term, stable patterns of exchange, an organization composed of magicians and a committed laity cannot be sustained.

P98 Magicians will serve individual clients, not lead an organization.

P99 Magicians are much less powerful than religious specialists.

P100 The explanations of magic are not a cultural system.

P101 In dealing with the disconfirmation of their explanations, magicians tend to generate large numbers of new and unconnected explanations.

P102 A society in which religious organizations with gods of great scope have differentiated, yet which possesses magic based on supernatural assumptions, will continue to postulate numerous demigods.

P103 To the extent that a religion provides relatively specific compensators as well as general compensators, it will tend to have a complex culture including demigods.

P104 To the extent that a religion provides specific compensators as well as general compensators, it will tend to oppose supernaturally-based magic and demigods outside its system.

P105 To the extent that a religion does not provide specific compensators, it will tolerate supernaturally-based magic and demigods outside its system.

P106 If a religion evolves until it has but one god of infinite scope, it can no longer provide supernatural specific compensators as part of its cultural system, and it will have little to offer most people.

P107 Explanations that assume the gods are rational offer greater certainty of reward than explanations that assume the gods are irrational.

P108 Distinguishing the supernatural into two classes – good and evil – offers a rational portrait of the gods.

P109 The more complex the culture, the clearer the distinction drawn between good and evil gods.

P110 The older, larger and more cosmopolitan societies become, the clearer the distinction drawn between good and evil gods.

P111 Humans seek to exchange with good gods, and to avoid exchanging with evil gods.

P112 Good gods will be preferred who are thought to protect humans from exchanges with evil gods.

P113 The more complex the culture, the more likely is belief in good gods that are more powerful than evil gods.

P114 The older, larger and more cosmopolitan societies become, the more likely they are to believe in good gods that are more powerful than evil gods.

P115 To the extent that good gods are thought to be more powerful than evil gods, the less likely it is that persons will exchange with evil gods.

P116 Sects come into being through schisms from existing organizations in their religious tradition.

P117 When a person is attached to an exchange partner, the person is willing to expend some costs to maintain the relationship with the partner.

P118 When a person has invested in an exchange, the person will tend to maintain the exchange relationship until the potential reward is achieved, or until the continuing cost of the relationship markedly exceeds the cost the person is willing to pay for the reward.

P119 When a person is involved in a set of exchanges, the person will have fewer resources to invest in alternative exchanges.

P120 When a person believes in a particular explanation, the person is unlikely to invest in competing explanations in which the person does not believe.

P121 Schisms in groups will be most likely along lines of social cleavage.

P122 Schisms will be most likely in groups that contain marked social cleavages.

P123 Schisms in groups will most likely take the form of secessions which appear to preserve the investments of the individuals seceding.

P124 Schisms in groups will most likely take the form of secessions which appear not to require great new investments on the part of the individuals seceding.

P125 Schisms will tend to take place in the form which the tradition of religious beliefs implies will be least likely to endanger previous investments.

P126 Schisms will tend to take place in the form which the tradition of religious beliefs implies will be most likely to facilitate the achievement of the desired rewards; that is, they will take place in accordance with the explanations in which the religious compensators are embedded.

P127 Schisms will be most likely to take place if the tradition of religious beliefs does suggest a form schism may take without endangering previous investment, and particularly if it suggests that such a form will actually facilitate achievement of the desired general rewards.

P128 Consumers will participate in a schism only if in so doing they can maintain exchange relationships with their most valued distributors, or can at very little cost switch to a new but similar distributor.

P129 Consumers will participate in a schism if they perceive that by so doing they can achieve an improved exchange ratio in pursuit of rewards.

P130 Schisms will be most likely if sets of individuals within the original religious group have markedly different exchange ratios or pursue markedly different rewards.

P131 The potential for group conflict over the distribution of rewards and the emphasis on compensators is present in all religious bodies.

P132 The greater the degree of power inequality in a religious organization the greater will be the potential for group conflict over the distribution of rewards and the emphasis on compensators.

P133 It is very difficult for individuals to achieve accurate evaluations of themselves.

P134 Every person seeks a positive self-evaluation.

P135 Persons desire a positive evaluation of the rewards they possess, including the explanations and the power-giving resources they possess.

P136 Explanations that imply positive evaluations of a person and the rewards the person possesses are themselves rewards, while explanations that imply negative evaluations are costs.

P137 Persons who possess a scarce reward will avoid explanations that identify the corresponding compensator as the real reward.

P138 Persons who possess a compensator for a scarce reward will avoid explanations that identify the corresponding reward as indeed the true reward.

P139 Contact with a scarce reward or with persons who possess the scarce reward constitutes a cost for persons who desire the reward yet lack the power to obtain it.

P140 Consumers of scarce rewards and consumers of the corresponding compensators tend to avoid relationships with each other.

P141 Consumers of scarce rewards and consumers of the corresponding compensators will advocate and follow distinctly different patterns of behavior.

P142 Tension with the surrounding sociocultural environment is equivalent to subcultural deviance, marked by difference, antagonism and separation.

P143 To the extent that religious groups are involved with compensators for scarce rewards, they are in tension with the sociocultural environment.

P144 The higher the tension of a religious group, the greater the number and perceived value of the compensators it can provide for scarce rewards.

P145 In any religious body, the less powerful will tend to prefer relatively higher tension with the external society.

P146 In any religious body, the more powerful will tend to prefer relatively lower tension with the external society.

P147 The lower the tension of a religious group, the greater and more valuable the supply of rewards it can earn from the outside and provide to members.

P148 The lower the state of tension of a religious group the greater the demand generated among the less powerful members for more efficacious compensators.

P149 Demand for more efficacious compensators creates an opportunity for those with some power to increase their supply of rewards by organizing a sect movement.

P150 When the potential gains offset costs, some moderately powerful but relatively deprived members will lead a sect movement.

P151 The greater the degree of coercion the external society imposes on religious deviance, the weaker the tendency for deviant religious organizations to form.

P152 If changes in the external environment result in an intensification of the need for (and the numbers in need of) efficacious compensators, the tendency toward sect formation is proportionally strengthened.

P153 In a culture with a dominant religious tradition, the emergence of sect movements increases the proportion of the population affiliated with religious organizations.

P154 If a substantial group of marginal members develops within a sect, who have much to gain from reduced tension but who lack the power to transform the sect, they will tend to form a schismatic church movement.

P155 The tendency to form a schismatic church movement will be reduced to the extent that members desiring lower tension with the sociocultural environment are free to transfer to established low-tension groups at little cost.

P156 Mentally ill persons often invent novel compensators and accept them as rewards.

P157 The more extensive a case of mental illness, the greater the number, deviance, and generality of novel explanations it may generate.

P158 Chronically mentally ill persons are poor in the resources required to establish and maintain social enterprises.

P159 Successful psychopathological cult invention is more likely to result from an episode of acute mental illness than from chronic mental illness.

P160 The skills required for successful operation of a religious organization are best acquired by intimate participation in a successful existing religious organization.

P161 The skills required for successful establishment of a new cult are best acquired by intimate participation in a successful, recently-founded cult.

P162 Entrepreneurs who found cults tend to have first served an apprenticeship working closely with the leaders of a successful earlier cult.

P163 The greater the number of successful cults in a society, the greater the number of entrepreneurs who will seek to found still more cults.

P164 Religious engineering may be undertaken either in order to practice deception or in the belief that the product constitutes a real value.

P165 To the extent that a cult founder has had exchange partners who were satisfied members of a similar cult, he will tend to accept their favorable evaluation of the kind of compensators he offers.

P166 To the extent that a cult founder has been the satisfied member of a similar cult in the past, he will already personally value the kind of compensators he offers.

P167 To the extent that a cult founder has exchange partners who are satisfied followers, he will tend to accept their favorable evaluation of the compensators he gives them.

P168 Honest entrepreneurial cult founders will tend to have been deeply involved in a cult similar to the one they themselves found.

P169 Honest religious engineering is most likely within a culture that trusts in a doctrine of cultural progress.

P170 Overt religious engineering will be most rewarded in a culture that trusts in a doctrine of cultural progress.

P171 Honest entrepreneurial cult founders tend to innovate in specific explanations while preserving the more general explanations they gained in prior experience with other cults.

P172 Entrepreneurs with prior experience in a single cult will innovate only slightly when founding a new cult.

P173 Entrepreneurs who innovate greatly in founding a new cult are apt to have had prior experience with two or more successful cults.

P174 The invention of religious culture is easier to the extent that the inventor is able to use elements and sub-systems from existing religious systems.

P175 Entrepreneurial cult leaders tend to continue innovating after founding their cults, adding to their systems whatever compensators appeal to their followers.

P176 Cults founded by entrepreneurs cluster in lineages, sharing transmitted cultural similarities.

P177 Cultural similarities between cults in a lineage tend to be greater the more direct the historical connection between the cults.

P178 Founding a new cult generally does not require an entrepreneur to increase his tension with the surrounding sociocultural environment.

P179 The proportion of cults founded by entrepreneurs, compared to those founded by the mentally ill, will be greater the less the costs imposed by the society upon participation in cults.

P180 Parties to an exchange sometimes are unable to provide their exchange partner with the reward they have promised to give.

P181 When a party to an exchange falls just short of providing the reward expected by his exchange partner, he is apt to offer a compensator in addition to whatever reward he is able to provide.

P182 The greater the value and difficulty of a reward to which a group has committed itself, the longer the series of exchanges in which the members will engage in pursuit of that reward.

P183 The longer the series of imperfect exchanges in which a group engages, the greater the number and generality of compensators they will generate.

P184 The more the members of a group value each other, the greater costs they will expend to provide valued rewards for each other.

P185 The more socially closed a group, the more readily it can generate and sustain compensators, through exchanges among members.

P186 The more thoroughly interconnected a group, the more readily it can generate and sustain compensators through exchanges among members.

P187 Given sufficient time, groups that commit themselves to highly valued but unobtainable rewards tend to become religious cults.

P188 The greater the number and generality of compensators a group possesses at the beginning of incremental compensator-generation, the greater the number and generality it will possess at the end.

P189 Magical cults tend to evolve into religious cults if participants have long-term relationships with each other.

P190 The members of a group engaged in incremental compensator-generation will become exchange partners of increasing value to each other.

P191 A group engaged in incremental compensator-generation will experience social implosion.

P192 An unchecked process of incremental compensator-generation will result in a high-tension cult based in a thoroughly closed social group.

P193 Groups that become cults through incremental compensator-generation tend to be small enough for each member to have a relationship with every other member.

P194 To the extent that a society does not punish religious innovation, small sects tend to evolve into cults.

P195 The higher the tension of a small sect, the more likely it is to evolve into a cult.

P196 If changes in the external environment result in an intensification of the need for (and the numbers in need of) efficacious compensators, the tendency toward cult formation is proportionally strengthened.

P197 When cultural change or other factors produce new needs and new conditions of life for numbers of people, the rate of cult formation will increase proportionally.

P198 The ability to exchange novel compensators depends upon the relative efficacy, availability and cost of competing compensators.

P199 The religious organizations that encompass the majority of persons in any society will always contain a significant minority who desire more efficacious compensators than are available from these organizations.

P200 Potential cult converts always exist within more conventional religious organizations.

P201 In all societies and all organizations, people vary in the degree to which they have stakes in conformity.

P202 Persons with low stakes in conformity are relatively deprived in terms of rewards, compensators and self-esteem.

P203 Persons with low stakes in conformity are relatively free to deviate.

P204 Persons with low stakes in conformity tend to have less favorable evaluations of conventional explanations than do persons with higher stakes in conformity.

P205 Persons with low stakes in conformity have relatively much to gain and little to lose by creating novel compensators.

P206 Persons with low stakes in conformity have relatively much to gain and little to lose by accepting novel compensators.

P207 In any society, a significant supply of potential cult founders exists.

P208 In any society, a significant supply of potential followers for utterly new cults exists.

P209 Persons with a relatively negative self-evaluation are most likely to conceptualize religious affiliating as conversion.

P210 Persons who belong to social groups with relatively negative self-evaluations are most likely to conceptualize religious affiliating as conversion, even if they themselves have positive self-evaluations.

P211 Groups that recruit persons who possess and constitute rewards of relatively low value will tend to conceptualize affiliating as conversion.

P212 The greater the degree of coercion the external society imposes on religious deviance, the greater the probable cost experienced by an individual who joins a deviant religious organization.

P213 The greater the degree of coercion the external society imposes on religious deviance, the greater the value of desired reward required to bring an individual to join a deviant religious organization.

P214 The greater the degree of coercion the external society imposes on religious deviance, the more restricted the range of persons likely to join deviant religious organizations.

P215 The victim in a coercive exchange relationship will seek means to remove the coercion.

P216 People who perceive themselves to be victims of a repressive state will seek to organize their own cultural means of coercion against the state.

P217 Victims of a repressive state will tend to join high-tension religious movements if the state is sufficiently powerful to suppress political rebellion.

P218 Victims of a repressive state will tend to affiliate with millenarian religious movements if the state is sufficiently powerful to suppress political rebellion.

P219 Persons who desire limited rewards that exist, but who lack the social power to obtain them, will tend to affiliate with sects, to the extent that their society possesses a dominant religious tradition supported by the elite.

P220 Persons who desire limited rewards that exist, but who lack the social power to obtain them, will tend to affiliate with cults, to the extent that their society does not possess a dominant religious tradition supported by the elite.

P221 Persons who desire specific but nonexistent rewards will tend to become customers of client cults.

P222 If a single explanation in a cultural system fails, people tend to seek another to replace it, without disturbing the rest of the system.

P223 When explanations in a cultural system fail, people will seek the most modest revision of it that will apparently repair the damage.

P224 A person who is convinced that religion will provide great rewards, yet has failed to receive these rewards from one religious organization, will tend to seek another religious organization with distinctly different specific explanations.

P225 When two or more explanations fail, and are connected by a single explanation more general than they, participants in the cultural system will tend to seek a substitute for the more general explanation, and this tendency will be greater the larger the proportional value of explanations under it that have failed.

P226 Failure of numerous lower-level explanations in a cultural system tends to be communicated upward until the failure compounds to disconfirm much of the system.

P227 Persons who have experienced great misery and continued failure in obtaining rewards and effective compensators from religion will be more apt than others to accept radical religious explanations.

P228 When a person transfers from one religious affiliation to another, the tendency for him to pass through a stage of religious seekership is greater the greater the increment in tension with the sociocultural environment entailed by the transfer.

P229 When a person transfers from one religious affiliation to another, the tendency for him to pass through a stage of religious seekership is less the more cosmopolitan the society in which he lives.

P230 Persons with acute unmet needs for relatively specific rewards are more likely than other people to become religious seekers.

P231 Persons with acute unmet needs for scarce or nonexistent relatively specific rewards are more likely than other people to become chronic religious seekers.

P232 Religious seekers who are of less value to groups they contact than they initially appear will tend to become chronic seekers.

P233 Religious seekers who have already experienced a number of cycles of affiliation and disaffilation are apt to continue in chronic seekership.

P234 Chronic religious seekership is most common around high-tension religious groups.

P235 A chronic seeker tends to stay at about the same level of tension while going from group to group.

P236 Persons are more likely to join religious movements at turning points in their lives.

P237 People who repeatedly experience turning points in their lives are more likely than other people to become chronic religious seekers.

P238 Religious seekers will not accept new compensators, and be willing to expend costs over time to maintain them, until they experience repeated rewarding exchanges with other persons who already accept the compensators.

P239 Persons who believe in some parts of a strict cultural system will tend to believe in the other parts as well, although they will be prepared to expend the greatest costs for those parts of the system that directly meet their personal needs.

P240 Members of a religious organization tend to reward others who support the beliefs of the religion and tend to punish or break off relations with those who oppose the beliefs.

P241 Newcomers to a religious organization will be influenced through exchanges to accept the entire system of beliefs of the religion.

P242 Within a religious group, pressures toward doctrinal conformity are greater the higher the tension of the group.

P243 Members of high-tension religious groups tend to have a high proportion of their social relationships with other members, this tendency being limited primarily by the inability of members to give each other all commonly available desired rewards.

P244 Persons low in social relationships are more likely than others to become members of a new religious group.

P245 When a person's most rewarding exchange partners transfer to a new religious affiliation, the person is likely to transfer with them.

P246 Expanding religious movements will gain much of their new membership by chains of recruitment spreading through pre-existing networks of social relationships.

P247 A person whose valued exchange partners include many who lack the power to obtain scarce rewards is apt to become a member of a high-tension religious movement, under the influence of his partners, quite apart from the person's own power to obtain scarce rewards.

P248 The social networks of advantaged persons tend to be more extensive than those of the relatively deprived.

P249 New culture not exclusively oriented toward a particular non-elite subgroup in society tends to spread more rapidly through networks of the advantaged than of the relatively deprived.

P250 In cosmopolitan societies which possess a doctrine of progress, cults not designed to appeal to particular deprived groups spread more rapidly among advantaged members of society.

P251 Individual and social attributes which determine power are unequally distributed among participants in any new religious group at the time of its formation.

P252 High-tension religious groups with very narrow distributions of power among members are unlikely to decrease in tension.

P253 High-tension religious groups with medium distributions of power among members tend to move toward lower tension.

P254 High-tension religious groups with broad distributions of power among members are likely to undergo schism.

P255 High-tension religious groups formed in societies which impose great coercion on religious deviance are unlikely to decrease in tension.

P256 At formation, sects and cults tend to have relatively deprived members.

P257 At formation, sects and cults tend to have members with low stakes in conformity.

P258 At formation, sects and cults tend to have members with weak attachments to outsiders.

P259 At formation, sects and cults tend to be closed social groups.

P260 At formation, church movements tend to have few relatively deprived members.

P261 At formation, church movements tend to have members with strong attachments to outsiders.

P262 At formation, church movements tend to be open social groups, blending into the larger social network that surrounds them.

P263 If a new religious group keeps tension high and relies heavily on compensators to attract and keep converts, the powerlessness of converts will be maximized.

P264 If a new religious group keeps tension high and relies heavily on compensators to attract and keep converts, the outside attachments of converts will be minimized.

P265 High recruitment of powerless members will decrease the group's ability to avert or resist sanctions.

P266 Keeping tension high tends to maximize the extent to which the sect or cult is subjected to sanctions by the external society.

P267 The more severe the sanctions imposed on a new religious movement, the more it will tend to become isolated from the social environment.

P268 To the extent that a group is isolated, it will have great difficulty growing through recruitment.

P269 A high proportion of recruits to isolated religious groups are chronic social isolates.

P270 Isolated religious groups which initially recruit primarily chronic social isolates will subsequently find it almost impossible to grow through recruitment.

P271 Much of the time, it is impossible to predict the future course of an individual's fortune.

P272 The change in a person's net rewards from one time to another is greatly determined by random factors.

P273 In any category of people, the fate of any one individual will be an imperfect predictor of the fate of another.

P274 In any category of people initially at the same reward level, in future some will possess more than others.

P275 Social evaporation increases the average level of reward of members of a group.

P276 A moderate rate of social evaporation increases the commitment of members who remain in the group.

P277 The higher the tension of a religious group, the more strongly will social evaporation tend initially to increase the tension of the group.

P278 The lower the tension of a religious group, the more strongly will social evaporation tend to decrease the tension of the group.

P279 Social evaporation increases the ability of powerful members of a religious group to move it toward lower tension.

P280 Social evaporation reduces the pressures toward formation of church movements and sect movements.

P281 Moderate levels of social evaporation contribute to the success of a religious movement.

P282 Individuals with extreme levels of reward at one point in time will tend to be nearer the average for the society at a subsequent point in time.

P283 Individuals who join religious groups at times of extreme personal deprivation will tend to be less deprived at a later point in time.

P284 High-tension religious groups will be drawn by regression toward lower tension with the sociocultural environment.

P285 Sects and cults start out relatively small, smaller than their parent groups and considerably smaller than the dominant religious groups in the society.

P286 The period of initial organizational formation is a time of high availability of statuses in a new sect or cult.

P287 The period of initial organizational formation is a time of high exchange of compensators in a new sect or cult.

P288 The period of initial organizational formation is a time of high exchange of positive affect in a new sect or cult.

P289 The period of initial organizational formation is a time of high availability of rewards in a new sect or cult.

P290 Unless a new religious organization is too isolated socially, the period immediately following formation will be a time of rapid recruitment of new members.

P291 The initial characteristics and earliest achievements of a new religious movement tend to set the pattern for its future history.

P292 Religious movements which already are growing at a rapid rate tend to benefit from the tactic of raiding the memberships of other religious groups.

P293 Religious movements which fail to grow rapidly can increase the possibility of survival through social isolation.

P294 In a religious market, a few high-tension religious organizations will grow rapidly, while most will decline.

P295 In a religious market, a few high-tension religious organizations will become prosperous and will move toward lower tension.

P296 In a religious market, the majority of high-tension religious organizations will not prosper and will remain at high tension.

P297 Religious organizations socialize their members to the general norms required for successful human interaction.

P298 Religious organizations, except those at the highest tension, socialize their members to the specific norms required for success in the society.

P299 Relatively high-tension religious groups, except those at the highest tension, tend over time to increase the rewards received by their members.

P300 Successful, stable sects and cults tend to move toward lower tension.

P301 To remain successful, long after formation, religious groups rely greatly upon the tactic of revival.

P302 If they are to grow, religious movements must find means to expand the supply of attachments, investments and pleasures available through membership.

P303 If they are to grow, religious movements must increase stakes in conformity to the movement.

P304 As the membership of a sect or cult shifts from a converted to a socialized base, the compensator-oriented constituency will shrink relative to the reward-oriented constituency.

P305 Movement of a high-tension religious body toward lower tension creates both a cadre and a constituency for a new sect movement.

P306 Politics will emerge as a cultural system after religion has already done so.

P307 Science will emerge as a cultural system after politics has already done so.

P308 Cultural progress permits the development of cultural systems specializing in each major kind of reward that people publically exchange.

P309 As a society achieves a high level of cultural progress, its politics and science will evolve into cultural systems of great scope.

P310 Cultural progress reduces the market for magic.

P311 Cultural progress promotes the abandonment of magic by religion.

P312 The evolution of politics and science into cultural systems of great scope will promote the transformation of low-tension religion into a cultural specialty providing compensators of only the greatest generality.

P313 Belief in a single good god of infinite scope renders unnecessary the exchange of rewards to obtain religious compensators.

P314 Belief in a single good god of infinite scope severely reduces the ability of religious organizations and specialists to get others to give them rewards in exchange for compensators.

P315 It is impossible to sustain powerful religious organizations based on belief in a single good god of infinite scope.

P316 Cultural progress eventually curtails the ability of low-tension religious groups to provide compensators in exchange for valued rewards.

P317 As cultural progress reaches a high level, low-tension religion will accommodate its explanations to science, politics and any other successfully evolving secular cultural systems.

P318 Cultural progress multiplies cultural specialties.

P319 Cultural progress increases the number and reduces the average scope of exchange relationships for most individuals.

P320 The more cosmopolitan a society, the more common is individual social and geographic mobility.

P321 In cosmopolitan societies, social and geographic mobility tends to sever the ties of religious affiliation.

P322 Cosmopolitan societies tend to have rates of religious affiliation significantly lower than the maximum permitted by other characteristics of the societies.

P323 A high level of cultural progress produces secularization.

P324 Cultural specialties become cultural systems and forge their alliances with the state in the following order: religion, politics, science.

P325 Once political specialists have emerged in society, they will tend to combine in organizations seeking a political monopoly.

P326 In socially complex and cosmopolitan societies, a political organization can achieve an effective monopoly only through an alliance with the state.

P327 A political organization can sustain an effective monopoly only if it becomes the state.

P328 In socially complex and cosmopolitan societies, a political organization can achieve an effective monopoly by replacing the state.

P329 A political organization with an effective monopoly becomes the state.

P330 A state consisting of a political monopoly is a repressive state.

P331 A state consisting of a political monopoly will seek to repress religion.

P332 A state consisting of a political monopoly will seek an alliance with science in which it is the dominant party.

P333 When they become cultural systems of great scope, politics and science will severely limit the power of religion.

P334 When cultural progress curtails the ability of low-tension religious groups to provide compensators, sects will increase their share of the compensator market and recruit numbers of people they could not gain previously.

P335 In secular societies, persons without any religious affiliation and without strong stakes in conformity to political or scientific ideologies will be especially likely to join high-tension religious groups.

P336 Cosmopolitan societies tend to have high rates of denominational switching.

P337 Cosmopolitan societies have substantial rates of religious affiliation.

P338 Cultural progress cannot eliminate the need for highly general compensators or for every specific compensator.

P339 In the short run, secularization stimulates the development of sect movements.

P340 In the short run, secularization stimulates recruitment to sect movements.

P341 The existence in a secularizing society of one or more viable high-tension political organizations inhibits the growth of religious sects.

P342 To the extent that available political ideologies have been discredited by association with national enemies, popular and nationalist revolutions will tend to revive or create religious organizations in alliance with the state that are in high tension vis-a-vis other states.

P343 Cultural progress tends to disconfirm traditional systems of compensators.

P344 In the long run, cultural progress stimulates the emergence of cult movements.

BIBLIOGRAPHY

Abelson, Robert O.
1959 "Models of Resolution of Belief Dilemmas," *Journal of Conflict Resolution* 3: 343–352.

Abrahamson, Bengt
1970 "Homans on Exchange: Hedonism Revived," *American Journal of Sociology* 76: 273–285.

Ackerknecht, Erwin H.
1943 "Psychopathology, Primitive Medicine and Primitive Culture," *Bulletin of the History of Medicine* 14: 30–67.

Aguirre, B.E., and Jon P. Alston
1980 "Organizational Change and Religious Commitment," *Pacific Sociological Review* 23: 171–197.

Akers, Ronald L.
1985 *Deviant Behavior: A Social Learning Approach*. Belmont, California: Wadsworth.

Akers, Ronald L., Marvin D. Krohn, Lonn Lanza-Kaduce and Marcia Radosevich
1979 "Social Learning and Deviant Behavior: A Specific Test of a General Theory," *American Sociological Review* 44: 636–655.

Albrecht, Stan L., and Tim B. Heaton
1984 "Secularization, Higher Education, and Religiosity," *Review of Religious Research* 26: 43–58.

Allen, William Sheridan
1984 *The Nazi Seizure of Power*. New York: Franklin Watts.

Allport, Gordon W.
1960 *Religion in the Developing Personality*. New York: New York University Press.

Alston, Jon P. and B.E. Aguirre
1979 "Congregation Size and the Decline of Sectarian Commitment: The Case of the Jehovah's Witnesses in South and North America," *Sociological Analysis* 40: 63–70.

Altheide, David L. and John M. Johnson
1977 "Counting Souls," *Pacific Sociological Review* 20: 323–348.

Axelrod, Robert
1984 *The Evolution of Cooperation*. New York: Basic Books.

Bainbridge, William Sims
1976 *The Spaceflight Revolution*. New York: Wiley-Interscience.
1978 *Satan's Power: Ethnography of a Deviant Psychotherapy Cult*. Berkeley: University of California Press.

Bainbridge, William Sims
1982 "Shaker Demographics 1840–1900: An Example of the Use of U.S. Census Enumeration Schedules," *Journal for the Scientific Study of Religion* 21: 352–365.
1984a "The Decline of the Shakers: Evidence from the United States Census," *Communal Societies* 4: 10–34.
1984b "Religious Insanity in America: The Offical Nineteenth-Century Theory," *Sociological Analysis* 45: 223–239.
1985a "Cultural Genetics," in *Religious Movements: Genesis, Exodus and Numbers*, edited by Rodney Stark. New York.
1985b "Utopian Communities: Theoretical Issues." Pp.21–35 in *The Sacred in a Secular Age*, edited by Phillip E. Hammond. Berkeley: University of California Press.

Bainbridge, William Sims, and Laurie Russell Hatch
1982 "Women's Access to Elite Careers: In Search of a Religion Effect," *Journal for the Scientific Study of Religion* 21: 242–255.

Bainbridge, William Sims, and Daniel H. Jackson
1981 "The Rise and Decline of Transcendental Meditation." Pp. 135–158 in *The Social Impact of New Religious Movements*, edited by Bryan Wilson. New York: Rose of Sharon Press, (Chapter 13 in *The Future of Religion*).

Bainbridge, William Sims, and Rodney Stark
1979 "Cult Formation: Three Compatible Models," *Sociological Analysis* 40: 283–295. (Chapter 8 in *The Future of Religion*).
1980a "Client and Audience Cults in America," *Sociological Analysis* 41: 199–214. (Chapter 10 in *The Future of Religion*).
1980b "Scientology: To be Perfectly Clear," *Sociological Analysis* 41: 128–136. (Chapter 12 in *The Future of Religion*).
1980c "Sectarian Tension," *Review of Religious Research* 22: 105–124. (Chapter 3 in *The Future of Religion*).
1981a "The 'Consciousness Reformation' Reconsidered," *Journal for the Scientific Study of Religion* 20: 1–16. (Chapter 7 in *The Future of Religion*).
1981b "Friendship, Religion, and the Occult: A Network Study," *Review of Religious Research* 22: 313–327. (Chapter 15 in *The Future of Religion*).
1981c "Suicide, Homicide, and Religion: Durkheim Reassessed," *The Annual Review of the Social Sciences of Religion* 5: 33–56.
1982 "Church and Cult in Canada," *Canadian Journal of Sociology* 7: 351–366. (Chapter 20 in *The Future of Religion*).
1984 "Formal Explanation of Religion: A Progress Report," *Sociological Analysis* 45: 145–158.

Balch, Robert W., and David Taylor
1977 "Seekers and Saucers: The Role of the Cultic Milieu in Joining a UFO Cult," *American Behavioral Scientist* 20: 839–859.

Balswick, Jack O., and Gary L. Faulkner
1970 "Identification of Ministerial Cliques: A Sociometric Approach," *Journal for the Scientific Study of Religion* 9: 303–310.
Bannan, Rosemary S.
1965 "The Other Side of the Coin: Jewish Student Attitudes Toward Catholics and Protestants," *Sociological Analysis* 26: 21–29.
Barker, Eileen
1981 "Who'd Be a Moonie?" Pp. 59–96 in *The Social Impact of New Religious Movements*, edited by Bryan Wilson. New York: Rose of Sharon Press.
Becker, Lee B.
1977 "Predictors of Change in Religious Beliefs and Behaviors During College," *Sociological Analysis* 38: 65–74.
Beeson, Trevor
1977 *Discretion and Valour: Religious Conditions in Russia and Eastern Europe*. Glasgow: Fount.
Bell, Daniel
1971 "Religion in the Sixties," *Social Research* 38: 447–497.
1980 *The Winding Passage*. Cambridge: Abt.
Bellah, Robert N.
1964 "Religious Evolution," *American Sociological Review* 29: 358–374.
1970 *Beyond Belief*. New York: Harper and Row.
Benedict, Ruth
1934 *Patterns of Culture*. Boston: Houghton Mifflin.
Berger, Peter L.
1967 *The Sacred Canopy*. Garden City, New York: Doubleday.
Berger, Peter L., and Thomas Luckmann
1966 *The Social Construction of Reality*. Garden City, New York: Doubleday.
Bibby, Reginald W.
1983 "Searching for Invisible Thread: Meaning Systems in Contemporary Canada," *Journal for the Scientific Study of Religion* 22: 101–119.
Bibby, Reginald, W., and Merlin B. Brinkerhoff
1974 "When Proselytizing Fails: Organizational Analysis," *Sociological Analysis* 35: 189–200.
Bixenstine, V. Edwin, and Joan Douglas
1967 "Effect of Psychopathology on Group Consensus and Cooperative Choice in a Six-Person Game," *Journal of Personality and Social Psychology* 5: 32–37.
Blau, Peter M.
1964 *Exchange and Power in Social Life*. New York: Wiley.
Boas, Franz
1966 *Race, Language and Culture*. New York: Free Press.

Bott, Elizabeth
1955 "Urban Families: Conjugal Roles and Social Networks," *Human Relations* 8: 345–384.
Braithwaite, Richard Bevan
1953 *Scientific Explanation*. London: Cambridge University Press.
Brown, J.A.C.
1967 *Freud and the Post-Freudians*. Baltimore: Penguin.
Brownsberger, Carl N.
1965 "Clinical Versus Statistical Assessment of Psychotherapy: A Mathematical Model of the Dilemma," *Behavorial Science* 10: 421–428.
Burgess, Robert L., and Ronald L. Akers
1966 "A Differential Association-Reinforcement Theory of Criminal Behavior," *Social Problems* 14: 128–147.
Burgess, Robert L., and Don Bushell, Jr.
1965 *Behavioral Sociology*. New York: Columbia University Press.
Cantril, Hadley
1941 "The Kingdom of Father Divine," Pp. 123–143 in *The Psychology of Social Movements*. New York: Wiley.
Capra, Fritjof
1975 *The Tao of Physics*. Boulder, Colorado: Shambhala.
Carden, Maren Lockwood
1969 *Oneida: Utopian Community to Modern Corporation*. Baltimore: Johns Hopkins.
Carroll, Michael P.
1983 "Visions of the Virgin Mary: The Effect of Family Structures on Marian Apparitions," *Journal for the Scientific Study of Religion* 22: 205–221.
1985 "The Virgin Mary at LaSalette and Lourdes: Whom Did the Children See?" *Journal for the Scientific Study of Religion* 24: 56–74.
Cavalli-Sforza, Luigi Luca, and Marcus W. Feldman
1981 *Cultural Transmission and Evolution*. Princeton, New Jersey: Princeton University Press.
Cavan, Ruth Shonle
1971 "Jewish Student Attitudes toward Interreligious and Intra-Jewish Marriage," *American Journal of Sociology* 76: 1064–1071.
Childe, V. Gordon
1951 *Man Makes Himself*. New York: New American Library.
Chirot, Daniel
1977 *Social Change in the Twientieth Century*. New York: Harcourt Brace Jovanovich.
Church of Scientology
1978 *What is Scientology*? Los Angeles: Church of Scientology.
Cipolla, Carlo M.
1977 *Clocks and Culture: 1300–1700*. New York: Norton.

Cohen, Albert K.
1955 *Delinquent Boys*. New York: Free Press.
Cohn, Norman
1961 *The Pursuit of the Millennium*. New York: Harper.
Coleman, James S.
1956 "Social Cleavage and Religious Conflict," *The Journal of Social Issues* 12: 44–56.
Committee on the Judiciary, United States Senate
1964–1965 *The Church and State Under Communism*. Eight volumes. Washington, D.C.: U.S. Government Printing Office.
Cook, Judith A., and Dale W. Wimberley
1983 "If I Should Die Before I Wake: Religious Commitment and Adjustment to the Death of a Child," *Journal for the Scientific Study of Religion* 22: 222–238.
Cooper, Paulette
1971 *The Scandal of Scientology*. New York: Tower.
Davies, James C.
1962 "Toward a General Theory of Revolution," *American Sociological Review* 27: 5–19.
Davies, Paul C.W.
1977 *The Physics of Time Asymmetry*. Berkeley: University of California Press.
Davis, Kingsley, and Wilbert Moore
1945 "Some Principles of Stratification," *American Sociological Review* 10: 242–249.
Della Fave, L. Richard, and George A. Hillery, Jr.
1980 "Status Inequality in a Religious Community: The Case of a Trappist Monastery," *Social Forces* 59: 62–84.
Demerath, Nicholas J.
1965 *Social Class in American Protestantism*. Chicago: Rand McNally.
Devereux, George (ed.)
1953 *Psychoanalysis and the Occult*. New York: International Universities Press.
Dittes, James E.
1971 "Typing the Typologies: Some Parallels in the Career of Church-Sect and Extrinsic-Intrinsic," *Journal for the Scientific Study of Religion* 10: 375–383.
Djilas, Milovan
1974 *The New Class*. New York: Holt, Rinehart and Winston.
Dodd, Stuart C.
1961 "Can Science Improve Praying?" *Darshana* 1 (4): 22–37.
Doherty, Robert W.
1967 *The Hicksite Separation*. New Brunswick, New Jersey: Rutgers University Press.

Dohrman, H.T.
1958 *California Cult*. Boston: Beacon.
Dollard, John, Neil E. Miller, Leonard W. Doob, O.H. Mowrer, and Robert R. Sears
1939 *Frustration and Aggression*. New Haven: Yale University Press.
Durkheim, Emile
1897 *Suicide*. New York: Free Press (1951).
1915 *The Elementary Forms of the Religious Life*. London: Allen and Unwin.
1933 *The Division of Labor in Society*. New York: Free Press.
Durkheim, Emile, and Marcel Mauss
1963 *Primitive Classification*. Chicago: University of Chicago Press.
Dynes, Russell R.
1955 "Church-Sect Typology and Socio-Economic Status," *American Sociological Review* 20: 555–560.
1957 "The Consequences of Sectarianism for Social Participation," *Social Forces* 35: 331–334.
Edgerton, Robert B.
1966 "Conceptions of Psychosis in Four East African Societies," *American Anthropologist* 68: 408–424.
1967 *The Cloak of Competence*. Berkeley: University of California Press.
Ekvall, Robert B.
1968 *Fields on the Hoof: Nexus of Tibetan Nomadic Pastoralism*. New York: Holt, Rinehart and Winston.
Eister, Allan W.
1972 "A Theory of Cults," *Journal for the Scientific Study of Religion* 11: 319–333.
Eliade, Mircea
1958 *Rites and Symbols of Initiation*. New York: Harper and Row.
1971 *The Forge and the Crucible*. New York: Harper and Row.
Ellis, Jane
1978 *Letters from Moscow: Religion and Human Rigths in the U.S.S.R.* San Francisco: Washington Street Research Center.
England, R.W.
1954 "Some Aspects of Christian Science as Reflected in Letters of Testimony," *American Journal of Sociology* 59: 448–453.
Evans, Christopher
1973 *Cults of Unreason*. New York: Dell.
Evans-Pritchard, E.E.
1937 *Witchcraft, Oracles, and Magic among the Azande*. New York: Oxford University Press.
1965 *Theories of Primitve Religion*. London: Oxford University Press.

Eysenck, Hans J.
1965 "The Effects of Psychotherapy," *International Journal of Psychiatry* 1: 99–144.
Faia, Michael A.
1976 "Secularization and Schorlarship Among American Professors," *Sociological Analysis* 37: 63–73.
Faris, Robert E.L., and H. Warren Dunham
1939 *Mental Disorders in Urban Areas*. Chicago: University of Chicago Press (1967)
Fischer, Claude S.
1975 "Toward a Subcultural Theory of Urbanism," *American Journal of Sociology* 80: 1319–1341.
Flora, Cornelia Butler
1973 "Social Dislocation and Pentecostalism: A Multivariate Analysis," *Sociological Analysis* 34: 296–304.
Flowers, Ronald B.
1984 *Religion in Strange Times: The 1960s and 1970s*. Macon, Georgia: Mercer University Press.
Fodor, Nandor
1971 *Freud, Jung and Occultism*. New Hyde Park, New York: University Books.
Frank, Jerome
1961 *Persuasion and Healing*. Baltimore: Johns Hopkins University Press.
Frankfort, Henri
1948 *Kingship and the Gods*. Chicago: University of Chicago Press.
Frazier, Kendrick (ed.)
1981 *Paranormal Borderlands of Science*. Buffalo, New York: Prometheus.
Freud, Sigmund
1924 *A General Introduction to Psychoanalysis*. New York: Washington Square Press (1952).
1927 *The Future of an Illusion*. Garden City, New York: Doubleday (1961).
1930 *Civilization and its Discontents*. New York: Norton (1962).
1939 *Moses and Monotheism*. Letchworth, England: Hogarth.
1946 *Totem and Taboo*. New York: Random House.
Gaede, Stan
1976 "A Causal Model of Belief-Orthodoxy: Proposal and Empirical Test," *Sociological Analysis* 37: 205–217.
Gans, Herbert J.
1962a "Urbanism and Suburbanism as Ways of Life." Pp. 625–648 in *Human Behavior and Social Processes*, edited by Arnold M. Rose. Boston: Houghton Mifflin.
1962b *The Urban Villagers*. New York: Free Press.

Gardner, Martin
1957 *Fads and Fallacies in the Name of Science*. New York: Dover.
Garrett, William R.
1974 "Troublesome Transcendence: The Supernatural in the Scientific Study of Religion," *Sociological Analysis* 35: 167–180.
Gerharz, George P.
1970 "Secularization as Loss of Social Control: Toward a New Theory," *Sociological Analysis* 31: 1–11.
Gibbon, Edward
1782 *The History of the Decline and Fall of the Roman Empire*. New York: Macmillan (1896).
Gilfillan, S.C.
1970 *The Sociology of Invention*. Cambridge: M.I.T. Press.
Glezer, Alexander
1976 "Religion and Soviet Non-Conformist Artists," *Religion in Communist Lands* 4: 16–19.
Glick, Rush G., and Robert S. Newsom
1974 *Fraud Investigation*. Springfield, Illinois: Thomas.
Glock, Charles Y.
1962 "On the Study of Religious Commitment," *Religious Education* (special issue).
Glock, Charles Y., and Robert N. Bellah (eds.)
1976 *The New Religious Consciousness*. Berkeley: University of California Press.
Glock, Charles, Y., and Rodney Stark
1965 *Religion and Society in Tension*. Chicago: Rand McNally.
1966 *Christian Beliefs and Anti-Semitism*. New York: Harper and Row.
Goode, Erich
1967 "Some Critical Observations on the Church-Sect Dimension," *Journal for the Scientific Study of Religion*. 6: 69–77.
Goody, Jack
1961 "Religion and Ritual: The Definitional Problem," *British Journal of Sociology* 12: 142–164.
Gorsuch, Richard L., and Craig S. Smith
1983 "Attributions of Responsibility to God," *Journal for the Scientific Study of Religion* 22: 340–352.
Granovetter, Mark
1973 "The Strength of Weak Ties," *American Journal of Sociology*, 78: 1360–1380.
Greeley, Andrew M.
1981 "Religious Musical Chairs." Pp. 101–126 in *In Gods We Trust*, edited by Thomas Robbins and Dick Anthony. New Brunswick, New Jersey: Transaction.

Greene, Penelope
1974 "Comment on 'A Behavioral Model of Man: Propositions and Implications,'" *American Sociological Review* 39: 467–470.
Grosser, Morton
1979 *The Discovery of Neptune*. New York: Dover.
Gurr, Ted Robert
1970 *Why Men Rebel*. Princeton, New Jersey: Princeton University Press.
Gustafson, Paul
1967 "UO-US-PS-PO: A Restatement of Troeltsch's Church-Sect Typology," *Journal for the Scientific Study of Religion* 6: 65–68.
Habermas, Juergen
1978 *Knowledge and Human Interests*. London: Heinemann.
Hadaway, Christopher Kirk
1978 "Denominational Switching and Membership Growth: In Search of a Relationship," *Sociological Analysis* 39: 321–337.
Hadden, Jeffrey K.
1969 *The Gathering Storm in the Churches*. Garden City, New York: Doubleday.
Haggett, Peter, and Richard J. Chorley
1969 *Network Analysis in Geography*. New York: St. Martin's.
Hagstrom, Warren O.
1974 "Competition in Science," *American Sociological Review* 39: 1–18.
Haley, Peter
1980 "Rudolph Sohm on Charisma," *Journal of Religion* 60: 185–197.
Hechter, Michael
1978 "Group Formation and the Cultural Division of Labor," *American Journal of Sociology* 84: 293–318.
Herman, Nancy J.
1984 "Conflict in the Church: A Social Network Analysis of an Anglican Congregation," *Journal for the Scientific Study of Religion* 23: 60–74.
Herrnstein, Richard J.
1971 "Quantitative Hedonism," *Journal of Psychiatric Research* 8: 399–412.
Hilty, Dale M., and Rick Morgan
1985 "Construct Validation for the Religious Involvement Inventory: Replication," *Journal for the Scientific Study of Religion* 24: 75–86.
Hilty, Dale M., Rick L. Morgan, and Joan E. Burns
1984 "King and Hunt Revisited: Dimensions of Religious Involvement," *Journal for the Scientific Study of Religion* 23: 252–266.
Hindelang, Michael J., Travis Hirschi, and Joseph G. Weiss
1979 "Correlates of Delinquency: The Illusion of Discrepancy Between Self-Report and Offical Measures," *American Sociological Review* 44: 995–1014.
Hirschi, Travis
1969 *Causes of Delinquency*. Berkeley: University of California Press.

Hobsbawm, E.J.
1959 *Primitive Rebels*. Manchester: Manchester University Press.
Hofstadter, Douglas R.
1979 *Goedel, Escher, Bach: An Eternal Golden Braid*. New York: Basic Books.
Hollingshead, August B., and Frederick C. Redlich
1958 *Social Class and Mental Illness*. New York: Wiley.
Homans, George C.
1950 *The Human Group*. New York: Harcourt, Brace and World.
1967 *The Nature of Social Science*. New York: Harcourt, Brace and World.
1974 *Social Behavior: Its Elementary Forms*. New York. Harcourt Brace Jovanovich.
1984 *Coming to My Senses: The Autobiography of a Sociologist*. New Brunswick, New Jersey: Transaction.
Hood, Ralph W., Jr., and Ronald J. Morris
1983 "Toward a Theory of Death Transcendence," *Journal for the Scientific Study of Religion* 22: 353–365.
Hostettler, John A.
1968 *Amish Society*. Baltimore: Johns Hopkins University Press.
1974 *Hutterite Society*. Baltimore: Johns Hopkins University Press.
Hubbard, L. Ron
1954 "The Use of Scientology Materials," *Professional Auditor's Bulletin* number 36.
Huizinga, Johan
1950 *Homo Ludens*. Boston: Beacon Press.
Hunsberger, Bruce E.
1983 "Apostasy: A Social Learning Perspective," *Review of Religious Research* 25: 21–38.
Hutten, Kurt
1964 *Seher, Grubler, Enthusiasten*. Stuttgart: Quell-Verlag der Evang. Gesellschaft.
Jacobs, Janet
1984 "The Economy of Love in Religious Commitment: The Deconversion of Women from Nontraditional Religious Movements," *Journal for the Scientific Study of Religion* 23: 155–171.
James, William
1902 *The Varieties of Religious Experience* New York: Longmans, Green.
1963 *Pragmatism and Other Essays*. New York: Washington Square Press.
Jencks, Christopher
1972 *Inequality*. New York: Basic Books.
Johnson, Arthur L., Milo L. Brekke, Merton P. Strommen, and Ralph C. Underwager
1974 "Age Differences and Dimensions of Religious Behavior," *Journal of Social Issues* 30: 43–67.

Johnson, Benton
1957 "A Critical Appraisal of the Church-Sect Typology," *American Sociological Review* 22: 88–92.
1963 "On Church and Sect," *American Sociological Review* 28: 539–549.
1971 "Church and Sect Revisited," *Journal for the Scientific Study of Religion* 10: 124–137.
1977 "Sociological Theory and Religious Truth," *Sociological Analysis* 38: 368–388.
1982 "Taking Stock: Reflections on the End of Another Era," *Journal for the Scientific Study of Religion* 21: 189–200.

Johnson, Paul
1979 *A History of Christianity*. New York: Atheneum.

Johnson, Weldon T.
1971 "The Religious Crusade: Revival or Ritual?" *American Journal of Sociology* 76: 873–890.

Kanter, Rosabeth Moss
1972 *Commitment and Community*. Cambridge: Harvard University Press.

Katz, Elihu
1960 "Communication Research and the Image of Society: The Convergence of Two Traditions," *American Journal of Sociology* 65: 435–440.

Katz, Elihu, and Paul F. Lazarsfeld
1955 *Personal Influence*. Glencoe, Illinois: Free Press.

Kay, D.W.K.
1978 "Assessment of Familial Risks in the Functional Psychoses and their Application in Genetic Counselling," *British Journal of Psychiatry* 133: 385–403.

Keim, Albert N. (ed.)
1975 *Compulsory Education and the Amish*. Boston: Beacon.

Kennedy, John G.
1967 "Nubian Zar Ceremonies as Psychotherapy," *Human Organization* 26: 185–194.

Kiev, Ari
1972 *Transcultural Psychiatry*. New York: Free Press.

King, Morton
1967 "Measuring the Religious Variable: Nine Proposed Dimensions," *Journal for the Scientific Study of Religion* 6: 173–190.

Kline, Morris
1980 *Mathematics: The Loss of Certainty*. Oxford: Oxford University Press.

Kluckhohn, Clyde
1962 "Values and Value-Orientations in the Theory of Action: An Exploration in Definition and Classification." Pp. 388–433 in *Toward a General Theory of Action* edited by Talcott Parsons and Edward Shils. New York: Harper.

Kowalewski, David
1980a "Religious Belief in the Brezhnev Era: Renaissance, Resistance, and Realpolitik," *Journal for the Scientific Study of Religion* 19: 280–292.
1980b "Trends in the Human Rights Movement." Pp. 150–181 in *Soviet Politics in the Brezhnev Era*, editied by Donald R. Kelley. New York: Praeger.
Kuhn, Thomas S.
1959 *The Copernican Revolution*. New York: Vintage.
Kunkel, John H., and Richard H. Nagasawa
1973 "A Behavioral Model of Man: Propositions and Implications," *American Sociological Review* 38: 530–543.
Kunz, Phillip R., and Merlin B. Brinkerhoff
1970 "Growth in Religious Organizations: A Comparative Study," *Social Science* 45: 215–222.
La Barre, Weston
1969 *They Shall Take up Serpents*. New York: Schocken.
1972 *The Ghost Dance*. New York: Dell.
Leach, Edmund R.
1954 *Political Systems of Highland Burma*. London: Bell.
1962 "Pulleyar and the Lord Buddha," *Psychoanalysis and the Psychoanalytic Review* 45: 80–102.
Laumann, Edward O., Peter V. Mardsen, and Joseph Galskiewicz
1977 "Community-Elite Influence Structures: Extension of a Network Approach," *American Journal of Sociology* 83: 594–631.
Lederer, Wolfgang
1959 "Primitive Psychotherapy," *Psychiatry* 22: 225–265.
Lemert, Edwin
1967 "Paranoia and the Dynamics of Exclusion." Pp. 246–264 in *Human Deviance, Social Problems and Social Control*. Englewood Cliffs, New Jersey: Prentice-Hall.
Lenski, Gerhard
1966 *Power and Privilege*. New York: McGraw-Hill.
1976 "History and Social Change," *American Journal of Sociology* 82: 548–564.
Leuba, James
1916 *The Belief in God and Immortality*. Boston: Sherman French.
1934 "Religious Beliefs of American Scientists," *Harper's* 169: 291–300.
Levi-Strauss, Claude
1963 "The Sorcerer and his Magic." Pp. 161–180 in *Structural Anthropology*. New York: Basic Books.
Lewis, Gordon R.
1966 *Confronting the Cults*. Grand Rapids: Baker.
Lewis, Ioan M.
1971 *Ecstatic Religion*. Baltimore: Penguin.

Liebmann, Charles S.
1966 "Changing Social Characteristics of Orthodox, Conservative and Reform Jews," *Sociological Analysis* 27: 210–222.
Lipset, Seymour Martin
1960 *Political Man*. Garden City, New York: Doubleday.
Lofland, John
1966 *Doomsday Cult*. Englewood Cliffs, New Jersey: Prentice-Hall.
Lofland, John, and Rodney Stark
1965 "Becoming a World-Saver: A Theory of Conversion to a Deviant Perspective," *American Sociological Review* 30: 862–875.
London, Ivan D., and Nikolai Poltoratzky
1957 "Contemporary Religious Sentiment in the Soviet Union," *Psychological Reports* monograph supplement 3: 113–130.
Long, Theodore E., and Jeffrey K. Hadden
1983 "Religious Conversion and the Concept of Socialization: Integrating the Brainwashing and Drift Models," *Journal for the Scientific Study of Religion* 22: 1–14.
Lowie, Robert H.
1937 *The History of Ethnological Theory*. New York: Holt, Rinehart and Winston.
Luckmann, Thomas
1967 *The Invisible Religion*. New York: Macmillan.
Lumsden, Charles J., and Edward O. Wilson
1981 *Genes, Mind, and Culture*. Cambridge: Harvard University Press.
MacDougall, Curtis D.
1958 *Hoaxes*. New York: Dover.
Malinowski, Bronislaw
1948 *Magic, Science and Religion*. Garden City, New York: Doubleday.
Malko, George
1970 *Scientology: The Now Religion*. New York: Delacorte.
Mamiya, Lawrence H.
1982 "From Black Muslim to Bilalian: The Evolution of a Movement," *Journal for the Scientific Study of Religion* 21: 138–152.
Mandelbaum, David G.
1966 "Transcendental and Pragmatic Aspects of Religion," *American Anthropologist* 68: 1174–1191.
Mannheim, Karl
1936 *Ideology and Utopia*. New York: Harcourt, Brace and World.
Maris, Ronald
1970 "The Logical Adequacy of Homans' Social Theory," *American Sociological Review* 35: 1069–1081.
Martin, David
1978 *A General Theory of Secularization*. New York: Harper and Row.

May, Phillip R.A.
1971 "For Better or for Worse? Psychotherapy and Variance Change: A Critical Review of the Literature," *Journal of Nervous and Mental Disease* 152: 184–192.
Mayhew, Bruce H., and Roger L. Levinger
1976 "On the Emergence of Oligarchy in Human Interaction," *American Journal of Sociology* 81: 1017–1049.
McCall, Robert B.
1977 "Childhood IQ's as Predictors of Adult Educational and Occupational Status," *Science* 197: 482–483.
McCleary, Richard, Andrew C. Gordon, David McDowell, and Michael D. Maltz
1979 "How a Regression Artifact Can Make Any Delinquency Intervention Program Look Effective," *Evaluation Studies Review Annual* 4: 626–652.
McConaghy, N., and S.H. Lovibond
1967 "Methodological Formalism in Psychiatric Research," *Journal of Nervous and Mental Disease* 144: 117–123.
Medvedev, Zhores A.
1971 *The Rise and Fall of T.D. Lysenko*. Garden City, New York: Doubleday.
Medvedev, Zhores, and Roy Medvedev
1971 *A Question of Madness*. New York: Vintage.
Meeker, B.F.
1971 "Decisions and Exchange," *American Sociological Review* 36: 485–495.
Melton, J. Gordon
1978 *Encyclopedia of American Religions*. Two volumes. Wilmington, North Carolina: McGrath/Consortium.
Merton, Robert K.
1968 "Social Structure and Anomie." Pp. 185–214 in *Social Theory and Social Structure*. New York: Free Press.
1970 *Science, Technology and Society in Seventeenth-Century England*. New York: Harper and Row.
1973 *The Sociology of Science*. Chicago: University of Chicago Press.
Messing, Simon D.
1958 "Group Therapy and Social Status in the Zar Cult of Ethiopia," *American Anthropologist* 60: 1120–1126.
Mihajlov, Mihajlo
1976 *Underground Notes*. Kansas City: Sheed, Andrews, and McMeel.
Milgram, Stanley
1977 "The Small World Problem." P. 281–296 in *The Individual in a Social World*. Reading, Massachusetts: Addison-Wesley.
Miller, Neil E., and John Dollard
1941 *Social Learning and Imitation*. New Haven: Yale University Press.

Miller, Robert L'H.

1976 "The Religious Value System of Unitarian Universalists," *Review of Religious Research* 17: 189–208.

Milosz, Czeslaw

1953 *The Captive Mind*. New York: Random House.

Moberg, David O.

1967 "The Encounter of Scientific and Religious Values Pertinent to Man's Spiritual Nature," *Sociological Analysis* 28: 22–23.

Morioka, Kiyomi

1975 *Religion in Changing Japanese Society*. Tokyo: University of Tokyo Press.

Murdock, George P.

1949 *Social Structure*. New York: Macmillan.

Murphy, Jane M.

1976 "Psychiatric Labeling in Cross-Cultural Perspective," *Science* 191: 1019–1028.

Nagasawa, Richard H., and John Kunkel

1974 "Models and Probabilities: Reply to Greene," *American Sociological Review* 39: 470–473.

Nagasawa, Richard H., and Philip von Bretzel

1977 "The Utility of Formalization in Constructing Theories in Sociology," *Pacific Sociological Review* 20: 221–240.

Nagel, Ernest

1961 *The Structure of Science*. New York: Harcourt, Brace and World.

Nagel, Ernest, and James R. Newman

1958 *Goedel's Proof*. New York: New York University Press.

Nelson, Geoffrey K.

1969 "The Spiritualist Movement and the Need for a Redefinition of Cult," *Journal for the Scientific Study of Religion* 8: 152–160.

1972 "The Membership of a Cult: The Spiritualists National Union," *Review of Religious Research* 13: 170–177.

Niebuhr, H. Richard

1929 *The Social Sources of Denominationalism*. New York: Henry Holt.

Nietzsche, Friedrich

1872 *The Birth of Tragedy*. New York: Random House (1967).

Nordhoff, Charles

1875 *The Communistic Societies of the United States*. London: John Murray.

Nordquist, Ted

1978 *Ananda Cooperative Village*. Uppsala: Borgstroems.

Noyes, John Humphrey

1870 *History of American Socialisms*. Philadelphia: Lippincott.

Nozick, Robert

1974 *Anarchy, State, and Utopia*. New York: Basic Books.

O'Dea, Thomas F.
1966 *The Sociology of Religion*. Englewood Cliffs, New Jersey: Prentice-Hall.
Ogburn, William Fielding
1922 *Social Change*. New York: Huebsch.
Orrmont, Arthur
1961 *Love Cults and Faith Healers*. New York: Ballantine.
Parsons, Talcott
1957 "Motivation of Religious Belief and Behavior." P. 380–385 in *Religion, Society and the Individual*, edited by J. Milton Yinger. New York: Macmillan.
1964 "Evolutionary Universals in Society," *American Sociological Review* 29: 339–357.
Parsons, Talcott, and Edward Shils (eds.)
1962 *Towards a General Theory of Action*. New York: Harper.
Peters, Victor
1965 *All Things Common*. New York: Harper.
Phillips, Derek
1967 "Social Participation and Happiness," *American Journal of Sociology* 72: 479–488.
Pickering, W.S.F.
1984 *Durkheim's Sociology of Religion*. London: Routledge and Kegan Paul.
Pollin, William, Martin G. Allen, Axel Hoffer, James R. Stabenau, and Zidnek Hrubec
1969 "Psychopathology in 15,909 Pairs of Veteran Twins: Evidence for a Genetic Factor in the Pathogenesis of Schizophrenia and its Relative Absence in Psychoneurosis," *American Journal of Psychiatry* 126: 597–610.
Pope, Whitney
1976 *Durkheim's Suicide: A Classic Analyzed*. Chicago: University of Chicago Press.
Pope, Whitney, and Nick Danigelis
1981 "Sociology's 'One Law,'" *Social Forces* 60: 495–516.
Popper, Karl R.
1959 *The Logic of Scientific Discovery*. New York: Harper and Row.
1962 *Conjectures and Refutations*. New York: Basic Books.
Pratt, William F.
1969 "The Anabaptist Explosion," *Natural History* (February): 6–23.
Quine, Willard Van Orman
1959 *Methods of Logic*. New York: Holt, Rinehart and Winston.
Quinley, Harold E.
1974 *The Prophetic Clergy*. New York: Wiley-Interscience.
Rachman, Stanley
1971 *The Effects of Psychotherapy*. Oxford: Pergamon.

Reed, Meyer S., Jr.
1974 "The Sociology of the Sociology of Religion," *Review of Religious Research* 15: 157–167.

Richardson, James T.
1878 "An Oppositional and General Conceptualization of Cult," *Annual Review of the Social Sciences of Religion* 2: 29–52.

Richardson, James T., and Mary Stewart
1977 "Conversion Process Models and the Jesus Movement," *American Behavioral Scientist* 20: 819–838.

Richardson, James T., Mary White Stewart, and Robert B. Simmonds
1979 *Organized Miracles*. New Brunswick, New Jersey: Transaction.

Rieff, Philip
1968 *The Triumph of the Therapeutic*. New York: Harper.

Roberts, Bryan R.
1968 "Protestant Groups and Coping with Urban Life in Guatamala City," *American Journal of Sociology* 73: 753–767.

Roberts, Michael K., and James D. Davidson
1984 "The Nature and Sources of Religious Involvement," *Review of Religious Research* 25: 334–350.

Robbins, Thomas, Dick Anthony, and James Richardson
1978 "Theory and Research on Today's 'New Religions.'" *Sociological Analysis* 39: 95–122.

Rochford, E. Burke, Jr.
1982 "Recruitment Strategies, Ideology, and Organization in the Hare Krishna Movement," *Social Problems* 29: 399–410.

Rogers, Everett M.
1960 *Social Change in Rural Society*. New York: Appleton-Century-Crofts.

Roheim, Geza
1955 *Magic and Schizophrenia*. Bloomington: Indiana University Press.

Rokeach, Milton
1981 *The Three Christs of Ypsilanti*. New York: Columbia University Press.

Ronan, Colin
1971 "The Man who Curbed the Planets," *New Scientist* (30 December): 271–273.

Rosmarin, Trude Weiss
1939 *The Hebrew Moses: An Answer to Sigmund Freud*. New York: Jewish Book Club.

Russell, Bertrand
1962 *The Scientific Outlook*. New York: Norton.

Sargant, William
1959 *Battle for the Mind*. New York: Harper and Row.

Scarr, Sandra, and Richard A. Weinberg
1978 "The Influence of 'Family Background' on Intellectual Attainment," *American Sociological Review* 43: 674–692.

Scheff, Thomas J.
1966 *Being Mentally Ill.* Chicago: Aldine.
Schein, Edgar, H., and Warren G. Bennis
1965 *Personal and Organizational Change Through Group Methods.* New York: Wiley.
Schmookler, Jacob
1966 *Invention and Economic Growth.* Cambridge: Harvard University Press.
Schoenbaum, David
1966 *Hitler's Social Revolution.* New York: Doubleday.
Schoenherr, Richard A., and Andrew M. Greeley
1974 "Role Commitment Process and the American Catholic Priesthood," *American Sociological Review* 39: 407–426.
Schweitzer, Albert
1948 *The Psychiatric Study of Jesus.* Boston: Beacon Press.
Scott, John Finley
1971 *Internalization of Norms.* Englewood Cliffs, New Jersey: Prentice-Hall.
Selznick, Philip
1960 *The Organizational Weapon.* Glencoe, Illinois: Free Press.
Shupe, Anson D.
1976 "'Disembodied Access' and Technological Constraints on Organizational Development: A Study of Mail-Order Religions," *Journal for the Scientific Study of Religion* 15: 177–185.
Silverman, Julian
1967 "Shamans and Acute Schizophrenia," *American Anthropologist* 69: 21–32.
Simon, William, and John H. Gagnon
1976 "The Anomie of Affluence: A Post-Mertonian Conception," *American Journal of Sociology* 82: 356–378.
Simpson, John
1984 "High Gods and the Means of Subsistence," *Sociological Analysis* 45: 213–222.
Singer, Burton, and Seymour Spilerman
1976 "The Representation of Social Processes by Markov Models," *American Journal of Sociology* 82: 1–54.
Skinner, B.F.
1938 *The Behavior of Organisms.* New York: Appleton-Century.
Smelser, Neil J.
1962 *Theory of Collective Behavior.* New York: Free Press.
Smith, Ralph Lee
1968 "Scientology – Menace to Mental Health," *Today's Health* (December): 35.

Snow, David A., and Richard Machalek
1983 "The Convert as a Social Type." Pp. 259–288 in *Sociological Theory – 1983*, edited by Randall Collins. San Francisco: Jossey-Bass.
1984 "The Sociology of Conversion," *Annual Review of Sociology* 10: 167–190.
Snow, David A., and Cynthia L. Phillips
1980 "The Lofland-Stark Conversion Model: A Critical Reassessment," *Social Problems* 27: 430–447.
Snow, David A., Louis A. Zurcher, and Sheldon Ekland-Olson
1980 "Social Network and Social Movements: A Microstructural Approach to Differential Recruitment," *American Sociological Review* 45: 787–801.
Spencer, Herbert
1893 *The Principles of Sociology*. Vol. II. New York: Appleton.
Spiro, Melford E.
1964 "Religion and the Irrational." Pp. 102–115 in *Symposium on New Approaches to the Study of Religion*, edited by June Helm. Seattle: University of Washington Press.
1966 "Religion, Problems of Definition and Explanation." Pp. 85–126 in *Anthropological Approaches to the Study of Religion*, edited by Michael Banton. New York: Praeger.
Srole, Leo, Thomas S. Langner, Stanley T. Michael, Marvin K. Opler, and Thomas A.C. Rennie
1962 *Mental Health in the Metropolis*. New York: McGraw-Hill.
Stanner, W.E.H.
1956 "The Dreaming." In *Australian Signpost*, edited by T.A.G. Hungerford. Melbourne, Australia: Cheshire.
Stark, Rodney
1963 "On the Incompatiblity of Religion and Science," *Journal for the Scientific Study of Religion* 3: 3–20.
1964 "Class, Radicalism and Religious Involvement in Britain," *American Sociological Review* 29: 698–706.
1968 "Age and Faith: A Changing Outlook or an Old Process?" *Sociological Analysis* 29: 1–10.
1971 "Psychopathology and Religious Commitment," *Review of Religious Research* 12: 165–176.
1972 "The Economics of Piety: Religious Commitment and Social Class." Pp. 483–503 in *Issues in Social Inequality*, edited by Gerals Thielbar and Saul Feldman. Boston: Little, Brown.
1980 "Estimating Church-Membership Rates for Ecological Areas," National Institute of Juvenile Justice and Delinquency Prevention, L.E.A.A., U.S. Department of Justice. Washington, D.C.: Government Printing Office.
1981 "Must all Religions be Supernatural?" Pp. 159–177 in *The Social Impact of New Religious Movements*, edited by Bryan Wilson. New York: Rose of Sharon Press.

Stark, Rodney
1984a "Religion and Conformity," *Sociological Analysis* 45: 273–282.
1984b "The Rise of a New World Faith," *Review of Religious Research* 26: 18–27.
1985a "Europe's Receptivity to Cults and Sects." in *Religious Movements: Genesis, Exodus and Numbers*, edited by Rodney Stark. New York: Paragon (Chapter 21 in *The Future of Religion*).
1985b "Church and Sect." Pp. 139–149 in *The Sacred in a Secular Age*, edited by Phillip E. Hammond. Berkeley: University of California Press.
Forthcoming "The Rise and Decline of Christian Science."
Forthcoming "Modernization, Secularization and Mormon Success."

Stark, Rodney, and William Sims Bainbridge
1979 "Of Churches, Sects, and Cults: Preliminary Concepts for a Theory of Religious Movements," *Journal for the Scientific Study of Religion* 18: 117–131. (Chapter 2 in *The Future of Religion*).
1980a "Networks of Faith: Interpersonal Bonds and Recruitment to Cults and Sects," *American Journal of Sociology* 85: 1376–1395. (Chapter 14 in *The Future of Religion*).
1980b "Secularization, Revival, and Cult Formation," *The Annual Review of the Social Sciences of Religion* 4: 85–119. (Chapter 19 in *The Future of Religion*).
1981a "American-Born Sects: Initial Findings," *Journal for the Scientific Study of Religion* 20: 130–149. (Chapter 6 in *The Future of Religion*).
1981b "Secularization and Cult Formation in the Jazz Age," *Journal for the Scientific Study of Religion* 20: 360–373. (Chapter 19 in *The Future of Religion*).
1985 *The Future of Religion*. Berkeley: University of California Press.

Stark, Rodney, William Sims Bainbridge, and Daniel P. Doyle
1979 "Cults of America: A Reconnaissance in Space and Time," *Sociological Analysis* 40: 347–359. (Chapter 9 in *The Future of Religion*).

Stark, Rodney, William Sims Bainbridge, and Lori Kent
1981 "Cult Membership in the Roaring Twenties," *Sociological Analysis* 42: 137–162. (Chapter 11 in *The Future of Religion*).

Stark, Rodney, William Sims Bainbridge, Robert Crutchfield, Daniel P. Doyle, and Roger Finke
1983 "Crime and Delinquency in the Roaring Twenties," *Journal of Research in Crime and Delinquency* 20: 4–23.

Stark, Rodney, Daniel P. Doyle, and Lori Kent
1980 "Rediscovering Moral Communities: Church Membership and Crime." Pp. 43–52 in *Understanding Crime*, edited by Travis Hirschi and Michael Gottfredson. Beverly Hills: Sage.

Stark, Rodney, Daniel P. Doyle, and Jesse Lynn Rushing
1983 "Beyond Durkheim: Religion and Suicide," *Journal for the Scientific Study of Religion* 22: 120–131.

Stark, Rodney, Bruce D. Foster, Charles Y. Glock, and Harold E. Quinley
1971 *Wayward Shepherds*. New York: Harper and Row.
Stark, Rodney, and Charles Y. Glock
1968 *American Piety*. Berkeley: University of California Press.
Stark, Rodney, Lori Kent, and Daniel P. Doyle
1982 "Religion and Delinquency: The Ecology of a 'Lost' Relationship," *Journal of Research in Crime and Delinquency* 19: 2–24.
Stark, Rodney, and Lynne Roberts
1982 "The Arithmetic of Social Movements: Theoretical Implications," *Sociological Analysis* 4: 53–68. (Chapter 16 in *The Future of Religion*).
Steinberg, Stephen
1965 "Reform Judaism: The Origin and Evolution of a Church Movement," *Journal for the Scientific Study of Religion* 5: 117–129.
Stewman, Shelby
1975 "Two Markov Models of Open System Occupational Mobility: Underlying Conceptualations and Empirical Tests," *American Sociological Review* 40: 298–321.
Stone, Merlin
1976 *When God was a Woman*. New York: Harcourt Brace Jovanovich.
Stonequist, Everett V.
1937 *The Marginal Man*. New York: Scribner's.
Stump, Roger W.
1984a "Regional Divergence in Religious Affiliation in the United States," *Sociological Analysis* 45: 283–299.
1984b "Regional Migration and Religious Commitment in the United States," *Journal for the Scientific Study of Religion* 23: 292–303.
Sutherland, Edwin H., and Donald R. Cressey
1974 *Principles of Criminology*. Philadelphia: Lippincott.
Swanson, Guy E.
1960 *The Birth of the Gods*. Ann Arbor: University of Michigan Press.
1975 "Monotheism, Materialism, and Collective Purpose: An Analysis of Underhill's Correlations," *American Journal of Sociology* 80: 862–869.
Thrasher, Frederic M.
1927 *The Gang*. Chicago: University of Chicago Press.
Tillich, Paul
1948 *The Shaking of the Foundations*. New York: Scribner's.
Tiryakian, Edward A.
1972 "Toward the Sociology of Esoteric Culture," *American Journal of Sociology* 78: 491–512.
Tittle, Charles R., Wayne J. Villemez, and Douglas A. Smith
1978 "The Myth of Social Class and Criminality," *American Sociological Review* 43: 643–656.

Toby, Jackson
1957 "Social Disorganization and Stake in Conformity: Complementary Factors in the Predatory Behavior of Hoodlums," *Journal of Criminal Law, Criminology and Police Science* 48: 12–17.

Toch, Hans
1965 *The Social Psychology of Social Movements.* Indianapolis: Bobbs-Merrill.

Tombaugh, Clyde W., and Patrick Moore
1980 *Out of the Darkness: The Planet Pluto.* New York: Mentor.

Toulmin, Stephen
1960 *The Philosophy of Science.* New York: Harper and Row.

Turner, Jonathan H.
1974 *The Structure of Sociological Theory.* Homewood, Illinois: Dorsey.
1977 "Building Social Theory: Some Questions about Homans' Strategy," *Pacific Sociological Review* 20: 203–220.

Tylor, Edward B.
1871 *Primitive Culture.* New York: Brantano's (1924).

Underhill, Ralph
1975 "Economic and Political Antecedents of Monotheism: A Cross-Cultural Study," *American Journal of Sociology* 80: 841–861.

Van den Berghe, Pierre
1973 *Age and Sex in Human Societies.* Belmont, California: Wadsworth.

Van Gennep, Arnold
1960 *The Rites of Passage.* Chicago: University of Chicago Press.

Viereck, Peter
1965 *Metapolitics: The Roots of the Nazi Mind.* New York: Capricorn.

Volinn, Ernest
1982 *Lead Us from Darkness: The Allure of a Religious Sect and its Charismatic Leader.* New York: Columbia University, unpublished doctoral dissertation.

Vrga, Djuro, and Frank J. Fahey
1970 "The Relationship of Religious Practices and Beliefs to Schism," *Sociological Analysis* 31: 46–55.

Wallace, Anthony F.C.
1956 "Revitalization Movements," *American Anthropologist* 58: 264–281.
1959 "The Institutionalization of Cathartic and Control Strategies in Iroquois Religious Psychotherapy." Pp. 63–96 in *Culture and Mental Health,* edited by Marvin K. Opler. New York: Macmillan.
1966 *Religion: An Anthropological View.* New York: Random House.

Wallis, Roy
1976 *The Road to Total Freedom.* New York: Columbia University Press.
1982 "The Social Construction of Charisma," *Social Compass* 29: 25–39.

Weber Max

1946 *From Max Weber: Essays in Sociology*. New York: Oxford University Press.

1963 *The Sociology of Religion*. Boston: Beacon Press.

Welch, Kevin

1981 "An Interpersonal Influence Model of Traditional Religious Commitment," *The Sociological Quarterly* 22: 81–92.

1983 "Community Development and Metropolitan Religious Commitment: A Test of Two Competing Models," *Journal for the Scientific Study of Religion* 22: 167–181.

Welch, Michael R.

1977 "Analyzing Religious Sects: An Empirical Examination of Wilson's Sect Typology," *Journal for the Scientific Study of Religion* 16: 125–139.

Welch, Michael R., and John Baltzell

1984 "Geographic Mobility, Social Integration, and Church Attendance," *Journal for the Scientific Study of Religion* 23: 75–91.

Westfall, Richard S.

1958 *Science and Religion in Seventeenth-Century England*. New Haven: Yale University Press.

White, Harrison C.

1970 *Chains of Opportunity*. Cambridge: Harvard University Press.

White, Harrison C., Scott A. Boorman, and Ronald L. Breiger

1976 "Social Structure from Multiple Networks," *American Journal of Sociology* 81: 730–780.

White, Harrison C., and Ronald L. Breiger

1975 "Pattern Across Networks," *Society* (July-August): 68–73.

White, Leslie A.

1959 *The Evolution of Culture*. New York: McGraw-Hill.

White, Lynn

1962 *Medieval Technology and Social Change*. London: Oxford University Press.

White, Robert W.

1964 *The Abnormal Personality*. New York: Ronald Press.

Whitehead, Alfred North

1967 *Science and the Modern World*. New York: Free Press.

Whitworth, John McKelvie

1975 *God's Blueprints*. London: Routledge and Kegan Paul.

Whyte, William Foote

1943 *Street Corner Society*. Chicago: University of Chicago Press.

Wilson, Bryan

1961 *Sects and Society*. Berkeley: University of California Press.

1975 *Magic and the Millennium*. Frogmore, England: Paladin.

1979 "The Return of the Sacred," *Journal for the Scientific Study of Religion* 18: 268–280.

Wilson, Curtis

1972 "How Did Kepler Discover His First Two Laws?" *Scientific American* 226 (March): 93–106.

Wilson, Edward O.

1975 *Sociobiology – The New Synthesis*. Cambridge: Harvard University Press.

Winnicott, D.W.

1971 *Playing and Reality*. New York: Basic Books.

Wolf, Eric Robert

1969 *Peasant Wars of the Twentieth Century*. New York: Harper and Row.

Wuthnow, Robert

1976 *The Consciousness Reformation*. Berkeley: University of California Press.

1978 *Experimentation in American Religion*. Berkeley; University of California Press.

Wuthnow, Robert, and Kevin Christiano

1979 "The Effects of Residential Migration on Church Attendance in the United States." Pp. 257–276 in *The Religious Dimension*, edited by Robert Wuthnow. New York: Academic Press.

Yinger, J. Milton

1970 *The Scientific Study of Religion*. New York: Macmillan.

1977 "Countercultures and Social Change," *American Sociological Review* 42: 833–853.

Young, Michael, and Peter Willmott

1957 *Family and Kinship in East London*. Baltimore: Penguin.

1973 *The Symmetrical Family*. New York: Penguin.

Zukav, Gary

1979 *The Dancing Wu Li Masters*. New York: William Morrow.

Zweig, Stefan

1932 *Mental Healers*. New York: Viking.

INDEX

John E. Thiel

GOD AND WORLD IN SCHLEIERMACHER'S 'DIALEKTIK' AND 'GLAUBENSLEHRE'

Criticism and the Methodology of Dogmatics

Basler und Berner Studien zur historischen und systematischen Theologie. Vol. 43
ISBN 3-261-04810-7 253 pages paperback US $ 28.15*

*Recommended price - alterations reserved

This essay investigates the role played by Schleiermacher's philosophical lectures on 'Dialektik' in the methodology of his epoch-making dogmatics, the 'Glaubenslehre'. The God-world relationship, a central theme in both works, provides a focus for the author's contention that Schleiermacher employed his own epistemology as a standard of criticism for the dogmatic exposition of Christian doctrine.

Contents: The Principles and Methodologies of the 'Dialektik' and the 'Glaubenslehre' - The Role of Philosophy in Schleiermacher's Dogmatic Method - Proper Thinking and the Experience of Feeling - Proper Thinking and the God-World Relationship: The Doctrines of Creation and Preservation - Proper Thinking and the God-World Relationship: The Doctrine of the Divine Attributes and the Doctrines of the Original Perfection of Man and the World - Schleiermacher's Conception of Dogmatic Criticism.

PETER LANG PUBLISHING, INC.
62 West 45th Street
USA - New York, NY 10036

Second revised edition

David H. Turner

LIFE BEFORE GENESIS

A Conclusion
An Understanding of the Significance of Australian Aboriginal Culture

Toronto Studies in Religion. Vol. 1
ISBN 0-8204-0244-3 195 pages hardcover US $ 23.90*

*Recommended price - alterations reserved

Turner's 'conclusion' is that Australian Aborigines, having transcended the problem of incorporation and technology at a Stone Age level of development, achieved what eludes 'modern' society - peace, order and good government. The analysis is based on a comparison of Australian and Canadian aboriginal society and mythology following more than a decade of ethnographic work, numerous publications on the subject and a theoretical insight into the nature of the human condition. By reading the Book of Genesis in terms of his findings Turner discovers that he has gone some way to shattering the silence of the text. What emerges is a Prologue to the Judeo-Christian tradition which also hints at its Conclusion.

Contents: A distinction is drawn between 'incorporative' and 'confederative' historical traditions based on an analysis of Australian and Canadian aboriginal societies. The theoretical articulation of the traditions illuminates the book of Genesis.

PETER LANG PUBLISHING, INC.
62 West 45th Street
USA - New York, NY 10036